"In his fast-paced Critique of Psychoanalytic Reason, Nobus asks crucial questions about Lacan's theories and practice, not shying away from embarrassing issues like the use of variable sessions, the rationale of exorbitant fees, and traces of male chauvinism. Mapping the entire Lacanian field, this alert and funny book constructs a decagon—a polygon close to a circle—whose ten concepts are angles from which diagonals crisscross strategically. We follow effortlessly Lacan's histories, theories and inventions, effectively squaring the circle of Freudian Unreason."

Jean-Michel Rabaté, *Professor of English and Comparative Literature, University of Pennsylvania, USA; Fellow of the American Academy of Arts and Sciences*

"In this hugely impressive book, which is written with exemplary clarity, erudition and verve, Dany Nobus dares to ask profound and daunting questions about why Lacan remains such a vital and challenging motivator for thinking. Propelled by the force of this question ("Why Lacan?"), Nobus enters into the most vexed and enriching zones of psychoanalytic reflection and takes the reader along with him. The book is thought-provoking, wonderfully argued, pedagogical, and playfully lucid. It is also a gripping read that will help re-introduce Lacan to a new generation of thinkers."

Elissa Marder, *Professor of French and Comparative Literature, Emory University*

Critique of Psychoanalytic Reason

The highly arcane "wisdom" produced by the French psychoanalyst Jacques Lacan is either endlessly regurgitated and recited as holy writ by his numerous acolytes, or radically dismissed as unpalatable nonsense by his equally countless detractors. Contrary to these common, strictly antagonistic yet uniformly uncritical practices, this book offers a meticulous critique of some key theoretical and clinical aspects of Lacan's expansive oeuvre, testing their consistency, examining their implications, and investigating their significance.

In nine interrelated chapters, the book highlights both the flaws and the strengths of Lacan's ideas, in areas of investigation that are as crucial as they are contentious, within as well as outside psychoanalysis. Drawing on a vast range of source materials, including many unpublished archival documents, it teases out controversial issues such as money, organizational failure, and lighthearted "gay" thinking, and it relies on the highest standards of scholarly excellence to develop its arguments. At the same time, the book does not presuppose any prior knowledge of Lacanian psychoanalysis on the part of the reader, but allows its readership to indulge in the joys of in-depth critical analysis, trans-disciplinary creative thinking, and persistent questioning.

This book will appeal to researchers and students alike in psychoanalytic studies and philosophy, as well as all those interested in French theory and the history of ideas.

Dany Nobus is Professor of Psychoanalytic Psychology at Brunel University London, UK, Founding Scholar of the British Psychoanalytic Council, and former Chair and Fellow of the Freud Museum London. His previous books include *Thresholds and Pathways Between Jung and Lacan: On the Blazing Sublime* (edited with Ann Casement and Phil Goss, 2021), *The Law of Desire: On Lacan's "Kant with Sade"* (2017), and *Knowing Nothing, Staying Stupid: Elements for a Psychoanalytic Epistemology* (with Malcolm Quinn, 2005).

The Centre for Freudian Analysis and Research Library
Series Editors: Anouchka Grose, Darian Leader, Alan Rowan

CFAR was founded in 1985 with the aim of developing Freudian and Lacanian psychoanalysis in the United Kingdom. Lacan's rereading and rethinking of Freud had been neglected in the Anglophone world, despite its important implications for the theory and practice of psychoanalysis. Today, this situation is changing, with a lively culture of training groups, seminars, conferences, and publications.

CFAR offers both introductory and advanced courses in psychoanalysis, as well as a clinical training programme in Lacanian psychoanalysis. It can provide access to Lacanian psychoanalysts working in the United Kingdom and has links with Lacanian groups across the world. The CFAR Library aims to make classic Lacanian texts available in English for the first time, as well as publishing original research in the Lacanian field.

The Law of the Mother
An Essay on the Sexual Sinthome
Geneviève Morel

The Baby and the Drive
Lacanian Work with Newborns and Infants
Marie Couvert

Treating Autism Today
Lacanian Perspectives
Edited by Laura Tarsia and Kristina Valendinova

Critique of Psychoanalytic Reason
Studies in Lacanian Theory and Practice
Dany Nobus

www.cfar.org.uk

https://www.routledge.com/The-Centre-for-Freudian-Analysis-and-Research-Library/book-series/KARNACCFARL

Critique of Psychoanalytic Reason

Studies in Lacanian Theory and Practice

Dany Nobus

LONDON AND NEW YORK

Cover image: Life's Illusions, 1849, George Frederic Watts. Presented by Mrs Alfred Seymour 1902 © Tate

First published 2022
by Routledge
4 Park Square, Milton Park, Abingdon, Oxon OX14 4RN

and by Routledge
605 Third Avenue, New York, NY 10158

Routledge is an imprint of the Taylor & Francis Group, an informa business

© 2022 Dany Nobus

The right of Dany Nobus to be identified as author of this work has been asserted in accordance with sections 77 and 78 of the Copyright, Designs and Patents Act 1988.

All rights reserved. No part of this book may be reprinted or reproduced or utilised in any form or by any electronic, mechanical, or other means, now known or hereafter invented, including photocopying and recording, or in any information storage or retrieval system, without permission in writing from the publishers.

Trademark notice: Product or corporate names may be trademarks or registered trademarks, and are used only for identification and explanation without intent to infringe.

British Library Cataloguing-in-Publication Data
A catalogue record for this book is available from the British Library

Library of Congress Cataloging-in-Publication Data
Names: Nobus, Dany, author.
Title: Critique of psychoanalytic reason : studies in Lacanian theory and practice / Dany Nobus.
Description: Abingdon, Oxon ; New York, NY : Routledge, 2022. | Series: The Centre for Freudian Analysis and Research Library | Includes bibliographical references and index. |
Identifiers: LCCN 2021047992 (print) | LCCN 2021047993 (ebook) | ISBN 9781032172101 (hardback) | ISBN 9781032172118 (paperback) | ISBN 9781003252276 (ebook)
Subjects: LCSH: Lacan, Jacques, 1901-1981. | Psychoanalysis.
Classification: LCC BF109.L23 N63 2022 (print) | LCC BF109.L23 (ebook) | DDC 150.19/5--dc23/eng/20211012
LC record available at https://lccn.loc.gov/2021047992
LC ebook record available at https://lccn.loc.gov/2021047993

ISBN: 978-1-032-17210-1 (hbk)
ISBN: 978-1-032-17211-8 (pbk)
ISBN: 978-1-003-25227-6 (ebk)

DOI: 10.4324/9781003252276

Typeset in Times New Roman
by MPS Limited, Dehradun

For Oriana

Ames parentem, si aequus est, si aliter, feras

Contents

	List of Figures	xi
	Introduction	1
1	Lacan's *Écrits* Revisited: On Writing as Object of Desire	16
2	What Are Words Worth? Lacan and the Circulation of Money in the Psychoanalytic Economy	41
3	That Obscure Object of Psychoanalysis	62
4	The Sculptural Iconography of Feminine Jouissance: Lacan's Reading of Bernini's *Saint Teresa in Ecstasy*	87
5	*Esprit de Corps*, Work Transference, and Dissolution: Lacan as an Organizational Theorist	112
6	Psychoanalysis as *gai saber*: Towards a New Episteme of Laughter	131
7	Once He Was a Poet: On Psychoanalysis as Poetry in Lacan's Clinical Paradigm	151
8	Lacan's Clinical Artistry: On Sublimation, Sublation, and the Sublime	172

| 9 | Lacan with Antigone: On Tragedy and Desire in the Ethics of Psychoanalysis | 197 |

Bibliography	237
Acknowledgements	278
Photo Acknowledgements	282
Index	283

Figures

1.1	Jacques Lacan, *Écrits* (imaginary cover)	19
1.2	*La trahison de l'écriture*	24
1.3	Jacques Lacan, *Pas à lire* (imaginary book)	30
1.4	Schema of Sade's practical reason	33
1.5	Jacques Lacan, *a* (imaginary book)	34
4.1	The Cornaro Chapel	88
4.2	*Saint Teresa in Ecstasy* (detail)	94
4.3	*The Blessed Ludovica Albertoni*	96
4.4	*The Blessed Ludovica Albertoni* (detail)	97

Introduction

Much more than any other 20th-century psychoanalyst, Jacques Lacan will have had his name preceded by a forceful interrogative of "Why?". Much more than the books and papers engaging with other major figures in the history of psychoanalysis, those focusing on the life and works of Lacan will have started, implicitly or explicitly, with a section entitled "Why Lacan?", or some sort of justification as to why his presence is warranted. Juxtaposed with the name of Lacan, the question is everything but hospitable. It does not simply offer an opportunity for discussion; it is neither an invitation to contemplate, nor an encouragement to pause and reflect, even less a mere rhetorical figure—not requiring any answer whatsoever. Instead, the interrogative generally constitutes an intellectual assignment, a non-negotiable exhortation to work through the issue and to formulate a response that is both an explanation and a motivation. As such, it carries the same connotations as Heidegger's famous phrase "*Was heißt …?*", which he principally employed to incite thinking about thought itself (Heidegger, 2002[1954]). Whereas the phrase has been rendered into English as "What is called …?" (Heidegger, 1968[1954]), thus suggesting interpretations such as "What does it mean (to think)?", or "What does (thinking) mean", it really invokes the ratio of thought, and should therefore be interpreted as "What calls for (thinking)?", "What is responsible for (thinking) to occur?", or "What requires (thinking) to happen?". In a similar vein, the question "Why Lacan?" conveys an instigation, an obligation even, to account for the name's rationale, its *raison d'être*, and should therefore be taken as an injunction to think about "What calls for Lacan?".

The exigency and persistence with which this question presents itself often conceals an implicit accusation, prompting the need for an elaborate defence. Picture Jacques Lacan as a latter-day Josef K., who is arrested at the crack of dawn—someone must have been telling lies about him, because he knows he has not done anything wrong—and immediately brought to trial, the prosecution demanding: "Why Lacan?", "What calls for this man?", "What forces us to engage with him?", "What stops us from executing him,

DOI: 10.4324/9781003252276-1

or relegating him to the archives of oblivion?". Here is what a witness for the defence could say:

> Jacques Lacan is arguably the most important psychoanalyst since Sigmund Freud ... Lacan's work has transformed psychoanalysis, both as a theory of the unconscious mind and as a clinical practice. Over 50 per cent of the world's analysts now employ Lacanian methods. At the same time, Lacan's influence beyond the confines of the consulting room is unsurpassed among modern psychoanalytic thinkers. Lacanian thought now pervades the disciplines of literary and film studies, women's studies and social theory and is applied to such diverse fields as education, legal studies and international relations. For a student of the humanities and the social sciences today it is almost impossible not to engage with the ideas of Lacan at some level .... (Homer, 2005, p. 1)

These are the words of Sean Homer, an established academic who has himself engaged with Lacan's ideas in the fields of social and political theory. They appear in the opening paragraph of a short introductory volume, appropriately titled *Jacques Lacan*, under the even more appropriate heading "Why Lacan?". Few will disagree that, as a defence, the words carry a good deal of weight, although their assertive power does not preclude the need for further argumentation. The prosecutor is not satisfied with general claims and declarations. Why is Lacan the most important psychoanalyst since Freud? How has his work transformed psychoanalysis? Why is it that (give or take) 50 per cent of the world's analysts *do not* employ Lacanian methods? How does Lacanian thought pervade the humanities and the social sciences?

Let us assume, for a moment, that our witnesses do indeed have very good reasons for making these assertions. Let us assume that they would be able to substantiate each of their points, were they instructed to do so. In short, let us assume that our witnesses, as speaking under oath, are telling the truth. Then it would appear that the question *cum* accusation, to which the assertions offer a response *cum* defence, the question "Why Lacan?", could indeed only be formulated within an absurd, Kafkaesque universe. Were it to be true that someone's name is ubiquitous, that his contributions are seminal, path-breaking and earth-shaking, indispensable and incontrovertible, there is surely no reason to ask "Why?". Has anyone ever asked "Why Copernicus?", "Why Newton?", "Why Darwin?", "Why Einstein?". However, were we to assume that the question, instead of being absurd, represents a genuine exhortation to account for Lacan's existence as a *maître-à-penser*, then the answers cannot possibly be true, or they must contain some gross exaggerations and deliberate falsifications of the actual state of affairs, which implies that our witnesses run the risk of being charged with perjury.

Over the years, there has been no shortage of voices, witnesses for the prosecution, who have claimed that Lacan's defenders are inveterate liars, much like the man himself, and therefore deserve to be "dispatched", alongside their false prophet. Amongst the most impassioned of these anti-Lacanian voices is the imposing figure of Raymond Tallis, emeritus professor of geriatric medicine, prolific scholar, philosopher, poet, and playwright, who notoriously proclaimed in a highly publicized review of Élisabeth Roudinesco's intellectual biography of Lacan:

> [T]he French psychoanalyst Jacques Lacan … is one of the fattest spiders at the heart of the web of muddled not-quite-thinkable-thoughts and evidence-free assertions of limitless scope, which practitioners of theorhoea have woven into their version of the humanities … His lunatic legacy lives on in places remote from those in which he damaged his patients, colleagues, mistresses, wives, children, publishers, editors, and opponents—in departments of literature whose inmates are even now trying to, or pretending to, make sense of his utterly unfounded, gnomic teachings and inflicting them on baffled students. Aleister Crowley, the 20th-century thinker whom Lacan most resembles, has not been so fortunate in his afterlife. (Tallis, 1997, p. 20)

Similarly, scholars and clinicians such as François Roustang (1990), Mikkel Borch-Jacobsen (1991[1990]), Alan Sokal and Jean Bricmont (1998[1997]), Filip Buekens (2005), and Jacques Van Rillaer (2019), some of whom were themselves originally trained in the Lacanian tradition, have attempted to demonstrate that Lacan was but a self-obsessed, authoritarian nonsense-monger, a clinical charlatan and an inveterate plagiarizer, whose convoluted ideas and dubious intellectual and therapeutic footprint need to be permanently erased from our cultural memory. It is worth emphasizing, here, that not all of Lacan's detractors merely extrapolate their visceral aversion to psychoanalysis onto the easy target of an institutional maverick. Indeed, many of Lacan's fiercest critics are, and have historically always been, professionally trained psychoanalysts, some of whom—as I just pointed out—being former students of Lacan himself who, for one reason or the other, felt the need to defrock and dethrone the "master".

One may wonder, of course, why Lacan—should it be true that he was all the things his enemies hold against him—nonetheless succeeded in creating a substantial following, far beyond the borders of his native France. One may even be inclined to argue that the anti-Lacanian arguments must be flawed, simply on account of the fact that "50 per cent of the world's analysts" cannot possibly be wrong. Yet the witnesses for the prosecution will no doubt protest, here, that propagation and consensus are just about the weakest criteria for judging the truth-value of a system of thought, and that Lacan's widespread influence is but an empty fad, conditioned by a common desire amongst young intellectuals for non-mainstream, anti-establishment, and "progressive" ideas, behind which one can just about discern—to use the title of Richard Wolin's critical dissection of postmodernism's surreptitious infatuation with, of all systems, the ideological tenets of fascism—the perennial seduction of unreason (Wolin, 2004). As Francis Wheen put it in his highly entertaining volume *How Mumbo-Jumbo Conquered the World*, notably with reference to Lacan's infamous statement, in "The Subversion of the Subject and the Dialectic of Desire in the Freudian Unconscious", that "the erectile organ can be equated with the $\sqrt{-1}$" (Lacan, 2006[1960], p. 697): What does it matter, Barbara Ehrenreich once asked, if some French guy wants to think of his penis as the square root of minus one? 'Not much, except that on American campuses, especially the more elite ones, such utterances were routinely passed off as examples of boldly "transgressive" left-wing thought'. Few progressives dared to challenge this tyranny of twaddle for fear of being reviled as cultural and political reactionaries—or, no less shamingly, ignorant philistines' (Wheen, 2004, p. 89). In response to Sokal and Bricmont, who have been far less indifferent towards Lacan's statement than Ehrenreich, insofar as they conceded in their *Intellectual Impostures* that they found it positively distressing to see their penises being equated with $\sqrt{-1}$ (Sokal and Bricmont, 1997, p. 27), Bruce Fink has endeavoured to demonstrate that Lacan's declaration is less nonsensical than it may appear at first (Fink, 2004), yet I am not at all persuaded that his careful unpacking of Lacan's text will in any way alter Sokal and Bricmont's diagnosis of Lacanian theory, let alone their distress about their penises—or the phallus for that matter. For even if reason can be restored behind the surface of unreason, the latter will still be regarded as Lacan's main, and most conspicuous accomplishment, with the added complication that it may very well have been a consciously crafted scheme for tapping into the vulnerable minds of the younger generation and for securing a large group of enthusiastic adherents.

Pitting our witnesses against one another—those claiming that "everything" calls for Lacan and those positing that "nothing" calls for him, apart from the fact that Western culture seems to require a regular dose of intellectual humbug to sustain its image as always being at the forefront of ground-breaking, innovative thought—they are unlikely to cancel each other out. And so the debate surrounding Lacan's significance is likely to continue for many years to come, although the question "Why Lacan?" may also lose some of its poignancy in the process. For if we believe that Lacan was definitely the greatest 20th-century psychoanalyst after Freud, for whatever reason, there is no need to ask "Why?". Indeed the interrogative becomes absurd. Yet if we believe that he was but another narcissistic villain who unfortunately succeeded in deceiving a large number of naïve citizens with his charismatic persona and strangely appealing balderdash, the question becomes equally obsolete, because its specificity is drowned in a quagmire of pseudo-rhetorical musings about the social threats of post-modernity. "Why Lacan?" becomes synonymous, then, with "Why L. Ron Hubbard?", "Why Bhagwan Rajneesh?", "Why Deepak Chopra?" or, in a more sinister vein, "Why Jim Jones?", "Why David Koresh?", "Why Warren Jeffs?".

In this book, the interrogative that will have presided, sometimes unnecessarily perhaps, over many a volume dedicated to the life and works of Lacan is silently preserved, if only because "Why"—even when re-interpreted as "What calls for?"—is an eminently psychoanalytic question, and there is no good reason why a psychoanalyst, be it Lacan, should not be subjected to the question that underpins the discipline he helped to advance. In keeping with my earlier line of reasoning, the preservation of the question, in all its specificity, presupposes and implies that I cannot and will not engage in a defence of Lacan, neither his person nor his work, yet neither will I seek to affiliate myself, although it would no doubt be perceived as a grand token of intellectual generosity, with the anti-Lacanian factions on this planet. Instead, I shall maintain the questions "Why?" and "What calls for?" in their pressing urgency and therefore in the undecidability of their answers. As such, the essays collected in this volume demonstrate, each in their own way, that the only possible response to the question, the only way one can address it without reducing its underlying exhortation, the only way to answer it so that it is actually left intact, is by echoing the interrogative. Why? Because of "why?" Of all the possible answers, this is the one that comes closest to what the theory and practice of psychoanalysis itself instigated, with varying degrees of success, in its students and practitioners. In addition, it may also be the answer that is most germane to what Lacan's work in itself calls for, both within and outside a psychoanalytic setting.

On three separate occasions, Lacan himself wondered about the place, function, and status of his actions within the psychoanalytic community. On two occasions, his soul-searching followed his exclusion from an established psychoanalytic organization; on one occasion, it coincided with his auto-exclusion from the organization he himself had established. In each case, however, the reflexive and rather self-indulgent question "Why me?" elicited a protracted critique of the operating structures and organizational principles pervading a psychoanalytic association (including his own) and their implications for the future of psychoanalysis.

When, in the summer of 1953, Lacan took his leave from the *Société psychanalytique de Paris* and joined the newly created *Société française de Psychanalyse*, in which he was rapidly recognized as the main intellectual figure, he did not hesitate to interpret his own marginalization as a symptom of the ailing body of psychoanalysis, as supported by the official institutions. In the preface to his seminal 1953 "Rome Discourse", which should not be passed off as the first text in which Lacan spoke in his own name, but rather as the first text in which he spoke in order to justify and consolidate his own name, he scorned the psychoanalytic establishment, as represented by the institution to which he himself had belonged before the secession, for their authoritarian regulation of psychoanalytic training, and for a "disappointing formalism that discourages initiative", i.e., for reducing analytic technique to a simple set of recipes (Lacan, 2006[1953], p. 199). If we take Lacan's critique at face value, here, the implication is that he might never have risen to psychoanalytic superstardom had the official institutions been less rigid and more accommodating in their conception of psychoanalytic theory and practice. This may only be wild speculation, for sure, although it cannot be denied that Lacan had not been particularly radical or innovative during the years of his membership of the Paris Psychoanalytic Society, and only seems to have had his creative agency unleashed when on the brink of relational breakdown, and especially after having been orphaned. In 1949, Lacan proposed a series of regulations to the Paris Society, in which he stated that "psychoanalysis is essentially a medical technique", "medical qualifications ... and especially a specialisation in psychiatry [being] most recommendable for psychoanalytic training", and that a psychoanalytic training process requires "a rhythm of four to five sessions per week, three being a minimum, and a total duration of at least two years" (Lacan, 1976[1949], pp. 33–34). No one in the Paris Society disagreed, but there is absolutely no reason why they should have, since Lacan was only reiterating principles that had been in force, rigidly and formalistically, for many years. Lacan's diagnosis of the institution's pathologies and his vituperative dismissal of its anti-psychoanalytic premises only came later, after an unpalatable power-struggle had left him in the lurch, and after his "variable-length sessions" had become a thorn in the side of his former companions. Hence, there may have been something in the way the Paris Society, and by extension the international psychoanalytic movement, was functioning that effectively called for Lacan, that prompted him to become the radical dissident he definitely had not been until then.

Like the circumstances leading up to Lacan's "Rome Discourse", his intellectual survivor's strategy is equally well-known. Throughout the 1950s Lacan justified his institutional position and his intellectual interventions by means of his famous "return to Freud". If Lacan made a name for himself during the 1950s, it was primarily because he managed to convince a growing number of people that he was returning to them what they had been deprived of for way too long: the real, unadulterated, naked Freud, a body of work which had not been embellished by the arcane language of academic science; an oeuvre which had been recovered from the language of unfaithful, ideologically tainted translations and standardizing interpretations. It is in the name of Freud, and for Freud's sake, that Lacan embarked on his personal journey, and it is with a view to rediscovering the psychoanalytic homeland that he set out from the psychoanalytic shores on which he had lived, and which he had helped to define for many years. During the 1950s, Lacan became Lacan because of Freud.

It is also worth emphasizing, here, that Lacan's Freud, the Freud that allowed him to become Lacan, was not only at odds with the Freud to which the mainstream psychoanalytic circles had committed themselves, but also different from the Freud that most people would assimilate after a cursory, leisurely glance at his work. For if the meaning of the return to Freud was in actual fact a return to Freud's meaning, as Lacan put it in 1955 (Lacan, 2006[1955b], p. 337), this did not imply that Lacan effectively returned a meaningful Freud. Explaining his project to a no doubt bemused Viennese audience, Lacan posited that he aimed "to put back into force" "the original meaning Freud preserved" in psychoanalysis, challenging his listeners with questions whose rhetorical value was by no means unequivocal:

> How could this meaning escape us when it is attested to in a body of written work of the most lucid and organic kind? And how could it leave us hesitant when the study of this work shows us that its different stages and changes in direction are governed by Freud's inflexibly effective concern to maintain its original rigor? (Ibid., p. 336)

The irony, of course, is that Lacan was precisely making the point that the "inescapable meaning" of Freud had nonetheless escaped the rulers of the psychoanalytic city. Yet the double irony is that Lacan was also intimating that it had escaped them *not* because they had failed to put their finger on it, but exactly because they were convinced that they had managed to capture it. Lacan accused the psychoanalytic establishment of domesticating Freud's meaning, of turning Freud's work into a known corpus whose meaning is undisputed or, as he put in an oft-quoted passage from the "Rome Discourse", of reducing Freud's legacy to a set of "concepts that are being deadened by routine use" (Lacan, 2006[1953], p. 199). To Lacan, Freud's "inescapable meaning" had escaped his followers because they were convinced that they had found it. In other words, the "inescapable meaning" Lacan attributed to Freud is that definitive, true meaning escapes. "Freud's discovery calls truth into question [*met en question la vérité*]", Lacan maintained (Lacan, 2006[1955b], p. 337), with the added suggestion that there is no reason why this truth should not be called into question in its own right. During the 1950s, Lacan's return to Freud's meaning thus epitomized, more than anything else, a de-stabilization of the meaningful Freud, in favour of a Freud whose inescapable meaning is that his meaning continues to escape.

As it happens, most people who read Freud come to the conclusion that his work is relatively easy to read; they are left with the impression that they are capable of reading and understanding what he writes. Lacan intended to challenge the readability of Freud. After having read Lacan's reading of Freud, Freud becomes less readable—not because Lacan's reading of Freud is as such unreadable (which is, of course, what many of his critics have proclaimed), but because it forces the reader to read differently, to pay attention to the twists and turns of the text, its internal contradictions, logical inconsistencies, and *non sequiturs*. In Lacan's hands, Freud became more inscrutable, less familiar, more enigmatic, less comprehensible. In short, he was granted back the status deserving of a psychoanalyst. But the upshot is that, if during the 1950s Lacan became Lacan in the name and for the sake of Freud, his ascendancy was neither conditioned nor galvanized by any kind of doctrinal allegiance. To the best of my knowledge, Lacan did not refer to himself as a Freudian during these years, and this could easily be explained with reference to the fact that those who considered themselves Freudians occupied the psychoanalytic camps Lacan had left behind and against which he was rallying. In placing a question mark above the psychoanalytic establishment, Lacan not only interrogated a certain ideological transformation of Freud's work, but relocated interrogation itself at the heart of the psychoanalytic discipline. This outlook prevented Lacan from being a new adherent of (the new, but original) Freud, yet it also somehow situated him in the same place as Freud. It stopped him from being a follower, yet as a result it destined him to become a leader, with a following of his own.

It is again well-known how, at the end of 1963, Lacan's own group decided to expel him as a training analyst in return for its continued recognition as a study group of the International Psychoanalytic Association. Resuming his teaching after less than two months, in a different location and with a different audience, Lacan designated his expulsion as a "major excommunication" and reflected, for the second time, upon what authorized his presence and his interventions in the field of psychoanalysis (Lacan, 1994[1973], pp. 1–13). "[My] position ... has changed", he disclosed during his inaugural lesson at the *École Normale Supérieure*, "it is not wholly inside, but whether it is outside is not known" (Ibid., p. 3). The inside/outside distinction evidently referred, here, to Lacan's place within the psychoanalytic community, yet it could easily be applied to his new position vis-à-vis his own teaching. Between 1953 and 1963, Lacan taught his "return to Freud's meaning" at the *Hôpital Sainte-Anne* in Paris, mainly to an audience of analytic candidates at the French Psychoanalytic Society. It is no coincidence, therefore, that he focused his weekly theoretical seminars on clinical-technical issues such as resistance, transference, repetition, psychosis, the formations of the unconscious, ethical issues, identification, anxiety, etc. Truthful to his own principled belief about the dubious value of ready-made psychoanalytic knowledge, Lacan did not regurgitate the known facts, and in this sense his lectures were far removed from any type of introductory module in psychoanalysis, yet he was nonetheless careful to ensure that his teaching (and the writings that emanated from it) unfolded within the confines of a psychoanalytic training programme. When Lacan took the stage at the *École Normale Supérieure* in January 1964 to resume his seminar again, he was officially barred from teaching analytic candidates as part of their training programme. He was no longer a training analyst and his audience no longer expected him to offer his lectures as psychoanalytic training. And so Lacan commenced his seminar anew, but under a different title. Instead of continuing with "The Names of the Father", which he had broken off at the end of the first session, the day after he had officially been struck off as a training analyst, Lacan started afresh, with *The Fundamentals of Psychoanalysis*, a title which would not be misplaced as the corollary of Psychoanalysis 101, later to be renamed as *The Four Fundamental Concepts of Psychoanalysis*. As David Macey has pointed out in his introduction to the English translation of this seminar, "Lacan's reference to "fundamental concepts" indicates his adoption of a new stance ... By 1964, he was clearly beginning to move away from his habitual scepticism and to enter a territory which was not really his own" (Macey, 1994, p. xxx).

Whether or not one agrees with Macey's definition of this foreign territory as the "philosophy of concepts", it is difficult to deny that from 1964, Lacan was no longer merely speaking for Freud's sake, but increasingly for the sake of his own theory of psychoanalysis. Instead of rethinking Freud, Lacan started to rethink his own thinking of Freud, thereby offering himself to his audience as an original thinker in his own right. Whereas during the 1950s, Lacan's seminars and writings had been littered with references to Freud's works, these Freudian bearings gradually disappeared during the 1960s and 1970s. For a period of ten years, Sigmund Freud was the most quoted source in Lacan's seminars; during the period after his "excommunication", the most quoted source was actually Jacques Lacan. One probably should not interpret this avalanche of self-references only as a tell-tale sign of Lacan's growing narcissistic infatuation with his own genius, but also as an indication of his hard-won confidence to safeguard the future of psychoanalysis by protecting it against its own practitioners. Again, one may venture the hypothesis, here, that Lacan would not have had to consolidate his own thinking in this way, if the psychoanalytic group to which he belonged had been less perfidious, and more concerned with the maintenance of their internal training standards than with the application of the formalistic rules of the psychoanalytic establishment. Lacan's "betrayal" at the hands of his own people liberated him from all institutional constraints and gave him the opportunity to re-invent psychoanalysis, but by the same token it allowed his audience to re-invent his re-invention of psychoanalysis as his own invention. From the mid-1960s until the late 1970s, Lacan's audience grew exponentially, and his reputation as a *maître-à-penser* also slowly but steadily permeated academic layers in the Anglo-American world. When, in 1966, Lacan's *Écrits* were unleashed on the French public, 5,000 copies were sold in less than two weeks (Roudinesco, 1997[1993], p. 328). It is probably fair to say, here, that the more Lacan's audience expanded, the less he made an effort to make himself understood, and the less effort he made to make himself understood, the more his audience expanded.

It is interesting to note that with the increase of Lacanians flocking around Lacan, Lacan himself increasingly identified as a Freudian. On the 21st of June 1964, eight months after losing his rights as a training analyst, Lacan created his own psychoanalytic organization, which he initially called the *École Française de Psychanalyse*, yet which was shortly afterwards renamed the *École Freudienne de Paris* (Lacan, 1990[1964], p. 97). Intellectual allegiance was thus substituted for national identity, and the work of Freud was honoured, perhaps for the first time in history, as the undisputable basis for an educational structure, with the militant aim of accomplishing a labour "which, in the field opened up by Freud, restores the cutting edge of his discovery" and which "through assiduous criticism, denounces the deviations and compromises that blunt its progress while degrading its use" (Ibid., p. 97). In this sense, Lacan explicitly opted, although not at first, to put his institution under the aegis of an orthodox psychoanalytic tradition, although it was of course radically different from all the traditions of Freudianism that had developed until then. Lacan's choice did imply, however, that he considered "Freud's meaning" to be sufficiently recalibrated for a tradition to be introduced and promoted in his name. In choosing to call his school the "Freudian School of Paris", Lacan institutionalized the question mark he had placed over Freud's legacy during the 1950s, and shifted the interrogation to his own reading of Freud. Yet, in situating himself within a Freudian lineage, and creating a Freudian school, he probably could not have anticipated that his constantly increasing number of followers preferred to call themselves Lacanians.

What does it mean to be a Lacanian? This is exactly the question asked by Jean Clavreul, one of Lacan's analysands, shortly before the creation of the *École Freudienne de Paris*, to a group of people who had decided to remain loyal to their analyst and teacher. Answering his own question, Clavreul argued that being a Lacanian neither requires having undertaken an analysis with Lacan, nor agreeing with everything he says, but is predicated upon the acceptance of certain theoretical points, most importantly that complying with common normative standards for the sake of personal recognition is but an imaginary enterprise, which as such inflates the ego but disregards the significance of symbolically regulated bonds (Clavreul, 1977[1964], pp. 141–142). Using Lacan's terminology, Clavreul clearly wanted his "theoretical point" to come across as a sneer at those who had decided to give up Lacan in exchange for official recognition, but simultaneously he also seemed to be concerned about the danger of Lacan's allies constructing their identity on the basis of an identification with the master. It is as if Clavreul also wanted to emphasize that the questions "Why Lacan?", "What calls for Lacan?", or "What calls me to Lacan?" should not be answered along the lines of "Lacan allows me to construct myself in his name", or

"Lacan gives me the opportunity to identify myself as belonging to a radical intellectual movement".

Perhaps Clavreul's warning was not sufficiently explicit. Perhaps he was too idealistic and naïve in thinking that Lacanians, by virtue of their knowledge of Lacan's theory, would be better protected against the imaginary trappings of social recognition. The fact of the matter is that the Lacanians proved to be at least as vulnerable to the ills of blind allegiance and self-promoting fanaticism as any other loyal adherents of an ideological doctrine. It is difficult to know whether Lacan loved it or hated it—perhaps he looked at it with "hateloving" (*hainamoration*), as he himself designated the intricate tangle of love and hatred (Lacan, 1998[1975], p. 90)—but it definitely did not leave him indifferent. On numerous occasions, he complained to his audience about their complacency, their diligent absorption of his exceedingly complex ideas, their dogged determination to capture and regurgitate his wisdom, and their ardent desire to transform him into a cultural phenomenon. Lacan wondered why, and often confessed to the impossibility of escaping his attributed position, as in the following excerpt from December 1974:

> I don't know why what I bring to you here would be less stupid than the rest. It would make understandable why someone slipped a banana peel under my foot by calling me up and asking me to go to Nice to give a lecture—I am not joking—on the Lacanian phenomenon. I do not expect to be a phenomenon ... If I persevere ... it is only because I believe to have grasped something ... of the analytic experience, which the analysts find difficult to bear. Hence, if there is a phenomenon, it can only be the lacanalyst, or even the laca-no-analyst [*laca-pas d'analyste*] phenomenon ... Of course, I wasn't going to tell those people in Nice: "You know, I'm not a phenomenon!". Because that would have been a *Verneinung* [negation] ... And then, ... I asked them to pose me some [questions] ... [U]nlike you, they posed them ... and these questions were striking in this way: they were pertinent, in a second zone of course ... And so I found myself in the situation whereby, without having challenged the Lacanian phenomenon, I ended up demonstrating it. The Lacanian phenomenon ... is that I have an effect on an audience which has only heard from afar, through repercussion, what I articulate here .... (Lacan, 1998[1975], pp. 99–100)

Much more than the dissemination of the Lacanian phenomenon, and the dilution of his teaching across the cultural landscape, it was probably the "lacanalytic" ideology permeating his own circle, in combination with the endless intra-institutional struggles over the procedure of the so-called "pass", which finally prompted Lacan, on 5 January 1980, to dissolve his own school (Lacan, 1990[1980]). The circumstances, objectives and implications of this act are complex, and this is certainly not the place to engage with the numerous, contradictory interpretations of it that have been formulated over the years. I can imagine many a member of the *École Freudienne de Paris* being taken aback by Lacan's decision and mumbling the inevitable question: "Why, Lacan?". "There is a problem with the École", Lacan claimed, and he went on to suggest that his School had become "an Institution, the effect of a consolidated group, at the expense of the discursive effect expected from an experiment, when it is Freudian" (Ibid., p. 130). The last term is significant, because Lacan repeated it in what would be his final public lecture, the famous Caracas seminar of 12 July 1980, in which he presented his Latin-American audience (or his "lacano-Americans", as he had put it in June 1980) with an unusual challenge: "It's up to you to be Lacanians if you wish. For my part, I'm a Freudian" (Lacan, 1981[1980], p. 103). Lacan did not say that he was not a Lacanian, which could have been regarded again, as he himself pointed out after his Nice conference, as a *Verneinung*, but identified instead in the same vein as he had done 16 years earlier, as a follower of Freud. Why, Lacan? Why would you have thought that the creation of a new school, based on a new allegiance to the "Freudian Cause", would dis-solve the old-school problems? Why would you have thought that in gathering a new group of adherents, solemnly committed to "assiduous criticism", you would be able to expel the "deviations and compromises" that the old school had nourished, you who had suggested so emphatically, at the very end of your *Television* performance, that an interpretation must be sufficiently nimble for an ongoing exchange to take place between the pervasiveness of pure loss and the worsening of paternity? (Lacan, 1990[1974], p. 46). Why, Lacan?

Earlier on, I stated that "Why?" is the psychoanalytic question par excellence, as in the unfortunate analysand who after many years of analysis finally allows himself to go on a holiday and expresses his newly found joy to his analyst with a short message on the back of a picture-postcard: "I am having the time of life. Just wish you were here to tell me why". However silly the joke may be, it shows that the question is first of all situated on the side of the analysand, and that the analyst is called upon to provide an answer. Many a psychoanalyst will have heard his or her "preliminary sessions" revolve around Why-questions: "Why can't I sleep?", "Why do I always fall in love with the wrong guy?", "Why do I hurt myself?" And if the patient does not come up with the correct interrogative, only an idle psychoanalyst would want to avoid trying to elicit it.

In many of his writings, including the case studies, Freud claimed to know why something had happened to his patients, and sometimes to himself. He claimed to know why he had had the dream of Irma's injection, why he forgot the name of Signorelli, why Little Hans was afraid of horses (amongst other things), why Dora was coughing, why the Rat Man wanted to cut his throat, why Schreber (whom he had never met) had become a raving lunatic, etc. Yet there were also things about which he confessed his ignorance: why certain boys protect themselves against castration anxiety with a fetish, whereas others become homosexual, and still others resolve the issue in a "normal" way; why some women leave the Oedipal drama with a masculinity complex, others decide to throw out their sexuality altogether, and still others prefer the option of motherhood. Freud did not know what determines the choice of neurosis (*Neurosenwahl*), and he definitely did not know what a woman wants.

When Lacan embarked on his return to Freud's meaning, his intention was not to answer the questions Freud had left behind, in order to be better equipped at answering his patients' questions whenever they would occur. If anything, Lacan believed that this is exactly what had to be avoided at all costs and what permitted him to rally against the contemporary closure of Freud's thought in the works of Marie Bonaparte, Otto Fenichel, and other systematizers. When Lacan started reading Freud properly in the early 1950s, Freud appeared with more questions than he himself would ever have thought he had. As I indicated earlier, even those passages that would have been quite clear to any cultivated reader acquired a high degree of ambiguity in Lacan's return to Freud. And he not only forced himself to place this question mark above Freud's concepts and constructions, but also managed to instil his audience with the same desire, as Jean Hyppolite experienced all too well when he was asked to comment on Freud's paper "Negation" (Freud, 1961[1925*h*]; Hyppolite, 2006[1956]; Lacan, 1988[1975], pp. 52–61).

In returning to Freud, Lacan thus asked what very few, if any of his contemporaries had dared to asked: "Why, Freud?", "What calls for this notion?", "What makes you say what you say?". And in asking Freud "Why?", the answer was, as could no doubt be expected, more often than not left in abeyance. Yet in not receiving ready-made answers from Freud, Lacan gradually developed his own tentative answers, hypothetical formulations at best, which subsequently matured into more solid theoretical principles, such as the famous formula that "the unconscious is structured like a language". With hindsight, Lacan's exclusion from the French Psychoanalytic Society was perhaps also fortuitous, because it forced Lacan to stop, to reflect, and to start afresh, examining the validity of the formulae he himself had produced as answers to Freud's questions. When Jacques Lacan had become the answer to Sigmund Freud, the time was rife to question, in a Freudian psychoanalytic vein, the answers of Jacques Lacan. As the "question and answer" sections in the published version of *Seminar XI* demonstrate, this is exactly what happened during the first year of Lacan's lectures at the École Normale Supérieure. However, as time went by, the formulae became ever more ingrained in an unimpeachable codex of Lacanian thought. Why Lacan? Because of Lacan!

Just as much as Lacan's return to Freud's meaning did not entail a process of sense-making, with a view to discovering the one and true meaning of Freud, his interrogative did not contribute to the historicization of psychoanalysis or to the study of its "developmental history"—as Freud himself would occasionally have put it in a term Lacan found particularly enigmatic (Lacan, 1988[1975], p. 150). Although he would demand that his listeners always bring a text to life "by what follows and what precedes" it (Lacan, 1993[1981], p. 149), and although he opened his "Rome Discourse" by stating that blunt concepts could regain their sharpness from a re-examination of their history (Lacan, 2006[1953], p. 199), these principles should not be interpreted as Lacan's radical commitment to the history of ideas. At the most, they signalled appropriate procedures for problematizing texts and concepts. Unlike Freud, Lacan did not believe that the present becomes more meaningful when reflecting upon the past and contextualizing the *hic et nunc*. The interrogation of the present does not end with an investigation of the past. Instead, Lacan ventured to replace the classic Freudian paradigm of "what has been", with a less deterministic perspective on "what will have been", the so-called "future anterior" (Lacan, 2006[1953], p. 247).

The implication of this alternative temporal structure is that the answer to the question "Why?"—should it not only be attached to Lacan's name, but also examined with the tools of Lacan's theory—does not lie in any historical state of affairs, but in what Lacan "will have been", given what he is "in the process of becoming" (Ibid., p. 247). Time will tell whether Lacan was the greatest psychoanalyst since Freud and whether he succeeded in radically transforming psychoanalytic theory and practice. And when the answers seem obvious at any given point in time, time will still continue to tell what Lacan will have been. As such, there is no definitive answer to the question "Why Lacan?". This is why I claimed earlier on that the only "Lacanian" answer to the question is an echo of the question itself. This answer is, however, neither theoretical nor practical, neither intellectual nor anti-intellectual, but ethical, insofar as it represents a subjective responsibility, a duty to endlessly construct and reconstruct an account of oneself in our relationships with others. Those who believe they have another answer, whether positive or negative, edifying or repudiating, will have to measure the doctrinal value of their response against the insistence of Lacan's own questioning, and against their commitment to the future of psychoanalysis.

The essays in this collection will hopefully contribute to this ethical assignment and enable readers to question the (Lacanian) psychoanalytic knowledge they have assimilated and accumulated, with a view to opening up new theoretical, clinical, and applied perspectives on the inescapable meaning of psychoanalysis, as a paradigm whose definitive meaning must always be allowed to escape. This book will not allow anyone to call themselves Lacanian, yet were it to contribute in any way to Lacanians and Lacanianism being put to the test and questioned to the core, I would consider my mission accomplished. In effect, Lacan's arcane psychoanalytic "wisdom" and the concrete clinical practice associated with it are either endlessly regurgitated and recited as holy writ by his numerous acolytes, who tend to worship him like a Western spiritual guru, or radically dismissed as unpalatable codswallop by his equally countless detractors, who often portray him as a cunning charlatan. By contrast with these common, strictly antagonistic yet uniformly uncritical practices, this book is intended as a meticulous critique of some key theoretical and clinical aspects of Lacan's expansive oeuvre, testing their consistency, examining their implications, and investigating their significance. Under the general heading of "psychoanalytic reason", it performs this task on three distinct levels: the issue whether anything in particular calls for Lacan (his *"raison d'être"*), the question as to how psychoanalytic reasoning was altered by Lacan's philosophical and linguistic reformulations of it, and the ongoing concern over the quality and relevance of Lacan's own idiosyncratic "rationalities". In a series of nine interrelated chapters, the book highlights both the flaws and the strengths of Lacan's ideas, in areas of investigation that are as crucial as they are contentious, within as well as outside psychoanalysis. The reader will learn about Lacan's peculiar attitude towards money, his dalliance with organizational failure, his advocacy of "gay thinking", his conception of clinical psychoanalytic work as poetry, his recognition of the female orgasm in a 17th-century baroque sculpture of a saint, and his revisionist interpretation of Sophocles' *Antigone*, amongst many other controversial subjects.

In sum, throughout these essays, I have endeavoured to take Lacan seriously by categorically refusing to always take him seriously and steering away from the cultish adoration of the master that rules over many a Lacanian "school". As such, stale, institutionalized (Lacanian) knowledge will reveal itself as an epistemic structure of epiphanies, flashes of genius, risks, threats, fallacies, illusions, and make-believe. Unlike many other books on Lacan, the essays in this volume neither passionately endorse nor wholeheartedly reject Lacan's ideas, but subject them to detailed, critical scrutiny. At the same time, this book does not presuppose any prior knowledge of Lacanian psychoanalysis on the part of the reader, but allows its readership to indulge in the joys of in-depth critical analysis, transdisciplinary creative thinking, and persistent questioning.

Chapter 1

Lacan's *Écrits* Revisited: On Writing as Object of Desire

Maybe it was a patent case of morphogenetic resonance *avant la lettre*.[1] Maybe it was a mere occurrence of simple acausal synchronicity. Whether on 15 November 1966 the undead soul of Carl Gustav Jung whispered ever so softly into the young ears of Rupert Sheldrake, analytical psychology gradually giving birth to formative causation, fact of the matter is that this remarkable Tuesday was a day of three mighty crashes—two of which carefully planned, a third definitely unplanned, two pre-scheduled and eagerly anticipated, a third totally unexpected, yet all three of them equally memorable and momentous. In the early hours of the morning, cargo flight Pan Am 708, departing from Frankfurt with a destination of Berlin, crashed on initial approach in what was then Eastern Germany, 15 kilometres from the landing strip at Tegel airport, killing all three crew members. Some 16 hours later, the American spacecraft Gemini 12 splashed down in the North Atlantic Ocean, less than 5 kilometres off target, after which the two crew members were safely picked up by a U.S. aircraft carrier. Both events made newspaper headlines around the world the following day, totally obfuscating the third crash, even though in many ways the latter would prove equally pivotal and consequential. If there is any truth in Jacques Dutronc's lyrical portrayal of Paris as waking up at 5am, the third probably already happened in the French capital quite some time before daybreak, yet various other cities in the provinces and around Europe would not have been spared the tremendous impact of a thumping doorstop, landing in huge quantities and colonizing large amounts of precious shelf space. For all I know, when the colossal paper scatter bomb inscribed *Écrits* (Lacan, 1966a) landed in the bookshops on Tuesday, 15 November 1966, it did not cause any casualties, yet no one could have predicted its triggering a small intellectual tsunami, at least in the francophone world, whose ripples would still be felt 50 years later.[2]

For all its explosive contents and its humongous size, Jacques Lacan's *Écrits* would have looked surprisingly plain to anyone daring to approach it and mustering the strength to pick it up. White as mortal sin graciously forgiven, with no image or drawing teasing or enticing the reader, it was as if the hefty

DOI: 10.4324/9781003252276-2

tome was afraid to disclose itself, drawing an unadorned ivory veil over its heavy haecceity, compelling curious hands to look for telltale signs elsewhere, or forcing scrutinizing eyes to discern themselves in the central space of the white paper jacket. Inviting both projection and reflection, the volume's uncannily empty cover is the learned man's intellectual equivalent of the white sleeve the Fab Four would use, almost exactly two years later, for their weighty ninth release. Equally uncommon for a book, its front cover featured the name of its author twice, once at the top and once at the bottom, once in red and once in black, once in the same large font as the name of the publisher, and once in a smaller font, just above the name of the publisher—the name of the author thus repeated, although not exactly in the same way, as if one mention would not have been sufficient as an index of authorial ownership and intentionality.[3]

More than any other cover, this doubly inscribed signboard infesting the French bookshops on that fateful morning of 15 November 1966 would have probably instigated an involuntary volte-face, from front to back, in a quick and easy sleight of hand. There, in what the French call "*la quatrième de couverture*", and what is designated in English rather more prosaically as the "back cover", more whiteness would await, yet now with a duplicated and colour-changed title and an anonymous précis, which was as much an explicit injunction to the reader as it was a succinct description of the volume's *raison d'être*. Turning the book around, like a leisurely browser checking out the song titles of an album after having admired its cover, here is what interested, intrigued, or bemused minds would discover.[4]

> One must have read this collection from cover to cover to realise that a single debate is pursued in it, always the same. Should it seem dated, it shall nonetheless prove to be that of the Enlightenment.
>
> For there is a field in which dawn itself is late in arriving: the field that runs the gamut from a bias of which psychopathology has not rid itself to the false evidence with which the ego entitles itself to flaunt its existence.
>
> Obscurity passes itself off as an object in this field and flourishes through the obscurantism that finds anew its values in it.
>
> No wonder, then, that it is precisely in this field that people resist the discovery by Freud, a term that may be extended here on the basis of an amphibology: Jacques Lacan's discovery by Freud.
>
> The reader will learn what is demonstrated in it, which is that the unconscious stems from pure logic—in other words, from the signifier.
>
> Epistemology will always be lacking here, unless it starts from a reform, which is the subversion of the subject.
>
> Its advent can only be produced in reality [*réellement*] and in a place that is currently occupied by psychoanalysts.

> For 15 years, Jacques Lacan has been transcribing this subversion for analysts on the basis of their everyday experience.
> The thing is of too much concern to everyone not to make a ruckus.
> With these writings [*écrits*], Lacan enjoins us to ensure that this subversion is not hijacked by the culture industry.
>
> (Lacan, 1966a, back cover)

At the risk of straying into slightly self-indulgent, and always already fictionalized autobiographical reminiscences, when I assimilated these words for the first time in the original French, back in the mist of time, some time during the autumn of 1984, I had absolutely no idea what they meant. But then again, as Lacan himself intimated in the opening sentence, a proper appreciation of the nature and the stakes of the debate would have required my having read the entire volume, from beginning to end, all 900-odd pages of it. Inquisitive as I am, I followed Lacan's unequivocal exhortation to read. Almost 40 years later, I am still as curious as I was back then, and I still find myself reading, occasionally wondering what I missed, or whether I should re-read what I have already read numerous times over. In all sincerity, despite endless re-readings, I still cannot claim that I fully appreciate what Lacan was trying to convey here, from which culture industry he was trying to rescue his subversion, and to which persistently obscure field he had addressed his *Fiat Lux*.

Be that as it may, the back cover of *Écrits* indicates that Lacan placed his book firmly under the aegis of the Enlightenment, a statement which many a reader would no doubt have acknowledged, and probably long before having scrutinized the volume from cover to cover, as supremely ironic, given that what appears to reign supreme in these 900 pages, from beginning to end, presents itself as being exactly the opposite. Rather than signalling the end of obscurity and celebrating the long-awaited arrival of a new dawn, *Écrits* would seem to take its readers on an O'Neillian or Célinesque voyage into the darkest depths of the night, towards an intellectual hadopelagic zone, where eternal blackness reigns and where no ordinary mortal is sufficiently well equipped to find his bearings, let alone survive.[5] Returning to the empty white expanse on the book's front cover and choosing, as other publishers undoubtedly would have done, a suitable work of art to fill in the blank space—capturing a key feature of what lies beneath the surface with a view to inflaming the reader's imagination—it would thus not be Eugène Delacroix's *La liberté guidant le peuple* that might impose itself, as a latter-day pictorial emblem of the French Enlightenment tradition, but a version of the undisputed highlight of suprematism, Kazimir Malevich's infamous *Black Square* (see Figure 1.1).

And what are we supposed to make of the book's peculiar title? In her *Lacan: In Spite of Everything*, Élisabeth Roudinesco averred that, as a summa which constitutes "the founding Book [*sic*] of an intellectual system", Lacan's volume resembles both Ferdinand de Saussure's *Course in*

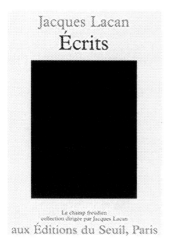

Figure 1.1 Jacques Lacan, *Écrits* (imaginary cover).

General Linguistics (Saussure, 1959[1916]) and Hegel's *Phenomenology of Spirit* (Hegel, 2018[1807]; Roudinesco, 2014[2011], p. 99). Whereas I broadly concur with the status Roudinesco accords to *Écrits*, I respectfully disagree with the comparisons that are being made, irrespective of the fact that neither Saussure's nor Hegel's book refer to writing (*écrit; écriture*) in their titles. For although it is self-evident that Saussure's book was written, it was not actually written by himself, but by Charles Bally and Albert Séchehaye, two of his students, based on lecture notes. As to Hegel's *Phenomenology of Spirit*, this was written over a very short period of time and under great duress, which partly explains why the substance of the book is measurably less well developed than its preface and introduction (Pinkard, 2018, p. xvi).

Restricting myself to the title of Lacan's doorstop, there is a small handful of books in French with exactly the same title (see, for example, Ensor, 1950; Janáček, 2009; Malévitch, 1975; Munch, 2011; Rigaut, 1970). What unites these books, in all their diversity, is that they invariably concern posthumous collections of written texts by people who are primarily known for other creative accomplishments (in painting, music, or poetry for instance). In other words, in these cases, the title *Écrits* is meant to retain the reader's interest, purely by virtue of the fact that the author is not primarily recognized as a writer. Whenever the title *Écrits* is employed to describe a collection of works by established authors of fiction or non-fiction, it is generally expanded through the addition of a classifying adjective denoting a unifying quality of the writings presented, as in Jean-Paul Sartre's *Écrits de jeunesse* (Sartre, 1990), or Victor Hugo's *Écrits politiques* (Hugo, 2002). In this case, *Écrits* would not suffice as a descriptive noun for the book's contents, precisely because the author is already principally known for being a writer.

In simply calling the book *Écrits*, the author, publisher, and/or editor thus decided that the title did not have to be about anything at all for the book to be about something specific, because the name of the author somehow guaranteed the contents of the volume and the subject under discussion, since he was not directly associated with writing. Indeed, even though he was 65 years old when *Écrits* appeared, and he had intermittently published innovative essays in specialized journals, Lacan had primarily gained a name for himself as a speaker. To the French intellectual community of the mid-1960s, the name of Jacques Lacan would have been synonymous with a weekly seminar on psychoanalysis, whose audience had grown exponentially from January 1964, when it started taking place at the famous "École Normale Supérieure" in the rue d'Ulm, under the auspices of the "École pratique des Hautes Études" (Lacan, 1994[1973], p. 1). Speaking about his intellectual trajectory to trainee psychiatrists in Bordeaux on 20 April 1967, Lacan disclosed that he himself had chosen the title of his book:

> I collected together something I had to call *Écrits*, in the plural, because it seemed to me that that was the simplest term to designate what I was going to do. I brought together under that title the things I had written just to put down a few markers, a few milestones, like the posts they drive into the water to moor boats to, in what I had been teaching on a weekly basis for 20 years or so… In the course of those long years of teaching, from time to time I composed an *écrit* and it seemed to me important to put it there like a pylon to mark a stage, the point we had reached in some year, some period in some year. Then I put it all together. It happened in a context in which things had gained ground since the time when I started out in teaching.
>
> (Lacan, 2008[2005], pp. 60–61)[6]

On 12 May 1971, when Lacan delivered "Lituraterre" at his weekly seminar in Paris, he further disclosed to his audience that his title *Écrits* was effectively "more ironic than one might think: when it concerns either reports, a function of conferences, or let's say "open letters" where I bring into question a facet of my teaching" (Lacan, 2013[1971a], p. 328).[7] Hence, the essays collected in *Écrits* had allegedly fallen out of Lacan's weekly teaching to psychoanalytic trainees, or out of his presentations at conferences and his public lectures, as the tangible material residues of an ephemeral discourse, with the proviso that in some cases the texts had been prepared before, and with the explicit purpose of being read out loud.[8]

On 9 January 1973, at the very beginning of a lecture on "the function of the written" (*la fonction de l'écrit*)—although this title would have been added afterwards, notably when the lecture was edited and prepared for publication as part of that year's seminar—Lacan conceded that when it came to choosing a title for his book, he could not think of anything better than to call it *Écrits* (Lacan, 1998[1975], p. 26). I have no good reason to think that he was disingenuous when he said he had not been able to come up with anything else, much as he was broadly correct in saying that most of the texts included in the book had originally been written for conferences, or published as meticulous distillations of one or the other aspect of his teaching. However, there is no doubt in my mind that the publisher accepted Lacan's suggestion, because they knew very well that, in the autumn of 1966, he was already sufficiently well-known—although evidently not as a writer—for this book of writings to find a readership in the absence of a more specific title, or indeed that the very lack of a specific title would effectively increase the book's appeal, because both in name and in size it would suggest a more or less complete summa (to use Roudinesco's term) of the author's work. After all, except for the book's Appendix I, which included the transcript of a presentation by France's pre-eminent Hegel-scholar Jean Hyppolite on Freud's paper "Negation" (Freud, 1961[1925*h*]) at Lacan's seminar in February 1954 (Hyppolite, 2006[1956]), and some ancillary materials by Jacques-Alain Miller, all the texts in the book had effectively been written by Lacan, so to call it *Écrits* may have been slightly vague and a trifle highfalutin, but nonetheless unquestionably truthful and indisputably accurate.[9]

However, all of this should not detract us from reconsidering the relationship (and the disparity) between the book's short and snappy title (one single word) and its everything but short and snappy contents (some 375,900 words). The first thing to note, is that *Écrits*, at least when written, is visibly plural, so that the book's content has not only been written, but *de facto* includes a multiplicity of writing*s*. Anyone who has ever picked up a copy of Lacan's book, whether in the original French or in translation, and who has looked at its table of contents, which appears at the very end in the original edition and at the very beginning in the English translation, will have been able to acknowledge this, so much so that my point probably comes across as blatantly obvious at best and totally stupid at worst.[10] Nonetheless, and distinctly counterintuitive as it may seem, I wish to argue that the multiplicity inscribed by Lacan in his book's title, and which appears both at the front and at the back, is by far the most deceptive aspect of its name. Multiple, plural, and manifold in its writing, the book is singular, monadic, and unitary in its written presentation, although this should not be taken to imply that it is complete, finished, and definitive. Put differently, although the title *Écrits* clearly suggests plurality when written, and Lacan himself referred to his work as a collection (*un recueil*) on the back cover and in his introduction to it (Lacan, 2006[1966b]), what landed with a loud bang in the French bookshops on 15 November 1966 is far from a jumbled miscellany, a Gallic smorgasbord or an intellectual liquorice all sorts. Lacan's ingredients may have been produced over a period of 30-odd years, when it came to pulling them out of their original soil and allowing them to supplement each other in a rich psychoanalytic broth, Lacan showed himself to be an excellent restaurateur, carefully recooking and rebalancing his diversified produce to create a coherent and consistent *plat de résistance*, quelling the reader's appetite with a gigantic dish of many different components and a wide variety of flavours, none of which were supposed to show their exact age or even their precise origin. *Écrits* was released in November 1966, and 1966 was to be the time of the book, even though some of its ideas went as far back as the mid-1930s.

To make my argument more persuasive and compelling, I can refer to four distinct features of *Écrits* that have attracted relatively little attention, or at least less interest than its more substantive components, i.e., the constitutive writings in themselves. First, avoiding the standard template of a conventional collection of papers, Lacan interspersed the essays selected for inclusion in the volume with five "connecting texts" and two addenda, four of which explicitly dated 1966, yet all clearly written when the book was under construction.[11] As historicizing and contextualizing essays, these inter- or binding texts function as conceptual bridges between and within the initial sections of the volume, and could therefore be considered part of the cement that keeps the edifice together. Indeed, when in mid-October 1966, Jacques Lacan was introduced to another, ever so slightly brilliant Jacques, and went on to confess to Derrida that he was primarily concerned that his forthcoming collection might not hold up (*ça ne va pas tenir*) (Derrida, 1998[1996], p. 52), one should not just interpret Lacan's trepidation literally, as an ostensibly futile or deviously exaggerated concern over the quality of the binding, but equally and perhaps more importantly as an entirely justifiable worry that his book would not be able to stand up, would not fall into place, might be falling apart, would not hang together, especially compared to those of his "structuralist" rivals Lévi-Strauss, Foucault, Barthes, Greimas, Genette, and Todorov, all of whom had released important works earlier in 1966 (Barthes, 1987[1966]; Foucault, 1970[1966]; Genette, 1966; Greimas, 1983[1966]; Lévi-Strauss, 1973[1966]; Todorov, 1966), and most definitely compared to that one big book on which the cover of *Écrits* had been modelled and which had elicited nothing short of a full-blown tantrum–Paul Ricœur's *De l'interprétation. Essai sur Freud* (Ricœur, 1965; Roudinesco, 1997[1993], p. 324).[12] With his "binding texts", Lacan wanted to ensure that his *Écrits* would not come across as a mere anthology, or what in the Anglophone publishing world is sometimes called "a reader" (notice the term), but that it would be recognized, despite the format, as a monograph, in which one debate and one argument is being pursued—as Lacan himself was at great pains to emphasize on his back cover.

Second, with very few exceptions, all of the texts included in *Écrits* were revised and modified by Lacan prior to their being reprinted.[13] Occasionally, Lacan would draw the reader's attention to the fact that one or more paragraphs had been re-written anno 1966, as is the case for instance with "The Function and Field of Speech and Language in Psychoanalysis", his

1953 "Rome Discourse" (Lacan, 2006[1953], p. 267), or that he had added a new note, as with the long topological footnote to the text on psychosis (Lacan, 2006[1959], pp. 486–487), yet in most cases the alterations were performed in silence, without the reader being informed. Taken account of the fact that, when Lacan undertook this task, he was not just correcting typographical errors, adding cross-references, or updating bibliographical details, but regularly modifying the conceptual texture and scope of his essays, the reader of *Écrits* thus needs to know, yet most probably would not have known (and many undoubtedly still do not know), that she or he is reading essays whose date of composition is *de facto* 1966, regardless of the fact that their original publication date may have been 30 or 20 years earlier.

Third, apart from a name index and a list of Freudian concepts in German, *Écrits* contained an index of concepts like no other, and which may very well still be unique in the history of scholarly publishing.[14] Compiled by a 22-year-old *normalien* by the name of Jacques-Alain Miller, who would go on to marry Lacan's youngest daughter Judith three days before the publication of *Écrits*, this "Classified Index of the Major Concepts", which was endorsed by Lacan himself, is by no stretch of the imagination an index in the common sense of the word, and I would be extremely surprised if anyone—casual reader or devoted scholar, psychoanalyst or student—had ever employed it in this way. In fact, I would be extremely surprised if anyone had ever used it all. As Miller himself indicated in an extended clarification for the reader, his "index" constituted a "systematization" which, although it reflects an interpretation, was designed to encapsulate and convey the conceptual order Lacan was articulating (Miller, 2006[1966a], p. 852). In other words, if there is and always would be a certain chronology pervading the logic and progression of Lacan's book, Miller's "index" purported to demonstrate that the intellectual developments over time were driven by one solid set of theoretical principles whose architecture he proposed to set out.

Fourth, over and above the physical binding of the book and the mortar of the binding texts keeping the 27 building blocks together, Lacan insisted on securing the entire edifice with a single headstone, "The Seminar on 'The Purloined Letter'" (Lacan, 2006[1957a]), taken out of the strict chronology, and itself extensively rewritten and interspersed with two "binding texts" (the "Presentation of the Suite" and the "Parenthesis of Parentheses").[15] As Derrida put it so perceptively in May 1990: Lacan's seminar on "The Purloined Letter", "by coming at the beginning, is thereby given the "privilege" [Lacan's term] of figuring the synchronic configuration of the set and thus *binding* the whole together" (Derrida, 1998[1996], p. 49).[16] Using a different metaphor, one might say that Lacan's seminar on "The Purloined Letter" is the one ring to rule them all, the one ring to find them, the one ring to bring them all and in the darkness bind them… Considering all of this, I thus respectfully disagree with the editors of *Reading Lacan's Écrits*, when

Figure 1.2 La trahison de l'écriture.

they suggest that *Écrits* is not a book, and that what we are dealing with is but an alternative version of Magritte's *La trahison des images*, which could be entitled *La trahison de l'écriture* ("The Betrayal of Writing") (Vanheule, Hook and Neill, 2019, p. xix) (see Figure 1.2). *Écrits* is most definitely a book, and even—as Roudinesco (2014[2011], p. 99) put it—a Book, in every possible sense of the word. Many readers may not encounter, or experience it this way, yet this does not preclude Lacan wishing it to be acknowledged as such.

However, as I pointed out earlier, the fact that *Écrits* is very much a book, the multiplicity inscribed in its name being nothing more, nothing less than a sagacious decoy for what is essentially designed as a single slab of considerable theoretical weight, should not be taken to imply that this book, merely by virtue of the fact that it is what it is, i.e., a book, is also the "finished article", a definitive text containing everything it is supposed to contain, or everything Lacan wanted it to contain. I could substantiate this point simply, even simplistically, by highlighting the fact that the title does not say, or even insinuate *Écrits complets* (complete writings), and that by 1966 Lacan had written (and published) much more than what eventually came to rest under the cover of *Écrits*: a substantial series of clinical psychiatric papers (see, for example,

Lacan, 1931; 1933a; 1975[1933]), an extended encyclopaedia article on the family (Lacan, 1984[1938]), and various distinctly "Lacanian" essays, including a logical reflection on the number 13 (Lacan, 2001[1945–1946]), a tribute to Maurice Merleau-Ponty (Lacan, 1982–1983[1961]), and an homage to Marguerite Duras (Lacan, 1987[1965]). Were there to be only *one* edition of *Écrits*, one could easily argue that these writings were not selected for inclusion, because for one reason or the other Lacan had not considered them to be sufficiently suitable, perhaps disturbing the "order", or even putting the collection at risk of falling apart, not standing up, not hanging together. Yet, in all likelihood, at least some of these writings were not included, because Lacan forgot about them, or did not find the time to revise them and allocate them to their proper place in his book. I can say this, because in actual fact there are *two* versions of *Écrits*, one ever so slightly bigger than the other, although the first version is rarely if ever mentioned. The version everyone refers to as *Écrits* is effectively the second edition of the book, which Lacan had the opportunity to reconstruct when the first edition became an instant blockbuster and unexpectedly sold out in no time. Those, like most of us, who did not manage to lay their hands on this first edition would not have known that the second edition was different, because nowhere on the cover or the endpapers did the publisher indicate whether the book was the first or the second edition, or that the second (and most widespread) edition differed from the first, original edition. However, a simple comparison of the Table of Contents of the first and the second editions suffices to ascertain that the first edition included only one appendix (Jean Hyppolite's commentary on Freud's *Verneinung*) and only one commentary by Miller, i.e., his "Classified Index of Major Concepts". For the second edition, a second appendix was added—a short paper by Lacan entitled "Metaphor of the Subject" (Lacan, 2006[1961])—whereas another commentary by Miller, on Lacan's graphical representations, was included between the first commentary and the index of Freud's German terms (Miller, 2006[1966b]).

To many, these observations may just be a matter of largely irrelevant historical minutiae, yet to me they demonstrate that, when Lacan submitted his original manuscript of *Écrits* to François Wahl—his former analysand, and his assigned editor at *du Seuil*, who may deservedly be dubbed the "obstinate obstetrician" of *Écrits*—he did not regard the collection as complete or definitive.[17] Were this to have been the case, he would not have added "Metaphor of the Subject" when the opportunity arose for a second edition to be produced. Furthermore, the fact that, in this second edition, "Metaphor of the Subject" was included as an appendix rather than within the chronological sequence—between "Subversion of the Subject" and "Position of the Unconscious"—should probably not be seen as this text being of lesser importance than the others, but as a purely pragmatic decision by the publishers, taken in order to avoid the entire volume having to be re-set and re-paginated. *Écrits* is very much a book, then, but it is also an incomplete book, a book with a clearly identifiable and carefully identified beginning, but without a precise end, a book which could have been even longer and weightier than it already is, a book whose ending endlessly recedes into the distance, and which has only arrived at its destination in a certain form and size on pure practical grounds, much like the psychoanalytic process itself.

I could substantiate my point about *Écrits* being an open, unfinished, and incomplete book even further with reference to its first German translation. During the early 1970s, the Liechtensteiner Norbert Haas, who was a professor of German at the University of Darmstadt, suggested to Lacan that a team of translators be established to prepare a German translation of the full French text, in three separate volumes. At the time, Lacan's work was hardly known at all in the German-speaking world, including within psychoanalytic circles, which operated almost exclusively under the aegis of the International Psycho-Analytic Association (IPA), from which Lacan had been formally excluded in 1963. Lacan was highly enthusiastic about the proposal and even agreed to write a new introduction for the project (Lacan, 2001[1973b]). However, it suffices to look at the covers of these three volumes, which appeared in 1973, 1975, and 1980, respectively, and thus during Lacan's lifetime, that the German *Écrits*, or *Schriften* as they were called, is a rather different book than the French original, and not merely owing to the fact that it was divided into three parts (Lacan, 1973–1980). The order in which Lacan's essays appear in *Schriften* is different from that adopted in *Écrits*, but much more importantly *Schriften* includes two essays that had never been included in *Écrits* before, neither in the 1966 edition, nor in the two-volume pocketbook edition from the early 1970s: Lacan's 1938 essay on the family (Lacan, 1984[1938]) and his 1961 tribute to Maurice Merleau-Ponty (Lacan, 1982–1983[1961]). In his new introduction to the books, which was significantly longer than his 1966 overture to *Écrits*, Lacan did not say anything about the contents, the organization and the composition of the volumes. He did not say anything about the translation, nothing about the reception of his work in the German-speaking world, nothing about himself, and nothing whatsoever about the fact that these volumes were, or would be quite different from the original. But even if he had justified the addition of two new texts to the German edition of the work that had made his name, I am not sure he would have been able to explain why these essays had never been included in a French edition of *Écrits*.

In the sense that quite a few essays could have been added to it had Lacan been given the opportunity to do so, *Écrits* thus remains very much an open book, at least at one end, yet it is also open-ended in the sense that it was only a summa of Lacan's intellectual journey up to 1966, a momentary written punctuation in an intermittently circuitous trajectory that had started over 30 years earlier and which would continue for another 15 years, although without anyone evidently being able to predict this at the time.

During these 15 years that followed, Lacan did not shy away from regularly self-referencing his *Écrits*, or from weaving his own story through and around *Écrits*, despite or perhaps by virtue of his clever re-fashioning of the French "*publication*" into "*poubellication*". One could easily interpret this play on words as representative of Lacan's own ambivalence towards his published writings, or even as indicative of his distancing himself, in a crafty linguistic act of self-rejection, from his own main publication. Be that as it may, I shall venture exactly the opposite claim, notably that the pun condenses within itself a psychoanalytic theory of writing and (knowledge) transmission *qua* remainder, waste-product, remnant and residue, which was conceived at a time when Lacan would have been greatly preoccupied with assembling and revising his writings for inclusion in *Écrits*, whose birth was effectively facilitated by *Écrits*, and which would come of age in the aftermath of *Écrits*. In other words, *pace* its title, *Écrits* did not contain or synthesize a psychoanalytic theory of writing Lacan had developed over the years, but this very title re-focused Lacan's attention, and inaugurated extensive reflections on the status of the letter, which in this case represents a writing character and written text rather than a missive. In terms of its contents, *Écrits* thus constituted an integrated series of key milestones in the psychoanalytic itinerary Lacan had pursued over a period of 30 years. In terms of its title, however, the book opened a completely new horizon, stretching from the signifier to the letter, from linguistics to topology and knot theory, from speech to writing, from oral transmission to mathematical formalization, and from logocentrism to grammatology.

Lacan first presented this conception of writing and the letter as an irreducible excess at his seminar session of 15 December 1965, when he was undoubtedly already deeply engaged in preparing the manuscript for *Écrits*:

> Writing and publishing is really not the same thing... The fortuitous and unexpected conjunction of what is called written text [*l'écrit*], and which has a very close relationship with the object *a*, provides every conjunction of writings [*écrits*] with the characteristic of the dustbin [*poubelle*]. (Lacan, 1965–1966, session of 15 December 1966)

Yet as it happens, this approximation between writing and the object of desire (*a*) had already been envisaged in two of the texts that would be included in *Écrits*—once explicitly in "Kant with Sade" (Lacan, 2006[1962]) and once implicitly in "The Seminar on 'The Purloined Letter'" (Lacan, 2006[1957a])—although Lacan himself would not fully realise its contours in the latter text until 1966, and thus retroactively, "with hindsight", in a flash insight of "deferred action", as an "already there" that was not properly appreciated when it revealed itself for the first time in the present.

Lacan's theory of writing and (knowledge) transmission directly revolves, here, around the conceptualization of the letter as a figuration of the object *a*, the elusive object-cause of desire (Lacan, 2014[2004], p. 101), which is simultaneously the object of anxiety and the object of (surplus) *jouissance*, and which Lacan himself at one point designated as his only real contribution to psychoanalysis (Lacan, 1973–1974, session of 9 April 1974). Cutting a long and complicated story short, I shall restrict myself to a succinct recapitulation of some of the passages in Lacan's work in which this theory of writing as object of desire takes shape, which should suffice for me to open, by way of conclusion, a certain perspective on the transmission of (Lacanian) psychoanalysis, to which *Écrits*, as everyone unquestionably accepts, has massively contributed—not only during the years before the publication of Lacan's seminars, i.e., before 1973, when the first of Lacan's seminars was officially released in French (Lacan, 1973), but also afterwards, as a versatile theoretical training tool, a seemingly inexhaustible source of arcane wisdom and, on occasion, as a blunt instrument of intellectual torture.

At the start of his seminar session of 9 January 1973, after having admitted that, back in 1966, he could not think of anything better than to call his book *Écrits*, Lacan disclosed that he was well aware of the fact that these *Écrits* were widely regarded as not being an easy read, to which he added that this is exactly what he himself had thought, to the point where he had even considered the possibility that they were "not meant to be read" (Lacan, 1998[1975], p. 26). The French expression, here, is *pas à lire*, which could also be translated as "not to be read"; "not for reading"; or even as "unreadable", "illegible", and "unintelligible". Lacan's little quip unmistakably resonates with the experience of many a first, uninformed reader, yet even the seasoned reader may recognise some truth in this declaration, if only because some of Lacan's prose is so cryptic and hermetic that whatever "reading strategy" is being adopted, the lock remains firmly in place. Nevertheless, *pas à lire* should not be taken to imply that Lacan did not *want* his book to be read, that he did not care whether it found a readership, or that he was totally indifferent about the way it would be read. Six weeks after having said that his *Écrits* were *pas à lire*, Lacan complimented, without irony, the authors of *Le titre de la lettre* (Lacoue-Labarthe and Nancy, 1990[1973]; Nancy and Lacoue-Labarthe, 1992[1990]), although without mentioning their names.[18] "[I]f it is a question of reading", he proclaimed, "I have never been so well read—with so much love" (Lacan, 1998[1975], p. 65). On the back cover of *Écrits*, Lacan opened his précis with a direct imperative, which was as much an exhortation to the reader as it was a precondition for the book's message to arrive at its destination: "*Il faut avoir lu ce recueil, et dans son long*" ("One must have read this collection from cover to cover", see above). Lacan also expressed his desire for the *Écrits* to be read in various talks and interviews he accorded following the book's publication. In April 1967, he said to his audience in Bordeaux:

> Even if you do not understand it very well, reading what I have written has an effect, holds your interest, is of interest. It is not that often that you read an *écrit* that is necessarily something urgent [*nécessité par quelque chose qui urge*], and which is addressed to people who really have something to do, something it is not easy to do. (Lacan, 2008[2005], p. 62)[19]

Quizzed by Italian journalists as to the obscurity of *Écrits* in 1974, Lacan reiterated:

> I did not write them in order for people to understand them, I wrote them in order for people to read them. Which is not even remotely the same thing... What I have noticed, however, is that, even if people don't understand my *Écrits*, the latter do something to people. I have often observed this. People don't understand anything, that is perfectly true, for a while, but the writings do something to them. (Lacan, 2013[2005], pp. 69–70)[20]

Lacan's desire for *Écrits* to be read can also be gauged from some of the handwritten dedications on the complimentary copies he sent out to colleagues and friends. The inscription on the copy he sent to Jean Beaufret, the French philosopher who facilitated Heidegger's reception in France, reads: "*Puis-je espérer un autre lecteur que vous?*" (May I hope for a reader other than you?) (Lacan, 1966b). And on Maud and Octave Mannoni's copy, he wrote: "*Avec ça la discussion peut dépasser le verbe n'est-ce pas et même le cuir chevelu*" (With this, the discussion may exceed the spoken word, don't you think, and even the scalp) (Lacan, 1966c).

Lacan's desire for people to read what he had written may even be inferred from how he had dealt with some of the individual papers included in *Écrits*. For example, in the opening lesson of *Seminar V, Formations of the Unconscious*, Lacan relayed the hope that his audience had read his recently published essay "The Instance of the Letter": "[M]y hope... is that you who make the effort to listen to what I have to say also make the effort to read what I write, since in the end it's for you that I write it" (Lacan, 2017[1998], p. 3). As Jacques-Alain Miller put it, in his own back cover précis for the centenary collection of Lacan's *Autres Écrits*: *pas à lire* "is like "Dangerous Dog", "No Entry", or even "*Lasciate ogni speranza*". It's a challenge, made for tempting desire" (Miller, 2001). *Pas à lire* does not signal, then, yet another way of saying that what was included in *Écrits* should be instantly relegated to the dustbin (*poubelle*), at least not before it had been dutifully read. A book entitled "Not to be read" or "Unreadable" is more likely to be read than a book entitled "Read me!", for the simple reason that the prohibition awakens the reader's desire to do exactly the opposite (see Figure 1.3).

Figure 1.3 Jacques Lacan, *Pas à lire* (imaginary book).

Here we encounter a first connection between writing and desire, prompted by Lacan's brief remark in January 1973, six-and-a-half years after the publication of *Écrits*. Yet the connection already appears inside *Écrits*, although it must be said that it is far from self-evident or clear-cut. Indeed, for a massive book entitled *Écrits*, it is distinctly odd that writing hardly receives any detailed attention in it, the more so as Lacan himself spent much of his early years as a psychiatrist studying and conceptualizing the function and characteristics of (psychotic) writing (Lévy-Valensi, Migault and Lacan, 1931; 1975[1931]), devoting some of his own clinical writings to the significance of psychotic writing(-style) (Lacan, 1975[1933]), and organizing his own doctoral dissertation around a clinical case he accessed and opened up through the patient's writings (Lacan, 1975[1932]).[21] Of course, *Écrits* consistently deals with writings (in the plural), those of Freud more than anyone else's, yet also those of Edgar Allan Poe, Henri Ey, Ernest Jones, André Gide, Immanuel Kant, D.A.F. de Sade, and innumerable others. Nonetheless, over and above Lacan's meticulous unpacking of their style and contents, the status of these writings, and the place and function of writing in general, is hardly a matter of theoretical and clinical concern in it. As I indicated previously, it is only in the aftermath of the publication of *Écrits*, and to a large extent by virtue of *Écrits*, i.e., of Lacan's designation of his book as *Écrits*, that the question of writing would become, or perhaps I should say re-become, a central focus of attention.[22]

The connection between writing and (the object of) desire appears first of all in Lacan's "Seminar on 'The Purloined Letter'", with the caveat that it is quite unlikely for any reader to have identified it without Lacan himself having shown the way, and even to have done so in the presence of his directives, which appear in a couple of quite enigmatic, yet exceedingly precious paragraphs at the end of his overture to *Écrits*. Lacan wrote:

> It is here [in his essay on "The Purloined Letter"] that my students would be right to recognize the "already" [*le "déjà"*] ... For I decipher here in Poe's fiction ... the division in which the subject is verified in the fact that an object traverses him without them interpenetrating in any respect, this division being at the crux of what emerges at the end of this collection that goes by the name of object *a* (to be read: little *a*). It is the object that (cor)responds to the question about style [Lacan's writing style] that I am raising right at the outset. (Lacan, 2006[1966b], pp. 4–5)

Translated into an idiom that ordinary mortals can understand, Lacan is essentially stating here that in all those cases when people had been eager to demonstrate how Lacan's entire theory had already been contained *in nuce*, or *in statu nascendi* in his earlier writings, there was but one instance where this effort would not have been foolhardy, namely in the consideration of his "Seminar on 'The Purloined Letter'" as a text that already deals with the object *a*.

Where is the object *a* to be found, then, in Lacan's "Seminar on 'The Purloined Letter'"? Lacan does not tell us explicitly, yet after having contemplated the question persistently for the past 30 years, I have come to the conclusion that it is neither in the circuit of the letter—its journey from one location to another, from the Queen's boudoir to the Minister's apartment to Dupin's little back library—nor in its material support, i.e. in the missive itself. Allusive and oblique as many of his statements may be, Lacan left no doubt that he regarded the letter (the missive) as "a pure signifier" (Lacan, 2006[1957a], p. 23), and its circuit as a simile for how the signifying chain organizes and determines subjectivity. If the object *a* is to be found anywhere in "The Purloined Letter", and in Lacan's reading of it, it is precisely in the remainder that is left behind once the letter *qua* signifier has moved to another place. For nowhere in Poe's story does the letter travel from one place to another without its former existence in each place being marked by a substitute object, which constitutes the detritus of the letter's transition to another location. When the Minister steals the Queen's incriminating letter, he leaves an unimportant "replacement letter" of his own on the table (Poe, 1988[1844], p. 321). When Dupin cunningly succeeds in purloining the letter from the Minister's apartment, he leaves behind a similar missive in the card-rack above the fireplace (Ibid., p. 332). And even at the moment when Dupin hands over the letter to the Police Prefect, it is only on condition that the latter leaves behind another piece of paper, a cheque containing his hefty reward (Ibid., p. 325). What distinguishes these remainders from the actual letter, is that the reader knows that something is written on it—some insignificant scribbles in the Minister's hand, some verses from Crébillon in Dupin's hand, the amount of money as a recompense for Dupin's services in the Police Prefect's hand. Furthermore, these remainders do not enter their own symbolic circuit, insofar as they do not travel from one place to another, thereby affecting those who are in possession of it, but firmly stay in those places where they first appeared, as remainders and reminders of what was there before, and has now moved on.

Strange as it may seem, I believe that it is in these three written leftovers that Lacan recognized the object a—although after the fact, through a process of deferred action, when writing the overture to *Écrits* in 1966—as something that falls out of, and cannot be recuperated within the signifying chain. It is a trifle odd, because one may reasonably expect the incriminating letter to operate as the true object of desire and not its replacements, yet apart from the fact that this letter remains empty (its message is never disclosed) and continues to circulate, this letter-object is much more a symbolic, structuring force than an object of desire. By contrast, the three leftovers are material pieces of writing that trigger and sustain the desire of whomever comes across them—the Queen's desire to retrieve a lost possession, the Minister's desire for revenge, and Dupin's desire for proper compensation. At the same time, the three distinct replacement letter-objects, each written in different hands, are intrinsically worthless. The Queen is entirely "free to crumple up" the Minister's own letter, Lacan wrote (Lacan, 2006[1957a], p. 8). The Minister's fit of anger after he has discovered Dupin's taunting verses may prompt him to do the same. The bank teller will undoubtedly destroy Dupin's cheque once it has been cashed—yet for all their *Ersatz* value, which is far less compared to the value of the letter they have replaced, they bolster and maintain the desire of their recipients. In short, as material written waste-products of the circulation of the signifier, they do not satisfy, but cause desire.

The only other place in *Écrits* where Lacan identified, this time explicitly, writing with the object of desire occurs in "Kant with Sade" (Lacan, 2006[1962]). Investigating how the Sadean fantasy (Lacan, 2006[1962], p. 653)—the fantasy of absolute destruction and transcendental negation with which Sade endowed his fictional band of libertines in the space of his creative imagination and in thousands of pages of (published and unpublished) writings—might be applied to Sade's own outlook on life as a writer, Lacan generated a new schema, which some scholars have recognized as the "schema of masochism" (Fink, 2014b, pp. 123–127), but which (in a flash of probably not-so-brilliant insight) I have preferred to call the "schema of Sade's practical reason" (Nobus, 2017b, p. 74), by way of tribute to Kant and to avoid Sade's singular *Weltanschauung* being readily pathologized (Lacan, 2006[1962], p. 657) (see Figure 1.4).

The exact relationship between Lacan's first schema (of the Sadean fantasy) and this second schema, and the associated redistribution of the terms, should not concern us here. What matters is that what Lacan allocated to

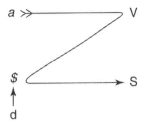

Figure 1.4 Schema of Sade's practical reason.

the place (and the function) of the object cause of desire (*a*) in the schema of Sade's practical reason—in the top left-hand corner, at the beginning of the vector—is nothing more, nothing less than Sade's libertine writings (Lacan, 2006[1962], p. 657), which landed him in a psychiatric institution with the diagnosis of "libertine dementia" for the last ten-and-a-half years of his life, even though they had only been circulating in clandestine editions, had been prohibited from public access, and were widely regarded as unreadable—*pas à lire*, both in the sense of "not to be accessed" and "illegible".[23] As such, "with Sade" Lacan had already reached the conclusion that (the act of) writing functioned outside the symbolic chain, and therefore outside the framework of meaning, as an object that is both gratifying and dissatisfying, and which can indeed be thrown or wiped away, before or after its potential benefits have been reaped, owing to its physical, material inscription.

What appeared, here, in a small corner of one of the most inaccessible essays in a volume that is not exactly known for its general accessibility, is that writing, its style and technique rather than its contents, functions as object *a*, causes rather than quells desire, if not in the author most definitely in its readership, because it forces them to examine the way in which they are implicated in what they have chosen to read, in what they have decided to pursue by way of reading, or *mutatis mutandis*, in what they have ignored or discarded as falling outside their scope of interest, or as being unworthy of further attention. Anticipating his response to the Italian journalists in 1974, Lacan argued in "Kant with Sade" that Sade's allegedly unreadable libertine novels not only urged readers to re-examine their relationships with other people, as Simone de Beauvoir had claimed previously (de Beauvoir, 1990[1950–1951], p. 64), but much more fundamentally that they compelled readers to investigate the relationships they entertain with themselves. As Lacan put it: "[A] fantasy [Sade's libertine writings], whose only reality is as discourse [as written text] and which expects nothing of your powers [in a physical sense], asking you, rather, to square accounts with your own desires" (Lacan, 2006[1962], p. 658). Much like Sade's libertine novels, Lacan told the Italian journalists in 1974 that his *Écrits* may have been unreadable, but that insofar as they operate in the place of object *a* they also force its readers to come to terms with their desire (see Figure 1.5).

Figure 1.5 Jacques Lacan, *a* (imaginary book).

In conclusion, I would like to say a few words about how Lacan's theory of writing as object of desire also informed his reflections on the transmission of psychoanalysis post *Écrits*, during the last 15 years of his career. During those years, Lacan became increasingly concerned about the transmission of his own work, which in this case cannot be dissociated from the question of psychoanalytic training. Troubled by what he perceived to be the ongoing proliferation and recurrent bestowal of spurious emblems of achievement in a formalistic system of psychoanalytic transmission, Lacan was at great pains to invent an alternative regulatory framework, in which trainees would not be given access to the profession on the basis of having demonstrated their understanding of psychoanalytic theory and technique in a series of essays and case-presentations or—God forbid—after having been "recognized" as suitable practitioners by a professional body. In this precise context, we need to situate his hugely controversial proposal of the pass (Lacan, 1995[1967]), which was formulated less than a year after the publication of *Écrits*, as an attempt to replace the monologistic, unified voice of the master who gives his blessing to the newly initiated, with a proto-Bakhtinian carnival of interpenetrating utterances (a formal heteroglossia), but also (counter-intuitive as this may seem) as an endeavour to capture the transmission of the object *a*, from its place as product-loss in the discourse of the master to its place as semblance-agency in the discourse of the analyst (Lacan, 2007[1991]). In this precise context, we also need to ascertain Lacan's progressive departure from speech and language, as the preferred vehicles for the transmission of knowledge, towards the mathematical and topological horizons of a new type of formalization, in which writing and the written would be placed centre stage. Whether he succeeded in this "grammatocentric" project is a different matter, and Lacan himself seems to have become increasingly despondent about the value of his new approach. During his customary closing address of the annual conference of the *École freudienne de Paris* in July 1978, which notably focused on the issue of transmission, he confessed:

> As I think about it now, psychoanalysis cannot be transmitted... [E]ach psychoanalyst is forced... to reinvent psychoanalysis... I have nonetheless tried to give a bit more substance to this; and this is why I have invented a certain number of writings [*c'est pour ça que j'ai inventé un certain nombre d'écritures*]. (Lacan, 1979[1978], p. 219)

With hindsight, one might also say that this is why he had published a certain number of *Écrits*—in fact no more than one, with occasionally one more.

Notes

1 An earlier version of this chapter was published in *Psychoanalytische Perspectieven*, 2018, 36(4), pp. 345–374. Materials from this earlier version are reproduced here with the permission of Dries Dulsster.
2 According to the French weekly news magazine *Le nouvel observateur*, 5,000 copies of *Écrits* were sold within a fortnight and before any reviews of the book had appeared in the press (Loriot, 1966). In the first volume of his monumental *History of Structuralism*, François Dosse reports that by 1984 sales for *Écrits* had exceeded more than 36,000 copies (Dosse, 1998[1991], p. 386). By 1993, when Élisabeth Roudinesco published her intellectual biography of Lacan, the single-volume had sold more than 50,000 copies, whereas the two volumes of the abridged paperback edition (Lacan, 1970; 1971a), which includes a generous selection of newly revised essays extracted from the single volume, had reached sales of over 120,000 for the first and over 55,000 for the second (Roudinesco, 1997[1993], p. 328). By contrast, the heavily truncated English edition of *Écrits*, which appeared in 1977 under the prestigious Tavistock imprint (Lacan, 1977), failed to attract a large readership, with the inevitable repercussion that the publishing company declined to take on any additional Lacan-translations (Smith, 1981). Speaking at a press conference in Rome on 29 October 1974, Lacan himself conceded that the overnight success of his *Écrits* had come as a total surprise to him and that he did not understand how it could have happened (Lacan, 2013[2005], p. 69).
3 Odd as the cover design for the original version of Lacan's *Écrits* may be for contemporary readers, it was actually identical to that of the volumes published in the series "L'ordre philosophique", which had been created in 1964 by Paul Ricœur and François Wahl, and which continues to exist to this day, although in a different format. *Écrits* thus appeared as if it were part of "L'ordre philosophique", in which seminal texts by Chomsky, Frege, Austin and others had

already been released, were it not for the fact that a publisher's mark on the front cover indicated that it belonged to "Le champ freudien", a book series edited by Lacan himself. However, the cover design of *Écrits* differed from that of the volumes published in "L'ordre philosophique" and other books released in "Le champ freudien" insofar as the back cover did not include a brief biographical presentation of the author. Those who did not know Lacan when picking up his *Écrits* would not have got to know anything about him simply from picking it up. Was it being assumed, here, that Lacan did not require an introduction? Was it the case that any biographical information about the author was considered a deterrent to potential buyers? Or was it a strategic decision in order to ensure that the ideas contained within the volume were presented as stemming from a disembodied voice and would survive beyond the lifespan of their creator? Over the years, the two volumes of the paperback edition of *Écrits* have been (re-)released with a number of different covers, ranging from abstract circles with a "bend sinister" to various photographs of Lacan himself, the latter again doubling the name of the author, although now with an image of his persona.

4 This précis was not included in the first English translation of *Écrits*—the one published in 1977 as a heavily abridged version of the original, containing just nine essays selected by Lacan himself (Lacan, 1977)—nor in the first complete English translation of the volume by Bruce Fink (Lacan, 2006[1966a]). The dustjacket of the first 1977 edition does include a contextualizing note about the author and his work, yet this was written by the translator (Alan Sheridan), probably with Lacan's consent. To the best of my knowledge, the précis has never been made available in English elsewhere. The translation provided here was originally produced by Bruce Fink for his complete English edition of *Écrits*. I am grateful to him for putting it at my disposal and I have reproduced it with some small modifications. Even though the précis is written in the third person and does not carry the name of an author, Lacan took away any doubt that he himself had composed it on two separate occasions. His first disclosure of authorship occurred in the session of 12 May 1971 of his seminar *D'un discours qui ne serait pas du semblant* (Lacan, 2006b), as well as in the published version of the essay entitled "Lituraterre" he read out on that occasion. In the seminar session of May 1971, he stated: "As for me, if I propose Poe's text [Edgar Allan Poe's 1844 short story "The Purloined Letter" (Poe, 1988[1844])], with all that is behind it, to psychoanalysis, it is precisely insofar as psychoanalysis cannot approach it without showing its failure. This is how I shed light on psychoanalysis, and it's already known, because it's on the back of my volume [*Écrits*], how in this way I also invoke the Enlightenment. Nonetheless, I shed light on it by demonstrating where psychoanalysis constitutes a hole" (Lacan, 2006b, p. 116). In "Lituraterre", these lines appear as: "As for me, if I propose to psychoanalysis the letter as being in abeyance [*en souffrance*], it is because it [psychoanalysis] shows its failure there. And it is through this that I shed light on it [psychoanalysis]: when I invoke in this way the Enlightenment, it is to demonstrate where it [psychoanalysis] constitutes a *hole*" (Lacan, 2013[1971a], p. 329). Apart from the French expression, the additional interpolations between square brackets, here, are based on the clarifications Lacan made during his seminar of 12 May 1971, when he read the text of "Lituraterre", and which have been reproduced in the published transcription of it (Lacan, 2006b, p. 116). In the alternative, "officially sanctioned" translation of "Lituraterre" by Khiara-Foxton and Price (Lacan, 2013[1971b]), some of the clarifications have been omitted, and so the text reads: "For my part, when I propose to psychoanalysis the letter as pending it is because it shows itself to fail therein. And it is in this way that I shed light on it: when I call upon the

enlightenment in this way it is to demonstrate where psychoanalysis forms a *hole*" (Lacan, 2013[1971b], p. 31). The latter translation thus potentially allows the reader to think that Lacan was suggesting that it is the letter, rather than psychoanalysis, which is failing, much like the published French text of "Lituraterre" could insinuate that it is not psychoanalysis, but the letter which constitutes a hole (Lacan, 2001[1971], p. 13). The latter (accidental or deliberate) mis-reading runs through a detailed commentary on "Lituraterre" by Laurent (2002[1999]), who categorically refuses to acknowledge Lacan's assertion that it is psychoanalysis which constitutes a failure and a hole, and that knowledge is "on the other side". Ironically, perhaps, Laurent's rather embarrassing Lacanian theory of the letter, and the fact that it was reprinted in a special issue of a journal entitled "Fictions in psychoanalysis", precisely proves Lacan's point: psychoanalytic knowledge fails, especially in those psychoanalysts who think they know. The second time Lacan referred to the précis as having been written by himself was on 4 November 1971, at the end of a lecture at Sainte-Anne Hospital in Paris, where he had delivered his seminar between 1953 and 1963: "The short note to be found on the back of the large pack of my *Écrits* mentions the Enlightenment. Why not admit it? I wrote it myself. Who else but me could have done so? My style has been recognized, and it's not badly written at all!" (Lacan, 2017[2011], p. 33).

5 It is worth emphasizing, here, that the inaccessibility of Lacan's writings is not a culturally or historically contingent feature, conditioned by specific circumstances—such as the reader not being French or not being a psychoanalyst—but an immanent characteristic, which was acknowledged in equal measure by Lacan's contemporaries, and even by those people operating in his circle of intimates. For example, on 26 November 1953, Daniel Lagache, the president of the newly established *Société française de Psychanalyse* (SFP), wrote a letter to his friend Michael Balint in which he commented on Lacan's report at the inaugural conference of the SFP in Rome: "On the whole, the report was considered difficult to read, but it nonetheless contains interesting and even important ideas. I hope to make a de-poeticized and more conceptual transcription of it, and to distribute these ideas to a larger audience" (Lagache, 1953). Many years later, Claude Lévi-Strauss told Didier Éribon in an interview that he often discussed the matter of reading Lacan with Maurice Merleau-Ponty, but that they always arrived at the conclusion that it would have taken them five or six readings to understand the text, and that time was just too short for that (Lévi-Strauss and Éribon, 1991[1988], pp. 73–74).

6 Lacan emphasized that the title is in the plural, because the last letter "s" of the word *Écrits* is silent when spoken, and the plural would only be heard when the word is preceded by a possessive pronoun, as in "*mes Écrits*", "*nos Écrits*", "*tes Écrits*", or "*ses Écrits*", a definite article (*les Écrits*), a genitive case (*des Écrits*), or a demonstrative adjective (*ces Écrits*).

7 Lacan had already made a similar point in a letter to Winnicott of 5 August 1960, and thus some six years before the publication of *Écrits*: "Everything that I have written in the last seven years takes on value solely in the context of my teaching" (Lacan, 1990[1960], p. 77).

8 This applies, for example, to "Presentation on Psychical Causality" (Lacan, 2006[1946]), "Presentation on Transference" (Lacan, 2006[1951]), "Psychoanalysis and Its Teaching" (Lacan, 2006[1957b]) and "The Signification of the Phallus" (Lacan, 2006[1958b]). The admission that his *écrits* were largely remnants, or indeed "waste-products" of his lectures, also emboldened Lacan on various occasions to refer to the publication of *Écrits* as a "poubellication", i.e. a "binification",

"trashification" or "garbagification". See, for example, Lacan (1965–1966, session of 15 December 1965), Lacan (2001[1968], p. 344) and Lacan (2018[2011], p. 195).

9 Hyppolite's text was originally published in the first issue of the journal "*La psychanalyse*" (Hyppolite, 1956). Following its inclusion in Lacan's *Écrits*, it was reprinted in the first volume of Hyppolite's collected writings, which were published three years after his death, notably with the subtitle *écrits* (Hyppolite, 1971[1956]). Apart from the English translation included in Lacan's *Écrits*, another English translation, by John Forrester, features as an appendix to the English translation of Lacan's *Seminar I* (Hyppolite, 1988[1956]; Lacan, 1988[1975]), despite the fact that it does not appear in the original French edition.

10 There is nothing suspicious about the fact that the book's Table of Contents changed place when *Écrits* was released in English. It is common practice in the French publishing tradition for a Table of Contents to appear at the back of a volume, whereas it is consistently placed at the front in texts published in English.

11 Only five of these seven texts are included in the book's Table of Contents, in which they have been italicized in both the French and the English versions. It should be noted that I am not referring to the appendices, here, which must be considered separately. I am also discounting the 1966 introduction to "Position of the Unconscious" (Lacan, 2006[1966*d*]).

12 At the time of the publication of *De l'interprétation*, in May 1965, Ricœur taught philosophy at the University of Paris. He had attended Lacan's seminars for quite a few years. Ricœur's massive volume was driven by a proposition to marry psychoanalysis with hermeneutics and phenomenology, and it opened with a chapter on psychoanalysis and language. However, the book's only in-text reference to Lacan did not appear until the third section, whereby Ricœur went so far as to question the originality of Lacan's thesis that the unconscious is structured like a language (Ricœur, 1970[1965], p. 395). At the same time, he also engaged extensively with the work of Lacan's pupils (and analysands) Jean Laplanche and Serge Leclaire, who had presented a joint paper in 1960 at the four-day conference on the unconscious that had been organized by Henri Ey at his psychiatric hospital in Bonneval, and which had already sparked Lacan's fury for its ostensible suggestion that language is not the condition for the unconscious (as Lacan himself had claimed), but that the unconscious is the condition for language. Lacan subsequently summarized his elaborate repartee to Laplanche and Leclaire's "betrayal" of his work in an essay entitled "Position of the Unconscious" (Lacan, 2006[1964]). For Laplanche and Leclaire's text, see Laplanche and Leclaire (1966[1960]; 1972[1960]). Ricœur's book was released in English in 1970 as *Freud and Philosophy: An Essay on Interpretation* (Ricœur, 1970[1965]).

13 The exceptions are those texts that had never been published before—"The Signification of the Phallus" (Lacan, 2006[1958*b*]) and "The Subversion of the Subject" (Lacan, 2006[1960])—and the transcript of his opening lecture for the seminar year 1965–1966, which reappeared as "Science and Truth" (Lacan, 2006[1965]). See, in this respect, the indispensable compendium by de Frutos Salvador (1994).

14 Although the name-index appears as very detailed, it features some glaring omissions. For example, the name of Georges Bataille, the ex-husband of Lacan's second wife was not included, and the same holds for Carl von Clausewitz, the famous Prussian theorist of war. Both omissions have been rectified in the English edition.

15 Neither of these is included in the Table of Contents of *Écrits*.

16 The word "privilege" appears in Lacan's "overture" to his *Écrits*, but is no longer detectable in the English translation. The French text reads: "Nous lui [le lecteur] ménageons un palier dans notre style, en donnant à *la Lettre volée* le privilège d'ouvrir leur suite [des écrits] en dépit de la diachronie de celle-ci [de la suite]" (Lacan, 1966a, p. 9). Fink has translated these sentences as: "I am offering this reader an easy entryway into my style by opening this collection with 'The Purloined Letter', even though that means taking it out of chronological order" (Lacan, 2006[1966b], p. 4). Given the privileged status Lacan accorded to his "Seminar on 'The Purloined Letter'", many a Lacan scholar may have wondered why he did not select this essay for inclusion in the 1977 abridged English edition of *Écrits* (Lacan, 1977). However, apart from the fact that Lacan's "Seminar on 'The Purloined Letter'" had already been published in English in 1972 (Lacan, 1972[1956]), the Pakistani-British psychoanalyst M. Masud R. Khan, who facilitated the publication of the selected *Écrits* and arranged for the book to be published under the Tavistock imprint, had asked Lacan to choose a sizeable number of primarily clinical or technical essays from *Écrits*, which rendered the "Seminar on 'The Purloined Letter'" otiose for the occasion (Lacan, 1976a). Lacan dutifully obliged, even though it implied excluding such key texts as "Kant with Sade" (Lacan, 2006[1962]) and "Science and Truth" (Lacan, 2006[1965]).

17 François Wahl was in analysis with Lacan from 1954 until 1960, and also attended Lacan's seminars during this period and for some time afterwards. Lacan had already signed a contract with Wahl for a new book series in April 1964, i.e., more than two years before the publication of *Écrits*, and the first book to be published in this series was Maud Mannoni's *L'enfant arriéré et sa mère*, which came out in May 1964, also with a stripped-down cover design of black and red lettering (Mannoni, 1964). Interviewed by François Dosse about his involvement in the production of *Écrits*, Wahl said: "To be honest, *Écrits* were published because of me: I found myself *de facto* in a central position, in the simple topographical sense of the word" (Dosse, 1998[1991], p. 386). For a detailed discussion of his involvement in the production of *Écrits*, see Roudinesco (1997[1993], pp. 319–331).

18 The English translation follows the second edition of the book, which was published in 1990. The order in which the authors appear on the cover and the endpages has been inverted in the English edition, probably because Jean-Luc Nancy was much better known in the Anglophone world than his co-author.

19 Lacan went on to claim that his *Écrits* are of course unreadable (*illisibles*) to all those who do not have anything important to do, or who are themselves in a hurry, as a result of which they only "pretend" to (have) read them. He also pointed out that the book had not attracted many reviews, which was blatantly untrue since at least 15 had been published in special newspaper sections and a range of learned journals by that time. For a large selection of the most important of these, see Arnoux, Berrebi, Boudet, and Germond (2016).

20 An Italian translation of *Écrits* by Giacomo B. Contri had been published shortly before this press conference. See Lacan (1974[1966]).

21 Speaking at Yale University in 1975, Lacan divulged that he had given pride of place to the case of "Aimée" in his doctoral dissertation, because "the person in question had produced numerous ... writings [*écrits*]" (Lacan, 1976[1975b], p. 9).

22 I do not doubt that Lacan's reconsideration of writing during the late 1960s and 1970s was also sparked by Derrida's trenchant critique of the logocentric tradition in Western philosophy, which moreover constituted the backdrop against which Nancy and Lacoue-Labarthe pursued their reading of Lacan in *Le titre de la lettre*. In addition, I should point out that there are of course numerous

passages in *Écrits*, including an entire essay (Lacan, 2006[1957c]), in which Lacan addresses the status of the letter, yet with very few exceptions these passages generally present the letter as an avatar of the signifier, and thus not as an instance or an agency that needs to be differentiated from the signifying chain. I first formulated this argument some 20 years ago (Nobus, 2002, pp. 26–27), based on such assertions by Lacan as "the letter exists as a means of power only through the final summons of the pure signifier" (Lacan, 2006[1957a], p. 23) and the letter is "the material medium [*support*] that concrete discourse borrows from language" (Lacan, 2006[1957c], p. 413). Since then, Tom Eyers (2012, pp. 50–54) has taken issue with my claim that until the mid-1960s Lacan situated both the signifier and the letter firmly within the register of the Symbolic by arguing that the letter was always already a pre-figuration of the Real, yet he can only do so by re-interpreting the "early Lacan" from the vantage point of the "late Lacan", which is to some extent what Lacan himself did, although with the greatest caution, in the overture to his *Écrits*. For a brief critical discussion of Lacan's often tacit critique of Derrida's emphasis on the primordiality of writing, see Nobus (2001). For an extensive critical analysis of the Lacan-Derrida debate, which was re-ignited during the early 1970s by Derrida's systematic deconstruction, in "Le facteur de la vérité" (Derrida, 1987[1975]), of Lacan's reading of "The Purloined Letter", see Major (2001), Hurst (2008), Alfandary (2016), and Earlie (2021).

23 Unfortunately, this connection between the object *a* and Sade's libertine writings in the schema of his practical reason is no longer evident from the English translation of *Écrits*, because the notation *a* has disappeared from the text, presumably because it was considered an index for the start of an enumeration which was not continued and therefore superfluous. In the first English translation of "Kant with Sade", by J. B. Swenson Jr., it has been preserved in its rightful place (Lacan, 1989[1962], p. 66).

Chapter 2

What Are Words Worth? Lacan and the Circulation of Money in the Psychoanalytic Economy

When Lacan died, on 9 September 1981, at the age of 80, he left behind a vast legacy, and not just in intellectual terms.[1] At the end of his life, Lacan was to all intents and purposes a fabulously rich man. In her biography of the psychoanalytic *maître-à-penser*, Elisabeth Roudinesco reports that in addition to the two adjacent apartments in the *rue de Lille*, where he had lived and practiced for 40 years, Lacan owned two other properties in Paris, as well as a large country house in Guitrancourt, near Mantes-la-Jolie, some 30 miles to the West of the French capital (Roudinesco, 1997[1993], pp. 397–398). His personal library at Guitrancourt alone amounted to more than 5,000 volumes and included many first editions of 16th- and 17th-century texts. He also possessed a fine collection of paintings and drawings by French masters, including works by Monet, Renoir, Picasso, Balthus, Derain, and Masson (who was his brother-in-law), and a large miscellany of ancient Asian and Mediterranean art objects (Roudinesco, 2005; 2014[2011], pp. 109–128).[2] Amongst his most prized possessions was the infamous 1866 canvas *L'origine du monde* by the French realist painter Gustave Courbet, which he had purchased at auction during the mid-1950s and which is currently held at the Musée d'Orsay in Paris (Barzilai, 1999, pp. 8–18). Still according to Roudinesco, towards the end of his life Lacan had become interested in gold, and had started collecting ingots. When he died, he had four bank accounts (Roudinesco, 1997[1993], p. 397).

To be fair, much like the amount of credit cards someone holds may not in itself be solid proof of personal wealth, the number of individual bank accounts is probably not a reliable indicator of richness, yet given Lacan's estimated annual income and expenditure, we may reasonably assume that the accounts contained significant sums of money. As a matter of fact, 14 years after Lacan's death, the French government accepted Courbet's painting *in lieu of* the inheritance tax that the family owed on Lacan's immoveable property and personal assets (see Musée d'Orsay). How did Lacan succeed in becoming so affluent? What allowed him to accumulate so much wealth that he could afford not only a personal secretary, but also a full-time butler?

DOI: 10.4324/9781003252276-3

The family into which he was born, although they were fairly successful middle-class businesspeople, would not have provided him with a hefty endowment or inheritance. He did not own a profitable private company, did not speculate on the stock market and, for all we know, had not won the lottery. He never occupied a senior position in any public- or private-sector organization; his weekly seminars and fortnightly clinical presentations, if not delivered *pro bono* are unlikely to have generated much income, and although he lectured widely outside Paris his honoraria would not have added up to large amounts of money. Although his second wife, Sylvia Maklès, had at one point been a promising French actress, after marrying Lacan she retired from the screen in order to devote herself entirely to domestic affairs (Roudinesco, 1997[1993], pp. 122–130).[3] And judging by his lifestyle, which involved regular lavish dinners in posh restaurants and bi-weekly visits to one of the top hairdressing salons in Paris, his fortune was not exactly the result of miserliness, or careful economizing.[4]

It is clear that Lacan derived the bulk of his income from seeing patients as a psychoanalyst in private practice. Starting some time during the mid-1930s, whilst he was still in training, over the years Lacan's practice developed into a hugely successful psychoanalytic business. As his seminars attracted more people, his work became more influential, and his name and fame spread more widely, Lacan's patients, too, became more numerous, more prominent, and more famous. For what it is worth, Roudinesco stipulates that during the last years of his life, Lacan conducted an average of 1,600 psychoanalytic sessions per month, at a rate of ten patients per hour, eight hours per day, and 20 days per month. Again, according to Roudinesco, Lacan's fee for a regular psychoanalytic session at the time varied between 100 and 500 French francs, and for supervision it ranged between 300 and 500 francs per session (Roudinesco, 1997[1993], p. 397). By comparison, the price of a private psychiatric consultation would have been roughly 180 francs, and the price of a regular medical consultation about 80 francs. If we take 300 francs as the average fee across the board, Lacan's monthly income would have been 480,000 francs gross. Taking into account the exchange rates at the time, this would have converted into roughly €72,000, £48,000, or $57,000 per month before tax. By today's standards, this is a significant amount of money; at the end of the 1970s, it would have been nothing less than a small fortune.

Envious as these sums may make us, Lacan's estimated wealth at the time of his death would presumably not give anyone any reason for concern had the source been hedge funds, investments, or real estate. Yet the fact that he derived it from charging patients large sums of money for private treatment is not by definition a problem either. Everyone knows that pursuing a treatment plan, or agreeing to surgery outside the public healthcare system or private insurance policies can be very expensive. In the United Kingdom, a top spinal surgeon will charge a patient £20,000 for posterior lumbar inter-body fusion, an operation lasting between two and three hours. Some spine surgeons perform more than 250 procedures like this per annum. It is evident that even the most renowned neuro-psychiatrist would not consider charging sums like these for a private consultation, yet fees of £200 to £300 per session are by no means unusual. If Lacan's accumulated wealth gives cause for concern, or may at least place some question marks over his clinical practice, and that of other psychoanalytic practitioners, it is for the way in which the money was generated, that is to say it is because his clinical approach may be seen as not meeting one or more of the standard "value for money" criteria of efficiency, economy, and effectiveness.

In an irreverent, and at times highly amusing collection of anecdotes about Lacan's psychoanalytic practice, his clinical presentations, and his place in the history of the psychoanalytic movement, Jean Allouch reports the following vignette:

> Having given Lacan a 500 franc note for his session, he [the patient] waits for his change. In vain. Lacan has pocketed the money and is already occupying himself with another analysand. But he's taken everything from him! And now he has nothing left! He can't bring himself to leave the premises and raises his voice to talk about the hotel, the train and especially about this 'nothing left'. Every time Lacan leaves his office, he tries to intercept him, but he is being ignored, or looked at without being seen. In the end, he goes to see Gloria [Lacan's secretary]. 'What do you want me to tell you?', she says. He did it because he had his reasons. He must have had his reasons. And then incisively: 'Next time, you'll pay attention!' (Allouch, 2009a, pp. 63–64)

Here is another one:

> At the end of the first preliminary session, Lacan asks the potential analysand about his income. He says he's not rich, and quite gently (given the value of this sum at the time) Lacan asks him for 100 francs. Yet when he opens his wallet, three 100 franc notes can be seen. Lacan corrects himself: 'Give me 300 francs; that's what I normally take for the first session'. He pays. For his second session, the analysand makes sure that he only has 100 francs in his pocket. When it comes to paying, Lacan interrogates him: 'How much did you give me last time?' '300 francs', the analysand says. 'Give me the same then'. Some time later, the analysand can no longer continue paying 300 francs per session, so he reminds Lacan of their first encounter. Lacan says: 'You were absolutely right in giving me 300 francs. When are you coming back?' 'It is impossible for me to continue like this', the analysand replies. To which Lacan responds: 'In that case, I'm kicking you out. Goodbye'. (Ibid., pp. 93–94)

All of the vignettes included in Allouch's book have been dutifully anonymized, which makes it difficult to establish to what extent they are true and accurate accounts of Lacan's financial "arrangements", rather than malicious gossip or Chinese whispers, urban myths, or persistent rumours. Nonetheless, the first "situation" mentioned above appears in almost identical terms at the end of Jean-Guy Godin's account of his analysis with Lacan:

> He [Lacan] doesn't give any change, no. Not that he's lacking in change, but out of principle. The misfortune can happen to the one who settles his session with a 500 franc note—small sum, actually. With this gesture, the analysand may have just fixed the new price for his sessions, without realizing it. He waits for his money, in vain, because it doesn't come. With Lacan having pocketed the note, he doesn't have to count on seeing his change, and it makes little difference whether he needs it or not. (Godin, 1990, p. 181)

In what follows, Godin repeats the text of Allouch's book almost *verbatim*, which may indicate that Allouch actually lifted the story from his colleague's work when compiling his collection of anecdotes.

Both aforementioned "scenes" are also very similar to those described by Gérard Haddad in his riveting narrative of his 11-year-long analysis with Lacan. At the end of the first session, Lacan tells Haddad that he will see him three times a week, and that each session will cost 200 francs. Haddad recalls:

> With my engineer's salary of 3,000 francs [per month] in 1969, this sum of 200 francs seemed quite considerable to me; actually, it struck me as inhumane. I had mentioned to Lacan that I did have some savings, and he had referred to them with a term that seemed rather odd to me: 'your little nest egg' [*votre petit pécule*].

Lacan immediately noticed my hesitation and explained:

> This is the honorarium for an analyst of my standing and it's not expensive. However, if you don't like the look of me, I can refer you to other analysts, my pupils who are, let's say, my equals. But I don't recommend that you go and see analysts who are beginners. (Ibid., p. 86)

Haddad arrives 15 minutes late for his first session, because he is held up in traffic. During the session, he returns to the vexed issue of the fee.

> 'I knew your lateness had other reasons,' Lacan says. Didn't you tell me that you had a nest egg? Look, this sum [of 200 francs per session] is the price of my consultation. But this is not what I will ask you ... It will be ... let's say half, 100 francs, so for three weekly sessions, taking into account

holiday breaks, about 1,000 francs per month, a third of your income, which is the accepted norm for the cost of an analysis. (Ibid., p. 89)

If this sounds like a good, or at least "reasonable" deal, then Haddad soon discovers that Lacan is not all that committed to keeping his side of the bargain: as time goes by, the price of the session first increases to 150 and then to 200 francs, and Lacan also accelerates the frequency of the sessions from three times a week to a daily appointment, and sometimes to two appointments per day, without thereby reducing the fee. Inevitably, Haddad has to tap into his "nest egg", but when that is about to dry up, he becomes worried about how to continue his analysis without it breaking the bank and impoverishing his family. On one occasion, Lacan insists on Haddad paying for a session that he had allegedly missed, but that had actually never been scheduled and which Lacan would not even have been able to conduct since it would have taken place on a bank holiday, when Lacan was in the habit of taking the day off at his country-house in Guitrancourt. (Ibid., pp. 308–309). Over time, Haddad's variable-length sessions also become shorter and shorter, to the point of being almost constantly reduced to zero:

> 'I could hardly say more than three or four words. Sometimes the session was finished before I had even opened my mouth, by an 'Until tomorrow', which didn't leave me with any choice' (Ibid., p. 312). Haddad starts his session: 'In cutting me off like that, you want to ...' 'Exactly,' says Lacan—end of the session (Ibid., p. 312).[5]

Stories like these are evidently celestial music to the ears of Lacan-bashers—proof that the charismatic psychoanalyst was just an ordinary exploiter or, as some would say, a ruthless "charlacan". Those who remain enthralled by Lacan's persona will no doubt try to minimize the importance of these transactions, or (echoing Lacan's secretary) refer them back to the inscrutable, yet unassailable *bona fide* intentions of the wise master: he must have had his reasons, that is to say the act must have been motivated by his desire to steer the patient's analysis in a certain direction, or to produce a momentary (in this case, "monetary") analytic effect. And indeed, although it puts him and his family in a state of severe financial hardship, Haddad too continued to believe in Lacan's sincerity as a psychoanalyst, and often recuperated the highly peculiar and financially draining demands to which he was being subjected within the semantic framework of his own analytic journey. Lacan's request to be paid for a session that was supposed to have taken place the day before, but could never have happened, is retrospectively "interpreted" by Haddad as an absolutely brilliant analytic equivocation on the signifier *pas hier* (not yesterday), which to him conjures up the name of the French journalist and writer Aimé Pallière, whose lifelong spiritual fluctuations between Christianity and Judaism had recently been the subject of one of Haddad's papers, and whose protracted religious indecisiveness reflected much of Haddad's own internal neurotic conflict (Ibid., pp. 308–309).

Irrespective of Lacan's ostensible greed, here, one is left wondering why his patients accepted to pay such elevated fees, including for missed sessions that never really existed in the first place, especially when the length of the session and the analyst's labour within it seemed to count for very little, almost nothing.[6] Of course, from the Lacanian analyst's perspective, the value of a psychoanalytic session, or indeed of the entire analytic process, ought not be measured in terms of its duration. A short session may be more analytically productive than a longer one, and the imposition of a strict temporal regularity upon the process, with a pre-agreed frequency and schedule of consultations and a fixed duration for each session, could very well have counter-productive effects—good value for money as it may seem. This is why, some time during the early 1950s, Lacan opposed the classic "50-minute hour" and argued in favour of variable-length sessions, thus attracting the odium of the psychoanalytic establishment, who saw in it a dangerous extension of the psychoanalyst's clinical power (Eissler, 1954).[7] In Lacanian psychoanalysis, "analytic value" is not directly proportional to the length of time an analysand spends in a session nor, for that matter, to the entire length of the analysis as such. In addition, "analytic value" is not a function of the volume, but of the quality of the psychoanalyst's interventions (interpretations, constructions), and is more fundamentally conditioned by the analysand's rather than the analyst's labour. In remaining silent throughout, or offering the analysand but a small discursive punctuation, more may be accomplished than through a long, laborious exposition of the latent, unconscious significance of the analysand's associations. And in throwing the analysand off balance with a sudden, unexpected intervention such as the cutting of the session mid-sentence, or after a very short period of time, the analyst may achieve more than in adhering to a standard, formal set of rules and regulations. As Schneiderman put it:

> The combined pressure of the shortness of the sessions and the unpredictability of their stops creates a condition that greatly enhances one's tendencies to free-associate … Almost by definition the ego can never be the master of the short session. (Schneiderman, 1983, pp. 133–134)

In some cases, patients know about all of this before their first consultation with a Lacanian analyst. In some cases it is their prefabricated knowledge of the way in which a Lacanian process unfolds that precisely draws them to it. In some cases, patients do not know anything about the approach that the Lacanian analyst will take, in which case they learn about it during the first preliminary session, either experientially or because the analyst explains it to them. Yet whatever the state of the analysands' knowledge as regards the process, they will end up paying the analyst for work that they themselves will be expected to do, under temporal conditions over which they themselves have little or no control.

If we accept this principle, the implication can only be that the psychoanalytic economy, and *a fortiori* its Lacanian avatar, is substantially worse than capitalism. In a capitalist ideology, the worker agrees to sell his labour in return for a sum of money (wages) of which he knows that it does not accurately represent the actual value of what he has agreed to contribute to the production process, thus allowing the employer to make profit and enrich himself. In the psychoanalytic paradigm, the analysand does not get paid for the work she does, and it is difficult to see how she would be able to sell her work to the analyst anyway, given that she herself is the main, and maybe even the sole benefactor of her labour. Of course, one may argue that a patient's work in analysis is of benefit to the analyst too, insofar as it allows him to gain more experience, thus improving his training and facilitating the application of certain insights to other cases. However, analytic work is primarily of use to the person who actually performs it. In this way, the analysand is more or less self-employed, were it not for the fact that she does not reap the financial benefits of her work, and is only really allowed to do it on condition that she agrees to pay for it. As Bruce Fink put it succinctly: "Psychoanalysts require analysands to work, but instead of paying them for their work, we make *them* pay for the privilege of working" (Fink, 2012, p. 64). Worse than capitalism: the analysand agrees to work, and is expected to do so within the parameters of the treatment setting, yet instead of being paid for his labour, he has to pay *for* it, sometimes so much that his only way of covering the cost is by getting another job.

If that sounds bad enough already, consider this. In a capitalist market economy, product manufacturers, service providers, and retailers are very keen to guarantee customer satisfaction, and on occasion it may even appear that the satisfaction customers derive from what they have purchased is actually more important to retailers than the products (goods or services) they sell. In many cases, stores also offer a "money-back guarantee" if the customer is not completely satisfied with the merchandise. In practice, few people are likely to take advantage of this commitment, but at least customers are led to believe that in return for parting with their cash they are expected to be satisfied, more satisfied, entirely satisfied, and that whoever takes the money is dedicated to ensuring that the whole experience is a satisfying one. In the psychoanalytic economy, there is no such thing as a reimbursement if the analysand is not completely satisfied with the outcome of the treatment for which he has paid. The analysand is not entitled to get her money back if she is not entirely happy with her analysis, for the pure and simple reason that, at least in a Lacanian framework, it is a certain loss of enjoyment (*jouissance*) and a certain reduction of (the illusion of) complete happiness, rather than an enhancement of satisfaction, that is aimed for. In other words, the analysand would not be in a position to ask her money back if at one point she comes to the conclusion that she is not entirely satisfied with what she gets out of her analysis, because *less* rather than more satisfaction is what she has been paying for! Paradoxically, only the analysand who comes out of his analysis with a sense of complete satisfaction would technically be entitled to a refund, were it not for the fact that precisely this newly acquired state of completion would undoubtedly prevent him from seeking compensation in the first place. Psychoanalysis is worse than capitalism: the analysand pays in order to work, and is not even supposed to enjoy what he gets out of it.

Unless someone is a complete masochist, why would anyone want to do this? Or, as Fink (2012) would have it: why would anyone in their right mind pay for an analysis (costing that much)? Maybe we should turn the question into an assertion, here, and say that anyone who pays for an analysis is, by definition, not in their right mind. And, of course, in many cases those people seeking out psychoanalytic treatment are not in their right mind at all, insofar as they may suffer from a plethora of disturbing symptoms, among which we may want to include the persistent desire to become a psychoanalyst ... Confused and conflicted, disturbed and distracted, the patient may thus lack the *compos mentis* to realize that it is actually inappropriate or wholly unnecessary to pay so much for work that he himself has to carry out, and which will actually leave him feeling less satisfied than before. The psychoanalyst who sets an exorbitant fee, and takes the willing patient's money, is therefore not only at risk of being perceived as a greedy, "rogue trader", but also as someone who is unscrupulously exploiting his patients' physical and emotional vulnerability for his own financial advantage.[8] Again, analysts and analysands themselves may see these pecuniary matters in a very different light, as an essential part of the analytic treatment, or as a necessary regulatory mechanism that prevents patients from having to feel grateful or indebted. The analogy is no doubt uncouth, but one is involuntarily reminded, here, of how the Indian guru Bhagwan Shree Rajneesh's collection of 95 Rolls Royce cars was to many non-believers solid evidence of his being a callous confidence operator who knew exactly how to defraud legions of infatuated soul-searchers, whereas for the so-called *sannyasins* themselves it was simultaneously a brilliant satirical take on Western people's obsession with luxury cars, and a wise attempt at bringing out and purging the core of jealousy in his followers' inner consciousness.

Inasmuch as someone is prepared to comply with the psychoanalytic economy, and pay a lot of money for the work she herself will be doing in her sessions, giving up a certain quantum of satisfaction on top, one is also tempted to ask what the analysand is actually paying for, especially when the clinical regime is based upon the temporal and financial principles adopted by Lacan. If the patient who starts an analysis is not purchasing any material goods, but rather paying for a type of "personal service", much like he would pay for legal advice or a health assessment, what kind of service is the psychoanalyst offering? It is definitely not to be compared with that offered by a life-coach, for instance, insofar as the analyst does not dispense genuine professional and personal advice, let alone individually tailored support and guidance. The psychoanalyst could not be further removed from the position of the "skilled helper" (Egan, 1982), less because he lacks clinical skills, but primarily because he deliberately steers away from offering the patient aid, counsel and assistance. To seemingly make matters worse again, the analyst is not even supposed to be animated by a desire to heal. On 25 January 1909, Freud wrote to Jung: "I often appease my conscious mind by saying to myself: Just give up wanting to cure; learn and make money, those are the most plausible conscious aims" (McGuire, 1974, pp. 202–203). Three years later, in his "Recommendations to Physicians Practising Psycho-Analysis", he declared: "Under present-day conditions the feeling [*Affektstrebung*] that is most dangerous to a psycho-analyst is the therapeutic ambition [*therapeutische Ehrgeiz*] to achieve by this novel and much disputed method something that will produce a convincing effect upon other people" (Freud, 1958[1912e], p. 115). In his 1915 paper on transference-love, he stated even more forcefully that "human society has no more use for the *furor sanandi* than for any other fanaticism" (Freud, 1958[1915a], p. 171). When he accepted the commission to write a paper on "Variations on the Standard Treatment" for the prestigious *Encyclopédie médico-chirurgicale*, Lacan uncompromisingly embraced Freud's position:

> Clearly advised by Freud to closely examine the effects in his experience of the danger sufficiently announced by the term *furor sanandi*, he [the psychoanalyst] does not, in the end, wish to appear to be motivated by it. While he thus views cure as an added benefit [*la guérison comme bénéfice de surcroît*] of psychoanalytic treatment, he is wary of any misuse of the desire to cure. (Lacan, 2006[1955a], p. 270)

Put differently, if during the course of his analysis the analysand does start to feel better, either because his symptoms have become less debilitating, or because he has found a way to cope with them, this is to be regarded as a beneficial side-effect, a fortunate yet unintended outcome, pure serendipity.[9] Hence, the patient entering analysis does not pay for the specialist care that will allow her to regain her mental health, at least not in the traditional sense of paying for a special treatment plan that has been purposefully designed to alleviate the symptoms and improve the patient's overall sense of wellbeing. So, if the (Freudo-Lacanian) analyst does not fit the standard description of a "healthcare professional", insofar as he does not seem to care all that much about the health of his patients, or is at least not supposed to allow himself to be guided primarily by a desire to heal and cure, what on earth is the patient paying for?

Reflecting upon her experience of being in analysis with Lacan during the 1960s, the acclaimed French writer and journalist Françoise Giroud (1990) conceded that Lacan's art of knowing how to interpret, the way in which he knew how to bring her to the point where she could read her unconscious, was totally invaluable, and in itself worth the high price of the sessions. And so it has been said that the patient is not just paying for the work he himself has to do, but also for the analyst's interpretations, his punctuations, citations, articulations, and oracles, in short for his precious words, no matter how sparse they may be. One could even extend this principle into an argument that the most valuable of the analyst's words are those that remain unspoken, those that do not feed anything more to the analysand than the pregnant sound of a non-judgmental, receptive taciturnity. As Theodor Reik put it at the end of a lecture before the Vienna Psychoanalytic Society in 1926:

> Beethoven once noted: 'The most important thing in music is not the notes'. Also in analysis what is said as such is not the most important thing. More important, it seems to us, is to recognize what our speech conceals [*verschweigt*], and what our silence betrays [*spricht*]. (Reik, 1968, p. 186)

The patient thus also pays for the analyst's golden silence, for the quiet acquiescence of his existence as an attentive listener, or *mutatis mutandis* for the right to remain silent himself when the words escape, or when speech cannot do justice to the meaning of the experience. The analysand pays for the presence of the analyst, which is not tantamount to a position of passive attendance or, as Freud would have it, to a mere offer of "evenly suspended attention", but which epitomizes the analyst's constant re-creation of an open depository, where the analysand can store his trials and tribulations, without running the risk of them being rejected.[10] As Bruce Fink has argued:

> Analysts willingly play a part, or rather many parts, as many as we [the analysands] thrust upon them. They do not—or at least most of them know they should not—say, 'Stop projecting, I'm not the kind of person you're acting as though I am. I'm not your mother'. They agree to stand in for the mother provisionally so that something about our relationships with our mothers can be worked through. They accept the projections and try not to take them personally, which is not always easy. They get paid to be actors, to play all the roles in our daytime and night-time dramas. We [the analysands] pay so that we can assign the analyst to whatever role we want, knowing that the analyst will accept to serve as a placeholder. (Fink, 2012, p. 65)

If this makes perfect sense as a clinical principle, then it can be deemed acceptable for the patient to be asked to pay for the special privilege of being listened to, and heard in a non-judgmental way. The question remains, however, why the analysand has to pay *so much* for this. Controversial as it may be for the analyst not to be expected to act upon a *furor sanandi*, what if he or she has no reservations acting upon a *furor pecuniam*? What if Lacan did indeed use the technical principle of the variable-length session as a pretext for consistently cutting analytic sessions short—to the point of their being almost reduced to zero—not with a view to producing analytic effects, but in order to be able to see as many patients as possible in the space of an hour, thereby maximizing the financial returns from his clinical work?[11]

In a thought-provoking passage of his 1958 paper "The Direction of the Treatment", Lacan wrote:

> [I]f love is giving what you don't have, it is certainly true that the subject can wait to be given it, since the psychoanalyst has nothing else to give him. But he does not even give him this nothing, and it is better that way—which is why he is paid for this nothing, preferably well paid, in order to show that otherwise it would not be worth much. (Lacan, 2006[1958a], p. 516)

Lacan seems to be intimating, here, that purely on account of his presence the analyst could easily be seen as giving the patient his love, immaterial as this may be and as though the analyst (much like, or more than anyone else for that matter) would actually possess this "thing called love". Yet precisely in order to avoid that the analysand experiences the analyst's presence as a gift of love, the analyst is being paid, and preferably a large sum, because annihilating the "nothingness" of love, neutralizing the connotation of love that the patient may project upon the analyst's receptive, accommodating presence is hugely expensive.

Once again, the psychoanalytic economy appears as far worse than capitalism. Irrespective of the "money-back guarantee" or any other policy that allows goods to be returned or exchanged whenever a customer is not entirely satisfied with the products or services that she has bought, she may (and is, in a sense, expected to) still acknowledge the high-quality "customer care" in the way she has been dealt with. Employees selling their labour may very well realize that they are being underpaid, or that their employer is making substantial profits through the sale of the goods that they have produced, but they may simultaneously feel that they are being valued for what they do, and that the company truly cares about its workforce. This is very much the message that private sector organizations wish to convey to their employees: even under tough economic circumstances, which may impose unwelcome efficiency savings and austerity measures, we will be there to support you in any way we can, by virtue of various employee assistance programmes, including career transition counseling and outplacement services. In the psychoanalytic economy, the analyst actively avoids being perceived by the analysand as someone who is loving and caring. More fundamentally, although the analysand may love his analyst, he cannot expect this love to be reciprocated. The analyst may always be there for her patients, but this presence is not an act of love. Regardless as to the quality of the "analytic service" that is being provided by the analyst, the analysand should not assume that it is delivered with love.

The analysand's payment thus serves the technical purpose, here, of evacuating the meaning of love that could be attributed to the analyst's mere *acte-de-présence*. But it also prevents the analysand from feeling that he actually owes the analyst something, that he is indebted to the analyst, or that he should be deeply grateful for what he has been offered which, as Freud pointed out in his essay "On Beginning the Treatment", may greatly exacerbate neurotic resistance, to the detriment of the analytic process (Freud, 1958[1913c], p. 132).[12] In his *Seminar II*, in the context of a discussion of the hefty reward of 50,000 francs that C. Auguste Dupin receives for having retrieved the purloined letter in Edgar Allan Poe's eponymous short story, Lacan elaborated on Freud's point as follows:

> I don't mean to insist on it, but you might gently point out to me that we [psychoanalysts], who spend our time being the bearers of all the purloined letters of the patient, also get paid somewhat dearly [*nous nous faisons payer plus ou moins cher*]. Think about this with some care—were we not to be paid, we would get involved in the drama of Atreus and Thyestes, the drama in which all the subjects who come to confide their truth in us are involved. They tell us their damned stories [*de sacrées histoires*], and because of that we are not at all within the domain of the sacred and of sacrifice [*l'ordre du sacré et du sacrifice*]. Everyone knows that money doesn't just buy things, but that the prices which, in our culture, are calculated at rock-bottom [*calculés au plus juste*], have the function of neutralizing something infinitely more dangerous than paying in money, namely owing somebody something. (Lacan, 1988[1978], p. 204)[13]

Paying an analyst is rather similar, here, to paying a prostitute. Or rather, the money the analyst requires the patient to pay serves a similar purpose to the money a prostitute charges the client: it stops the "service user" from thinking that the "service provider" may feel inclined to "doing it" out of love, or it prevents the user from thinking that he should give the provider something in return. When the client is indeed someone who is using the services of a sex worker, the former's realization that the provider is only motivated by money may not make much of a difference—as long as the service is good (value for money!)—but to the client who is seeking the help of a psychoanalyst the same realization may seriously affect the continuation of the treatment, if only because it will by definition affect the transference. If the premium fee of the psychoanalytic session is justified as a technical tool for ensuring that the treatment can take place outside the semantic sphere of love, then the analyst would presumably not want to be perceived by the analysand as someone who is *only* doing it for the money. But how could this be prevented? If the analysand's money is meant to neutralize the analyst's love, how can the analyst by the same token avoid being re-invested with another love, notably the love of money? The issue is exacerbated by the fact that, whereas the sex worker at least does something tangible from which the client derives a certain degree of satisfaction, the psychoanalyst can easily be perceived as doing very little, almost nothing—as giving next to nothing in return for the patient's hard-earned cash. And if the analyst's "doing" is effectively reduced to an "act of being", then this in itself may instill the thought in the analysand's mind that it is the love of the filthy lucre that has prompted him to choose this seemingly undemanding and rather lucrative profession.

As an aside, it is worth mentioning that Lacan's designation of money as a neutralizing signifier, that is to say as a symbolic unit of exchange, is in itself indebted to Saussurean linguistics, who had in turn "borrowed" the homology between money and speech from the Italian economic sociologist Vilfredo Pareto. In his *Course on General Linguistics*, Saussure asserted:

> To determine what a five-franc piece is worth one must therefore know: (1) that it can be exchanged for a fixed quantity of a different thing, e.g. bread; and (2) that it can be compared with a similar value of the same system, e.g. a one-franc piece, or with coins of another system (a dollar etc.). In the same way a word can be exchanged for something dissimilar, an idea; besides it can be compared with something of the same nature, another word. (Saussure 1959[1916], p. 115)

Although Saussure's structuralist semiotics of money, which emphasizes the symbolic reference point of financial transactions and, by extension, of any type of economic exchange, was quite influential, it is by no means the only, and not even the most prominent account of how money functions within socio-economic interactions.[14] Yet whenever Lacan raised the issue of money—admittedly, on very few occasions—he stayed truthful to the Saussurian model of money *qua* signifier. For example, in "The Function and Field of Speech and Language in Psychoanalysis" (the 1953 Rome Discourse), he referred to money as a symbolic gift, whose function is similar to that of words in traditional forms of economic exchange, and he compared the exchange of old and worn, meaningless words to the use of coins that have changed hands so many times that their denomination and inscription are no longer visible (Lacan, 2006[1953], pp. 209, 256).[15] Much later on, in *Seminar XVI*, Lacan reiterated the Saussurian paradigm by positing that money does not have use-value but only exchange value (Lacan, 2006a, pp. 284–285). The fetishization of money, as exposed by Marx in his critique of the capitalist economy, only contributes to the maintenance and development of the economic system if it *does not* prompt the capitalist to accumulate wealth through saving, but rather through parting with the funds in such a way that they can re-enter the financial circuits of exchange, commerce, and investment.

Returning to the idea that the analysand's payment is necessary for the analyst's act to become devoid of any attribution of love, the question remains as to how one can set a price on this. How much money does the analysand need to pay for the meaning of love to be neutralized? Why does the analyst have to be paid "dearly"? Why is he "preferably well paid" in this process of semantic neutralization? In a remarkably frank podcast on the website of the *École de la Cause freudienne*, the Lacanian analyst Pierre-Gilles Guéguen justified the vexed issue of the high cost of an analysis as something that is absolutely crucial to its internal dynamics. First of all, referring to one of Lacan's remarks that an analysis should cost a lot (*beaucoup, beau-coup*, "a lot" and "a beautiful catch"), he goes on to say that it is never the analyst's intention to financially ruin a patient, but to nonetheless ensure that he pays a little bit more (*un tout petit plus*) than he can actually afford, which allegedly requires a great deal of subtlety on the part of the analyst, but which prevents the patient from relating to his analysis as an object of consumption—say a packet of cigarettes—and which forces him to commit himself to it, in a way that is fully engaged (Guéguen, 2012). Guéguen's take on the monetary reality of analysis seems slightly different, here, from Lacan's argument about the patient's semantic neutralization of the analyst's presence, yet in a sense it is just the flipside of the process. The large sum of money that the analysand pays the analyst—if not in real terms at least relative to his means—simultaneously precludes the analyst being seen as "doing it" out of love and defines the analysand as someone who is not only committed, but also dedicated and devoted. Being found willing to pay more for something than one can actually afford must necessarily indicate that one loves it very much, so much that one is prepared to go the extra financial mile.

Some people will no doubt regard these technical explanations as spurious excuses or retrospective justifications for analysts cashing in on their patients' symptomatic sensibilities and infatuations, which make them particularly vulnerable to exploitation. It is extremely difficult to discard critical reservations such as these, especially when one is looking at Lacan's idiosyncratic technique. In addition, the type of financial regime imposed by Lacan may easily constitute a new and not insignificant threat to the transference. For it may very well be the case that the analysand who pays a substantial fee for her analytic sessions is prevented from seeing her analysis, on the side of the analyst, as a labour of love, but it will not necessarily stop her from regarding her analyst as a ruthless profiteer, a greedy exploiter, someone who merely takes advantage of her vulnerable state of mind in order to enrich himself. Surely, she could say, it suffices for my analyst to stop the session after five minutes, to kick me out before I even had the chance to say anything—as Lacan seemed to have been in the habit of doing towards the end of his life—for me to realize that he is not there for me just because he loves me. And the fact that I keep coming back despite being "treated" in this way is in itself an indication that I do take all of this seriously. Why do I have to pay on top, and more than I can afford? The risk, here, is that the evacuation of the meaning of love in the patient's perception of the analyst's reasons for "being there" indeed coincides with a new semantic investment of the analyst as animated by *furor pecuniam*. This is not just about the analysand thinking that the analyst is only there, as the pure presence of being, out of a love of money, but that he takes advantage of his being there for the patient *in order to* satisfy his greed. Whereas the patient's payment allows the analyst to be de-invested as a loving figure, his position gets contaminated with a new set of attributions around the central suspicion of financial exploitation.

Just as much as the patient's attribution to the analyst of charitable, caring and loving intentions is not, by definition, problematic for the unfolding of the transference, but something that needs to be worked through during the course of the analysis, the same is no doubt true for the opposite perspective. In some circumstances, the analyst's being perceived as greedy may even open up analytically productive strands of work. Let me illustrate this with a famous example. In an influential paper on the significance of the fee in psychoanalytic treatment, the eminently respectable psychoanalyst Kurt R. Eissler painstakingly canvassed the great many different situations in which the psychoanalyst could find himself with regard to fee-setting, offering sensible answers and practical solutions to such thorny issues as to how to proceed when a severely depressed patient is no longer in a position to pay, or what to do when a child's parents cannot afford the treatment anymore. As a comprehensive technical guide for how to deal with money matters psychoanalytically, the paper probably served numerous clinicians, but in an addendum to the text, Eissler ended on what he called an "interesting question": should one "accept a fee when one analyses a call girl?" "I would surmise," he continued, "that the analysis has a far better chance of success if the payment of a fee is postponed until such time as the patient has made a new professional choice" (Eissler, 1974, p. 99). If the question is strange, the admittedly tentative answer, here, has always struck me as even stranger. Considerations of so-called "hot" (untaxed) money aside, why would the analysis be at risk of failing if the analyst accepts a fee from his call girl-patient? Why would it have a higher chance of success if the analyst waives the fee for as long as the patient continues to work in this profession? What would be her motive for making "a new professional choice" if this change of profession coincides with her having to start paying for her sessions? Doesn't Eissler's reluctance to charge a prostitute reflect his own moral values about what is considered acceptable income, regardless of the issue that he himself would be expected to pay tax on income that, although properly incurred, was derived from a concealed and illegal source? And to what extent is his decision to offer free analysis influenced by his wanting to avoid being perceived as just another pimp?

In a perceptive reading of this case, the psychoanalytic historian John Forrester agreed with Eissler and suggested that it is only when the woman thinks the analyst is doing it for love, not money, that the seduction essential to analysis will start to unfold. The call girl is too much like the analyst to be seduced—she knows what the price of love is, she knows what an hour is worth—no ambiguity. Only when money and love no longer correspond with each other will the seduction start, will her words begin to fill up with ambiguity. The analyst knows too well how to weigh words, just as the call girl knows that the whore with a heart of gold is an effect of language. (Forrester, 1990, p. 47)

With all due respect to Eissler and Forrester, I tend to disagree with their justifications. For one, I am not at all sure call girls understand the "price of love". They may know something about the "cost of sex" in all its permutations, but I would be surprised if their professional duties equip them with a better grasp of the monetary value of love, whatever that may mean. After all, their clients do not buy love, and are being charged for the sexual service in accordance with a certain "price-list", which also includes an agreement over the actual duration of the service, in order to prevent the spectre of love from looming on the horizon.[16] Secondly, although the analyst's offer of free sessions may indeed prompt the call girl to think that the analyst, since he is clearly not doing it for money, must therefore be doing it for love, I remain unconvinced that this will trigger the "essential seduction" and fill up her words with ambiguity. The call girl will have grown used to exchanging sex for money. In waiving his fee, the analyst runs the risk of placing himself in the same position as her clients, insofar as he may elicit in her the idea that he is giving her what she wants (psychoanalytic treatment) without expecting any other form of compensation than a certain sexual service. In perceiving her analyst as but another of her clients, it is unlikely that the "essential seduction" will unfold; it would seem much more likely she is confirmed in the belief that, whatever she decides to do, she is always reduced to being a whore. In light of this, it may be much more productive, here, if the analyst charges the call girl an elevated fee for her sessions, because this is much more likely to trigger the "essential seduction" in all its semantic complexities. It may make her think that the analyst is greedy, maybe even greedier than her pimp, but it may also make her realize that the analyst is not after her body, that she may have something else to offer than a sexual service, that she is not just defined in terms of what she does, and how she makes a living, but also in terms of what she does not do, i.e., quite literally being a client in her own right.

Let me arrive at some conclusions. Ever since Freud discussed the issue of money as primarily a psychological problem for the patient, which is governed by the anal stage of libidinal development (Freud, 1959[1908*b*]), but never really more than a practical problem for the analyst, insofar as he too has to earn a living and therefore somehow needs to ensure that he is being paid handsomely for his work (Freud, 1958[1913c]), many psychoanalysts have endeavoured to come up with more nuanced, subtle, and sophisticated perspectives on the circulation of money in the psychoanalytic economy (see Berger and Newman, 2012; Herron and Rouslin Welt, 1992; Krueger, 1986; Murdin, 2012; Reiss-Schimmel, 1993; Viderman, 1992; Vasse, 2008). Over the years, it has become clear that money is sometimes just a practical problem for the patient, and sometimes also a psychological problem for the analyst, and that this "reversed perspective" is more likely to manifest itself during times of economic recession, when more people are out of work and the competition for patients is more severe. Under conditions of austerity, fewer patients may be inclined to seek out psychoanalytic treatment, and more patients may be forced to interrupt the treatment they have already started, whilst more psychoanalysts may feel the need to unnecessarily prolong the treatment or increase the frequency of the consultations for those patients who can afford it, and fewer psychoanalysts may be inclined to offer challenging interpretations out of fear of losing their patients.

If we accept that psychoanalysis—as I have laid out in this chapter, although not without a certain degree of irony—is in many ways worse than capitalism, because the patient has to pay for her own work, without a guarantee of success, without a proper "return policy", without the analyst caring, and without her even being supposed to enjoy the outcome, then Lacan's idiosyncratic psychoanalytic *nouvelle cuisine*, which seemed to have revolved around the patient paying more for less, must come across as pure exploitation, whose severity is exacerbated by the fact that the one who is being exploited is someone who is suffering, or who has been ravaged by blind infatuation. In my view, there is no solid evidence that Lacan practiced psychoanalysis with the sole purpose of enriching himself at his patients' expense—literally and metaphorically—even when he reduced the time (but not the frequency) of the sessions to almost nothing. It is fair to say that his price was high, became higher as the years went by, and was no doubt higher than that of many other analysts at the end of his life when, quite paradoxically, his clinical acumen often seemed to have been clouded by physical ailments and other preoccupations. Yet this in itself does not constitute a good enough reason to assert that he was a money-hungry charlatan who took advantage of his patients. It seems to me that the issue is more complicated than that, for the pure and simple reason that when it comes to psychoanalysis it is impossible to place the operation on a scale of value, whereby it would enter into a monetary calculus. The same problem, which is commonly designated as the issue of commensuration, also applies to other commodified objects, such as body parts, works of art and intellectual property, but in the case of psychoanalytic treatment, which does not involve the procurement of material goods and in which the exact nature of the service remains opaque, it would seem particularly acute. Anno 2022, the fee for psychoanalysis in London ranges from £30 to £300 per session, largely depending on the seniority, fame and reputation of the analyst—although some prominent practitioners do operate with a so-called "sliding scale". So one analyst can be substantially more expensive than another, merely owing to his rank and esteem, which implies that the cost of the treatment is not so much a function of the severity of the presenting problem and the associated complexity of the intervention—as it would generally be the case for a standard medical issue—but conditioned by the presumed prestige of the person offering it. In psychoanalysis, the patient does not just pay for his analysis, he also pays for his analyst, and the more so as the analyst is more notable, more renowned, and more experienced.

In an intervention at a conference in Aix-en-Provence in 1972, Lacan claimed, without irony: "I think it's impossible to say something about the function of money [in the analytic discourse] without asking oneself, from the beginning, whether money is situated at the place of the analyst ..." (Lacan, 1972, p. 205). Neither rhetorical, nor entirely open, the question definitely deserves to be asked, not as an invitation to reflect upon how psychoanalysts may be affected by greed, but as an exhortation to think about how money is a driving force for the direction of the psychoanalytic treatment.[17] Much like the sophists in Ancient Greece, psychoanalysts expect to be paid, and rather dearly or, in Lacan's case, exorbitant amounts, for dispensing valuable words of wisdom or opening up precious spaces of silence.[18] This does not by definition make them into professional swindlers, although it does not by definition preclude the existence of swindling professionals either. The value of the psychoanalyst's presence is inestimable, in the sense that its benefits cannot be measured accurately by any reliable standards, so that the costs associated with it will be equally incalculable, or may only be evaluated in terms of their fairness retrospectively, long after the treatment has finished. If many people who were in analysis or supervision with Lacan during the 1970s seemed to complain about the premium fee, then few if any subsequently indicated that the experience was not worth it, that they would have been better off without it, or that they felt betrayed or ripped off.

This is not the perspective of the satisfied customer, who consoles himself with the thought of having received good value for money, but rather the view of someone who is capable of reflecting upon the value of their own work, and who in doing so arrives at the conclusion that it was to some extent a complete waste of time (but not money), because it was built upon the spurious expectation of it generating some form of material benefit. To realize this can indeed be very expensive. How expensive it is should not be conditioned by the analyst's symptom or his fantasy, but it is definitely the analyst who, on account of the position he occupies within the treatment, is expected to establish the financial logic of the psychoanalytic economy, and who should therefore be held accountable for it. If, as Lacan would have it, money is to be situated at the place of the analyst within the psychoanalytic discourse, this can only mean that it is not aimed for as a psychoanalytic product—neither for the analysand, nor for the analyst—but represents something to be employed as a special tool for advancing the psychoanalytic process and facilitating effects. The implication is that whatever the analyst decides to charge the patient, this fee (and the entire monetary regime in which it is set) should be justified with reference to the direction of the psychoanalytic treatment and not, for example, in terms of socio-economic factors (the analyst's professional reputation, the going "market rate" for psychoanalysis, the general cost of living), let alone in terms of personal honoraria or narcissistic rewards. The analyst should be held accountable for the fees that he imposes or negotiates, and should be able to explain how a certain fee is appropriate for the maintenance of the psychoanalytic economy in each and every individual case. To the best of my knowledge, Lacan never explained himself on the point of his elevated and seemingly excessive fees—apart from the brief mention of his "analytic standing" in his first meeting with Haddad—but that in itself does not mean that he did not take responsibility for them, or would have been unable to do so had he been asked. The least one should expect is that a considered explanation *can* be given, and that the considerations constitute a reflection of what the analyst wants to achieve psychoanalytically, that is to say that they are in accordance with what Lacan himself would have designated as the "ethics of psychoanalysis".

Notes

1 This chapter is adapted from an article originally published in Volume 38.2 of *Modern Psychoanalysis* and is reproduced here with the permission of the publisher.
2 Some of Lacan's art objects were put up for auction by his second daughter Sibylle in 1991, together with his psychoanalytic couch and various other pieces of furniture from Paris and Guitrancourt. The couch made news headlines by fetching 98,000 French francs (roughly €15,000, £10,000, or $12,000 at the time). See Loudmer (1991).
3 Between 1930 and 1950, Sylvia Maklès appeared in 31 French films, her most memorable role being that of Henriette Dufour in Jean Renoir's 1936 featurette *Partie de campagne*. In a rare interview conducted by an American PhD student shortly before her death, Sylvia stated: "I could no longer make films because of my husband ... He was awful. When I was working on a film, he would come onto the set when the light was red, when it was forbidden for anyone to enter, he would stride across the set while we were in the midst of a scene ... [My] husband [Lacan], with the actors, he was ... horrible. He despised them ... They annoyed him. He didn't like them" (Hunt, 1995, pp. 169–173). See also Hunt (1998).
4 For an entertaining interview with Karolos Kambelopoulos, Lacan's hairdresser at the famous Carita salon in the Faubourg Saint Honoré, see Psaroudakis, Parker, and Burman (2012).
5 For similar accounts of Lacan cutting his analysands' sessions extremely short, see Godin (1990, p. 49), Rey (1989, pp. 84–85), Schneiderman (1983, pp. 132–133)

and Geblesco (2008, p. 93). Another poignant example is included in Schoonejans (2008, p. 17), yet this is undoubtedly fictional, serving the purpose of painting a dramatic picture of the analyst rather than relaying actual historical circumstances.
6 Most of the people writing about their analysis with Lacan mention the exorbitant fee, yet in some cases Lacan also seemed to have accepted a substantially reduced charge. At the end of the 1960s, the Lebanese neuro-psychiatrist Adnan Houbbalah "only" paid 100 francs per session for supervision with Lacan, and even managed to get him to agree to 50 francs when his financial situation became rather precarious (Houbbalah, 2007, p. 51).
7 Judging by the various accounts, the "variable-length session" became virtually synonymous with the "short session" towards the end of Lacan's life, whereas at the beginning of his clinical career he was clearly more versatile in his manipulation of time, and in the way he would direct the analytic sessions in general. For example, Jean Clavreul, who entered analysis with Lacan during the late 1940s and who became one of his most loyal followers, disclosed that when he had to be admitted to hospital during his analysis Lacan came to visit him there on some 20 occasions so that the work could continue. See Clavreul (2001, p. 31; 2007, p. 28).
8 According to the iconoclastic sociologist Frank Furedi (2003), it is actually the whole of contemporary Western culture that is to blame for driving people into the hands of ruthless therapists, vulnerability being the defining feature of 21st-century citizenship.
9 The analytic side-effect of symptom-relief is not even to be regarded as *de facto* beneficial, insofar as it may very well constitute a "flight into health", driven by the unconscious force of resistance, and staged as a defense against the work of psychoanalysis proper.
10 On "evenly-suspended attention" [*gleichschwebende Aufmerksamkeit*], see Freud (1958[1912e], pp. 111–112). In his *Seminar XI*, Lacan posited that the presence of the analyst is "in itself a manifestation of the [patient's] unconscious" (1994[1964], p. 125), and should not be disconnected from the transference. In this way, he distanced himself from the views of Sacha Nacht, who had recently defined the presence of the analyst as a "constant availability and unconditional reception, an unlimited patience and a capacity for giving, which resumes for him [the patient] this love from which he had felt separated since childhood, and which he needs in order to learn how to live" (Nacht, 1963, p. 3).
11 This is effectively what has been insinuated on a number of occasions by Élisabeth Roudinesco. See Roudinesco (1997[1993], p. 397; 2014[2011], p. 113–114).
12 After World War I, Freud relaxed his principles regarding the key importance of the psychoanalytic fee, and argued strongly in favour of the creation of free psychoanalytic outpatient clinics, which would accommodate the poor, the unemployed, and the working class. In February 1920, the Berlin *Poliklinik für Psychoanalytische Behandlung Nervöser Krankheiten* was opened on this basis. See Freud (1955[1919a], p. 167) and Danto (2005).
13 An almost identical statement appeared in "The Seminar on 'The Purloined Letter'", the article that Lacan subsequently devoted to Poe's story, although here it is formulated as a rhetorical question: "And is it not the responsibility their transference [of the purloined letters that the analysand deposits in the analyst] entails that we [as analysts] neutralize by equating it with the signifier that most thoroughly annihilates every signification—namely money?" (Lacan, 2006[1957a], p. 45). In the passage from *Seminar II*, Lacan's "*calculés au plus*

juste" does not actually mean "at rock-bottom", i.e., at the lowest possible level—as the translation would have it—but rather "as fairly as possible" or "in the best possible way".

14 For a detailed overview of various contemporary perspectives on the social significance of money, see Maurer (2006).

15 Interestingly yet puzzlingly, Lacan also suggested in this context that Freud's decision to pay the Wolf Man a stipend, with which he effectively inversed the financial regulation of the analytic process, was a decisive factor in the triggering of his patient's psychosis. For in-depth discussions of money *qua* signifier in Lacanian theory, see Arnaud (1999; 2003a), Carrington (2016), Forrester (1997), Gibeault (1989), Goux (1990[1973–1978]), and Martin (1984).

16 The only thing that would put a call girl in a better position to understand the "price of love" is the very fact that she is used to negotiating the "cost of sex", yet that in itself would only make her understand the real price of love if she allows the cost of sex to be reduced to nothing …

17 For another reading of this passage, which situates it in the context of Lacan's theory of the four discourses, see Nobus (2012).

18 As to Lacan's own views on the psychoanalyst as a contemporary sophist, see Cassin (2020[2012]). I am grateful to Mladen Dolar for drawing my attention to Cassin's work.

Chapter 3

That Obscure Object of Psychoanalysis

Objectivity and Subjectivity

In a famous line from the opening paragraph of his 1856 essay on the "pathetic fallacy", the English art critic John Ruskin asserted, in all seriousness yet not without hyperbole, that "objective" and "subjective" are "two of the most objectionable words that were ever coined by the troublesomeness of metaphysicians" (Ruskin, 1906[1856], p. 161).[1] Anyone familiar with the history of Western philosophy will immediately recognize Ruskin's metaphysicians, here, as the venerable cast of characters called German idealists and British empiricists. Roughly from the late 17th century, they persistently opposed the certainty of self-consciousness and the duality of mind and matter in the Cartesian tradition, in order to advance more sophisticated epistemological systems, without therefore always agreeing with each other as to the precise nature of the relationship between (knowing) subject and (known) object. While these philosophers all acknowledged that Descartes' distinction between *res cogitans* and *res extensa*—as the two fundamental, independent ontological categories—could not be sustained, Kant took issue with Berkeley's empirical idealism, Fichte criticized Kant's transcendental idealism, Schelling could not accept Fichte's ethical idealism, and Hegel's absolute idealism somehow aimed to "sublate" all disagreements in the ultimate synthetic proposition of the subject-object identity, without of course reconciling anything or anyone (Beiser, 2001, p. 3). With undisguised contempt for the philosophical "desire for mystification", which in his view had merely favored the proliferation of semantic ambiguities, Ruskin proposed a return to "plain old English", so that the phrase "It is objectively so" may be replaced with "It *is* so" and its counterpart "It is subjectively so" is simply rendered as "It does so" or "It seems to me" (Ruskin, 1906[1856], p. 161). As such, Ruskin did not dispute the actual distinction between objectivity and subjectivity, if it is taken to represent the difference between what something is on account of its intrinsic, discrete properties, and how something appears and is experienced by an observer, on account of his or her own (limited and potentially flawed)

DOI: 10.4324/9781003252276-4

faculties of perception. If anything, by using "plain old English" he implicitly advocated—at least within the realms of aesthetics, artistic expression, and art appreciation—a return to the Cartesian ontological dichotomy, with the added recommendation that artists should shy away from "fallaciously" attributing subjective qualities (pathos) to the objects they are representing, the naturalistic style of representation being more truthful and not at all less artistically valuable.

Terminological preference and personal taste aside, Ruskin was of course fully aware that the practice of art, however different it may be from scientific research, cannot be conceived without the pre-supposition of a knowing, creative agency who describes, explains, interprets, evaluates, and represents a certain (internal and/or external) reality, regardless as to whether this reality factually exists in the absence of the knowing agency. Even if the painter restricts himself to representing "what is", rather than what "seems" to him, he is nonetheless involved in the process of representation as a carrier and instrument of knowledge production, whether the source of this knowledge is located in him- or herself or in the reality that is being represented. Hence, even without the "objectionable" terms "objective" and "subjective", it seems virtually impossible to extract the "subject-object" dialectic from any sustained reflection upon the representability of reality and the validity of claims to knowledge—an impossibility which Ruskin's recourse to "plain old English" makes all the more poignant.

Despite, or perhaps by virtue of Hegel's proposed "subject-object identity", the debate concerning the vexed relationship between the (knowing) subject and the (known) object has by no means been resolved, although it is no doubt fair to say that scientists tend to be less concerned about the issue than philosophers. With the exception, perhaps, of particle physicists studying quantum mechanics, few if any contemporary scientists, including those working within the human and social sciences, would consider anything but a realist or materialist position as the essential epistemological stance governing the process of scientific discovery. This is not to say that contemporary scientists radically ignore the researcher's implication in the research process, and all the sources of bias that this ineluctable involvement may contain, nor that they completely disregard the social embedment of the scientific enterprise. It just so happens that genuine science has allegedly developed the means to detach itself from these influences, or to control and reduce their significance, in its reliance on robust codes of practice, strict research protocols, advanced statistical tests and the abstract language of mathematics. Never shy of a strongly worded assertion, the British chemist Peter Atkins put it as follows:

> There is certainly a considerable social element in the pursuit of knowledge, and in particular in the control of spurious claims, but that does not logically imply that the knowledge so obtained is socially

engineered any more than that the outcome of a complex experiment is necessarily a complex aspect of nature. (Atkins, 1995, p. 97)

It should be noted, here, that Atkins does not restrict science to a particular set of academic disciplines—physics, chemistry, biology, etc.—but designates it, in the broadest possible sense, as a procedure, a mode of discovery, in short a specific methodology for "exposing fundamental truths about the world" (Ibid., p. 97). Knowledge that deserves to be called scientific is knowledge that has been generated through rigorous empirical research, irrespective of the object of study. In other words, objectivity in science does not depend on the nature of the object that is being investigated, but on the way in which the investigative process is conducted. Any known object can be examined in isolation from the knowing subject that is examining it, provided the knowing subject follows the rules and regulations of scientific experimentation.[2]

Compelling as this outlook may seem, matters become rather more complicated when the object of study is not just a material substance, but also and primarily a subject, a knowing agency, a human being endowed with self-consciousness, exercising the power of intellect and participating in the discursive deployment of social structures. In its academic remit, the issue is no doubt of particular importance for the epistemology of psychology, were it not for the fact that precisely psychology has gradually moved away from any serious consideration of subjectivity in its central object of study. As a result of its aspiration to distance itself from the odium of (mental) philosophy, and driven by its intention to be recognized and respected amongst the natural sciences, psychology has effectively forfeited any in-depth reflection upon what makes us, as human beings, stand out from other living entities.[3] Ever since the late 19th century, when Wilhelm Wundt started testing people's reaction time to a variety of sensory stimuli under controlled laboratory conditions, and maybe with the exception of researchers working within the psychological sub-disciplines of clinical and counseling psychology, psychologists have studied human beings as if they were working with any other living, or indeed non-living entity. Despite the fact that people selected for psychological research are now called participants, they are generally engaged as passive respondents, objectifiable and objectified units, individuals in the literal sense of the term, whose reactions, functions, and mechanisms can be examined in the same way as the elementary particles in an inanimate substance in a physics laboratory. In *From Anxiety to Method in the Behavioral Sciences*, the French-Hungarian anthropologist and psychoanalyst George Devereux polemically posited that, in adopting this approach, psychology proceeds to studying human beings by virtue of actually killing them in their very nature and structure as human beings (Devereux, 1968). And this "homicidal methodology" (my term rather than his), he argued, is in itself an epistemological defense against the researcher's anxiety of losing his position of epistemic authority when having to concede that he is not only observing and interpreting a participant, but that this participant is also simultaneously observing and interpreting him as a researcher. It may seem ironic, then, that Devereux himself subsequently focused on an exploration of what would happen if researchers were to abdicate their position of control, and become more aware of their own status as an observed entity, with all the uncertainties that it entails, rather than on the characteristics of the subject-object that is the observing and interpreting research participant. Fact of the matter is, however, that Devereux did not believe in the possibility of extracting these characteristics of the observed subject-object from those of the observing subject. The participants' responses are triggered by, and therefore crucially conditioned by the researcher's actions, so that the former are always already a reflection of the latter. The known object of study is therefore not just also a knowing subject, but the knowing subject of the observer/researcher also inevitably infiltrates and contaminates the realm of the observed subject-object, so that the known object as a knowing subject cannot be isolated from (and is fundamentally a reflection of) the knowing subject who believes to be in a position of epistemic authority as the principal investigator of the research project.

In developing this argument, Devereux made it quite explicit that his main source of inspiration was the discipline (theory, practice, and methodology) of psychoanalysis, yet he could probably have justified his position as easily with reference to Kant's transcendental idealism or Hegel's vision of the subject-object identity. Where philosophy is drawn upon to criticize the scientific *modus operandi*, scientists are unlikely to be bothered, galvanized as they will be by their robust research protocols, and emboldened also by the fact that there is no such thing as a unified philosophical theory of knowledge, but just a series of seemingly sterile philosophical disputes about the validity of scientific claims—so much so that the Canadian philosopher Charles Taylor at one point felt it necessary to argue that the whole construal of epistemology urgently needs to be overcome (Taylor, 1995). Where psychoanalysis enters the critical equation, scientists are unlikely to be bothered either, if only because both the philosophical and the scientific foundations of the edifice have intermittently been exposed in all their fundamental flaws and fallacies. Whereas philosophy still enjoys a certain degree of legitimacy amongst natural, social, and human scientists, psychoanalysis has been relegated to the dustbin of history as a fraudulent fiction by philosophers and scientists alike.[4]

Nonetheless, the discipline of psychoanalysis deserves a higher degree of scrutiny, here, precisely because of its historically uneasy and traditionally ambivalent relationship with philosophy and science. Unlike epistemology within modern philosophy, psychoanalysis has never really had the ambition to develop a coherent theory of knowledge production in order to reflect upon the relationship between known object and knowing subject, let alone to extend such a theory and reflection beyond the boundaries of its own theoretical and clinical sphere of action. And this is precisely why it is worthy of attention. What, if anything, can psychoanalysis still contribute to existing philosophical and scientific discussions about objectivity and subjectivity? Neither strictly philosophical nor strictly scientific, neither to be situated exclusively amongst the human and social sciences nor to be restricted to the arts and humanities, what does psychoanalysis have to offer with regard to the subject-object relationship, as it unfolds and operates within its own confines, and beyond? How does psychoanalysis conceive of "subject" and "object", and what philosophical and scientific importance should we attach to this conception? And what does Lacan, who was by far the most philosophically minded psychoanalyst of his generation, have to contribute to this debate?

Freud's Ego-subject

On account of his recognition of the unconscious as an irreducible mental "scene" and fundamental epistemic structure, Freud did not regard the human being as a fully integrated individual or, for that matter, as a more or less unified and self-transparent personality, purely acting upon voluntary, conscious intentions and endowed with immutable "character traits" that condition the interactions with others and the relationship one has to oneself. Freud's *Mensch* is someone who is not completely in control of his or her thoughts and actions, someone who does things he does not really want to do, and vice versa. Pleasure-driven as the human being may be, consciousness is hugely restricted in the influence it may exercise over the course and manifestation of this drive. However hard we try, we cannot decide, for example, over the contents of our dreams. We cannot consciously design the *dramatis personae* and the story-line facilitating a nocturnal emission, just as much as we cannot consciously interfere to cease painful patterns of repetitive nightmares—the latter no doubt constituting one of the best arguments against the commonly held neuro-scientific idea that dreams are just random firings of neurons.[5] For Freud, the ego (*Ich*) is "in its very essence a subject" (*ist ja doch das eigentlichste Subjekt*) (Freud, 1964[1933a], p. 58), yet the problem is that this ego "is not master in its own house" (*daß das Ich nicht Herr sei in seinem eigenen Haus*) (Freud, 1955[1917a], p. 143), so that the ego as subject is limited in its ambitions to express itself as a knowing agency by the fact that its sovereignty is intermittently attacked by epistemic forces operating from the inside, within the boundaries of its own perceived sphere of influence. Hence, from a classic Freudian perspective, there is no such thing as a knowing subject—at least not in the traditional meaning of the term—because the subject is animated by knowledge (representations, thoughts, ideas) over which it has no control. Not fully known to itself, and therefore partially ignorant about its own mental powers, the subject is literally subjected to the knowledge that is at work outside its realm of consciousness, which implies that, from the perspective of the unconscious, the knowing subject is being known (as a passive object) rather than being knowledgeable. On account of the force of the unconscious, the subject is objectified as an "un-known known", that is to say as something that is being exercised by (its own) knowledge, without it having any awareness of how, when, where, and why this process is taking place.

Yet this is not the only way in which the ego, as subject, appears as an object in psychoanalysis. "The ego can take itself as an object", Freud argued, "can treat itself like other objects, can observe itself, criticize itself, and do Heaven knows what with itself" (Freud, 1964[1933a], p. 58).[6] What he evidently had in mind, here, was the function of the super-ego, whose ferociousness Freud compared to the Kantian categorical imperative, and which turns the ego-subject into an ego-object every time it exposes the ego to the prohibitions and injunctions that emanate from its role as the mental guardian of conscience, morality, and the ego ideal (Freud, 1961[1923b], pp. 34–35; 1961[1924c], p. 167). The "splitting of consciousness" (*Spaltung des Bewußtseins*), which Freud had originally detected in his psychoanalytic work with hysterical patients, and which captures the previously described antagonism between conscious and unconscious knowledge, is extended, here, to encompass an additional "split", whereby the ego "during a number of its functions—temporarily at least" reduces its subjectivity in the critical objectification of its own knowledge (Freud, 1964[1933a], p. 58).[7] Whereas in the first process of objectification, the ego-subject's knowledge is put at risk and appears as ignorance due to the uncontrollable interference of knowledge and thoughts coming from a place that is inaccessible to the ego, a location where the subject does not exist, this second type of objectification exposes the value of the knowledge that the ego-subject does believe to possess in its very existence as properly constituted, intellectually accurate, and morally acceptable knowledge. The knowing subject, who is already challenged by the knowledge erupting from the unconscious, is criticized, judged, directed, and indeed isolated as a known object by a literally superior agency, which is held to occupy the moral and intellectual high ground.[8]

To this dual objectification of the ego-subject, a third one could no doubt be added. In "The Ego and the Id", Freud formulated no less than three distinct hypotheses to account for the emergence of the ego, each of them showing that the ego is not part of human nature, does not exist at birth, is developmentally constituted rather than constitutionally given (Freud, 1961[1923b]). Drawing on an explanation he had initially proposed a couple of years earlier, in "Beyond the Pleasure Principle" (Freud, 1955[1920g]), Freud contended first of all that the ego is an extension of the psychic system of "Perception-Consciousness" (Pcpt.-Cs.), which is in itself derived from and established against the external stimuli that threaten its integrity and sustainability (Freud, 1961[1923b], p. 28). As such, the ego "is the representative in the mind of the real external world" (Ibid., p. 28). Secondly, Freud designated the ego as a "bodily ego", "not merely a surface entity, but... the projection of a surface" (Freud, 1961[1923b], p. 26). Here, the ego-subject appears as the mental representative of the anatomo-physiological structure that is the living body, which receives, registers, and processes various types of sensory information. Thirdly, and most importantly, Freud regarded the ego as the result of a series of identifications with objects that had previously been invested (cathected) erotically under the influence of the pleasure principle. Yet it is not just the "shadow of the object" [*Schatten des Objekts*] that falls upon and is assimilated within the ego, the psychic energy (libido) is in itself redirected towards the ego, after it has been withdrawn from the external objects, where it then gives rise to narcissism.[9] The ego is therefore some kind of archive of formerly eroticized objects, which is also capable of taking itself as an object of erotic satisfaction. Although he did not claim to fully understand the exact mechanism by which abandoned objects are established in the ego, Freud was nonetheless convinced of its significance:

> When it happens that a person has to give up a sexual object, there quite often ensues an alteration of his ego which can only be described as a setting up [*Aufrichtung*] of the object inside the ego... [T]he process, especially in the early phases of development, is a very frequent one, and it makes it possible to suppose that the character of the ego is a precipitate [*Niederschlag*] of abandoned object-cathexes and that it contains the history of those object-choices. (Freud, 1961[1923b], p. 29)[10]

Each of these hypotheses would deserve to be unpacked in its conceptual and empirical (clinical) foundations, yet for the purpose of my argument, here, it will be sufficient to identify their common denominator. In all their distinctiveness, and mutually exclusive as they may seem, Freud's hypotheses all suggest that the ego-subject is fundamentally an object-function. Whether formed as a result of the living organism's visceral contact with external objects (stimuli coming from the outside world), as a mental reflection of complex bodily sensations, or as the repository of the remnants of formerly eroticized entities in the social environment, the ego-subject is an object-derived and object-based function. Even when Freud lyrically compares the ego to "a man on horse-back, who has to hold in check the superior strength of the horse", he is quick to concede that, unlike the rider, the ego can only perform this task by drawing on "borrowed forces" (Freud, 1961[1923b], p. 25).

The conclusion to be drawn from this is perhaps as puzzling as it is surprising: insofar as psychoanalysis is traditionally regarded as a discipline (theory, practice, and method) which accords the highest importance to subjective experience, the very notion of the subject appears as particularly problematic, not only because subjectivity is de-centered as a mental function, but mainly because it is objectified in its being subjected to and dependent upon the influences of the unconscious, the super-ego and the outside world. In all fairness to Freud, he hardly ever used the term "subject" (*Subjekt*) or, for that matter, self (*Selbst*), and the aforementioned passages are amongst the very few in his published works in which "subject" occurs in a non-trivial context. Instead of "subject", Freud consistently opts for ego (*Ich*) or—outside the abstract field of his metapsychological speculations—for "human being" (*Mensch*), "person" (*Person, Persönlichkeit*), and the more clinically pertinent terminology of "patient" (*Patient*), sick person (*Kranke*), "analyzed" (*Analysierte*), neurotic (*Neurotiker*), etc.[11] Freud's ostensible reluctance to employ the term "subject" has been attributed to his highly critical stance towards (idealist) philosophy, in which it holds pride of place as the constitutive locus of (the phenomenology of) self-consciousness, and this despite the fact that his own formulations regarding the subjective quality of sensory perception and the resulting unknowability of the external reality are sometimes explicitly linked to Kant's argument that the thing-in-itself cannot be objectively known, but only subjectively thought.[12] Regardless of Freud's motives, here, what matters is that the ego, which is explicitly designated as the "essential subject", comes into existence as an object, and is objectified in its status as a knowing agency when it is taken to task by the unconscious, the super-ego, and external reality. Hence, if Freud's unconscious exists as a Kantian noumenon, only ever to be experienced and apprehended as an appearance, then the appearance itself is no longer governed by an autonomous subject, who acts as the conscious receiver and interpreter of the sensory manifestations of reality. Unlike Kant's subject, Freud's ego-subject is in its very essence always already an object, a *perceptum* rather than a *percipiens,* something that is acted upon rather than someone who acts. Whereas in his transcendental idealism Kant subjectified the object—what is always subjectively thinkable yet never objectively knowable qua object—Freud proposes exactly the opposite: an objectified subject, which is always objectively thinkable but never subjectively knowable qua subject.[13]

Lacan's Object *a*

If the subject is fundamentally problematic in psychoanalysis, then the same cannot be said for the object, at least not from a conceptual point of view. Indeed, there is a veritable proliferation of the object in Freud's theory, and it probably does not come as a surprise that this Freudian object, regardless of its intrinsic qualities, whether animated or inanimate, is always to some extent sexualized. Freud did not hesitate to assert that the sexual object is the most original object and the first object to be known in the child's prototypical attachment to the mother('s breast) (Freud, 1958[1912b], p. 105; 1963[1916–1917], pp. 328–329).[14]

As such, the Freudian object is by definition the object of the sexual drive, with the caveat that the sexual drive is not a unitary force which is geared towards the simultaneous realization (and concurrent gratification) of all aspects of human sexuality, but a "partial drive" (*Partialtrieb*), that is to say a drive which is not one but rather a component part of a unity, whereby the latter only comes into being when all the partial drives work together in a coordinated fashion.[15] Yet unlike its other three constituents (the source, the pressure, and the aim), the object is the most replaceable element of the drive:

> It is what is most variable about an instinct and is not originally connected with it, but becomes assigned to it only in consequence of being peculiarly fitted to make satisfaction possible. The object is not necessarily something extraneous: it may equally well be a part of the subject's own body [*ein Teil des eigenen Körpers*]. It may be changed any number of times in the course of the vicissitudes which the instinct undergoes during its existence.... (Freud, 1957[1915c], pp. 122–123)

Freud does not provide any reasons as to the variability of the object, and one is led to wonder why it would be exchanged in the first place once it has been found totally adequate as a suitable wellspring of sexual satisfaction. It seems much more logical to assume that an object is replaced because it no longer provides the expected and formerly experienced gratification. The variability and endless exchangeability of the object of the drive, then, may not be primarily conditioned by the vicissitudes of the drive itself, much less by the fact that it is "peculiarly fitted to make satisfaction possible", but by its being particularly "unfit" to fulfill its function as a sexual prop.

This, at least, would be in accordance with Freud's thesis, formulated at the end of his *Three Essays on the Theory of Sexuality*, that the "finding of an object is in fact a refinding of it" [*Die Objektfindung ist eigentlich eine Wiederfindung*] (Freud, 1953[1905d], p. 222).[16] The object that is allocated to the (fundamentally partial) sexual drive, so that it can achieve its aim of satisfaction, is presented, here, as a retrieved, re-discovered object—an object which has somehow been found back after it had gone missing. However, it is never the original object as such which is re-found, but only ever a substitute, and so the satisfaction it brings can only pale in comparison. The implication is that, on the one hand, the sexual object contains nothing new, is not in any way an original find, because it is only identified insofar as it can be modeled on an old, definitively lost object, whereas on the other hand it is also unable to generate a sustained experience of full satisfaction, because it is only an approximation, a simulacrum of the original object and the satisfaction that it provided.

Throughout his seminar on object-relations (Lacan, 2020[1994]), Lacan insisted on the importance of this tortuous and ultimately disappointing process of the re-finding of an object in Freud's theory, in order to demonstrate that in Freudian psychoanalysis a fully satisfying, perfectly adequate, intrinsically consistent, harmonious sexual object is but a neurotic illusion. In doing so, he radically opposed the proponents of the so-called object-relations movement in psychoanalysis, who were convinced of the possibility of a human being establishing a completely satisfying and therefore non-conflictual relationship with an external sexual object, under the aegis of (heterosexual) genitality, and who advocated this possibility both as the paragon of mental health and as the final aim of the psychoanalytic treatment, against which its success may then be measured. The theoretical foundations for this view, which proved immensely popular during the first decades after World War II, had been laid by Karl Abraham, one of Freud's most loyal adherents, in an extended 1924 essay on the development of the libido, which was published shortly before his premature death (Abraham, 1954[1924]). In the second part of this study, Abraham constructed a six-fold hierarchy of the developmental stages of psychosexuality, in which the libido was assumed to evolve from an oral to a final genital phase, with the simultaneous substitution of wholesale object-love for the original auto-erotism. According to Abraham, genital object-love epitomizes the most accomplished stage of psychosexual development, because at this level a human being is capable of approaching the sexual object in its entirety and without any ambivalence (*ambivalenzfrei*). The unified object thus only emerges with the advent of genitality, and it is a "total entity" (*Gesamtheit*) because it is eroticized in its totality qua object and because the eroticization is unconditional, pure, unrestrained by any opposing tendencies. By contrast, the pre-genital stages of object-love are always characterized by some form of partiality, inasmuch as the sexual object (mouth, anus) only represents a part of the total object that is libidinally invested in the genital stage. Pre-genital love is therefore partial love (*Partialliebe*) and the objects that are singled out to satisfy the drive are only object-parts, partial, or part-objects (*Objektteile*) (Ibid., 1954[1924], pp. 480–501).

Loyal to a fault, Abraham felt that in promoting this view he was merely organizing ideas and systematizing propositions that had already been formulated by Freud. Unfortunately, he did not live long enough to appreciate the master's serious reservations regarding the impact of genitality. If the first genital stage, which only involves the phallus and which coincides with the Oedipus complex, does not spontaneously develop into fully formed genitality, which involves the recognition of the male as well as the female genital, but is actually followed by a so-called latency period, then the actual dissolution of the Oedipus complex itself is rather complicated and rarely complete, especially for girls but also for boys (Freud, 1961[1925*j*], pp. 251–258). When full genitality is finally reached, during the years of puberty, it is therefore haunted by the phallic specters dwelling amongst the ruins of the Oedipus complex. Or, as Freud put it in one of his last works:

> The complete organization [of sexuality] is only achieved at puberty, in a fourth, genital phase... This process is not always performed faultlessly... The situation is complicated by the fact that as a rule the processes necessary for bringing about a normal outcome are not completely present or absent, but *partially* present [*dass sie sich* partiell *vollziehen*]... In these circumstances the genital organization is, it is true, attained, but it lacks those portions of the libido which have not advanced with the rest and have remained fixated to pregenital objects and aims. (Freud, 1964[1940*a*], pp. 155–156)

Quite apart from the fact that genitality is by no means hailed, here, as the final, most advanced stage of psychosexual development, Freud also crucially recognizes within it an ongoing element of partiality, something that remains lacking in terms of libidinal attraction.

Taking his lead from Freud's own conception of the object, Lacan vehemently disputed the theoretical and clinical paradigm of a harmonious genitality, without therefore rejecting Abraham's manifold contributions to a psychoanalytic theory of the object, and even less those of the latter's onetime collaborator and former patient, Melanie Klein. The reason is simple. Except in the illusory ideal of the final genital stage, part-objects feature prominently in Abraham's (Freudian) account of the developmental path of the libido, and the same can be said for Klein's theory of sexuality, in which genitality is situated at a much earlier phase of sexual development, no longer championed as an unblemished type of object-relation, and generally conceptualized in its inherent connections with other, pre-genital trends (Klein, 1993[1957]). In "The Direction of the Treatment and the Principles of its Power", Lacan posited: "This theory [of object relations], however much it has degenerated in France in recent years, has... a noble origin. It was Karl Abraham who opened up this field and the notion of the part-object is his original contribution" (Lacan, 2006[1958*a*], p. 505). For Lacan, following Freud, partiality not only characterizes the sexual drive, but also typifies each and every sexual object. What for Abraham and his successors is but a passing phase in the evolving organization of the libido—or, as it happens, a pathological fixation on a partial, immature form of love—is to Lacan the hallmark of every possible approach to the object. Partial love and the inherently inadequate part-objects for which it is expressed are neither transient phenomena nor clinical exceptions but quite simply the erotic or amorous norm. Hence, Lacan's infamous formula "there is no such thing as a sexual relationship" (*il n'y a pas de rapport sexuel*) (Lacan, 2007[1991], p. 116; 1998[1975], p. 7). Instead of an object-relation, Lacan suggested that there can only ever be a relation with a flawed (lacking) object, with an object that, in its partiality, does not live up to the expectation of fullness.

"What makes it such that the object presents itself as broken and decomposed is perhaps something other than a pathological factor", Lacan declared (Lacan, 2006[1958a], p. 507). Tentative as this statement may be, he was actually convinced that any approach to the sexual object comes with an "essential difficulty" [*une difficulté essentielle*], which stems from an "internal order" [*qui est d'ordre interne*] (Lacan, 2020[1994], pp. 51–52). The difficulty follows an internal order, because it is not the result—as had been argued by Wilhelm Reich (1971) and Herbert Marcuse (1966), for instance—of the socio-cultural suppression of the sexual drive, but of an intra-psychic mechanism, which regulates the object-relation in such a way that relational harmony is excluded.[17] In a much more radical way than Foucault did in *The History of Sexuality* (Foucault, 1978[1976], pp. 15–49), Lacan ruled out the so-called "repressive hypothesis" of sexuality—sexual dissatisfaction resulting from the suppressive rules of social institutions—postulating instead that the restrictive attitude towards sexuality in the family, the social community and society in general is in itself a reflection of the fact that these regulatory systems have been created by human beings, and therefore something that should be understood as an effect rather than a cause. As he put it in *Television*:

> Freud didn't say that repression *comes from* suppression... [A]s he progressed there, he leaned more toward the idea that repression was primary... So that's why we reexamine the test case, taking as a starting point the fact that it is repression that produces suppression. Why couldn't the family, society itself, be creations built from repression? They're nothing less. That, however, may be because the unconscious ex-sists, is motivated by the structure, that is, by language. (Lacan, 1990[1974], pp. 27–28)[18]

The internal order that presides over the essential difficulty which pervades any encounter with the sexual object appears, here, as the order of language, which Lacan also designated as the symbolic order or, quite simply, the Other (Lacan, 1988[1978], pp. 235–247). If complete satisfaction in relation to a perfectly adequate object is impossible, it is because the entire process is embedded in a linguistic structure of symbolically articulated needs and demands. In other words, the re-found object is essentially flawed and only ever presents itself as a part-object, because it cannot reinstate the original experience of satisfaction, but more crucially because this pure, perfect and unmediated experience of satisfaction has suffered a "primary repression", became radically excluded with the assimilation of language and the integration of symbolic rules and regulations.[19]

In order to give some theoretical and clinical consistency to the status of this part-object in psychoanalysis, Lacan at one point introduced and gradually consolidated the notion of the object *a* (*objet petit* a), which he advanced as his key invention (Lacan, 1966–1967, session of 16 November 1966; 1973–1974, session of 9 April 1974; 2006a, p. 45).[20] To claim that with the object *a* Lacan aspired to a more stable and robust conceptualization of the part-object than the one proposed by Freud (Abraham and Klein) may seem a massive overstatement, here, in light of the fact that the object *a* appears in Lacan's theory under a multitude of different guises: as object (cause) of desire, as object of the fantasy, as object of the drive, as object of anxiety, as a substitute (*Ersatz*) object, as surplus-enjoyment (the psychoanalytic equivalent to Marx's notion of surplus-value), as the object-agency in the discourse of the psychoanalyst, etc. Nonetheless, each of these "avatars" of the object *a* is designed to situate its impact and significance as a figuration of the point where an object presents itself as lacking (flawed, partial, incomplete, broken, inadequate), owing to the symbolic structures that govern the way in which all objects are approached. As such, not all objects function as objects *a*, yet every object, insofar as it enters a symbolically regulated network of relationships, contains the object *a* function. In a sense, Lacan's object *a* is nothing more, nothing less than the very *a* as object, whereby *a* should be interpreted as the linguistic index of what is missing, lacking or lost.[21] The object *a* is literally the "shadow of the object"; it represents an object that is not or no longer materially present, or the place where the object appears as incomplete, so that the actual object (as a complete material presence) can only be inferred (imagined) from what it has left behind.[22]

It is interesting to note, here, that Lacan's invention of the object *a* represents not so much a creation *ex nihilo*, but rather the rediscovery and subsequent naming of an object that had somehow been missed in one of Freud's works, and indeed in one of his own texts from the 1950s. As he disclosed in a 1972 lecture at the University of Louvain: "When one day I invented the object *a*, it's because it was already included in 'Mourning and Melancholia'" (Lacan, 1981[1972], p. 11).[23] The object is never found, but only ever re-found. Similarly, when in 1966 Lacan published his *Écrits*, a massive collection of papers spanning 30 years of intellectual labour, he was reluctant to accept that some of the later concepts and ideas had already been foreshadowed in the earlier work, with one exception: the object *a*. Lacan agreed that it "is here that my students would be right to recognize the 'already' [*reconnaître le 'déjà'*]" (Lacan, 2006[1966b], p. 4), because he felt that he had effectively adumbrated the object *a* in his detailed analysis of Edgar Allan Poe's "The Purloined Letter", the paper which he had decided to place at the head of the collection (against the chronological order in which all the other texts had been placed) (Lacan, 2006[1957a]). The object *a* was thus in itself re-found, by its founder, once again, and this time as a finding in his own text. Quite annoyingly, Lacan did not actually state where exactly he believed to have already outlined the object *a* in his reading of Poe's story. And so I would like to rekindle the hypothesis, here—which I elaborated in Chapter 1 of this book—that the object *a* appears every time the incriminating letter which, we are led to believe, the Queen has received from her lover, is removed from its place and a replacement (less valuable, less powerful, and less gratifying) object is left behind, as its placeholder, by the person who takes it away: it is the "unimportant" letter which the Minister leaves behind on the table after he has purloined the one belonging to the Queen, but also the facsimile left behind in the card-rack by Dupin, when he in turn purloins the letter from the Minister, and finally the cheque which the Police Prefect gives to Dupin when he takes hold of the latter's prized possession. In each and every instance, the replacement piece of paper (unimportant letter, facsimile of the coveted missive, cheque) does not only serve as a poor return gift or an aide-memoire of the lost possession, and thus as a "reminding remainder", but as factual proof that the original object has been removed from its place. Although Poe tells us that the Queen "saw, but, of course, dared not call attention to the [Minister's] act" (Poe, 1988[1844], p. 321), had she not seen it, she would still have been able to conclude that Minister D had stolen it, as opposed to her having accidentally mislaid it or (God forbid) her spouse having laid hands on it, precisely by virtue of the replacement letter that is left behind. Similarly, when Dupin leaves behind his facsimile, with the handwritten inscription on it, and without the Minister's noticing the theft, the latter will come to realize that he has been forever deprived of his instrument of blackmail and who was behind the act, precisely on account of the substitute that sits in its place. This, it seems to me, is exactly how Lacan conceived of the object *a*: it is the object, or that aspect of the object which occupies the place of what is no longer present, and therefore proves that what, at one point in time, may have been available is no longer accessible.[24]

The object *a* being what it is, an inadequate part-object or, better still, that essential part of the object where it shows its inadequacy and which results in desire being triggered and inflamed (caused) rather than quenched, one is evidently left to wonder how a relation with this type of non- or *a*-object can be established, if at all. What, if anything, may support the way in which the object *a* is apprehended, acknowledged or, indeed, known? What kind of subject, if any, can we reasonably assume to enter into a relationship with the object *a*? Conversely, how does the object *a* influence, affect and ascertain the subject that stands in relation to it? With regard to the Queen's acknowledgement of the unimportant letter that the Minister has left on her table, Lacan suggests that she "is now free to crumple [it] up" (*peut maintenant rouler en boule*) (Lacan, 2006[1957*a*], p. 8), and we may assume that the same is true for the Minister himself when he finds Dupin's facsimile letter in the card-rack, and that this fate will even befall the Police Prefect's cheque after Dupin has cashed it.[25] What does it mean for all objects to be relational, apart from the object *a*, "which is an absolute" (Lacan, 2016[2005], p. 101), especially if we take into consideration that the object *a* can be conceived as part of any object?

Alienation and Separation

At this point, it is necessary to return to the vexed issue of the subject in psychoanalysis which, as I indicated previously, is a notion hardly ever used by Freud and which, when it does enter his discourse, barely comes with any material substance or intentionality attached to it, objectified as it is by the unconscious, the super-ego, and the shadows of the abandoned objects that have fallen upon it. With Lacan, however, the subject reemerges as a conceptual cornerstone of the psychoanalytic edifice, so much so that it occupies virtually every page of his writings. To some, Lacan's insistence on the subject is but a way to render explicit what had remained obscure in Freud, whereas to others this reintroduction of the subject (and the associated concepts of truth and foundation, for instance) demonstrates Lacan's spurious allegiance to a certain philosophical doctrine, and notably the metaphysical assumptions with which psychoanalysis is invariably contaminated.[26]

As is well-known, Lacan regarded the subject as "divided" (*divisé*), or "barred" (*barré*), which should not be understood as it having two or more constitutive parts, thus being divided between two or more components, but rather as it being disconnected, barred from entering, or split off from proceedings. Although it could easily be justified with reference to Freud's concept of the unconscious as an autonomous set of repressed representations, or as an elaboration of his idea of the "splitting of the ego" (*Ichspaltung*) (Freud, 1964[1940a], pp. 202–204; 1964[1940e]), Lacan sees the divided subject initially as an effect of the symbolic order (the Other of language, but also the discourse of the unconscious), which prevents speaking beings from having direct, unmediated access to the naked, absolute reality (the real) that surrounds them. The implication is that the essence of being (what Freud aptly referred to as *Kern unseres Wesen*), irrespective of its precise nature (material or immaterial, human or non-human, dead or alive), remains in itself barred from being fully accessed through reason and knowledge (Freud, 1953[1900a], p. 603; 1964[1940a], p. 197).[27] For once it is accepted that a speaking being is intrinsically limited, incomplete, and fractured, the knowledge produced by this "knowing subject" is equally restricted, unfinished and cracked. However reliable and valid a body of knowledge may be, and regardless of the sophistication of the tools that are being used to support and facilitate its production, the knowledge will always inevitably refer to and end up being referred to another knowledge, which is no more accomplished, coherent, and consistent than its previous incarnation.

When attempting to elucidate the constitution of the divided subject ($) in relation to the Other, during his 1964 seminar on the foundations of psychoanalysis, Lacan reminded his audience of his algebraic formula for the fantasy, $ ◇ a, the central part of which (the lozenge) he decomposed into two distinctive operations called "alienation" and "separation" (Lacan, 1994[1973], pp. 203–229; 2006[1964], pp. 712–721).[28] The alienation Lacan introduced, here, is not the Hegelian alienation (*Entfremdung*), but rather a logical operation of disjunction (in Latin *vel*), which coincides with the lower section of the lozenge $ ∨ a. As an added, yet crucial complication, Lacan emphasized that the disjunction of alienation is neither inclusive nor exclusive (following the two types of disjunction that are conventionally distinguished in formal logic) and therefore rather "exclusive". Unlike the standard exclusive disjunction, which is only valid when one *or* the other proposition is true, and unlike the inclusive disjunction, which is valid when one *or* the other proposition is true *and* when both propositions are true, the Lacanian disjunction is *only* valid in one of the two cases when one *or* the other proposition is true, thus further excluding one of the two options that are regarded as valid in the exclusive disjunction.

Lacan's most memorable example of this particular disjunction, which also serves as an allegory for the constitution of the divided subject, is that of the highwayman who confronts his victim with the choice (*vel*): "Your money or your life" (Lacan, 1994[1973], p. 212; 2006[1964], p. 713). Would someone prefer to relinquish his life than his money, he is likely to lose both, because the highwayman does not have much of a reason to leave the money behind once he has taken his victim's life. And even were the highwayman to be completely satisfied with someone's life, the dead person would evidently no longer be in a position to enjoy his capital. The peculiar choice with which the unfortunate victim is confronted does not actually leave him with much of an option at all, because one of the "choices", i.e., money, is by definition forfeited as soon as the question is posed. Put differently, in accordance with the Lacanian disjunction of alienation *only* the situation in which life is preserved is considered valid and viable.[29] Lacan argued that a similar dynamic presides over the constitution of the divided subject, whereby the terms of the alternative can be described as "being (*l'être*) or meaning (*le sens*)" or "subject or Other". The only viable options in these disjunctions are "meaning" and "Other", because just as money without life (to support it) is unthinkable, being cannot be thought without meaning, and the subject cannot persist without the Other. Yet in deciding, as a "forced choice", for meaning and the Other, the latter options become lacking in themselves. What for the highwayman's victim becomes a life without money, appears in the constitution of the divided subject as meaning deprived of (access to full) being and an Other deprived of (full, conscious) subjectivity. As such, alienation causes full being and the subject (as full being) to disappear, and what Lacan conceptualizes as the divided subject, then, is nothing else than the manifestation of a crack in the speaking being's forced engagement with the meaningful Other. In a different register, the disappearance of full being in the process of alienation is of course also tantamount to the loss of a state of complete self-fulfillment. The net result is therefore similar to what Freud described as the radical disappearance of an original experience of satisfaction.

In a sense, Lacan's outlook on the constitution of the divided subject, here, is less radical than it may seem, because it can no doubt be regarded as a mere amplification of Freud's perspective on the ego-subject, which is reduced to the point of nothingness in its very status of a knowing, acting subject. However, alienation is only the starting point of the divided subject's causation, insofar as it is followed by what Lacan calls separation, the second "fundamental operation", which coincides with the upper section of the lozenge, $ ^ a$. Separation follows the logical principle of conjunction (in Latin *et*), although once again Lacan adds the twist that the conjunction of separation, unlike the classical conjunction, which is valid *only* when two propositions are simultaneously true, is *only* valid when *neither* of the two propositions is true. Applied to the example of "your money or your life", separation implies that not only money, but life itself becomes an impossible choice or, more radically, that the highwayman does not even pose the question, but simply exclaims: "You are dead!" Of course, the victim, after he has been robbed of his money, may also come to the conclusion that a life without capital is not worth living and proceed to kill himself. This too, in Lacan's book, would count as a separation. Indeed, the endpoint of separation always unavoidably coincides with the annihilation of life. This is why Lacan, in his discussion of separation, referred to Freud's controversial concept of the death drive and the suicide of Empedocles (Lacan, 2006[1964], p. 715). Applied to the alternative "being or meaning", separation involves the eradication of meaning (the Other), which would in turn lead to the elimination of the divided subject and the restoration of full being. "*Separare*, separating", Lacan stated, "ends here in *se parere*, engendering oneself" (Ibid., p. 715). In light of the previous example, which ends in certain death, the idea of self-engendering seems paradoxical, here, were it not for the fact that what is at stake is not the death of the human being, but the death of the divided subject. "Here the subject proceeds from his partition [in the Other] to his parturition", Lacan added, with the proviso that this process "does not imply the grotesque metaphor of giving birth" to oneself, but rather "a determination to succeed" in obtaining some form of civil status, whereby the subject is no longer purely dependent on the Other but is capable of asserting and representing himself (Ibid., p. 715). The problem is, however, that the Other can never be fully erased, that the subject can never completely free itself from the Other's stronghold in order to become its own cause, so that the divided subject is only ever thrown back on its constitutive "lack-of-being" and the ensuing "want-to-be" (*manque-à-être*) (Lacan, 1994[1973], p. 29).[30] Separation remains stuck, therefore, in an endless attempt at "self-extraction" from the symbolic order, which only ever results in a new alienation. This is why Lacan also refers to separation as a *"refente"*, literally a re-splitting or re-division, and why he considers the two operations of alienation and separation to be circular, yet non-reciprocal: they are circular, because one leads to the other, *ad infinitum*, but at the same time they are non-reciprocal, because one does not compensate for the other (Lacan, 2006[1964], p. 714).[31]

The question that remains, of course, is who or what is responsible for setting the process of separation in motion. Lacan's answer is that separation is triggered not by the splitting of the subject in itself, but by the "splitting of the object", which results from the original alienation. It is the object *a*, as the inadequate part-object that has come to replace the lost experience of full satisfaction, which triggers separation and the renewed division of the subject.[32] One more return to the example of the highwayman may help explain this. Assuming that the victim does what he is supposed to do, i.e., hand over his money in order to stay alive, then we can reasonably expect him to try and recuperate the lost sum, irrespective of how much money he still has left after the robber has taken the cash. Yet whatever capital he manages to accumulate afterwards, the funds will never be entirely adequate, less so because they will never compensate for the loss in monetary terms—indeed, the victim may become wealthier than before—but more because they will never be able to erase the memory of the robbery: the replacement funds are not fully identical to what was lost, and the victim will realize that one's life can depend on the "kindness" of robbers. What operates on the place of the lost capital, here, is Lacan's object *a*, which is in itself a flawed, lacking object, and which therefore elicits the subject's desire to return to the original state of full satisfaction, with the known result of a renewed division.

The Potentiality of Being

I have taken my discussion of the way in which the subject and the object have been theorized in psychoanalysis, at least in its Freudian and Lacanian versions, far enough to formulate some conclusions as to what psychoanalysis may contribute to the ongoing debate concerning the subject-object relationship in science, philosophy and epistemology. In particular, it will be important to tease out what type of relationship is still conceivable between a divided subject ($) and an inadequate part-object (*a*), and how this relationship underpins the way in which objects are apprehended by subjects outside the sphere of psychoanalysis, in a conventional empirical research setting for instance.

The first thing to note is that the psychoanalytic divided subject has no substance whatsoever; it is merely an effect of symbolic alienation and a failed attempt at radical separation from the Other, in confrontation with the inadequate part-object that is the object *a*. This type of conceptualization of the subject subverts all theories that promote the realization of an inner, true self, because at the place where one is expected to find oneself, there is nothing at all, no unified "one-self", no true identity.[33] Following Aristotle's conception of the material cause, in which matter is connected to something underneath (a *hypokeimenon*), Lacan regarded the subject as a foundation, but only insofar as it is subservient to the materiality of language and the absolute inaccessibility of the real nature of the object:

> There is no way of escaping this extraordinarily reduced formula that there is something underneath. But precisely, there is no term that we can designate this something by. It cannot be an *etwas* [a (some)thing], it is simply an underneath, a subject, a *hypokeimenon*. (Lacan, 2007[1991], p. 48)[34]

In advocating the substitution of an intangible, fleeting subject for a core, autonomous, and solidified self, Lacan may seem to prefigure, then, postmodernist constructionist paradigms in which the subject appears as an undifferentiated, purely contextual factor, which is the product of symbolic, discursive formations. Yet the divided subject only really fits into these perspectives, when it is conceived as a negativity, caused by the human being's ineluctable embedment in a symbolic system. The subject radically transcends discursive determinism from the moment it attempts to realize itself through its separation from the Other. The divided subject is therefore not simply a symbolically dependent non-entity, but also a desire that tries to emancipate itself from the forces that presided over its constitution. It is a *hypokeimenon*, a subjected non-being, but also more than a *hypokeimenon*, since it is continuously in the process of replacing non-being with being. Of course, by adding separation to alienation, and emphasizing the non-reciprocal circularity of the operations, Lacan averred that the ontological status of the subject is neither about being, nor about non-being, but about the relentless shift between being and non-being. The divided subject is thus a permanent inchoate element, whose ontology may be captured with Schelling's notion of the "potentiality of being" (*Sein können*), with which he designated the unique ability of human beings to come in contact with the Absolute (Schelling, 2006[1809]).

More importantly, however, is the role Lacan assigns to the object *a* in all of this. As a part-object, the object *a* is not objectified by the subject, if only because the latter can lay no claim whatsoever to any form of agency. Matters are rather the other way round, the divided subject, having already been deprived of its substance, being objectified by the object. In Freudian terms, this is again the shadow of the abandoned object that falls upon the ego, whereas in Lacanian terms it can be interpreted as the divided subject being re-caused, re-divided by the desire that the object *a* elicits in it. The subject is therefore simultaneously caused by the Other and by the object *a*, without ever being *causa sui*, and without this process of causation ever being finished. This does not imply that the subject is purely object, nor that the object is merely subject nor, for that matter, that the Hegelian subject-object identity finds its ultimate guarantee in the psychoanalytic relationship between the divided subject and the object *a*. As Lacan put it in the overture to his *Écrits*: "the division in... the subject is verified in the fact that an object traverses him [*le traverse*] without them interpenetrating [*sans qu'ils se pénètrent*] in any respect" (Lacan, 2006[1966b], p. 4).[35] The subject is traversed by the object, much like the shadow of the object falls onto the ego, without the subject entering into the reciprocal arrangement of in turn traversing the object. The object *a* does not enter into a proper relationship with the subject, because the part-object cannot be reduced. When she sees the "unimportant letter" on the table, the Queen is definitely free to crumple it up, but getting rid of the material remainder will not erase the fact that she has been deprived of something precious, and is now keen to get it back.

The resulting picture is complex, yet far removed from any of the classic realist or idealist positions in the philosophy and epistemology of science. Insofar as it is embedded in a symbolic structure of language—a set of rules, a code of conduct, a research protocol—any object of study must necessarily appear as something that resists symbolization and that can therefore not be entirely integrated into a structure of knowledge. A known object can only ever be half-known and half-subjectified, the rest (object *a*) being that which forever escapes epistemic apprehension. This differs radically, of course, from the standard view in empirical science, which considers the object to be a completely de-subjectified, knowable entity, which can be fully known by a knowing subject. Ironically, however, as Žižek has pointed out: the object *a* "far from being 'independent of the subject'... is *stricto sensu* the subject's shadow among the objects, a kind of stand-in for the subject, a pure semblance lacking any consistency of its own" (Žižek, 1994, p. 33). The object *a*, the object in its Kantian noumenal quality of Thing, is correlative of the subject, which is in itself but a vanishing point, a locus of barred access, which can be represented without ever being fully representable. In this way, the part-object (that part of the object which constitutes an absolute unknown) indeed reflects and objectifies the subject as an unknown noumenon, which prompts the subject to know more and pursue allegedly higher strata of knowledge.

To end, it is worth recalling how Lacan proposes the two operations of alienation and separation as the two constituents of the fantasy, which governs and regulates the non-relationship between subject and object. It is only as a fantasy, which is in itself never fully consolidated, but always subject to some form of recalibration, that a relationship between subject and object can be established or that an object can be perceived by a subject as an adequate, satisfying and altogether knowable object. The rest is silence....

Notes

1 An earlier version of this chapter was first published in *Continental Philosophy Review*, 2013, 46(2), pp. 163–187. It is reproduced here with the permission of SpringerNature.
2 For an excellent critical analysis of how the scientific method developed over time, see Cowles (2020).
3 In keeping with the proposition that science is a procedure and that scientificity can be measured against the robustness of methodological principles for conducting empirical research, psychology has effectively exchanged the need to identify a distinctive object of study for the need to develop scientifically sound and statistically solid research methods. Long gone are the days that psychology focused exclusively on perception, attention and consciousness. Most psychologists will probably still agree that the human being remains central, yet which aspect of this human being—mind, brain, behaviour, personality, patterns of social interaction—should constitute the private hunting ground for psychologists has become less relevant than the implementation of a set of rigorous rules for (quantitatively and/or qualitatively) investigating these and other human aspects.
4 See, for example, Grünbaum (1984) and Macmillan (1997). For a more polemical collection of criticisms, see Meyer (2005) and Onfray (2010).
5 The widely accepted neuro-scientific theory of dreams as caused by random firings of neurons is a corollary of the so-called "activation-synthesis hypothesis", which was first formulated by Hobson and McCarley in 1977. Since then, Hobson has not let an opportunity go by to expose Freud's view of dreams (as unconscious wish-fulfillments) in all its flaws, without being able to tackle decisively clinical phenomena such as recurrent anxiety-dreams and the repetitive occurrence of identical dream-images. From a neuropsychological point of view, Hobson has also been taken to task by the neuro-psychoanalyst Mark Solms for assuming that dreaming is simply synonymous with the REM state of sleep. See Hobson and McCarley (1977), Hobson (2002, pp. 17–34), Hobson (2011), Solms (1997), and Solms and Turnbull (2002, pp. 181–216).
6 An almost identical phrase appears in Freud (1957[1917e], p. 247).
7 For "splitting of consciousness", see Freud (1962[1894a], pp. 46–47) and Breuer and Freud (1955[1893a], p. 12).
8 The precise origin of the super-ego and the reasons for its severity should not really concern us here. Suffice it to say that for Freud, the super-ego is "as much a representative of the id [the least accessible part of the unconscious, which coincides with the repressed] as of the external world" (Freud, 1961[1924c], p. 167).
9 For "shadow of the object", see Freud (1957[1917e], p. 249). In an influential 1987 book, Christopher Bollas took his lead from this idea in order to conceptualize the pre-verbal locus of an "unthought known", which acts as a powerful drive in the unconscious (Bollas, 1987). For the re-direction of object-libido towards the ego and the function of narcissism, see Freud (1957[1914c], pp. 74–75).
10 The problem with this explanation is that it seems to pre-suppose what is being accounted for. If the ego is a repository of identifications with objects whose libidinal investment has been abandoned, then what is responsible for setting the de-eroticization and subsequent identification in motion, if not some form of ego? In a protracted philosophical reflection on subjectivity and power, Judith Butler has detected similar contradictions and ambiguities in Foucault's and Althusser's conceptions of the subject. See Butler (1997).
11 The latter terms all appear, for example, in the 1912 technical paper "The dynamics of transference", although this can no longer be gauged from the standard

English translation, in which *Mensch* is rendered as "individual", *Person* as "subject" and *Analysierte* as "patient". See Freud (1958[1912b]).
12 On the absence of the notion of the subject in Freud, see Borch-Jacobsen (1988[1982]; 1993[1991]). In both texts, the author develops a trenchant critique of the epistemological underpinnings of psychoanalysis, arguing that Freud's rationalistic view of the unconscious as a set of representations (*Vorstellungen*) inevitably implies the implicit pre-supposition of a subject, who is both the re-presenting agency of these representations and what is represented in them. For a thorough philosophical investigation of these and other unresolved antinomies in Freud's non-conception of the subject, see Tauber (2010). For Freud's Kantian position on the unconscious as a thing-in-itself that can only be experienced indirectly, through the phenomenal traces that it leaves behind, see Freud (1957[1915e], p. 171) and Freud (1964[1940a], p. 196).
13 Borch-Jacobsen recognizes the object-quality of the Freudian subject, yet he is at great pains to demonstrate that the subject is being insidiously re-inscribed at various points in Freud's theory as a self-representing agency, which for him signals both Freud's failure to properly acknowledge and understand the possibility of unrepresented thought and, by the same token, the failure of psychoanalysis, which is thus inadvertently driven back into the domain of metaphysics. See Borch-Jacobsen (1993[1991], pp. 22–24).
14 Once again, it needs to be emphasized that the knowing agency, here, is not a conscious subject. Freud persistently avoids attributing the so-called "development of the libido", which proceeds from auto-erotism to narcissism to external object-choice, to any form of subjective intentionality. Although in English translation, the subject regularly re-appears, for example in the phrase "the subject's own body", Freud uses much more generic phrases such as "*am eigenen Körper*" or describes the process as an automatic mechanism, which follows its course without any interference or direction from a central mental faculty.
15 The standard English translation of *Partialtrieb* is "component (sexual) instinct". See, for example, Freud (1963[1916–1917], p. 328). In a number of places, Freud argued that the partial drives become unified under the influence of the advent of genitality, which subsumes the oral, anal, sadistic, masochistic and other drive-components under the primacy of sexual procreation, and also as a result of a fully accomplished object-choice, which overrules the auto-erotic libidinal organization that gives free reign to all types of partial satisfaction. However, a full-fledged genitality and an established object-choice are in themselves dependent upon a properly dissolved Oedipus complex, which Freud considered to be an ideal rather than an actually occurring event (Freud, 1963[1916–1917], pp. 328–337). In other words, genitality is the most problematic stage in the development of the libido for all human beings.
16 In the first session of his 1956–1957 seminar on object-relations, Lacan indicated that the re-finding of an object is the first and most important context in which the question of the object in psychoanalysis should be addressed (Lacan, 2020[1994], pp. 6–8), a context which Freud had already sketched in his posthumously published *Project for a Scientific Psychology* (Freud, 1966[1950a]). And indeed, in this text, which was originally written in 1895, he designated the object as an "object wished-for" (*Wunschobjekt*), which may be perceived in the outside world or otherwise merely hallucinated, and which is based on the memory of an initial experience of satisfaction (Freud, 1966[1950a], p. 322).
17 In "Civilization and its Discontents", Freud himself argued that the sexual life of human beings is severely impaired owing to the restrictions and prohibitions imposed by "civilized society", yet only to conclude on a note of caution:

"Sometimes one seems to perceive that it is not only the pressure of civilization but *something in the nature of the function* [the sexual function] *itself* which denies us full satisfaction and urges us along other paths" (Freud, 1964[1930a], p. 105, italics added).

18 For Freud on "primal repression" (*Urverdrängung*), see Freud (1957[1915d], p. 148). In "Civilization and its Discontents", Freud refers in this respect also to an "organic repression" [*organischen Verdrängung*] (Freud, 1964[1930a], p. 99-footnote 1 and p. 106).

19 As with all of Lacan's formulations, this process should not be interpreted in developmental terms—first there was pre-verbal harmony, then there was symbolic loss, and then an inadequate part-object to compensate for it—but rather as a retrospective construction: the symbolically determined experience of dissatisfaction comes with the nostalgic image of a lost state of bliss, which the sexual object is by definition unable to restore.

20 For an excellent critical survey of Lacan's development of the object *a* between the mid-1950s and the mid-1970s, see Le Gaufey (2012).

21 Although Lacan originally derived the object *a* from the first letter of *autre* (other, the neighbor as alter ego), *a* subsequently acquired the connotations of a mathematical function or an algebraic sign, which should therefore not be translated. By extension, *a* could also be linked to the grammatical "privative alpha", which conveys the absence of the quality with which it is associated (as in a-moral or a-sexual). It could even be seen as the original nothingness in the Biblical sense, since "in the beginning was God" (*berechit bara Elohim*) (Genesis, 1) and therefore *beth* rather than *aleph*. For a further exploration of these points, see Porge (2005, pp. 191–202).

22 The object *a* substitutes for what Lacan calls the imaginary phallus (-φ), which to some extent coincides with the object that the Freudian boy-child, when confronted with sexual difference, imagines to have been in the girl's possession prior to her losing it (and thus being "castrated"). The imaginary phallus epitomizes a point where the object would have been complete, and thus in a state of full satisfaction (enjoyment, *jouissance*). The object *a* that replaces it may still generate some sort of satisfaction, but it is only surplus-jouissance (*plus-de-jouir*), which is simultaneously "in excess" and never enough.

23 "Mourning and Melancholia" is, of course, the paper in which Freud referred to the "shadow of the object" (Freud, 1957[1917e], p. 249).

24 In his text, Lacan does mention the Minister's substitute letter as an important residue of the theft, yet without developing the point further: "A *remainder* [*reste*] that no analyst will neglect, trained as he is to remember everything having to do with the signifier even if he does not always know what to do with it: the letter, left on hand by the Minister, which the Queen is now free to crumple up" (Lacan, 2006[1957a], p. 8). Equally, he singled out the importance of both Dupin's factitious letter, especially its handwritten inscription, as well as his hefty remuneration, for the structural dynamics of the narrative, yet without linking these remainders to the previous one, and without elaborating much on their function. For an incisive discussion of these "neglected remainders" in Lacan's text (and Poe's story), as well as Derrida's subsequent "neglect of the neglect" in his influential critical reading of Lacan, see Davis (2010, pp. 114–124). Had he looked beyond his *Écrits*, Lacan would no doubt also have re-encountered a shadow of the object *a* in his close reading of Plato's *Symposium*, more particularly in the "divine and golden images" (*agalmata*) which Alcibiades, in his strange eulogy on Socrates, claimed to have seen behind the philosopher's hideous Silen's mask. See Lacan (2015[2001], pp. 134–148). Needless to say,

Alcibiades' paean to Socrates' virtues is not to be taken at face value, here. It is totally insincere, not so much because he is inebriated, but because he is profoundly annoyed by the philosopher's superior wisdom and, even more so, by his recurrent refusal to respond to the young man's insistent advances. See Plato (2003, pp. 212–219).

25 Insofar as it is a precious love-letter, the Queen is unlikely to destroy her missive after it has been returned to her, despite its incriminating content, just as much as neither the Minister nor Dupin (nor the Police Prefect) would care to destroy it, because of the power that it grants. Poe himself does not say anything about what happens to the three replacement documents and leaves Dupin to wonder about the Minister's "precise character of his thoughts, when, being defied by her whom the Prefect terms 'a certain personage', he is reduced to opening the letter" which he has placed in the card-rack. See Poe (1988[1844], p. 332).

26 The underlying metaphysical dimensions of Lacan's work were brilliantly, although some would say undeservedly exposed by Jean-Luc Nancy and Philippe Lacoue-Labarthe in their 1973 book *The Title of the Letter*, a volume which Lacan himself recommended, without irony, to his audience as an excellent example of good reading. See Nancy and Lacoue-Labarthe (1992[1990]) and Lacan (1998[1975], p. 65). For an excellent study of the Lacanian subject, which can also be used as an authoritative introduction to his work, see Fink (1995).

27 In the latter text, Freud writes: "The core of our being [*Kern unseres Wesens*], then, is formed by the obscure *id*, which has no direct communication with the external world and is accessible even to our own knowledge only through the medium of another agency" (Freud, 1964[1940a], p. 197).

28 In the latter text, which is in many ways a condensed version of the 1964 seminar, Lacan talks about "the two fundamental operations with which the subject's causation should be formulated" and describes these operations (alienation and separation) as "circular, yet nonreciprocal" (Lacan 2006[1964], p. 712). My reading of the subject-object relation within these two operations is indebted to Sipos (1994, pp. 105–122 and pp. 198–209), Fink (1990), Fink (1995, pp. 49–55), Laurent (1995), and Verhaeghe (1998; 2004, pp. 212–220), although it also diverges from these interpretations in a number of ways. For a terrific exposition of the two operations in the context of Lacan's conceptualization of the unconscious, see Verhaeghe (2019).

29 Because the money is gone as soon as the question is formulated, the choice immediately shifts towards another alternative: life or death. In this way, the question "your money or your life" really conceals another question, namely "life or death". This is a genuine alternative, because none of the two options is already excluded in advance, so that the victim does have the freedom to decide whether he wants to live or die, assuming of course that the highwayman is to be trusted and will not proceed to kill his victim anyway after he has taken the money.

30 Lacan recognizes the principle also in Augustine's theology, insofar as his desire for a personal and personalized God forces him to oppose the idea of God as *causa sui*. See Lacan (2006[1964], p. 713).

31 It should be noted that the term *refente* has simply been rendered as "splitting", here.

32 This allows us to understand why Lacan links separation to Freud's later notion of *Ichspaltung*, as it appears, for instance, in the unfinished and posthumously published paper "Splitting of the Ego in the Process of Defence" (Freud, 1964[1940e]). In this text, Freud discussed *Ichspaltung* in relation to the creation of a fetish-object, as a means to overcome the threat of castration. Although the

fetish-object dampens down the anxiety associated with castration, and thus generates a certain amount of satisfaction (what Lacan would have termed surplus-jouissance), it also serves as a constant reminder of the object (the imaginary phallus) that had presumably been lost in the mist of time. Hence, *Ichspaltung* is based, here, on an essential splitting of the object (Freud, 1964[1940e], pp. 276–278).
33 Of course, in certain quarters the self has been re-injected into Freud's and Lacan's works, and the entire so-called ego-psychology movement in psychoanalysis has been geared towards re-establishing the ego as an integrated, conflict-free zone of mental activity.
34 In their critical readings of Lacan, both Nancy and Lacoue-Labarthe (1992[1990]) and Borch-Jacobsen (1993[1991]) persistently seem to ignore the fact that, although the subject is foundation, it is neither substance nor presence, neither truth nor agency. If truth speaks, as Lacan argued, it is only ever half-said in the subject's statements, so that the truth is not spoken by the subject, but the subject is spoken for by truth.
35 In a very rare gloss on this passage, Egginton unfortunately misses the significance of the object and reduces the "relationship" which Lacan outlines to the division between fiction and truth (Egginton, 2007, p. 83).

Chapter 4

The Sculptural Iconography of Feminine Jouissance: Lacan's Reading of Bernini's *Saint Teresa in Ecstasy*

> A swoon so sweet
> Should have eternal guise;
> But since suffering does not rise
> To the Heavenly Portal
> Bernini in this stone made it immortal.
> (Pietro Filippo Bernini, on his father's *Saint Teresa*)

Ecstasy in the Chapel

Amongst the innumerable architectural splendors of Rome, the church of *Santa Maria della Vittoria*, in the Sallustiano area of the city, is an unusually modest example of early 17th-century Baroque design.[1] Situated on a street corner, and hemmed in by adjacent buildings at the back and to the right, anyone approaching the edifice from the Piazza di San Bernardo feels rather underwhelmed by how the whole of its left side is but a plain terracotta rendered wall, with no artistic features other than a rectangular stained glass window above a small oriel. For the church's travertine façade, Giovanni Battista Soria took inspiration from Carlo Maderno's design for the façade of the nearby church of *Santa Susanna*, yet it does not incorporate the latter's rich decorations and is far more restrained in its use of figurative sculpture. And so nothing in this rather unassuming exterior can prepare visitors for the sumptuous spectacle inside. From the resplendent cantoria on the counterfaçade to the frescoed dome, from the lavish nave to the eight ornate side chapels, each and every part of the small church bathes in the glory of Baroque prodigality. Even the nave's monumental Corinthian pilasters of coloured marble, with their gilded capitals in support of a richly exaggerated entablature, exude a sensation of grandeur, and contribute integrally to the overwhelming visual extravaganza.

For all its aggregate magnificence, many people would probably not be drawn to the church were it not for one particular sculpture, *Saint Teresa in Ecstasy* by Gian Lorenzo Bernini (1598–1680), which Simon Schama has dubbed "the most astounding peepshow in art" (Schama, 2006, p. 78).

DOI: 10.4324/9781003252276-5

Released from a single slab of white Carrara marble, the sculpture is the centerpiece of the large funerary chapel to the left of the church's transept. The chapel was commissioned in January 1647 by the wealthy Venetian Cardinal Federico Cornaro (1579–1653) for the staggering amount of some 12,000 silver papal *scudi*, in honour of his esteemed family members and of his admired Teresa of Ávila (1515–1582), the Spanish mystic who had been canonized by Pope Gregory XV 25 years earlier.[2] It took Bernini and his associates five years to complete the work, but when it was finally unveiled in the summer of 1652 Roman public opinion echoed Cornaro's own view that the highly theatrical combination of sculpture, painting, and architecture had resulted in a timeless masterpiece—a *bel composto* of sublime beauty (see Figure 4.1).[3] The widespread acclaim could probably have been predicted, because it is hard to believe that Bernini would have been prepared to take serious artistic risks in conceiving the chapel, in which case he would not only have been in danger of offending his generous patron, but also of undermining his own stellar reputation within the ecclesiastical hierarchy, both within the Vatican and further afield, and any additional commissions that may have stemmed from it.

Figure 4.1 The Cornaro Chapel.

For almost four centuries, a plethora of historians, art critics, novelists, philosophers, men and women of God, and members of the general public have stood in front of the Cornaro chapel, either endorsing the initial response to the work, or expressing anger and dismay at what they consider to be a shameless sacrilegious depiction of Saint Teresa's vision, or dismissing Bernini's sculpture as a typical example of the deplorable excesses of Baroque art—a corruption of aesthetic principles, animated by hubris, and executed in bad taste. Shortly after the unveiling of Bernini's equestrian statue *The Vision of Constantine* in 1670, an anonymous pamphlet started to circulate in which the author denounced both the artist's recent work and some of his earlier sculptures. Of *Saint Teresa in Ecstasy* it was said that Bernini had "dragged that most pure Virgin not only into the Third Heaven, but into the dirt, to make a Venus not only prostrate, but prostituted" (Anonymous, 1976[1670], p. 53).[4] When none other than the Marquis de Sade, travelling incognito in Italy, visited the chapel some time during the autumn of 1775, his impression could not have been more different, yet he too identified a lingering ambiguity in the representation. "The piece is sublime", he wrote in his diary,

> because of the air of truth that characterizes it, but when seeing it one has to keep reminding oneself that she is a Saint, because from Teresa's ecstatic appearance, and from the fire that embraces her expression, one could be easily mistaken. (Sade, 1995[1775–1778], p. 87)

During the Enlightenment period, mysticism was generally dismissed as misplaced spirituality—a type of religious fanaticism Kant would have discarded as *Schwärmerei*, pathological enthusiasm, "monstrosities on reason" (Kant, 1997[1788], p. 101)—which stands in the way of the true liberation of human thought. And so the French magistrate, writer, and rationalist Charles de Brosses quipped: "If that is divine love, then I know it, and one may see numerous natural examples of it in the netherworld" (Brosses, 1986, pp. 64–65). When, from the early 19th century, European culture developed a strong taste for neoclassical art, the entire Baroque period was vilified as an aesthetic aberration, unworthy of serious consideration, and Bernini's *Saint Teresa* was widely regarded as the apotheosis of obscene vulgarity. In a massive critical compendium of Italian art, originally published in 1855, the influential Swiss art historian Jacob Burckhardt wrote: "Here [in *Saint Teresa in Ecstasy*] we clearly forget all simple questions of style, owing to the outrageous degradation of the supernatural" (Burckhardt, 1855, p. 709). On the continent, the tide started to turn towards the late 1900s, but in the English-speaking world Bernini was not rehabilitated until the second half of the 20th century. When the German-American art historian Rudolf Wittkower published a new *catalogue raisonné* of Bernini in 1955, it was praised by Irving Lavin—the world's foremost Bernini historian—for its bold and courageous attempt at countering the "profoundly unberninesque", Anglo-Saxon "penchant for reticence and understatement in aesthetic matters" (Lavin, 2007, p. 2).

Élisabeth Roudinesco has speculated that Jacques Lacan entered *Santa Maria della Vittoria* sometime in early February 1934, when he was on honeymoon in Italy with his first wife (Roudinesco, 1997[1993], p. 79). Although it would have been his first visit to the Eternal City, it was not to be his last, so he may have stood in front of the Cornaro chapel on more than one occasion. We do not have a record of what Lacan thought of Bernini's sculpture in 1934. Unlike Sade, he did not keep a diary of his voyage to Italy and unlike de Brosses he did not send regular reports of his adventures to his friends back home. Telegrams from Rome to his former lover were too short and personal to include reflections upon works of art. Picturing the newly-weds looking up at *Saint Teresa in Ecstasy*, what words did they exchange? In 1934, Dr Lacan was a recently qualified psychiatrist training to become a psychoanalyst. Could he have proffered a Freudian interpretation of the scene? Would he have known that Freud's co-author, Josef Breuer, had at one point described Teresa of Ávila as "the patron saint of hysteria" (Breuer and Freud, 1955[1895*d*], p. 232), thereby echoing Freud's master Jean-Martin Charcot, who had diagnosed Teresa as an "undeniable hysteric" (Charcot, 1897, p. 10), in tune with quite a few other late 19th-century medical doctors?[5] Enthralled by the artistic experiments of the surrealist movement, and particularly intrigued by Salvador Dalí's method of paranoia-criticism, which allowed for two completely different objects to be represented at the same time, did he see in Bernini's statue a perfect illustration of a double image—pain and pleasure, agony and bliss, death and sexuality?[6]

It was not until almost 40 years later that Lacan made a comment in public about Bernini's *Saint Teresa*. At the end of the seventh session of his 1972–1973 seminar *Encore*, delivered on 20 February 1973 in front of a packed lecture theatre at the Law Faculty on the *Place du Panthéon* in Paris, Lacan extolled the virtues of mysticism, invoking Saint John of the Cross, Hadewijch of Antwerp, and Teresa of Ávila. Casually comparing the experiences of the latter two women, he identified a common trait:

> *Mais pour la Hadewijch en question, pour Sainte Thérèse, enfin disons quand même le mot. Et puis en plus vous n'avez qu'à aller regarder dans une certaine église à Rome la statue du Bernin pour comprendre tout de suite—enfin quoi?—qu'elle jouit, ça ne fait pas de doute! Et de quoi jouit-elle? Il est clair que le témoignage essentiel de la mystique, c'est justement de dire ça—qu'ils l'éprouvent mais qu'ils n'en savent rien.*[7]

Succinct as it may have been, this remark on the jouissance of Hadewijch and especially Saint Teresa would prove to be inescapable as a clear indication of Lacan's problematic views on femininity for countless scholars working on the intersections between psychoanalysis, women's, and gender studies. All in all, critics have taken issue with no less than four different aspects of Lacan's statement: (i) the fact that Lacan decided to look at Bernini's statue, rather than read Saint Teresa's personal account of the event; (ii) Lacan's declared certainty with regard to what Bernini's statue reveals about the nature of Saint Teresa's experience; (iii) Lacan's interpretation of Saint Teresa's sculpted vision as a particular type of feminine jouissance; (iv) Lacan's assertion that women merely testify to this experience, without knowing anything about it.

In this chapter, I will briefly consider each of these four contentious aspects of Lacan's reading of *Saint Teresa in Ecstasy*, probing into the source and origin of the criticism, gauging its validity and impact, whilst at the same time trying to understand Lacan's own perspective. In doing so, I will show that Lacan's controversial comment on Bernini's *Saint Teresa* is not at all dissimilar to Bernini's own disputed exteriorization of the mystic's inner world, insofar as both men have essentially been taken to task for imposing a male fantasy upon an intimate experience from which they remain fundamentally barred, but which they nonetheless wish to capture, domesticate, and recuperate within the epistemic structure of their own phallic economy. The larger problem, then, is not about the specific definition of jouissance, but about who is entitled to define it, and about the way in which certain definitions are believed to be surreptitiously contaminated by the jouissance of the one who formulates them.

A Certain Look

Shortly after Lacan's seminar *Encore* was released in France, Luce Irigaray wrote a paper for a conference on "Sexuality and Politics" in Milan, in which she staged a vehement rebuttal of Lacan's conceptual elaboration of a specific form of jouissance that would be supplementary to the more ordinary, typically masculine "phallic jouissance", and therefore situated beyond the phallus as a distinctly feminine jouissance.[8] Although Lacan believed that his "discovery" would "give another consistency to the women's liberation movement" (Lacan, 1998[1975], p. 74), Irigaray rejected the whole idea as nothing but the corollary of a psychoanalytic master's unyielding reliance on the supremacy of the male principle, especially in the realms of speech, language, and discourse. To her, Lacan's reading of Bernini's *Saint Teresa* constituted one of the most poignant illustrations of the phallic assumptions underpinning his psychoanalytic take on feminine sexuality. Rather than following his exhortation to see Teresa's jouissance in the Cornaro chapel, she famously wrote:

> In Rome? So far away? To look? At a statue? Of a Saint? Sculpted by a man? What pleasure [jouissance] are we talking about? Whose pleasure

[jouissance]? For where the pleasure [jouissance] of the Theresa (*sic*) in question is concerned, her own writings are perhaps more telling. (Irigaray, 1985[1976]), p. 91)

Irigaray wondered why Lacan chose to send his listeners to Rome, as if there were no relevant feminine, or even mystical experiences to be discovered closer to home, but she was particularly critical of the fact that as a man he encouraged them to ascertain a certain type of feminine jouissance by looking at a statue (a speechless, dead object) of a woman sculpted by another man, rather than by reading the woman's own description of the event that had subsequently been carved into stone. And, indeed, what is striking about Lacan's juxtaposition of Hadewijch and Saint Teresa is that he invites his audience to read some texts by the former, whilst remaining silent about the voluminous works produced by the latter. Lacan disclosed that "a very nice person" had brought him a book by Hadewijch and that he had read it immediately (Lacan, 1998[1975], p. 76), but when it comes to Saint Teresa, he somehow preferred looking at the sculpture rather than reading the specific passage in her autobiography which had inspired Bernini's composition.[9]

Of course, statues are generally there to be looked at, but in this case Lacan's visual epistemology of mysticism may indeed appear as silencing and objectifying. As Cristina Mazzoni has put it:

> By stressing the visual dimension of the mystic's utterance, that is, by affirming the sufficiency of looking at the mystic in order to understand her message ... Lacan is clearly making a reductive and patronizing move. Not only does he rely on a man's graven image of a woman's verbal account, but he also regresses to the positivistic attitude of Charcot and his school at the Salpêtrière, where doctors, wrapped up in their visual contemplation and compulsive photography, did not bother to listen to the hysteric's and the mystic's words .... (Mazzoni, 1996, pp. 46–47)[10]

The point is exceptionally well-made, but it is nonetheless assumed, here, that Teresa's autobiography would have allowed for a more nuanced perspective, or would have generated a different kind of knowledge altogether about her experience, as though the text of the vision were intrinsically more ambiguous than Bernini's statue. Would Lacan have come to a different conclusion had he decided to interpret Teresa's description of the episode, rather than Bernini's representation of the event? Irigaray definitely did not believe that he would have been able to read Teresa's text without reconfirming his masculine bias, but if his reading of the text had been similar to his interpretation of the statue, would this really prove the pervasive influence of male chauvinism? Before Bernini started carving, quite a few male painters had captured the transverberation in a much more serene way.[11] Were they more truthful to Teresa's text, less at the mercy of phallic fantasies, or simply more restrained for fear of being accused of blasphemy and profanation? What if Bernini's sensuous exhibition of Teresa's "spiritual pain" was not just an artistic sublimation of his private sexual fantasy, but a carefully crafted reflection of late 17th-century religious conceptions of the ecstatic nuptial union between God and an ascetic virgin? Vice versa, some female readers of Teresa's autobiography have come up with interpretations similar to those emanating from Lacan's visual contemplation of the statue, and long before Lacan expressed his own views. In addition, in his influential 1957 volume *Eroticism*, Georges Bataille categorically opposed straightforward sexual interpretations of the mystic's visionary experience, whether captured in writing or in marble (Bataille, 2001[1957], pp. 223–226). All of this would indicate that the content of the interpretation is perhaps less dependent on the gender of the interpreter than Irigaray wanted her own readers to believe.[12]

Maybe the real issue is not that Lacan decided to look rather than read, or that his interpretation of *Saint Teresa in Ecstasy* was predicated upon a male gaze, but that his look is that of a voyeur, because Bernini's statue offers Teresa's transverberation up for eroticized observation. Of course, in staging the spectacle of ecstasy, it turns every spectator into a voyeur, someone who is by definition too entrenched in his or her own jouissance to fully understand what is there to be seen.[13] If there is a highly charged eroticism in Bernini's sculpture, then, it would not just be because of the way in which Teresa's inner state has been visualized by a male sculptor, but also and primarily because the emphatically theatrical setting forces the spectator into a certain spatial position, from which he or she can only escape by effectively leaving the scene. Purely by virtue of its textual description, Teresa's own account of her vision leaves more to the reader's imagination, insofar as it places the reader in the position of a confessor rather than an observer, yet this in itself does not exclude the attribution of eroticism to her story, on the contrary. It is not just that Teresa's words are evocative, but that the reader *qua* confessor is asked to receive and validate a woman's candid testimony of a most intimate physical and spiritual experience, from which this reader has been excluded, and which may therefore easily instill a sensation of erotic tension.[14] In other words, whether Teresa's experience is considered via her own text or via Bernini's sculpture, it is the position of the interpreter, as confessor or observer, as much as the contents of the work, that is responsible for the effect. Ecstatic as Teresa's experience may have been, it is the interpreter's ineluctable position of witness that generates the attribution of a certain form of jouissance, and which may be celebrated as much as it may be despised, glorified as much as it may be ignored or rejected.

When Lacan invited his listeners to go and look at Bernini's statue, it is quite unlikely that he wanted them to inspect the graceful little seraph, the

Figure 4.2 Saint Teresa in Ecstasy (detail).

gilded rays illuminating the scene, the richly flowing drapery of the saint's habit, or her hands and feet. More than anything else, looking at *Saint Teresa in Ecstasy* involves looking at the expression on Teresa's face, and there is no reason to believe that Lacan's look would have been directed elsewhere, at least not in the first instance (see Figure 4.2).

Over the years, numerous descriptions of Teresa's facial expression have entered the literature, perhaps none better than an early 20th-century impression by Walther Weibel:

> The wonderful head ... is bent back on the neck as if from the painful thrust of a dagger. The eyes are half closed under leaden, fallen lids and rolled back almost completely so that the iris is only visible as a faint shadow on the upper edge of the white of the orb. The depression

around the whole eye further strengthens the impression that a serious crisis shakes this frail woman. The nostrils seem to quiver; the mouth is convulsively opened, not in a scream, but barely in a deep moan. The lids, the nostrils, and the mouth are sharply undercut to create an effect of long shadows. (Weibel, 1976[1909], p. 84)

To the best of my knowledge, Bernini was the first to exteriorize Teresa's mystical experience by endowing her eyes and mouth with the same swooning quality as the rest of her body, thus enriching her physical levitation with an inchoate countenance that is profoundly suggestive of a transportive emotional communion. Of all the visually arresting elements of *Saint Teresa in Ecstasy*, the saint's face is the furthest removed from Teresa's own account of her vision, in which she did not mark out her own facial expression (assuming that this would have been possible in the first place), and it is unquestionably the feature of the statue that sets it most apart from all previous representations of this vision.[15] If this is how a 17th-century man visualized divine love, is this also the look of religious ecstasy? Is it the unequivocal sign of the saint's *unio mystica*? Does it symbolize holy rapture or is it, more prosaically, the facial expression of mundane eroticism?

Some time towards the end of 1673, Cardinal Paluzzo Paluzzi launched a competition for the design of a large marble sculpture of his great-great-grandmother, the Blessed Ludovica Albertoni (1473–1533)—a Roman noblewoman who had entered the lay Franciscan order of the *Penitenti* after the death of her husband, and who had recently been beatified by Pope Clement X for her tireless devotion to the poor people of Rome. The sculpture was to be installed in the newly refurbished Altieri chapel of the church of *San Francesco a Ripa*, in Rome's Trastevere district. When Bernini won the competition, he promised to deliver the sculpture within six months, free of charge, purportedly in exchange for his disgraced younger brother Luigi being pardoned for having raped a young boy (Mormando, 2011, pp. 312–315). Bernini's sculpture of Ludovica Albertoni is placed above the altar, and shows the pious woman in a semi-recumbent position on her bed, with her knees bent and her hands reaching towards her chest. Her body is almost completely engulfed by the intricate folds of her tousled drapery (see Figure 4.3).

Once again, however, it is the woman's facial expression that commands attention, not in the least because it is almost an exact copy of Saint Teresa's in the Cornaro chapel, so much so that Weibel's aforementioned description of Saint Teresa's countenance could be applied equally to Ludovica Albertoni, and that a naïve visitor to the Altieri chapel may be led to believe that Bernini sculpted a second Saint Teresa (Figure 4.4).

Nonetheless, whereas Saint Teresa is meant to be at the mercy of her ecstatic vision, Ludovica Albertoni is supposed to be gasping in expiration on her deathbed. Pleasure or pain? Ecstasy or agony? Most viewers looking

Figure 4.3 The Blessed Ludovica Albertoni.

at Saint Teresa's facial expression have settled for ecstasy rather than agony, and have shifted the statue's ambiguity towards the conflation of earthly and divine love, despite Teresa's own admission that the transverberation caused her both sweetness and intense pain (Ávila, 1957[1588], p. 210). In the case of Ludovica Albertoni, the scholarly community remains divided as to the precise nature of the woman's experience, with some authors claiming she is dying, others arguing she is in ecstasy, and others either confessing to be unsure or maintaining that, in good mystical fashion, hers is the painful pleasure of a love-death.[16]

When Lacan looked at Saint Teresa's facial expression, he immediately understood what was going on. He did not doubt for a moment that what he was seeing was the unequivocal representation of a certain form of feminine jouissance. In the terms of his own so-called "logical time"—a threefold structure which he had articulated a propos of the "sophism of the three prisoners"—one could say that he minimized the "time for comprehending" to the point where the "moment of concluding" coincided with the "instant of the glance" (Lacan, 2006[1945], pp. 169–172). Yet, whereas in the sophism of the three prisoners, the truth-value of the conclusion is only ever established retrospectively, after it has been drawn, so that certainty is always bound up in a process of nervous anticipation, Lacan's conclusion about Teresa's

Figure 4.4 The Blessed Ludovica Albertoni (detail).

jouissance would appear to be pre-validated, if not to say pre-formed or pre-fabricated. Given Lacan's own lifelong misgivings about quick and easy understanding, his lack of doubt vis-à-vis Bernini's Saint Teresa definitely comes across as extremely puzzling.[17] Why was he so sure? In a fascinating study of representations of "deviant femininity" in art, the art historian Mary D. Sheriff suggested that Lacan may have felt convinced, because so many other people, men and women alike, had already interpreted the statue in the same way before him (Sheriff, 2004, p. 92). Back in 1978, long before *Encore* was translated into English, Stephen Heath was much less generous towards Lacan, insofar as he saw the psychoanalyst's "confidence of knowledge", and his not showing "the trace of any difficulty" when reading Bernini's sculpture, as indicative of his unconscious need to buttress a masculine interpretive ideology and, more insidiously, of profound sexist prejudice (Heath,

1978–1979, p. 52).[18] In order to situate and evaluate Lacan's certainty, here, I believe it is necessary to consider what exactly he was certain about—not the object of contemplation, i.e., Teresa's facial expression *per se*, but what this object signifies in terms of the Saint's lived experience. Although it is driven by a look—both his own look and that on the saint's face—Lacan's certainty cannot be dissociated from what his own look prompted him to discern *behind* the look on Teresa's face, notably a type of jouissance that is uniquely feminine.

Knowledge of Jouissance

Commenting on the way in which Bernini had captured Saint Teresa's ecstasy, Lacan told his audience: "[*E*]*lle jouit, ça ne fait pas de doute*". In Cormac Gallagher's unofficial English translation of Lacan's seminar, which relies on literal transcriptions of the lectures, the sentence reads: "That she is having an orgasm, there is no doubt about it".[19] In the official English translation, which follows the version of *Encore* edited by Jacques-Alain Miller, the comment has been rendered more informally as "[S]he's coming. There's no doubt about it" (Lacan, 1998[1975], p. 76), and this is how Lacan's remark has usually been adopted in the Anglophone literature.[20] Nowadays, it is common practice in English-language works on Lacan for the term jouissance to be left untranslated, because none of the available options—enjoyment, satisfaction, bliss, orgasm—are deemed to do full justice to the wide semantic spectrum of the French word.[21] In the passage from Irigaray's paper quoted previously, jouissance has been rendered as pleasure, yet from the late 1950s, Lacan insisted that jouissance is only related to pleasure inasmuch as it is limited by it (Lacan, 2006[1960], p. 696). Jacques-Alain Miller has detected no fewer than six different paradigms of jouissance in Lacan's works, yet in none of these is the term jouissance clearly defined, and rather than succeeding or replacing one another over time, the paradigms often blend in with each other, before diverging again (Miller, 2000, p. 15). As David Macey put it:

> The connotations of the terms [jouissance and *jouir*] shift considerably over the years, but they never shed their earlier meanings. Their final acceptations tend therefore to be the result of a process of semantic-conceptual accretion, and their meanings are contextual rather than definitional. (Macey, 1988, p. 201)

In his Seminar *Encore*, Lacan distinguished between at least eight different types of jouissance, without ever glossing one of these as strictly synonymous with orgasmic satisfaction: jouissance of the Other, jouissance of the body, jouissance of being, feminine jouissance, perverse jouissance, phallic jouissance, sexual jouissance, surplus jouissance (*plus-de-jouir*) (Lacan,

1998[1975]). Assuming that not all of these terms are synonyms, the fact that sexual jouissance is singled out for special mention can only suggest that some of the other types of jouissance are a-sexual and, we may reasonably assume, an-orgasmic.

Strange as it may seem, given how jouissance (and especially the verb *jouir*) definitely connotes orgasm in everyday French, one therefore needs to avoid according a strictly sexual, orgasmic meaning to Lacan's term in each and every context in which it occurs.[22] And so it should not be readily assumed that Lacan was certain about Bernini's *Saint Teresa* having an orgasm, regardless as to what the sculptor himself may have had in mind. Lacan may have been certain that she was in the throws of jouissance, but that should not compel us, as interpreters of Lacan, to designate this particular jouissance as a sexual phenomenon. One may reprimand Lacan for being certain, here, about the jouissance displayed on the face of Bernini's Saint Teresa, but one should not berate him for being convinced that she was showing all the telltale signs of orgasmic enjoyment. Lacan's point was much more subtle, which is also borne out by his admonishment of Charcot and his followers for reducing mysticism to mere "questions of cum" (*affaires de foutre*) (Lacan, 1998[1975], p. 77). In a sense, Lacan's certainty is echoed, then, in the translators' certainty, yet the latter alters the referent of the verb "*jouir*" to exactly the opposite of what he seems to have had in mind. For Lacan's entire trajectory in *Encore* prior to his discussion of mysticism was effectively geared towards the delineation of an Other jouissance—or a jouissance of the Other—which is not at all sexual, but situated within the sphere of pure bodily existence, and which would allegedly be reserved to those speaking beings who are called "women". Of course, this does not make Lacan's reading less problematic, because Bernini's visual representation of this Other jouissance, as readily identified by Lacan, is strikingly similar to common (male) visualizations of the female orgasm. And so one is left wondering how Lacan allowed his own knowledge about what Teresa's facial expression reveals to reach out beyond the standard interpretation of female orgasm. If a woman's sexual enjoyment is already less verifiable in a reliable body event than a man's orgasm, because it cannot be conflated with ejaculation, how is her non-sexual jouissance legible, with any degree of certainty, within a spatial framework that only allows access to visual inspection?[23]

Teasing out the intricacies of Lacan's argument in *Encore* is a hugely challenging task, for at least three reasons. Firstly, in his lectures Lacan elaborates on various principles and ideas first adduced during the two previous years' seminars—respectively entitled "*D'un discours qui ne serait pas du semblant*" (On a Discourse that Might not be made of Semblance) (Lacan, 2006b) and "... *ou pire*" (... or Worse) (Lacan, 2018[2011])—and in an essay called *L'étourdit* (Lacan, 2001[1972]), without making any concessions to the uninitiated.[24] *Encore* is very much part of a "work in progress", and as an extension of Lacan's earlier explorations on sexual difference it articulates new insights, without offering definitive truths. Secondly, in *Encore* Lacan combines a number of counter-intuitive formulae, such as "There is no such thing as a sexual relationship" (Lacan, 1998[1975], p. 9) and "Woman does not exist" (Lacan, 1998[1975], p. 7), in a highly abstract theoretical framework that also relies on logic, mathematics, and knot theory. Thirdly, Lacan's discourse in *Encore* is typically apophantic, elliptical and allusive. Apart from the fact that he tends to assert rather than argue, his statements are often vague and seemingly lacking in precision. In order to integrate Lacan's ideas into a consistent and coherent theory, readers are required to overcome ostensible contradictions, test alternative interpretations, approach well-known concepts from new angles, and relinquish their own acquired certainties and understanding for the sake of a new body of knowledge.

All of this applies *a fortiori* to Lacan's notion of jouissance, and the multiple guises under which it appears in *Encore*. Lacan is certain that Bernini's *Saint Teresa* experiences a particular form of jouissance, but how this jouissance should be understood is not at all certain, not even for Lacan himself, and its precise status remains a matter of debate, even amongst seasoned Lacan scholars.[25] What he recognized, without a trace of doubt, on Teresa's facial expression is a jouissance "beyond the phallus" (Lacan, 1998[1975], p. 74), a jouissance that is "supplementary" rather than "complementary" to the phallus (Ibid., p. 73), which is non-sexual, and which can also be designated as a "jouissance of the Other" (Ibid., p. 82). If the latter term already appears to contradict Lacan's claim from the early 1960s that the Other (the symbolic order, the structure of language) prohibits jouissance, and that the jouissance of the Other does not exist (Lacan, 2006[1960], pp. 696–700), it also contains a fundamental ambiguity in that it can be read as an objective or a subjective genitive. Who is experiencing the jouissance in this "jouissance of the Other"? Does the notion "jouissance of the Other" refer to a subject who is capable of deriving jouissance from the Other, because the Other constitutes an object of satisfaction in the subject's libidinal economy, or does it refer to a jouissance on the side of the Other, to the Other being a locus of jouissance in its own right? Or are both options intended? And how should the Other be understood, here? In sharp contract with his previous work, Lacan's notion of the Other in *Encore* is no longer synonymous with the symbolic order, but also seems to connote a range of "other" realities, such as the subject's physical body, the pure experience of being, and even God. To complicate matters further, in *Encore* Lacan did not distinguish between masculinity and femininity by reserving phallic jouissance to the former and jouissance of the Other to the latter, but by restricting masculinity to the realm (and the inherent failures) of phallic jouissance, and associating femininity with both phallic jouissance and jouissance of the Other. In terms of jouissance, femininity is indeed not the "complement" of masculinity, then, which is what would pave the way for the establishment of a harmonious sexual relationship between the two, but something that is "there [in masculinity] in full (*à plein*)", whilst also being "something more" (*en plus*) (Lacan, 1998[1975], p. 74). To the universal identity of a phallic masculinity, Lacan opposed the undecidable division of a femininity that is both phallic and "meta-phallic", whereby the latter form of jouissance constitutes a genuine alternative to the conventional, sexual or sexualized experience of jouissance.[26]

When he looked at Bernini's *Saint Teresa*, Lacan understood immediately that she was experiencing jouissance—not the ordinary phallic jouissance that is conditioned by the symbolic order, but an extra-ordinary jouissance of the Other, of which the mystics say "that they experience it, but know nothing about it" (Lacan, 1998[1975], p. 76). Apart from the fact that one may wonder how Lacan detected this particular jouissance in Teresa's facial expression—unless he discerned it, without saying so, in other features of the composition, such as the body's levitation, which would not necessarily solve the problem—there is a clear tension, here, between the certain ignorance that Lacan ascribes to a woman's jouissance of the Other, and the certain knowledge from which he himself operates when ascribing this ignorance. In the opening lesson of *Encore*, Lacan treated his audience to yet another counter-intuitive formula when he posited that the "superego is the imperative of jouissance" (Lacan, 1998[1975], p. 3).[27] Applying this axiom to his own position, Lacan's expression of certainty with regard to Teresa's jouissance, could therefore be regarded as his demanding jouissance from her, in an act that is not just egoistical but "superegoistical", which is exactly what stirred Irigaray's anger.[28] And the fact that the jouissance in question is allegedly not phallic, but "of the Other" only aggravates matters, because it takes away a woman's ability to counter the psychoanalyst's certainty with her own experiential knowledge. In knowing for sure that Bernini's *Saint Teresa* displays a type of jouissance of which she herself knows nothing, Lacan may thus be seen as invalidating in advance any counter-argument formulated by the one to whom the jouissance is attributed. Were Teresa to claim that she does know something about her jouissance, Lacan would argue that the jouissance in question is phallic rather than "from the Other", and so his own knowledge would remain intact. Were she to agree that she does not know anything about her jouissance, then this would "no doubt" be seen as proof of her jouissance of the Other, and so once again the knowledge of the psychoanalyst would be confirmed.

As I pointed out earlier, Lacan was clearly sure about the jouissance of the Other in Bernini's *Saint Teresa*, but he was not all that sure about how this jouissance of the Other should be understood. Reflecting upon the statue, he asked himself "*[D]e quoi jouit-elle?*", which Fink has rendered as "What is she getting off on?" (Lacan, 1998[1975], p. 76), and which raises the issue of how both the source and the object of the jouissance of the Other should be envisaged—the subject being unequivocally allocated, here, to the Saint herself. In a thought-provoking commentary on this question, Jacqueline Rose has stipulated that the answer may lie in the very act of transverberation (Lacan, 1982, p. 52, footnote 17). In this reading, Saint Teresa's jouissance would simply stem from her being "penetrated" by the angel's "great golden spear" (Ávila, 1957[1588], p. 210): she is getting off on the fact that her body is being pierced several times by a short, but very beautiful, male messenger of God. Looking at Bernini's statue, and reading the Saint's autobiography, Rose's answer to Lacan's question cannot but strike as self-evident, but Lacan did not give it a moment's consideration. The reason, I suspect, is that he categorically refused to accept that a woman's jouissance of the Other might be caused by a mere act of phallic penetration, which would not only contradict his claim that jouissance of the Other is firmly situated "beyond the phallus" (Lacan, 1998[1975], p. 74)—as something that is independent from it—but also undermine his thesis that it is "supplementary" to phallic jouissance, i.e. something that is neither the counterpart, nor the reciprocal correlate of phallic jouissance.

Suggestive of a perfectly balanced nuptial union as Bernini's composition of Saint Teresa and the angel may be, Lacan did not see in it the epitome of an ideal relationship, in this case between a devout woman and a divine agency. To Lacan, Saint Teresa definitely experiences jouissance of the Other, yet this is not because of God. Irrespective of what she stated in her autobiography and regardless of Bernini's representation of the transverberation, Lacan did not believe that Saint Teresa is "getting off" on God, at least not at the point of her jouissance of the Other. Lacan's reasoning, here, is that God himself cannot be dissociated from the symbolic order: "It is indubitable [*hors de doute*—again, a point of certainty] that the symbolic is the basis of what was made into God" (Lacan, 1998[1975], p. 83). If jouissance of the Other is effectively situated beyond the phallus, and therefore beyond the symbolic, then God cannot have anything to do with it.[29] The fact that Teresa herself explained her delightful pains with reference to an act of transverberation is nothing but a retroactive phallicization of her own mystical experience, both insofar as she is producing a symbolic account of it, and inasmuch as she is describing it as the effect of a divine intervention. For Lacan, phallic jouissance is sexual as much as it is symbolic, and it generates satisfaction at the level of speech and language (Lacan, 1998[1975], p. 64), as much as it may give subjects the impression that there is a sexual relationship after all. It may not be a coincidence, then, that Lacan insisted on his audience looking at Bernini's statue instead of their reading the Saint's autobiography. Precisely because the former does not speak, and does not require anyone to listen, but drives spectators into the (eroticized) position of a silent observer, something Other than phallic jouissance may be revealed.

Critics will no doubt reiterate at this point that Lacan's refusal to consider Saint Teresa's jouissance as being the outcome of a phallic act of divine transverberation does not make his alternative interpretation more palatable. For one could argue that Teresa's jouissance of the Other is the mere result of Lacan's own epistemo-phallic piercing, Lacan ignoring the smiling seraph with the great golden spear, because he himself is too busy smiling (or enjoying) when he sees how Teresa is surrendering her body and soul to his own ruthless penetration of her entrails with the blunt weapon of psychoanalytic knowledge. For some, Lacan's rhetorical strategy in *Encore* is "arrogant, manipulative, by turns seductive and pejorative" (Cook, 1999, p. 86), because under the guise of challenging phallocratic assumptions of femininity he continues to operate within his own phallic sphere of knowledge. Others, like Toril Moi, have argued that in situating femininity (or at least part thereof) outside the symbolic, Lacan continued to believe that the symbolic order, the organized language of reason, is exclusively masculine, thus relegating femininity not only to a place beyond the phallus, but also to a space of unreason (Moi, 2004, p. 864), from which they can only mutter unrecognizable words, at the risk of being perceived as possessed or mad. And this is exactly the fate that befell Saint Teresa, both under the watchful religious eyes of the Spanish Inquisition and under the diagnostic lenses of 19th-century medical doctors. The fact that for Lacan Teresa is the patron saint of femininity, rather than the patron saint of hysteria, does not make much of a difference, then, in terms of how the feminine body is inscribed, because the underlying symbolic logic remains driven by a phallic principle.

Liberating as it may seem for Lacan to select an exceptional female figure—humble in her beliefs, yet determined in her actions—as the emblematic representative of a typically feminine form of jouissance, Teresa's mystical devotion, her pious seclusion and her commitment to absolute poverty drives her femininity outside a socially sanctioned norm, which may at best be regarded as a celebration of Goethe's already deeply problematic "eternal feminine" and at worst as a devious strategy of exclusion, purely orchestrated for the perpetuation of masculine jouissance.[30] Bernini's *Saint Teresa* is again more ambiguous, here, than Teresa's own autobiography, because spectators are more likely to reinterpret the sculptural iconography of the Saint's mystical vision as a mystification, or to place the spectacle of her mysticism somewhere between the mythical and feminine mystique. However, Lacan's own re-interpretation of Bernini's interpretation would seem to reduce this ambiguity insofar as it takes its cue from an epistemic certainty about Teresa's jouissance of the Other. Be that as it may, whereas Bernini has been taken to task for profaning Teresa's sacred vision by endowing her with the facial expression of "earthly love", Lacan could thus be taken to task for re-sacralising Bernini's Saint Teresa by recognizing in the statue a uniquely feminine, transcendental experience of a-sexual jouissance beyond the phallus, from a perspective that is at least as phallic as the one adopted by the baroque sculptor. Although Bernini and Lacan would appear to have arrived at different conclusions about the precise nature of Teresa's physical and emotional pain, in their very act of definition they do not seem to have been able to escape a certain phallocentrism. The question as to how feminine jouissance should be defined accordingly shifts towards a question as to whom is entitled to define it, and from which position acceptable definitions may be formulated.

The Saint and the Sphinx

In the summer of 1972, Lacan was invited to contribute to the 50th-anniversary celebrations of the Henri-Rousselle Hospital—the first psychiatric outpatient clinic and the first "open" psychiatric institution in France—where he had completed his clinical training in psychiatry, and where for a number of years he had been conducting biweekly clinical presentations. For the first part of his intervention, Lacan chose to summarize and elaborate on the main lines of his seminar ... *ou pire* (Lacan, 2018[2011]), which had just come to an end, whereby he paid particular attention to how his logical formulae of "sexuation" simultaneously confirmed and extended Freud's conceptions of the Oedipus complex and castration anxiety.[31] At the end of this section, and before treating his audience to a bit of topology, Lacan summed up the result in a rhetorical tour-de-force:

> You've satisfied me, little man. You've understood, that's what was necessary. Go then, of the amasaid [*étourdit*] there is not too much out there, for it to return to you in the afternoon [*après-midit*], after all the half-truths have been said. By virtue of the hand that will respond to you, when you call it Antigone, the same that can devour you because I'm sphinxing my notall [*pastoute*], you might even know towards the evening how to make yourself the equal of Tiresias, and like him, in having played the part of the Other, divine what I have said to you. (Lacan, 2001[1972], p. 468)

Although it may not be immediately clear, Lacan was speaking here as an incarnation of the sphinx of Thebes, who is addressing a little man by the name of Oedipus who has just succeeded in abolishing her tyranny and liberating the city by giving the correct answer to her deadly riddle. After having said to Oedipus that she is satisfied, that he has satisfied her, she issues a stark warning: in the afternoon of your life, the truth of what you have just said in response to my riddle will come back to haunt you, because you will marry your mother, blind yourself when you realize that you have committed both incest and parricide, be forced into exile and spend the evening of your life wandering at the hand of your daughter Antigone, until you die in a small grove called Kolonos. On the one hand, the sphinx has to admit that a little man has broken her spell, and brought her to her knees, yet on the other hand she tells Oedipus that what he regards as his victory will also be his downfall, and that he will only start to see clearly after he has become blind, much like the prophet Tiresias—blinded by Hera for agreeing with Zeus, and notably from personal experience, that in matters of sex a woman has much more pleasure than a man. In this small allegory, Lacan imagined what the Sphinx would say to Oedipus after her enigma has been solved, and in the hour of her own death, yet he also surmised what a woman would say to a man who has just fathomed her mystery. And he implicitly wondered what response he would get from a woman—be it a sphinx or a saint—to his own, Oedipal *cum* phallic theory of feminine jouissance. In saying that my jouissance of the Other is supplementary to the phallus, you have satisfied me, Dr Lacan, so now go away and accept your terrible fate, which you won't be able to escape, and which will not resolve anything about feminine jouissance, until you gauge out your eyes and allow yourself to be guided by a woman's hand, without knowing exactly where she is leading you.[32]

In a brilliant introductory essay to a selection of texts by Lacan on feminine sexuality, Jacqueline Rose has argued that "Lacan was implicated in the phallocentrism he described, just as his own utterance constantly rejoins the mastery which he sought to undermine" (Rose, 1982, p. 56). And so, even when he articulated the Sphinx' words to little Oedipus, one could say that he continued to speak for her, putting his own masculine words into her mouth, in a self-serving, self-congratulatory rhetorical ploy. To his credit, Lacan seems to have been aware of this complication, because in the very first session of *Encore* he questioned his own relation to the knowledge his audience expected him to produce, simultaneously professing his profound ignorance, his desire not to know, and his intention to know more (Lacan, 1998[1975], p. 1). In addition, during the years following *Encore*, Lacan was at great pains to reinvent his own phallic symbolic order, both in an implicit attempt to tackle the criticism of phallogocentrism that had been leveled against him by Derrida and others, and in an effort to secure the transmission of psychoanalytic knowledge in a less fictional, more formalized, less metaphorical and more rigorous way. After having posited in *Encore* that "there is no such thing as a prediscursive reality", insofar as every "reality is founded and defined by discourse" (Lacan, 1998[1975], p. 32), Lacan did not simply reiterate that femininity can only be supposed and constructed as a meta-discursive reality within the boundaries of an inherently phallic discourse. Instead, he aspired to challenge the phallic principle of sexual difference, which makes femininity *de facto* synonymous with negativity and otherness, and which turns a woman by definition into the symptom of the one who is encumbered with this phallus (Lacan, 1982, p. 168). Contrary to what he had been advancing since the 1950s, Lacan now argued that the phallus is "what gives body to the Imaginary", and what endows the hole of the Symbolic with a dimension of imaginary consistency (Lacan, 1975b, p. 18). At the same time, he exchanged his former reliance on the Symbolic, as the function and field of speech and language, for a new allegiance to writing, mathematics, topology and knot theory—practices and disciplines that would come closer to the Real. During the 1970s, Lacan could be seen spending more and more time re-examining the connections between his three registers of the Symbolic, the Imaginary, and the Real, via the physical manipulation of the so-called Borromean knot. If the notion of the phallus did not disappear altogether from his intellectual radar, it was relegated to a secondary role, in favour of a "new signifier"—a signifier which does not make any sense whatsoever, or whose sense is at least balanced against other, non-semantic dimensions, and which opens up onto the Real (Lacan, 1977–1979[1976–1977], 17/18, p. 23).[33]

After his casual, yet controversial comment on Bernini's *Saint Teresa* in *Encore*, Lacan also revisited on various occasions his notion of the jouissance of the Other, emphasizing how it concerns an ek-sistence (*Ek-stasis*, a "standing beside" or "going out") of the Symbolic, within the Real and the Imaginary.[34] Saint Teresa's ecstasy would thus ek-sist somewhere on the intersection between her written account of the transverberation, without which it would not have been transmitted to her confessors (and to all of us) as a real event, and Bernini's sculptural exteriorization of it, without which the real event would not have been given a certain phallic imaginary consistency. In this respect, the ecstasy would be neither pre-discursive, nor meta-discursive, but indicative of an alternative discursivity, which stands outside speech and language, and which may therefore be more evocative than anything spoken words can articulate. It is a hypothesis every visitor to the Cornaro Chapel may wish to test, either by bringing a copy of Saint Teresa's autobiography, or by reading the passage from the book on one of the cards that have been placed in front of the central crucifix on the altar. Bringing a copy of Lacan's seminar *Encore* is optional.

Notes

1 The essay on which this chapter is based appeared previously in *The Comparatist*, 2015, 39(1), pp. 22–46. Materials from this earlier version are reproduced here with the permission of Zahi Zalloua.
2 On the cost of the chapel, see Barcham (1993) and Napoleone (1998). In order to appreciate the sum of the commission, one should take account of the fact that, according to Spear, a "family of five in Rome around 1600 could live modestly on 90 *scudi* a year" (Spear, 2003, p. 312). The church of *Santa Maria della Vittoria* was originally built by friars of the Discalced Carmelites, a mendicant religious order founded by Teresa of Ávila and John of the Cross. Hence, merely by virtue of its location Cornaro's sepulchral chapel was already a tribute to his favourite Saint. On the life and times of Cornaro, see Barcham (2001).

3 In his biography of Bernini, Franco Mormando quotes one of the Roman news bulletins (*avvisi*) of the time as saying that "the Cavalier Bernini received and continues to receive a universally favorable response and great applause for the extraordinary perfection, beauty and originality of both the statue and the chapel" (Mormando, 2011, p. 159).
4 The manuscript is in the Vatican Library. For excerpts of it, see Previtali (1962).
5 The most detailed pathography of Teresa as a hysteric was published in 1883 by Guillaume Hahn SJ, a Belgian Jesuit *cum* professor of physiology at the University of Louvain, who drew extensively on Charcot's theories. In 1882, the manuscript of Hahn's book had won a prize in Salamanca, on the occasion of the 300th anniversary of Saint Teresa's death. See Hahn (1883) and Weiser (2019).
6 On the link between the surrealist look and Baroque forms of representation, see Caws (1999).
7 This is my own literal transcription of what Lacan said on 20 February 1973. A recording of the session can be found at http://www.valas.fr/IMG/mp3/07-encore-73-02-20.mp3. When Lacan's Seminar was officially published in January 1975, the sentences were edited by Jacques-Alain Miller, as approved by Lacan himself, with some minor modifications to the original: "*Pour la Hadewijch en question, c'est comme pour Sainte Thérèse—vous n'avez qu'à aller regarder à Rome la statue du Bernin pour comprendre tout de suite qu'elle jouit, ça ne fait pas de doute. Et de quoi jouit-elle? Il est clair que le témoignage essentiel des mystiques, c'est justement de dire qu'ils l'éprouvent, mais qu'ils n'en savent rien*" (Lacan, 1975a, pp. 70–71). For reasons that will become clear later on, I shall not provide an English translation at this point. In the published version of Lacan's Seminar, the session of 20 February appears as the sixth rather than the seventh of the series, because the second session, which included a lengthy presentation by François Recanati, is considered a complement to the first session, and thus not listed separately. It is also worth noting that Lacan's comment on Bernini's *Saint Teresa* was reproduced on the back cover—the so-called *quatrième de couverture*—of the French volume, and that a reproduction of the statue adorned the front cover, so that Lacan's entire Seminar was literally held together by Bernini's *Saint Teresa*.
8 Irigaray's paper "Così Fan Tutti" was first published in French in October 1976, in an edited volume on *La jouissance et la loi* (Irigaray, 1976). It was reprinted in 1977 in her *Ce sexe qui n'en est pas un* (Irigaray, 1977[1976]), and subsequently included in the English translation of this book, which was published in 1985 (Irigaray, 1985[1976]). The title of the essay evidently alluded to Mozart's opera *Così Fan Tutte* (Thus do all women), but in writing *Tutti*, Irigaray suggested that "All men are the same", and that Lacan was no different from all the others.
9 The passage occurs at the end of Chapter 29 of Teresa's autobiography: "Beside me, on the left hand, appeared an angel in bodily form ... He was not tall, but short, and very beautiful; and his face was so aflame that he appeared to be one of the highest rank of angels, who seem to be all on fire ... In his hands I saw a great golden spear [*un dardo de oro largo*], and at the iron tip there appeared to be a point of fire [*un poco de fuego*]. This he plunged into my heart several times so that it penetrated to my entrails. When he pulled it out, I felt that he took them with it, and left me utterly consumed by the great love of God. The pain was so severe that it made me utter several moans [*aquellos quejidos*]. The sweetness caused by this intense pain is so extreme that one cannot possibly wish it to cease, nor is one's soul then content with anything but God. This is not a physical, but a spiritual pain, though the body has some share in it—even a considerable share.

So gentle is this wooing [*requiebro*] which takes place between God and the soul that if anyone thinks I am lying, I pray God, in His Goodness, to grant him some experience of it" (Ávila, 1957[1588]), p. 210). This vision became known as Teresa's "transverberation", i.e., her "striking through", and it would prove crucial for her canonization (see Slade, 1995, pp. 127–132). There is no evidence that Cornaro instructed Bernini to focus on this particular episode of Teresa's life when executing his commission. In all likelihood, it was a source of inspiration for the artist because in the era's cultural imagination this was the vision most commonly associated with the life of Saint Teresa. In addition, Mormando has stipulated that if Bernini did not read the passage in Teresa's autobiography, he could have relied on one of the numerous Italian retellings of the vision (Mormando, 2011, p. 162). For an excellent study of Teresa's autobiography, which is commonly referred to as the *Vida*, see Eire (2019).

10 In *Lacan in Contexts*, David Macey makes a similar point when he states that Lacan reduced Saint Teresa to "the silent object of a male gaze", but he goes on to extend the argument to Lacan's theory of femininity in general, which he deems to be fundamentally driven by a scopic economy of women as *to-be-looked-at-ness* (Macey, 1988, pp. 200–207).

11 Representations of the transverberation pre-dating Teresa's canonization include engravings by Karel van Mallery (1609), Adriaen Collaert and Cornelis Galle (1613), and Anton Wierix (1614), as well as an altarpiece by Peter Paul Rubens (1614), and a painting by Palma il Giovane (1615). All of these depict the scene in a resolutely earnest manner. After the canonization, Italian artists such as Bernardo Strozzi and Giulio Cesare Procaccini painted a much more ecstatic Saint, whereas Spanish and Latin American artists continued to prefer the solemn image. See, for example, Wilson (1999).

12 In 1948, Princess Marie Bonaparte—a prominent psychoanalyst of the *Société Psychanalytique de Paris*, whose membership also included Lacan—published an extended paper on the essential ambivalence of Eros, in which she designated Teresa's delightful physical and emotional pain as a "violent venereal orgasm" (Bonaparte, 1948, p. 193). One year later, Simone de Beauvoir posited in *The Second Sex*: "St Theresa's writings hardly leave room for doubt, and they justify Bernini's statue, which shows us the saint swooning in an excess of supreme voluptuousness" (de Beauvoir, 1997[1949], p. 682). Less crudely than Bonaparte, she went on to argue that Teresa's description of her mystical experience clearly shows how it is a mere continuation of an embodied eroticism, without implying, therefore, that the former can be reduced to the latter. See also Hollywood (2002, pp. 120–145).

13 That Bernini clearly intended it to be this way is evidenced by the fact that he constructed a theatre box on each side of the proscenium (see Figure 4.1), in which members of the Cornaro family seem to be leafing through a programme, or heavily debating matters that have no doubt been sparked by the spectacle on the stage, despite the fact that it seems to be taking place beyond their sightlines.

14 Teresa's writings were never made publicly available during her lifetime, and even after they were published, in 1588, high-ranking members of the Spanish Inquisition still campaigned for the books to be banned, because they regarded them as emblematic of the nun's demonic, erotic possession. See Weber (1990, pp. 159–165).

15 Without focusing on Teresa's facial expression, Mormando has pointed out that Bernini took one major liberty when interpreting Teresa's vision. Whereas Teresa was in her mid-forties when she experienced the transverberation, and her body

would have already suffered tremendously from various physical ailments as well as from self-inflicted mortifications of the flesh, in Bernini's sculpture the nun has been transformed into a young, attractive, sensuous and glamorously dressed woman—a transformation which Mormando unashamedly interprets as a manifestation of Bernini's strong libido ... (Mormando, 2011, pp. 164–165).

16 Those who maintain that Ludovica Albertoni is dying include Hibbard (1965, pp. 220–227), Perlove (1990, p. 44), and Boucher (1998, pp. 142–143). For those who claim she is in ecstasy, see Avery (2006, p. 152) and Petersson (2002, p. 40). For a more nuanced interpretation, see Careri (1995, pp. 51–86).

17 During his first public seminar at Sainte-Anne Hospital, Lacan averred: "To interpret and to imagine one understands are not at all the same things. It is precisely the opposite. I would go as far as to say that it is on the basis of a kind of refusal of understanding that we push open the door to analytic understanding" (Lacan, 1988[1975], p. 73). Two years later, he repeated the point in an undisguised warning to trainee psychoanalysts: "It's always at the point where they [students, trainees] have understood, where they have rushed in to fill the case in with understanding, that they have missed the interpretation that it's appropriate to make or not to make" (Lacan, 1993[1981], p. 22).

18 For a trenchant critique of Heath's argument, whereby it is demonstrated how he himself becomes implicated in the epistemic certainty he is trying to discredit, see Gallop (1982, pp. 43–55).

19 See http://www.lacaninireland.com/web/wp-content/uploads/2010/06/Book-20-Encore.pdf.

20 Before the complete version of Lacan's seminar was officially released in English, a selection of texts by Lacan on feminine sexuality, including two sessions from *Encore*, was translated by Jacqueline Rose. In this volume too, Lacan's comment on Bernini's *Saint Teresa* is rendered in the informal way as "[S]he's coming, there is no doubt about it". See Lacan (1982, p. 147).

21 On the untranslatability of jouissance, see Cassin (2014, pp. 794–796). On the notion's semantic spectrum in French, see Van Reeth and Nancy (2014, pp. 47–65).

22 I agree with Toril Moi that in leaving the term untranslated we endow it with "the mystery of the exotic and the unknown" (Moi, 2004, p. 860), but if this is what Lacan intended, then it would only apply to the jouissance that resists signification because it operates outside the symbolic, beyond the phallus—precisely, the type of jouissance that he considered to be the prerogative of femininity—since in Lacan's view phallic jouissance is not all that mysterious.

23 For a fascinating analysis of the artistic and scientific visualizations of female orgasm, which takes its lead from Lacan's interpretation of Bernini's *Saint Teresa*, see Jagose (2013, pp. 135–174).

24 *L'étourdit* is just about the most hermetic essay in an oeuvre that is not exactly known for the clarity of its exposition. As of June 2021, the seminar *D'un discours qui ne serait pas du semblant* is not yet available in an official English translation.

25 Interpretations of Lacan's discussion of jouissance in *Encore* abound, especially in French, yet there is a wide divergence of opinion as to how the various modalities of jouissance that Lacan distinguishes there relate to each other, and how they may be integrated into a sound theoretical structure. See, for example, André (1985; 1999[1986]), Boussidan (2009), Chiesa (2014), Fink (2002), and Miller (2000; 2011). In addition, there is as yet no comprehensive study of Lacan's *Encore* seminar in English.

26 Lacan was adamant that the non-universal logic of feminine jouissance, which supplements the universal logic of masculine jouissance, should not be

re-interpreted as two opposing existential possibilities, as in "sóme are (phallic)" and "some are not (phallic)", but should be conceived instead as a proper undecidability, which follows the modal logic of contingency. See Lacan (2018[2011], pp. 183–186) and Miller (1994).
27 The formula is counterintuitive, because the Freudian super-ego, as the inheritor of the Oedipus complex, is traditionally regarded as the mental guardian of law and order, the seat of conscience and morality, and the relentless issuer of restrictions and prohibitions. Lacan's alternative perspective is derived from Saint Paul's epistle to the Romans: "(7) What shall we say then? *Is* the law sin? God forbid. Nay, I had not known sin, but by the law: for I had not known lust, except the law had said, Thou shalt not covet. (8) But sin, taking occasion by the commandment, wrought in me all manner of concupiscence. For without the law sin *was* dead. (9) For I was alive without the law once: but when the commandment came, sin revived, and I died. (10) And the commandment, which *was ordained* to life, I found *to be* onto death. (11) For sin, taking occasion by the commandment, deceived me, and by it slew *me*. (12) Wherefore the law *is* holy, and the commandment holy, and just, and good. (13) Was then that which is good made death unto me? God forbid. But sin, that it might appear sin, working death in me by that which is good; that sin by the commandment might become exceedingly sinful" (Paul the Apostle, 7: 7–13). In his 1959–1960 seminar *The Ethics of Psychoanalysis*, Lacan argued that it is only by virtue of the law (and, by extension, the superego) that sin acquires "an excessive, hyperbolic character". See Lacan (1992[1986], p. 84). He repeated the point in "Kant with Sade", where he wrote that the presence of the law makes sin "inordinately sinful". See Lacan (2006[1962], p. 667).
28 For a further development of this point, see Hayes (1999, pp. 332–333).
29 This has not stopped some scholars from arguing that the source of Teresa's jouissance is to be situated in an authentic religious experience, similar to the mystico-eroticism of the Tantric world. See Kripal (1995, p. 326) and Parsons (2003).
30 In an idiosyncratic reading of Lacan's notion of feminine jouissance, Žižek has argued that there is nothing mystical at all about the jouissance of the Other, because it is complicit with the feminine phallic jouissance, insofar as the former is "constitutive of the feminine seductive masquerade [for the man]: the way woman seduces and transfixes the male gaze is precisely by adopting the role of the Enigma embodied, as if her whole appearance is a lure, a veil concealing some unspeakable secret" (Žižek, 1999, p. 214). Rather than seeing the feminine jouissance of the Other from the angle of the masculine figure, Žižek attempts to understand it, here, from the perspective of femininity, yet he nonetheless draws the conclusion that it is being staged for the male gaze. According to Žižek, the only way a woman would be able to undermine the phallic economy is by relinquishing her position beyond the phallus, by declaring that there is no great secret Beyond, and by unconditionally surrendering herself to male jouissance ... (Ibid., p. 214). For a more detailed exploration of Žižek's argument, see Depoortere (2005).
31 No doubt because *Encore* was published without a contextualizing, critical apparatus, it is commonly held that the formulae of sexuation constitute one of *Encore*'s innovations, yet it should be emphasized that Lacan had already introduced these formulae two years earlier, and that in *Encore* he merely synthesized a long and laborious process of exposition.
32 For an alternative reading of this passage from *L'étourdit*, see Laurent (2011).

33 For an in-depth exploration of this "new signifier", see Chapter 7 of this book.
34 Saint Teresa herself defined *ekstasis* as a "period [that] is always short and seems to the soul even shorter than it really is", but when the soul eventually "returns to itself" it is unable to "doubt that God has been in it and it has been in God". See Ávila (1961[1588], p. 101). For an extensive discussion of Teresa's description, see Anderson (2006, pp. 341–344).

Chapter 5

Esprit de Corps, Work Transference, and Dissolution: Lacan as an Organizational Theorist

Introduction

Forty years after his death, Lacan's work remains clinically disputed yet theoretically vindicated. In times of evidence-based treatment plans, health economics, cost-effectiveness evaluations, and the ubiquitous neoliberal rationality of market competition, the clinical practice of Lacanian psychoanalysis is very much on a life-support machine in institutional mental healthcare settings, especially in the Anglophone world.[1] In addition, most clinical psychology and psychotherapy training programmes have relegated it to the dustbin of cultural history as a pseudo-scientific paradigm. By contrast, Lacan's theories have gone from strength to strength in academic departments of literature, cultural studies, modern languages, linguistics and rhetoric, media and communication studies, women's and gender studies, philosophy, and film theory. The versatile applicability of his concepts as solid tools for critical analysis is also demonstrated in the widest range of disciplines outside the traditional human and social sciences, and seems to gain more and more momentum on a daily basis, with architects, legal scholars, criminologists, educational scientists, theologians, and classicists now also engaging with his work (see e.g., Beattie, 2013; Caudill, 1997; Cho, 2009; Hendrix, 2006; jagodzinski, 2005; Miller, 2007a, 2007b; Milovanovic, 2003).

Since the late 1990s, Lacan's notions have also started to gain momentum in organization research, critical management theory, business studies, and public administration scholarship, on both sides of the Atlantic. Many of the new Lacanians in these fields have demonstrated how key Lacanian concepts such as the mirror stage, the divided subject, the object *a*, desire, jouissance, fantasy, and discourse can be used productively in order to understand, *inter alia*, how organizations function and become dysfunctional (see, for instance, Arnaud, 2002), how individuals operating within organizations maintain their professional identities and develop certain types of working relationships with their colleagues (Arnaud and Vanheule, 2007; Driver, 2009b, 2009c; Harding, 2007; Kosmala and Herrbach, 2006), how authentic leadership is established (Costas and Taheri, 2012), how work-related problems such as envy, stress, and burnout may be addressed (Bicknell and Liefooghe, 2010; Driver, 2014; Vanheule, Lievrouw and Verhaeghe, 2003; Vanheule and Verhaeghe, 2004; Vidaillet, 2007), how strategic and operational change management may be facilitated (Driver, 2009a; Kenny, 2009), how practices of human resource management affect individuals at work (Johnsen and Gudmand-Høyer, 2010), how executive coaching and consulting can be tailored to subjective as well as collective needs (Arnaud, 2003b), how entrepreneurship discourse is predicated upon the assumption of certain "work identities" (Jones and Spicer, 2005), how staff representatives react to the threat of factory closure (Vidaillet and Gamot, 2015), and how organizational processes are conditioned by broader socio-political and economic configurations (Bloom and Cederström, 2009; Fotaki, 2009; Glynos, 2011; Stavrakakis, 2008). If Lacan has not fully arrived yet in organization and critical management studies, then he is definitely making serious headway as a theoretical force to be reckoned with.

Why did it take so much longer for Lacan to be conceptually assimilated in organization studies compared to other disciplines? It is a question that quite a few scholars working in this area have asked themselves, and to which a number of tentative answers have been formulated. In their editorial introduction to a special issue of the journal *Organization*, Contu, Driver, and Jones surmised that "it may have something to do with the maturing of organization studies or equally something to do with the complexity of Lacan's work that repelled early efforts at boarding" (Contu, Driver and Jones, 2010, p. 310). As a non-specialist in the field, I cannot comment on the extent to which organization studies have indeed "matured" over the years, whatever that may mean, unless one would see the "Lacanianisation" of organization studies in itself as a clear sign of its coming of age. As to the hermetic complexity of Lacan's work, this is, of course, legendary and it has frustrated and infuriated many curious scholars, often dampening their initial enthusiasm and steering their projects in alternative directions. Yet Lacan's ostensible inscrutability has not prevented a plethora of people working in the arts and humanities from engaging with his work, and organizational research itself has regularly drawn upon other notoriously abstruse French theorists, such as Foucault, Deleuze, Guattari, Derrida, Lyotard, and Baudrillard (see e.g., Burrell, 1988; Carter and Jackson, 2004; Cooper, 1989; Letiche, 2004; Letiche and Essers, 2004; Linstead and Thanem, 2007). In their introduction to a volume of papers presented at the first international "Lacan at Work" conference, Cederström and Hoedemaekers stated their own reasons for Lacan's slow and delayed reception in organization studies:

> [W]hile organization studies include a broad register of phenomena, the main concern is with the study of organizations; and as far as we know,

there's not a single statement in Lacan's work directly addressing organizations or the life within the walls of the corporation. Lacan had many interests—from wigs and cars, to art and antique books—but the study of organizations was simply not one of them. Second, organization studies have traditionally been occupied by questions of performance, control and how corporations can be made more efficient, effective and profitable. Such a starting point seems particularly incongruent with Lacanian theory.

(Cederström and Hoedemaekers, 2010, p. xiv)

The second reason, here, cannot but persuade anyone vaguely familiar with the development and critical focus of Lacan's thought. The trials and tribulations of the corporate sector simply do not appear on his intellectual radar. Performance and productivity, although they could be adduced as accurate translations of Freud's notion of *Leistungsfähigkeit*, which occasionally crops up in his writings as a possible goal for the psychoanalytic treatment (see, for example, Breuer and Freud, 1955[1895d], p. 261), definitely do not feature highly on Lacan's agenda. Critical voices may also point out that when, during the 1970s, Lacan unashamedly started to adopt the "short-session treatment", which would have earned him an estimated monthly income of almost half-a-million French francs (Roudinesco, 1997[1993], p. 397), he was clearly interested in turning his psychoanalytic practice into a profitable business enterprise.[2] Yet it is fair to say that whenever he broached the issues of production and profit, such as in his seminars of 1968–1969 (Lacan, 2006a) and 1969–1970 (Lacan, 2007[1991]), it was not with a view to devising solid (psychoanalytic) strategies for building the economy, boosting company turnover, increasing profit margins and accumulating capital, but rather to expose the social and subjective fallacies of these very principles. If we restrict "organizational culture", then, to the classic structure of the corporate enterprise operating under economic conditions of high capitalism, Lacan indeed emerges as the anti-organizational psychoanalytic theorist par excellence, or the psychoanalyst who did not care at all about what was going on in that segment of society.

Nonetheless, I do not believe that this in itself explains why organizational theorists have been rather reluctant in adopting his work. Other 20th-century psychoanalysts, such as Elliott Jaques, Eric Trist, Isabel Menzies Lyth, and quite a few researchers affiliated with the Tavistock Institute of Human Relations, have been critical of the instrumental rationality principle pervading traditional corporate management structures and conventional practices of organizational development, without therefore being ignored or dismissed by organizational theorists.[3] Organization studies have not always been geared to finding ways to increase performance, efficiency, and effectiveness in the corporate sector and the profit-making industries. It would be wrong to think that organization studies have always uncritically embraced the principle of the *homo oeconomicus*, and have always stood in the service of traditional business values, as the academic lodestar of liberal enterprise.

As an anti-humanist and a fierce critic of the adaptation paradigm in ego-psychology and related psychoanalytic models, Lacan was profoundly weary of any developmental, corrective, and accumulative perspective on mental health, and of any clinical and theoretical outlook that regards the restoration of a patient's psychic economy and its return to a well-integrated state of stable equilibrium as a realistic aspiration (see, for instance, Lacan, 1988[1975], p. 25; 2006[1953], p. 204; Van Haute, 2002[2000]). By extension, Lacan was extremely sceptical of any social system that inscribes progress and growth as the most advanced accomplishments into its discourse, because he did not believe that the outcomes (goods and services) of a production cycle can be fully recuperated into the regulatory frameworks, the economic structures and the organizational mechanisms that condition and support the process (Lacan, 2006a, pp. 15–19). Lacan's is not a theory of gains, benefits, acquisitions, yields, returns, dividends, and credits, but a theory of lack, loss, waste, remainders, deficits, debits, costs, and perditions. Whenever Lacan considered the possibility of gains and benefits—at a subjective rather than a social level, psychically yet also economically—it was always to emphasize that these returns are intrinsically flawed, essentially incomplete, and fundamentally dissatisfying. The most poignant example of this can be found in his conceptualization of the so-called object *a*, the object of desire, which he designated not as the object which satisfies desire, but as the object which causes desire (on account of it being a substitute and therefore intrinsically lacking object), and as the object which simultaneously generates more and less satisfaction (jouissance) (Lacan, 2014[2004], p. 101; 2006[1962], p. 654).[4] Hence, it is correct that efficiency, effectiveness, and economy—the hackneyed axioms of sustainable productivity and high-quality service delivery in a neo-liberal organizational culture—are anathema to how Lacan interpreted the force field of mental processes and the dynamics of the social bond. Yet contrary to what Cederström and Hoedemaekers claim in the aforementioned passage, Lacan did consider how the "anti-organizational" forms of lack, loss and waste could be built into the walls of an alternative organization, how organizational life could be re-built, as it were, upon the foundations of incompleteness, as a non-totalizing entity in which hierarchical authority is balanced against a communal, libertarian, and solidaristic culture of exchange.

In this chapter, I endeavour to show that it is a mistake to think that Lacan was not interested in organizations, and that this is one of the reasons, perhaps the most important reason, why organizational theory has been slow in engaging with his ideas. If anything, I shall venture the exact opposite claim to Cederström and Hoedemaekers, notably that many organizational theorists may have found his work rather difficult to digest, precisely because Lacan had a lifelong intellectual and personal interest in organizations, and invented a number of radical, proto-anarchist arrangements for running an organization. The major corollary of this thesis is that a genuine appreciation of Lacan's contributions within the field of organization studies should not proceed from a demonstration of the critical applicability of one or the other of his concepts to the various aspects of organizational life, but should effectively start with a detailed analysis of the organizational theory that is already present and operative within Lacan's own work, and which resonates with the clinical and theoretical psychoanalytic project he pursued over a period of 40 odd years.

Esprit de Corps

In the late summer of 1945, Lacan spent five weeks in England, during which period he visited Hatfield House in Hertfordshire, which at the time accommodated a specialized centre for the rehabilitation of former prisoners-of-war and veterans who had been based overseas. Still a psychiatrist, yet also already a psychoanalyst, Lacan was far from endorsing and promoting psychiatric interventions, but what he saw at Hatfield—the complete liberty with which the patients were allowed to move around, the absolute freedom given to them as to how they wished to spend their time, the non-hierarchical seating arrangements between officers and residents in the shared dining facilities, the group therapy sessions inspired by the psychodrama-technique of Jacob Moreno, the diverse therapeutic programme of open workshops and discussion groups, and the organized visits to local factories—made a huge impression on him, so much so that upon his return to Paris he showered heaps of praise on this quintessentially English version of "democratic psychiatry". "To evaluate the importance of the work", Lacan declared to an audience of both French and British psychiatrists at the professional group of *L'évolution psychiatrique*,

> suffice it to say that 80% of the men [...] choose freely to go through this gradual reintegration process [*éclusage*] where their stay is on average six weeks, but which can be shortened or prolonged upon their demand [...] Thus, psychiatry served to forge the instrument thanks to which Britain won the war; conversely, the war has transformed psychiatry in Britain. (Lacan, 2019[1947], p. 45)[5]

Even more instructive than his visit to Hatfield was Lacan's long conversation with Wilfred R. Bion and John Rickman—"two men", he said, "of whom it can be said that the flame of creation burns in them" (*Ibid.*, p. 24). During the winter of 1942–1943, Bion had been put in charge of the rehabilitation of demoralized soldiers in the so-called "Training Wing" of the Northfield Military Hospital, near Birmingham (Harrison, 2000, p. 186). Rather than reinforcing the Wing's iron army discipline, and actively preparing the soldiers for their swift return to military service, which had often seemed to result in an exacerbation of their neurotic symptoms, Bion decided to let the collective neurosis reign, deliberately refusing to intervene when things would get out of hand. Remarkably, within a period of a mere couple of weeks, the Wing's atmosphere changed to the point where the men would start to take responsibility for organizing their own chaos. Instead of complaining, they would start to re-focus their energies on the accomplishment of specific group tasks and the management of inter-personal relationships. Rather than treating the soldiers' neurotic conditions as individual illnesses, Bion decided to turn neurosis itself into the collective enemy, thus recreating a positive *esprit de corps* (characterized by shared loyalty, solidarity, fellowship, and an implicit sense of duty) amongst the patients, by establishing within their ranks a mutual, common understanding of the destructive forces that threatened their co-existence. To realize this goal, and to turn the patients into "self-respecting men socially adjusted to the community and therefore willing to accept its responsibilities" (Bion and Rickman, 1961[1943], p. 13), Bion decided to act the part of an experienced officer who "knows some of his own failings, respects the integrity of his men, and is not afraid of either their goodwill or their hostility" (*Ibid.*, p. 13). In doing so, he imposed a concise set of simple rules, which involved (among other things) each man having to become part of one or more small groups with a particular educational, occupational or operational goal, whereby the men would remain entirely free to choose which group(s) they wanted to join, and would also be at liberty to set up their own group if their preferential activity was not already served by an existing group or if, for whatever reason, they were unable to join their preferred group (*Ibid.*, p. 16). Probably alerted by suspicious colleagues in the hospital section of the clinic, some officials from the War Office paid a surprise visit to the wing one night, and found the place in a state of total disarray. Without hesitation, they decided that the "experiment" had to be terminated, and that the two maverick doctors should be "relieved" from their duties (de Maré, 1985, p. 110; Harrison, 2000, p. 191; King, 2003, p. 41; Shephard, 2000, p. 260).

Lacan thought that this so-called "first Northfield experiment" was absolutely brilliant. Speaking to *L'évolution psychiatrique*, he stated: "[T]he lively details of this experience […] seem to me to be pregnant with a birth of sorts that is a new outlook opening upon the world" (Lacan, 2019[1947], p. 32). But he did not stop there. Apart from complimenting the way in which English psychiatrists had succeeded in tackling the problem of war neurosis in new and imaginative ways, Lacan also applauded the English take on recruiting army officers, especially Bion's so-called "leaderless group project", which had been conducted some years before the first Northfield experiment, under the auspices of the War Office Selection Boards. Some ten candidates eligible for being recruited to an officer's rank were placed in a group, without any specific indication as to its concrete organization or designated leadership. The group was then given a specific real-life challenge, which would only be achievable if the men found a way of channelling their individual energies towards the collaborative performance that was required for the completion of the set task. As Bion put it, during the experiment "it was the duty of the observing officers to watch how any given man was reconciling his personal ambitions, hopes and fears with the requirements exacted by the group for its success" (Bion, 1946, p. 78). Neither the observing officers, nor the advising psychiatrists, nor Bion himself for that matter, were acting upon a position of authoritative leadership, but rather "suspended" their leadership in favour of releasing the group's own internal dynamics, thus also questioning its propensity to expect shotgun solutions to be delivered by identified leaders. Reflecting upon the experiments and justifying the idea of "suspended leadership", Bion later commented: "The group always make it clear that they expect me to act with authority as the leader of the group, and this responsibility I accept, though not in the way the group expect" (Bion, 1961[1948–1951], p. 82). In his subsequent work with groups, Bion would consistently refuse to adopt a directive stance, instead allowing the group to evolve spontaneously and to follow its own internal laws, and only intervening when he believed he knew what was about to happen, which often left people in the group feeling puzzled and bemused.

Lacan strongly commended how English psychiatrists had made a major contribution to the war effort, but he was even more appreciative of the "democratic" principles supporting Bion's innovative recruitment device. First, rather than someone in an established position of authority recruiting and selecting the new officers, candidates are being given the opportunity to demonstrate *in vivo* what they are worth, and therefore to somehow self-select, in a situation of strict "fair play". Second, although the officers and psychiatrists assess individual contributions to the group task, they themselves only testify about what they have observed to a selection panel, so that theirs is only one voice among many, and the final decision is to a large extent based on what is conveyed in a "witness statement". Third, the objectivity and validity of the entire process are not driven by the controlled administration of psychometric tests or the use of conventional quantitative measures of physical and mental capacity, but rather by the careful elicitation and rigorous evaluation of strictly subjective phenomena (Lacan, 2019[1947], pp. 35–40). It is these very principles that Lacan would endeavour to situate at the heart of the psychoanalytic training programme in the *École freudienne de Paris* (EFP), the organization he founded in June 1964, some eight months after his exclusion from the International Psycho-Analytic Association (IPA).

Work Transference

Neither in his written texts, nor in any of his seminars did Lacan explicitly refer to Bion's work again, yet his most important contribution to organizational theory, namely his own foundation of the EFP and the fundamental pillars upon which it was built, was clearly inspired by Bion's experiments with leaderless groups and at Northfield. It should be mentioned, in this context, that up until the point when the EFP was established, Lacan had had a fair share of trouble with psychoanalytic institutions, not in the least with the IPA, from which he was definitively barred as a training analyst in November 1963 (Miller, 1977; Turquet, 2014). And so the organizational structure of the EFP may have looked very differently had the institutions to which Lacan belonged during the late 1940s and 1950s been more hospitable to his idiosyncratic views on the theory and practice of psychoanalysis. In other words, Lacan's own perspective on what makes a (psychoanalytic) organization up to the task of fulfilling its function may not have materialized if he, on a personal and professional level, had not felt the crushing weight of traditional institutional power. The key events are worth recapitulating, here, if only because they once again illustrate that, contrary to what some scholars have claimed, Lacan had a lifelong interest in organizations, clearly positioned himself vis-à-vis a certain type of organizational culture, and typically argued in favour of an organizational structure that is commensurate with the nature of the task to be accomplished.

In 1934, whilst still in analytic training, Lacan joined the *Société Psychanalytique de Paris* (SPP), then the only psychoanalytic organization in France, and rapidly made his way through its ranks, becoming a full member in 1938 (Roudinesco, 1997[1993], pp. 80, 86). When, after the Second World War, the SPP resumed its activities, Lacan became a member of the SPP's "Teaching Committee", and in this capacity he produced a paper outlining the procedures for the selection of new trainees, as well as the indicative contents of a psychoanalytic training programme, and the mechanisms for "recognizing" (appointing, endorsing) new psychoanalysts (Lacan, 1976[1949]). The document was fairly mainstream, apart from the fact that Lacan did not *de facto* wish to exclude non-medically trained candidates from the psychoanalytic profession, and that he also proposed a certain de-centralization of power, allowing more members to participate in decision-making processes pertaining to candidate-selection and the delivery of teaching. Then, during the Winter of 1952–1953, an acrimonious conflict erupted between Lacan and Sacha Nacht, the then president of the SPP, around the organizational structure of a proposed psychoanalytic training institute, whereby Lacan's main reservations concerned the seemingly unassailable power of the institute's directorate and the autocratic "examination" of the candidates' training by a sovereign group of self-appointed "officials". In the end, Lacan lost out and was forced to resign from the SPP, by which he also forfeited his membership of the IPA (Miller, 1976, p. 90).[6]

After the first split in the French psychoanalytic community, Lacan spent ten years delivering his weekly seminar at Sainte-Anne Hospital, as part of the analytic training programme of the newly created *Société Française de Psychanalyse* (SFP), whilst practicing as a psychoanalyst, entertaining people at his summer house in Guitrancourt, and generally having fun. At the SFP, he did not occupy any important administrative or managerial positions, yet generally supported the new organization's request to be considered for re-admission to the IPA (Etchegoyen and Miller, 1996, p. 48). However, throughout this period, Lacan also fired on all cylinders when considering the psychoanalytic establishment's practices and procedures, whereby he did not let an opportunity go by to ridicule the institutional hierarchy and its rigid, dogmatic attitudes towards analytic practice and training standards. Already in the 1953 "Rome Discourse", he suggested that the SPP's Training Institute was erected on the basis of a "disappointing formalism that discourages initiative by penalizing risk, and turns the reign of the opinion of the learned into a principle of docile prudence in which the authenticity of research is blunted even before it finally dries up" (Lacan, 2006[1953], p. 199). With undisguised sarcasm, he went on to compare the institute's conception of analytic training to "that of a driving school which, not content to claim the privilege of issuing drivers' licenses, also imagines that it is in a position to supervise car construction" (*Ibid.*, p. 200).

Lacan's finest moment came in 1956, in a paper published on the occasion of the centenary of Freud's birth. Dissecting the so-called "situation" of psychoanalysis and the contemporary condition of psychoanalytic training programmes, he painted a hilarious, satirical picture of the spurious distribution of power in the psychoanalytic establishment, in the great tradition of Swift and Rabelais. In "The Situation of Psychoanalysis and the Training of Psychoanalysts in 1956" (Lacan, 2006 [1956]), which remains one of Lacan's least studied papers, but also one of his most vehement repudiations of the hierarchical structure of (psychoanalytic) organizations, he designated those people who are in analysis as Little Shoes.[7] They more or less comply with institutional and clinical rules, do not dare to speak up for themselves outside the sessions, and generally follow the path imposed by the *soi-disant* Sufficiencies, that is to say those who have successfully finished their analytic training and have been given full access to the psychoanalytic profession—psychoanalysts, as the institution would call them. On the whole, Lacan asserted, the Sufficiencies do not say much either, because self-sufficient as they are they do not feel the need to start a conversation or engage in discussion. But then there are also the Beatitudes, in whom we can easily recognize the so-called "training analysts", and who have been appointed by the Sufficiencies, and put in charge (as superior members of the organization) of the Truly Necessary, i.e., those Little Shoes who do not come to see a psychoanalyst because they want to be relieved of some pressing personal problem but because they want to train as psychoanalysts. In carefully laying out the stakes of his elaborate exposition, Lacan conceded that no psychoanalytic society can exist without Sufficiencies (practicing psychoanalysts), with the caveat that as a professional rank this position can only ever be reached asymptotically and therefore never be fully attained, so that Sufficiency is but the momentary occupation of a certain clinical position and not the definitive realization of a certain professional stature—analysts only ever being able to approximate the category of Sufficiencies as perennial Truly Necessaries. Put differently, for Lacan, analytic training is never fully finished, and no one should ever have the right or the duty to say that he or she *is* or has effectively become a psychoanalyst. Critical as the presence of Sufficiencies may be for the survival of psychoanalytic organizations, Lacan was particularly disapproving, here, of the sovereign power they seem to have, not only in selecting the Truly Necessary (analytic trainees) and distinguishing them from the Little Shoes, but also in appointing the Beatitudes (training analysts) from their own kind, and deciding which of the Truly Necessary can become Sufficient on the basis of what the Beatitudes have managed to achieve with them. In short, Lacan disputed the doctrinal authority with which the psychoanalysts in the organization would concentrate all power within their own ranks, and exposed the psychoanalytic establishment as a ritualized, ceremonious, and formulaic institution, not dissimilar to the self-perpetuating leadership of the Catholic priesthood.

Could Lacan have anticipated, here, that the very organization whose self-serving rigidity he had exposed would also proceed to getting him formally expelled as a training analyst some seven years later, with the help and agreement of former allies in his own institution? Maybe not. Fact of the matter is that at the 23rd Congress of the IPA, the institution's central executive decided that the SFP could only maintain its status as a study group of the IPA, with a view to progressing to full recognition as a freestanding, constituent society, if and only if a certain Dr Lacan was removed from his functions as a training analyst (Miller, 1977, pp. 41–45). Pierre Turquet, the author of the report recommending that Lacan be defrocked, was a British psychiatrist who was working at the time as a consultant at the Tavistock Clinic, where he did research on organizational behaviour and group relations. During World War II he had been a major in the Royal Army Medical Corps, where he had contributed to the development of the War Office Selection Boards. When Lacan had shared his impressions of British psychiatry with his colleagues of *L'évolution psychiatrique* after his return from England, Major Turquet had been a member of the audience. Following the IPA's guideline, a majority of psychoanalysts in the SFP eventually decided that the master should be brought down. Much like the Sufficiencies had at one point promoted Lacan to the status of a Beatitude, they were also clearly capable of "de-selecting" him if they themselves were at risk of losing their official recognition as Sufficiencies. On Wednesday, 20 November 1963, the day after the deal was agreed, Lacan delivered the first and only session of his seminar on "The Names-of-the-Father", ending with the pregnant words: "I am not here in a plea for myself. I should, however, say, that—having, for two years, entirely confided to others the execution, within a group, of a policy [the request to be re-affiliated to the IPA], in order to leave to what I had to tell you its space and its purity—I have never, at any moment, given any pretext for believing that there was not, for me, any difference between yes and no" (Lacan, 1990 [1963], p. 95). Of course, less than two months later, Lacan continued anyway, or rather he started again, with a new seminar, in a new location and with a new audience. The topic was "the foundations of psychoanalysis", later to be modified into "the four fundamental concepts of psychoanalysis". At the beginning of the first lecture he could not resist reopening a barely healed wound, and so he started with the question "*En quoi y suis-je autorisé?*"—"What gives me the authority to do this?" or, as the English translator of the seminar renders the phrase: "Am I qualified to do so?" (Lacan, 1994[1973], p. 1). Clearly, the problematic "authorization" in question did not simply concern Lacan's position as a lecturer, but referred more specifically to his teaching about the foundations of psychoanalysis. The question should thus be understood as: "What authorizes a psychoanalyst who has just been officially removed from his training position in a psychoanalytic organization to lecture on the basic principles of his discipline?"

If the question was not entirely rhetorical, Lacan nonetheless decided that the "problem [be] deferred" (*Ibid.*, p. 1). But not for too long. At the Summer solstice of 1964, Lacan created his own school, the *École Française de Psychanalyse* (EFP), subsequently to be renamed as the *École freudienne de Paris*. In the opening paragraphs of its "Founding Act" he emphasized that the organization (*l'organisme*) had been established in order to accomplish a programme of work (*un travail*), with three distinct aims: (1) restoring the cutting-edge truth of Freud's discovery; (2) returning the practice of psychoanalysis to its proper duty (*devoir*); and (3) denouncing the deviations and compromises that blunt and degrade psychoanalysis (Lacan, 1990 [1964], p. 97).[8] Although he did not refer to Bion's distinction from the early 1950s between a productive work group and three inert basic-assumption groups (Bion, 1961[1952]), Lacan thus set out with the explicit goal of forming a "work group", whose working objective or primary task (*objectif de travail*) consisted in a "movement of reconquest" (*mouvement de reconquête*) (Lacan, 1990 [1964], p. 97). In order to ensure that the group would remain focused on the designated task and would not (as Bion would have had it) resort back to one or more "basic assumptions", Lacan proposed that the work be carried out by small groups of minimum three and maximum five people, *and* an additional person—the so-called "plus one"—who is in charge of selecting the concrete work topic, facilitating the discussion and determining the outcome of each individual group member's work (*Ibid.*, p. 97). After some time, the small groups would be expected to permutate, insofar as the individual members would be encouraged to leave in order to join another group. Lacan decided to call the small group a "cartel"—a name he glossed etymologically as being derived from the Latin *cardo*, meaning "hinge" (Lacan, 1990[1964], p. 101; Lacan, 1976[1975a], p. 221). It is important to note, here, that the cartel constitutes a temporary collective effort around the accomplishment of a set of specific individual tasks, from which the entire organization may benefit. Being a member of a cartel (the essential work group) was also a necessary and sufficient condition for being a member of the school (Lacan, 1990[1964], p. 100). In addition, Lacan stipulated that whoever is put in charge of "directing", be it the work of the cartels or (at a higher level) the work of the entire school, would not be seen as occupying a chiefdom (*chefferie*), on account of which he or she would then be given access to a higher rank. *Mutatis mutandis*, nobody in the school, regardless of rank and status, would be perceived as having been demoted if she or he engages in "base-level work" (*Ibid.*, pp. 97–98). Every individual enterprise (*enterprise personnelle*), regardless as to which position the individual occupies within the school, would moreover be subjected to institutional criticism and control, so that no hierarchical stratification makes someone inferior or superior, and a "circular organization" (*organisation circulaire*) is created (*Ibid.*, p. 98).

The idea of the cartel was exceedingly simple, and is redolent of the leaderless groups Bion set up when having to select new Army officers at the start of the Second World War, with the proviso that in Lacan's School the cartels were not designed to select or recruit individuals, nor to facilitate any kind of therapeutic results, but to contribute to the accomplishment of the school's normative primary task. As such, the Lacanian cartel drew both on the leaderless group and Bion's "work group", whereby institutional leaders are placed in positions of "suspended" authority.

Although the concept and structure of the cartel was discussed extensively in the EFP, it did not prove nearly as controversial as Lacan's proposals for safeguarding the quality of the work and guaranteeing its transmission. If the cartel is the format and the mechanism by which the work is executed, then a certain regulatory framework is required to ensure that the work is captured, evaluated, and communicated, internally as well as externally. What is required here, Lacan stated, is a "work transference" (*un transfert de travail*), which requires putting in place a system that enables the work to be transferred from one person to another, from one group to another, from the groups to the school, and from the school to its external environment (*Ibid.*, p. 103). The notion of *transfert de travail* may very well be a hapax in Lacan's work, but should clearly be understood in connection with what, in his 1958 text on the direction of the treatment, he had already defined as *travail du transfert* (the work of transference) and *travail de transfert* (transference work), both terms adduced as translations of Freud's concept of *Durcharbeitung* (working through), which is meant to capture the most advanced part of the clinical psychoanalytic process (Freud, 1958[1914g], p. 155; Lacan, 2006[1958a], pp. 498, 526). Traditionally, psychoanalytic institutions had guaranteed the transmission of their work, which in this case refers both to how psychoanalytic knowledge is being passed on generally, as well as to how new psychoanalysts are being trained, via a strict set of rules and regulations, controlled by an "executive board", which sits at the top of the institutional hierarchy. Possibly inspired by what he had observed in England during the autumn of 1945, and emboldened by what he himself had experienced in his tumultuous relations with representatives of the SPP and the IPA, Lacan decided to organize his own school in a radically different way, although for many of its members this would prove to be an unfeasible, potentially deleterious initiative.

Dissolution

Working from the basic axiom that a psychoanalytic institution cannot function without psychoanalysts, Lacan came up with the provocative claim that a psychoanalyst derives his authorization only from himself (*le psychanalyste ne s'autorise que de lui-même*) (Lacan, 1995[1967], p. 1), by which he meant that only someone's own analytic experience, i.e., the analysis that someone has undertaken, can equip him or her with the necessary "qualifications" to practice psychoanalytically, and not the successful completion of a "pseudo-academic" training programme, let alone the endorsement by an institutional hierarchy. Although many people (mis)interpreted this principle as Lacan effectively suggesting that anyone should have the right to call himself a psychoanalyst—with potentially disastrous consequences for the clinical standards, the public image and the future of the discipline—in practice he argued in favour of the recognition of one single criterion for evaluating whether someone could be considered a psychoanalyst, and be authorized to practice: the personal experience of having been through the process of psychoanalysis.

Nonetheless, when presenting this principle to the EFP in October 1967, Lacan also considered the possibility of the school formally recognizing that someone had effectively been trained as a psychoanalyst and was working psychoanalytically, whereby he outlined two avenues for this recognition. First, the school may decide to bestow the title of "Analyst Member of the School" (AME) upon those practicing psychoanalysts who have demonstrated their analytic ability, in whatever form, and without the psychoanalysts themselves asking for this recognition. Second, analytic trainees and practicing analysts may themselves ask for institutional recognition, in which case they are required to speak about their own psychoanalytic journey, individually and independently, to three "passers"—members of the school who are roughly at the same point of their own trajectory and therefore "equals"—who subsequently transmit what they have heard to a decision-making body (the so-called "cartel of the pass"), which then deliberates as to whether the candidate should be given the title of "Analyst of the School" (AE) (Lacan, 1995[1967], p. 1).

Lacan made it clear that these titles should not be interpreted in a hierarchical way, as the AMEs being superior to the AEs, or vice versa, but simply as different "steps" (*gradus*), each with their own duties and responsibilities. At the same time, he also reduced the power traditionally accorded to the training analyst, inasmuch as he no longer wished to differentiate between a training analysis and a "regular analysis".[9] Lacan did not see the need for potential analytic trainees to be treated differently from "normal patients", and did not want the training analysts to have the power to decide, or even to advise on how and when trainees should be recognized as psychoanalysts. In this non-hierarchical structure, and the radical decentralization of institutional power that Lacan attempted to bring about, here, we can once again detect an echo of Bion's ground-breaking experiments with leaderless groups. The recruitment and selection of new psychoanalysts is not left to people in a position of authority, but candidates self-select, insofar as they simply draw on their own analytic experience in order to apply their skills, demonstrate their capacity, or satisfy independent observers. Much like the selection panel had operated in Bion's leaderless group experiments, the actual decision-making body does not evaluate the candidates directly, but relies for its judgment on a set of non-partisan "witness statements". What matters is not whether someone has passed a requisite number of tests with flying colours—say a portfolio of examinations and coursework and the minimum amount of analytic sessions with a training analyst—but whether someone's subjective analytic experience shows sufficient clinical promise for that person to practice psychoanalytically.

So did it all work? In light of the fact that Lacan decided to dissolve his own school some 15 years after it was created, one may be tempted to respond with a resounding "no". However, much like the Stalinist atrocities may not in themselves be a sufficient reason for confirming the intrinsic failure of the great communist experiment, Lacan's dissolution of the EFP may not as such be a reliable indicator of the fact that the entire organizational edifice was built on extremely loose foundations. It is clear that, despite Lacan's well-meaning attempt to diffuse institutional power, the EFP did not live up to the grand expectations that were raised on the day of its first inception. In transforming traditional hierarchical patters of operation into a "circular organization", Lacan was firmly convinced that the work of the school could be accomplished, and that doctrinal inertia could be averted, yet the institutional "consistency" that he believed would come with experience did not materialize, or gradually transformed itself again into a more conventional series of arrangements, with teachers and pupils, thinkers and disciples, leaders and followers, masters and slaves.[10]

The problem, no doubt, was to a large extent Lacan himself, who would always be the superior "plus one", the one who would not only stand out from the others on account of having been the one to found the school (and therefore also being the only one who could subsequently legitimately disband it), but the one who was *de facto* intellectually unassailable, clinically infallible, institutionally unimpeachable. Much like Bion in his Northfield experiments, Lacan recognized that the school expected him to demonstrate his authority as the leader of the organization in his capacity of director of the school. Much like Bion, he accepted this responsibility, without therefore always complying with what the group was expecting of him. Yet this position of "suspended leadership", which constitutes an alternative position of agency—closer to that operating within the discourse of the analyst than that which is at work in the discourse of the master, following the distribution of functions in Lacan's famous "theory of the four discourses" (Lacan, 2007[1991])—gradually changed into a new, uncritical attribution of power. During the late 1960s and early 1970s Lacan regularly complained about the large following he was attracting, and the seriousness which seemed to animate his audience and the people working in his school. Lacan's innovative mechanism for securing the institutional recognition of psychoanalysts who wish to be recognized as such, which came to be known as the "procedure of the pass", gradually showed its fractures. Witnesses were not believed to be as non-partisan and independent as could be hoped for. Testimonials were believed to be contaminated by the witnesses' knowledge of the identity of the candidates' own psychoanalysts. The cartel of the pass was often suspected of cronyism and nepotism, and it was widely believed that being in analysis with a certain analyst vastly increased once's chances of being nominated as an AE. New artificial hierarchies started to emerge, and the work transference did not always manifest itself as creatively and productively as Lacan had wished for. Despite Lacan's explicit insistence that their would be no hierarchical difference between an AME and an AE, the latter gradually acquired the status of the most accomplished title in the school, reserved for the best analysts.[11]

In a letter of 5 January 1980, Lacan announced that the school he had created some 15 years earlier would be dissolved (Lacan, 1990[1980]). One could no doubt see Lacan's decision, here, as an act of despair or frustration, or as an act signalling his own admission of organizational failure, yet one could also interpret it in a different light, as the intentional initiation of necessary transformational change. In the opening paragraphs of his letter, Lacan reminded his readership of the main reasons as to why he had decided to create the EFP:

> [F]or a labor [...] which in the field opened by Freud restores the cutting edge of his truth—which brings the original praxis he instituted under the name of psychoanalysis back to the duty incumbent upon it in our world—which, through assiduous critique, denounces the deviations and compromises blunting its progress while degrading its use. (*Ibid.*, p. 129)

"I maintain [this objective]", Lacan posited, and that "is why I am dissolving" (*Ibid.*, pp. 129–130). Hence, the dissolution of the organization is a necessary precondition for the work towards the accomplishment of the normative primary task to be sustained. In order for the "circular organization" to survive, it must occasionally be dissolved and re-created, especially at a time when it seems to have reached a standstill, and when the members may be least expecting (or wanting) it, owing to the installation of a certain professional and socio-intellectual comfort. Like the work-group that is the cartel, the "circular organization" also has its life-span and must be disbanded, permutated and re-constructed in order to sustain itself as such. On 11 March 1980, towards the end of his last public seminar, Lacan invited the former members of his school to mourn, which also constitutes a kind of work, the death of their institutional home, and to become "de-Schooled" and "de-glued" (*d'écolé*), whilst at the same time announcing that a new organizational structure would be created, with the same structure of small working groups at its basis (Lacan, 1982[1980]). If a particular development of the institutional *esprit de corps*, which had adversely affected the work transference, had necessitated the dissolution, then no dissolution should stand in the way of the re-creation of a new *esprit de corps*.

Conclusion

Throughout his career as a psychoanalyst, Lacan accorded great importance to the study of organizational structures and institutional cultures, at first out of personal interest and curiosity, later on because he felt compelled to denounce the systems and practices which had contributed to his being ostracized from his own institution, and equally because he believed it was possible to actually conceive of an entirely new type of organization. Most of Lacan's contributions, here, centred on the specific organization of psychoanalytic institutions, yet all of the concerns Lacan expressed in his radical review of how psychoanalysis is institutionalized and of how psychoanalytic institutions organize themselves can easily be extrapolated to operational, strategic and managerial issues in non-psychoanalytic, public- and private-sector organizations.

As a critical theorist of psychoanalytic institutions, Lacan occupied himself with the recruitment and selection of candidates (for psychoanalytic training), with the way in which (psychoanalytic) training is delivered and monitored, with how the end of the training process should be conceived, with how candidates who have finished their training should be recognized institutionally, and with typical "managerial" processes of (analytic) appraisal, evaluation and promotion. He was concerned about the stratification, the hierarchical structure, the allocation of authority, the distribution of power and the function of leadership in (psychoanalytic) institutions. He was deeply involved in setting the parameters for assuring institutional quality and standards, guaranteeing the organization's normative primary task, and securing its social and epistemological sustainability. Although he was almost exclusively focused on how psychoanalytic organizations function, Lacan examined how and where decisions are being made, how people get to participate in decision making processes, how members of the organization are being appointed, how knowledge, information, and ideas are communicated and transmitted internally as well as externally, and how rules and regulations are being formulated and enforced.

All of these matters are strictly relevant to the study of organizational life outside the psychoanalytic institutions today, which implies that Lacan's ideas, context-specific as they may be, have potentially widespread significance, or may at least be employed directly in the design and delivery of a Lacanian organizational framework. Over the past decade, Lacanian psychoanalytic theory has shown its value for organizational studies and many researchers within critical management studies now regularly draw on his ideas. Yet instead of applying Lacan's concepts—desire, jouissance, object *a*, the fantasy, the divided subject, discourse—to organizational dynamics, there is another, potentially more fruitful way of appreciating the significance of Lacanian psychoanalysis for organizational analysis, and that is to extract and assess the explicit, practical and theoretical, contributions Lacan himself made to the study of organizations. In this chapter, I have not offered a detailed and comprehensive analysis of the development of Lacan's entire organizational theory. I have merely restricted myself to what I perceive to be some of its key milestones and central tenets, whereby I have organized the narrative around three notions: *esprit de corps*, work transference and dissolution. Over the years, Lacan's recurrent "victimization" at the hands of psychoanalytic officialdom, his uncompromising non-conformist position with regard to institutional rules, and his own institutional initiatives have been dissected in a large number of books and papers—some greatly appreciative and some overtly critical—yet most of these publications concentrate on the problematic institutionalization of the theory and practice of psychoanalysis, on the issues surrounding the establishment of a psychoanalytic training programme, and on the relation between masters and disciples in the advancement of psychoanalytic knowledge. For all I know, Lacan has never been properly studied as an organizational theorist in his own right. This work still needs to be done, yet my own modest contribution to it, which constitutes no more than a brief survey of its contours, will hopefully facilitate a new appreciation of Lacan as an organizational theorist in his own right, who deserves to be studied alongside Bion and other major figures in the history of the psychoanalytic study of organizations.

Notes

1 An earlier version of this chapter was published in *Psychoanalytische Perspectieven*, 2016, 34(4), pp. 355–378. Materials from this earlier version are reproduced here with the permission of Dries Dulsster.
2 For more details on Lacan's highly lucrative, private psychoanalytic business, I refer the reader back to Chapter 2 of this book.
3 Readers interested in pursuing this strand of psychoanalytic research will benefit from Jaques (1951), Trist et al. (1963), and Trist and Murray (1990).

4 For an in-depth analysis of the status of the object in Lacan's works, see also Chapter 3 of this book.
5 Both in the four French editions of Lacan's text and in the first of the two English translations of it, Hatfield has been misprinted as Hartfield, which makes me think that the editors did not investigate the circumstances of Lacan's visit nor, for that matter, the environment in which the work he described had been taking place. See Lacan (1947; 1986[1947]; 1987[1947]; 2000[1947]; 2001[1947]).
6 The focus of this chapter does not allow me to describe the tumultuous events within the French psychoanalytic community during the first half of 1953 in much detail. For a meticulous, chronological reconstruction of how the discussion (and the subsequent schism) unfolded, see de Mijolla (2012, pp. 279–432). Also, the minutes of the IPA business meeting of July 1953 indicate that Lacan's vehement attack on the Institute's hierarchical functioning may not have been the only problem, or that a vehement disagreement over organizational matters of psychoanalytic training was rapidly diverted towards a more personal issue. Indeed, Lacan was also perceived at the time as someone who would take great, potentially unacceptable liberties with firmly established clinical rules. As Marie Bonaparte, by far the most prominent member of the SPP, put it to the IPA committee: "[O]ne of these members [Lacan] [...] promised to change his technique [of variable-length clinical sessions], but did not keep his promise" (Eissler, 1954, p. 272).
7 For an alternative reading of Lacan's allegory and the entire essay in which it was set, see Gherovici and Steinkoler (2020).
8 It is often assumed that Lacan read his "Founding Act" for the new psychoanalytic school to some of those who had remained loyal to him at one or the other rented venue in Paris, yet Lacan's thespian character and the fact that he was profoundly shaped by the surrealist tradition meant that he turned the event into a proper performance. During the first weeks of June 1964, some 50 French psychoanalysts received an invitation to come to the apartment of Dr François Perrier on the *avenue de l'Observatoire* in Paris during the early evening of Summer solstice. Upon arrival that Sunday, they were led into Perrier's large drawing room, where a tape-recorder had been placed in the middle of a low table in the centre of the room. When the signal was given for the event to start, Perrier turned on the tape-recorder, from which Lacan's highly pitched, disembodied voice started filling the room: "I hereby found...". Midway through the performance, the door to the drawing room silently opened and Lacan himself entered, in order to take a seat at the back. When the tape-recording ended, after some 20 minutes, Lacan moved to the centre of the room and started commenting on his new initiative ... See Nasio (2014).
9 The principle was less original than it is often portrayed, because it had already been proposed by Sándor Ferenczi back in 1927 (Ferenczi, 1964[1927], p. 376).
10 And so it is fair to say that, despite Lacan's good intentions, almost all of his communal, libertarian, solidaristic principles of organizational functioning eventually failed. Yet this is to some extent true for all of the alternatives that have been proposed over the past 100 years or so within other psychoanalytic training organizations. In fact, I do not know of any psychoanalytic training organization that does not struggle with a series of crucial, yet largely intractable questions. Should there be a minimum criterion for the duration of a candidate's own analysis, and if so what should it be? Should the frequency and the duration of the candidate's analytic sessions be pre-established? Should a candidate be allocated a training-analyst by a training committee, or should trainees be allowed to choose their own analyst? If the latter, should the analyst be a

practitioner within the candidate's own training organization, or should the pool of qualified analysts be extended to all practicing psychoanalysts, irrespective of their affiliation and seniority? Should the training-analyst decide whether the candidate's analysis has sufficiently progressed for him or her to be "inducted into" the profession, or should this decision rest with the training committee? If the latter, which "assessment criteria" should the training committee employ, other than the authorized record of completion of the candidate's analytic sessions? What happens if the training committee decides that a candidate is not (yet) qualified to work as a psychoanalyst? Should candidates be allowed to see patients (under supervision), and if so at what stage in their training analysis? Should patients be assigned to candidates, or are candidates at liberty to take on any patients who come to them? Should the training analysis *de facto* end when the candidate is admitted to the profession? If not, is it entirely up to the candidate to decide how long the training analysis should continue? How does an analyst become a training analyst and/or analytic supervisor? Is it purely based on the number of years she or he has practiced, or should an analyst apply to the training committee or another institutional body? If so, which criteria will this institutional body use in order to assess the analyst's application? How many hours of analytic supervision should a candidate complete? Should the candidate be given the freedom to choose his or her own supervisor? If so, should the supervisor belong to the organization in which the candidate is training, or can he be chosen from a wider constituency of analytic supervisors? How will the supervisor evaluate the candidate's work? Is the supervisor expected to report back to the training committee, and if so what form should the supervisor's report take? And what about the theoretical components of the training-programme? Should psychoanalytic candidates sit exams, write essays, deliver presentations, participate in group-work, complete a dissertation? And then there is the even more vexed issue of entry criteria. If candidates are not to be selected on the basis of academic qualifications, what will the training committee be looking for? Which motivations for analytic training are deemed acceptable and which are deemed inadmissible? Should these criteria be made explicit? If not, how will those conducting the selection process be held accountable for their decision? Should candidates be of a certain age, and have certain professional or other qualifications before they can be considered? Should people with a history of mental illness or with a criminal record be *de facto* excluded from training? Should candidates be of good moral character?

11 This is still very much the case in the current *École de la cause freudienne*, insofar as I have heard numerous people boasting over the years that they have "passed the pass" and obtained the coveted recognition of AE.

Chapter 6

Psychoanalysis as *Gai Saber*: Towards a New Episteme of Laughter

Encounter with a Fantasist

Some time during the mid-1950s, Madeleine Chapsal, a 30-something journalist writing for *L'express*—the recently launched weekly supplement to the French financial daily *Les Échos*—attended a fancy dress party organized by the editorial board of Jean-Paul Sartre's journal *Les Temps Modernes*, where she was introduced to a certain Dr Lacan.[1] Many years later, Chapsal recalled the event as follows:

> The first time I saw Jacques Lacan he was wearing a bushy ginger-coloured wig, and he invited me to dance ... That night the famous psychoanalyst's head presented me with an image of him that I never forgot: he was a fantasist! (Chapsal, 1984, p. 31)

In her seminal biography of Lacan, Elisabeth Roudinesco drew on a personal conversation with Chapsal to elaborate on the story. According to Roudinesco, the young female journalist had adored Lacan's "penchant for disguise [*le côté travesti du personnage*], his auburn wigs, his love of social life and gossip, [and] the way he enjoyed theatrical situations" (Roudinesco, 1997[1993], p. 261). After their first encounter, Lacan and Chapsal immediately struck up an intimate friendship, leading to Chapsal being regularly invited to Lacan's country house at Guitrancourt, and her receiving a long series of amorous letters and notes, in which the psychoanalyst would sometimes ask his confidante for specific sartorial advice when he was preparing for another *bal masqué* (Chapsal, 1984, p. 38). Whether Dr Lacan was in the habit of wearing ostentatious wigs at fancy dress parties, I do not know. Whether he would also wear them in other situations, I do not know either. Maybe Chapsal was chuffed and charmed when she saw on the psychoanalyst's cranium a grotesque reflection of her own notorious ginger mop. Maybe she was just puzzled, bemused, and surprised. Fact of the matter is that on that particular evening, Lacan's exuberant hirsute display of colour made such an important impression on Chapsal that she was left

DOI: 10.4324/9781003252276-7

with an inerasable "flash-bulb" memory, gladly accepted all his invitations—to dance, to dine, to play, and to wine—and eventually conducted a long interview with him for *L'express*, in which he paid tribute to the revolutionary discoveries of his master Sigmund Freud, defended his own linguistic approach to Freud's legacy, and denounced how contemporary psychoanalysis was descending ever more into a "confused mythology" (Lacan, 1957, p. 22).[2]

To the best of my knowledge, no one apart from Chapsal ever reported similar occurrences of Lacan dressing up, disguising himself, or regaling an audience with odd accessories and idiosyncratic accoutrements. No one, that is, apart from Lacan himself. The day is Friday, 1 November 1974. In New York City, at the United Nations Headquarters, the UN General Assembly adopts Resolution 3212, which calls upon all states to respect the sovereignty, independence, territorial integrity, and non-alignment of the Republic of Cyprus. In Rome, in the splendorous concert hall of the *Accademia Musicale di Santa Cecilia*, Lacan speaks at the 7th Conference of the *École freudienne de Paris*, the school he himself had founded ten years earlier. In front of a packed auditorium, Lacan declares:

> There is not a single discourse in which make-belief [*le semblant*] fails to call the shots [*mène le jeu*] ... So, be more relaxed, more spontaneous when you receive someone who comes to speak to you in analysis. Don't feel so obliged to take on airs. Even as a buffoon, you are justified in being so. You only have to watch my *Television*: I am a clown. Take that as an example, and don't imitate me! The seriousness that spurs me on is the series that you constitute. You cannot be part of it [*en être*] and be it [*l'être*] at the same time.
> (Lacan, 2019[1974], p. 88, translation modified)

Anyone who has ever read the text called *Television* (Lacan, 1990[1974]), which was published shortly before Lacan's appearance on French television in March 1974, will probably seriously doubt the seriousness of Lacan's self-assessment, here, because alongside "Radiophonie" (Lacan, 2001[1970]) and "L'étourdit" (Lacan, 2001[1972]), both from the same period, it counts amongst the most conceptually abstruse and intellectually demanding of the psychoanalyst's later works. I have never come across anyone who admitted to having experienced uncontrollable fits of laughter at the reading of *Television*, or who thought that reading *Television* was great fun, or that the text was an inexhaustible source of amusement—intellectually or otherwise. But here is the twist: Lacan did not exhort his audience to *read* the text of *Television*, but to watch him *on* television, literally performing notes that would then be published with the eponymous title.[3] In telling his listeners in Rome, and particularly the psychoanalysts among them, that he was a clown when playing the text that was subsequently entitled *Television*, Lacan insisted on the sensory qualities of the spoken word—delivered with a highly distinctive tone of voice, and accompanied by a number of visually arresting mannerisms—and not on a particular feature of its written inscription. Something of the intentionally comical disappears, then, when the words become detached from the person speaking them, from the way in which they are articulated, with their particular punctuation and their carefully crafted timing. And yet, when the words are being re-connected to the image of the living body of the psychoanalyst who is declaiming them, in this case Jacques Lacan, they do not by definition generate laughter either, strange as the performance may be. Vocalizing a version of his own text *Television* on television, Lacan did not tell jokes, was not wearing a wig, did not dance and could rarely be seen smiling or laughing. But he did not want to be taken entirely seriously. Those who did take him seriously, so seriously that they were prepared to follow him, demonstrated both their captivation by what they perceived to be the image of the unassailable master, and their unwillingness to allow this image to fall from the superior position it was held to occupy. They may have gone so far as to laugh *with* him, but they would never have dared to laugh *at* him. In Rome in 1974, Lacan in a sense complained about the fact that too many psychoanalysts were lacking in humour, despite his best intentions to make them laugh or, better still, despite his consistent attempts at presenting himself as a risible figure.

In this chapter, I will demonstrate that the thespian side of Lacan's character, his keen eye for comedy, and his utter contempt for self-indulgent gravitas were not just *ad hoc* phenomena—"accidental" features of his private and public persona, frivolous flights of fancy elicited by particular social circumstances—but rather essential components of a consciously considered outlook on life, which also and most crucially informed his conception of psychoanalytic theory and practice. More specifically, I will argue that, when Lacan at one point went so far as to assert that he was gay, this "confession" was inspired by the same reasons that prompted homosexual people in the Anglophone world to adopt the word "gay" as the most apposite designation for their sexual orientation. Lacan aimed for a subtle, humorous resistance to normative practices and established conventions, and for him this principle of "gayness" was to be situated at the heart of psychoanalytic knowledge, both in its purely theoretical and in its clinical applications. At the end of the chapter I will propose, therefore, that my portrait of Lacan-the-psychoanalyst as a gay man, which is not at all antagonistic to how his master Sigmund Freud would come across in "nonofficial" representations, may offer us a useful paradigm for the way in which psychoanalytic knowledge should be advanced, as well as a valuable metaphor for how knowledge should be maintained in psychoanalytic institutions that want to remain truthful to the epistemic foundations of their discipline. As such, I will suggest that against the formalistic rigidity of institutionalized psychoanalytic knowledge, it is crucial for psychoanalysts to re-engage with the "dancing" thought of Nietzsche's Zarathustra, which encapsulates the prophet's most radical answer to the sterile status of ponderous, petrified reasoning, and to embrace an episteme of laughter.

Jacques Lacan Is Gay!

On two separate occasions, in public and without ostensible shame or irony, Lacan conceded that he was gay. The day is Sunday, 22 October 1967. In Washington, DC, thousands of young demonstrators storm the Pentagon out of protest against the Vietnam War. At the *Maison de la Chimie* on the *rue Saint-Dominique* in Paris, the Belgian-French psychoanalyst Maud Mannoni is presiding over a study weekend on psychosis, featuring presentations both by members of Lacan's *École freudienne de Paris* and by a number of high-profile external speakers, such as Donald Woods Winnicott, David Cooper, and Ronald David Laing. As would have been common, Lacan delivered the closing speech of the conference, during which he divulged:

> Everyone knows that I am gay [*je suis gai*], some would even say that I'm a bit childish [*gamin*]. Look, I'm having a good time [*je m'amuse*]. It constantly happens to me that, in my texts, I am giving myself over to all kinds of jokes [*plaisanteries*], which is obviously not to the taste of academics. But look, it's true, I'm not sad. Or more precisely, I only have one real sadness in what has been traced out for me by way of a career, and that is that there are fewer and fewer people to whom I can explain the reasons for me being gay, when I really do have them.
> (Lacan, 1968, p. 145)

One could easily dismiss this brief public "confession" as a facetious *fait divers*, not signaling much of a commitment, were it not for the fact that three-and-a-half years later, Lacan again disclosed his "subjective affectation", this time in front of a massive audience at his weekly seminar. The day is Wednesday, 12 May 1971. At the local town hall in St Tropez, Rolling Stones front man Mick Jagger is getting married to Bianca Pérez-Mora de Macias. At the great lecture theatre of the Law Faculty on the *Place du Panthéon* in Paris, Lacan is treating his audience to a performance of "Lituraterre", a text he has written for a special journal issue on psychoanalysis and literature (Lacan, 2013[1971a]; 2013[1971b]).[4] Telling the hundreds of devoted listeners how he has learnt to read some Chinese characters, Lacan goes on to describe his limitations when it comes to deciphering the handwriting:

> In the handwritten form, I can't recognize the character anymore, because I am a novice. But that's not what is so important really, because what I call the singular can actually support a firmer form. What

is important is what is added. It is a dimension or—in the way I've taught you to play with these things—a *demansion*, where something resides that I introduced to you in the previous seminar, or in the one before, with the word that I wrote, simply to amuse myself, as *papeludun* [a word play on *pas-plus-d'un*, no more than one]. It's the *demansion* of which you know that it allows me ... to install the subject into what I will call today, simply because I'm producing literature and I'm gay [*je suis gai*]—you will recognize it, because I've already written it under a different form—the *Hun-En-Peluce* [a word play on *Un-en-plus*, One more].[5]

It is worth noting, here, that the phrase "I'm gay" is not actually part of the text that Lacan was reading, insofar as it does not appear in any of the published versions of "Lituraterre". Much like something is "added" to the standard Chinese character when it is reproduced by a "subjective hand", which may effectively prevent non-experts from finding their way around the handwritten text, "I'm gay" represents the singular subjective "*demansion*" which Lacan himself added to the text, when he was speaking and performing the written words in front of a live audience. As such, this particular phrase already constitutes Lacan's own meta-textual interpretation of "Lituraterre", something he decided to add to it in the spur of the moment, as an explanatory reflection upon his persistent punning on words.

What could have prompted Lacan to tell his listeners that he was gay, and what reasons could he have had for being gay in the first place? For, as he pointed out in his lecture on 22 October 1967, he definitely had his reasons, despite the fact that there were progressively fewer and fewer people around to whom he could explain himself. Of course, one should not be deceived, here, by the fact that in the English-speaking world the word "gay" has acquired strong connotations of (male) homosexuality, which have now almost completely taken over its entire semantic field. At the end of the 1960s, such connotations were still uncommon, especially in France. No one should be misled, therefore, in thinking that, whilst the Pentagon was being stormed and Mick Jagger was getting married, Lacan was finally coming out of the closet as a homosexual cruiser. I could have chosen to render Lacan's "*je suis gai*" as "I am cheerful", "I am joyous", "I am joyful" or "I am happy", yet these terms would no doubt be better suited as translations of the French words "*enjoué*", "*joyeux*", or "*heureux*", and one would only really want to avoid the word "gay" on account of its current association with a certain sexual orientation, which at the time it just did not have.[6]

In fact, there are very good reasons for insisting on the significance of Lacan's being gay—as opposed to him being merely cheerful or joyous—and they are essentially the same as those that encouraged Walter Kaufmann to continue to render the title of Nietzsche's *Die Fröhliche Wissenschaft* as *The Gay Science*, from his first discussion of the book in his seminal 1950 revisionist account of the German philosopher (Kaufmann, 2013[1950]), up to his landmark 1974 translation of the work, which was released at a time when the word "gay" had already been adumbrated by the homosexual community in the English-speaking world (Nietzsche, 1974[1887]). Without going so far as to suggest that Nietzsche was homosexual, which he very well may have been, Kaufmann clarifies:

> [I]t is no accident that the homosexuals as well as Nietzsche opted for 'gay' rather than 'cheerful'. 'Gay science', unlike 'cheerful science', has overtones of a light-hearted defiance of convention; it suggests Nietzsche's 'immoralism' and his 'revaluation of values' ... What Nietzsche himself wanted the title to convey was that serious thinking does not have to be stodgy, heavy, dusty, or, in one word Teutonic. (Kaufmann, 1974, pp. 4–5)[7]

In his introduction to a more recent translation of *Die Fröhliche Wissenschaft*, Bernard Williams makes a similar point: "No one, presumably, is going to be misled by the more recent associations of the word 'gay'—it simply means joyful, light-hearted, and above all, lacking in solemnity" (Williams, 2001, p. x).[8] Likewise, for me to say that Lacan admitted to being gay, no one will presumably be led to believe that I want to insinuate that he actually confessed to being a homosexual, although the notion's connotations of spontaneous, undirected playfulness and its implicit purpose of demonstrating carefree civil disobedience served the homosexual community extremely well.

But there are other than purely linguistic reasons for emphasizing Lacan's and Nietzsche's gaiety. When Nietzsche "composed" *Die Fröhliche Wissenschaft*—not once, but twice between 1881 and 1886—he gave the second edition of his book the parenthetical subtitle "*la gaya scienza*", thus suggesting that his own German title was effectively already a translation, and that *fröhlich* was intended to render the adjective *gaya*. In addition, as Nietzsche pointed out in a passage of *Ecce Homo* published in 1888, one year after the second edition of *Die Fröhliche Wissenschaft*, the so-called "Songs of Prince Vogelfrei", which were added to this second edition, "are very clearly reminiscent of the Provençal concept of *gaya scienza*, that unity of *singer, knight,* and *free spirit* that is distinctive of the wonderful early culture of Provence" (Nietzsche, 2005[1888], p. 123). It is unclear how Nietzsche had come across the concept of *gaya scienza*. He may have discovered it via Ralph Waldo Emerson, with whose works he had become infatuated as a schoolboy and whose essays he ardently re-read whilst writing *The Gay Science*.[9] Alternatively, his knowledge of it may have stemmed from his own deep personal interest in Mediterranean culture, as represented in this case by the medieval troubadours of southern France.

In 1323, seven distinguished citizens of Toulouse founded the *Sobregaya Companhia del Gay Saber* (literally, "The super gay company of the gay knowledge"), with the aims of fighting sadness and boredom, celebrating joyful educational practices through song and dance, and establishing an annual poetry contest open to all *"dictador et trobador"* (Passerat, 2000). In order to evaluate the quality of the poems more rigorously, and with a view to promoting Occitan grammar, the seven members of the "gay company" then asked a lawyer by the name of Guilhem Molinier to compile a comprehensive handbook setting out the fundamental rules of lyrical poetry. The book was eventually published under the title *Las Leys d'Amors* (*The Laws of Language*), and became hugely influential in various parts of southern Europe as the standard treatise on the art of poetry (Anglade, 1919–1920; 1930; Lafont, 1966; Léglu, 2008; Stevens, 1986). Over time, the Toulousians became known in Occitan as the *Consistori de la Gaya Sciensa*, in Spanish as the *Consistorio del Gay Saber*, and in French as *La Compagnie des mainteneurs du Gai Savoir*, although the polyphony of languages and the amalgamation of cultures in the Mediterranean during the late Middle Ages often resulted in various hybrid designations such as *Consistori del Gai Saber*, *Consistoire de la Gaie Science,* and *Consistori de la Gaya Ciència*. The shift from *"sciensa"* to *"saber"* and *"savoir"* makes sufficiently clear, here, that the consistory did not so much intend to re-define the rules of scientific practice, or the practical (empirical) principles of science, but rather the language of knowledge, or the rhetorical and especially the poetic structures governing a certain type of knowledge production. *Gaya scienza* is in essence "gay knowledge", "gay learning", or "gay intelligence", rather than "gay science", although any kind of science (in the commonly accepted meaning of the word) will inevitably draw upon and generate bodies of knowledge. As such, Nietzsche was definitely right in rendering *scienza* as *Wissenschaft,* but the latter term should not be re-translated into English, as some Nietzsche scholars have done, as "wisdom". Apart from the fact that *Wissenschaft* never refers to wisdom in German, Nietzsche intended to advance a new type of scholarly investigation, resulting in a new kind of knowledge, which was not meant to be any less serious, disciplined and rigorous than conventional scientific practices and doctrines, but which would overcome the rigid, formalistic style of academic, professorial science, as it was to be found primarily in German (Teutonic) quarters. Although *Wissenschaft* (science) is, strictly speaking, the most accurate translation of *scienza*, we should interpret "science" in the broadest possible sense here, Nietzsche aiming his derision at all the representatives of humorless knowledge-production, at all those epistemic authorities who do not believe that serious knowledge can simultaneously be playful, light-hearted, and funny.[10] Had they been around at the time, he probably would have directed it also at those people who go by the name of Lacanians.

What characterizes *gai saber*, and what the didactic style of the *Leys d'Amors* may easily obfuscate, is the ludic and jocular approach to the composition of lyrical poetry, its deliberate recourse to semantic ambiguities, its recurrent re-creation of internal inconsistencies with regard to meter and rhyme, and its untroubled usage of apparent contradictions, making any literal or realistic interpretation impossible and therefore misguided. In a review of the 1967 French translation of Nietzsche's *Fröhliche Wissenschaft*, by Pierre Klossowski, the French critic and translator Jean-Louis Backès intimated that it was precisely this total defiance of contradictions or, viewed from a different angle, the pervasive simultaneous presence of seemingly incompatible experiences—happiness and sorrow, jubilation and despair—which may have attracted Nietzsche to the *gaya scienza* in the first place (Backès, 1968). As the Belgian medievalist Roger Dragonetti put it:

> It is entirely clear that the concept of *gay saber*, supported by the dionysiacal basis of *joy*, which the poets of courtly love celebrate with overwhelming fervor and a state of ravishing, supposes an entirely joyous, mocking and amusing side ... In a sense, the poets of the maternal idiom aimed to conquer knowledge through poetry, because for the *gay saber* of the troubadours it was all about turning the new literary language into a place for the most subtle findings [*trouvailles*] of reason, and at the same time for the play of letters and words. (Dragonetti, 1982, pp. 15–16)[11]

As serious as the Consistory may have been when it came to identifying the best *canço*, recognizing the "most excellent poet" (*plus excellen Dictador*) and awarding the coveted *violeta d'aur* (golden violet) at their annual poetry contest, they would not necessarily have been looking for the most serious-minded troubadour, or at least not for the poet who displayed the most rigorous understanding of the rules of lyrical poetry, but rather for a *joglar* (a minstrel, a performer) who was capable of demonstrating the most coltish, frisky, jaunty, merry, mirthful, spirited, and sprightly interpretation of the rulebook, so that something new and surprising was being invented. A true troubadour is someone who despises the humour-less gravitas of the formal form, someone who, when he gets down to do his business, cannot conform to any kind of accepted practice or standard pattern, neither within the symbolic framework of language nor within the rules of engagement that govern human interaction. As the troubadour Bertran de Born put it after spending time at a court in Normandy in 1182: "*Ja mais non er cortz complia on hom non grab ni non ria*" (Never is a court complete when no one jokes or laughs) (cited in Harvey, 1999, p. 8).[12]

When Lacan confessed publicly to being gay, on 22 October 1967, and again on 12 May 1971, there can be no doubt that he meant it. He was not joking about his affectation, and very much wanted to be taken seriously as a "gay psychoanalyst". By contrast with Nietzsche, there is no evidence that Lacan ever delved into Emerson, nor, for that matter, that he ever paid any serious attention to Nietzsche's "gay science".[13] Nonetheless, when he said he was gay, Lacan presented himself not just as being in a jolly, cheerful mood, but also and primarily as a self-identified "Professor of the Joyous Science"—one who is fully attuned to the poetic principles of the Provençal troubadours. And although he may not have known anything about Emerson, Lacan definitely knew something about the *gaya scienza*.

The day is Saturday, 26 September 1953. In Hannibal, MO, the CBS-affiliated KHQA TV channel 7 begins broadcasting. At the Institute of Psychology of the University of Rome, Lacan introduces the lengthy report entitled, "The Function and Field of Speech and Language in Psychoanalysis", which he has written during the summer, with a largely improvised address directed at the friends who have had the courage to follow him in the wake of a split in the Paris Psychoanalytic Society. At the end of his speech, Lacan exposes the grave errors committed by his fellow psychoanalysts, in the name of a spurious allegiance to the so-called "classical tradition", but he is also reassuring his audience that there is hope:

> If psychoanalysis is a source of truth, it is also a source of wisdom. And this wisdom has a face, which has never deceived anyone, ever since human beings have occupied themselves with its destiny. All wisdom is a *gay savoir*. It is being opened up, it subverts, it sings, it instructs, it laughs. It is all language. Nourish yourselves on its tradition, from Rabelais to Hegel. Open your ears to popular songs, to the marvelous dialogues of the street. You will receive the style through which humanity is revealed in human beings, and the meaning of language, without which you will never liberate speech. (Lacan, 2001[1953], p. 146).

During the question-and-answer session that follows, Lacan drives his point home with two additional references to the importance of the *gay savoir*, not drawing on examples from the troubadours but mentioning the satirical linguistic pyrotechnics of François Rabelais (Ibid., pp. 149, 152). Again, it is worth nothing, here, that *gay savoir* is what Lacan *adds* to the written text of his "Rome Discourse", when he is presenting it to the audience. When Rabelais is mentioned in the written text, there is no evocation of *gay savoir*.[14]

For all I have been able to establish, there are no further references to *gay savoir* in any of Lacan's written or spoken interventions until some 13 years later. That day is Wednesday, 19 January 1966. In India, Indira Ghandi is elected prime minister. In France, at Lacan's seminar at the *École normale supérieure*, which is focusing on the object in psychoanalysis, the audience is listening to a commentary by Thérèse Parisot (one of Lacan's numerous mistresses) on a paper by Roger Dragonetti, which deals with the function of the image in the works of Dante (Dragonetti, 1965). Following the presentation, Lacan gives his own views on the matter and states:

It is insofar as jouissance—I am not saying pleasure—is withdrawn from the field of courtly love that a certain configuration is established there which allows a certain equilibrium between truth and knowledge. It is properly what has been called ... *le gai savoir*. (Lacan, 1965–1966, session of 19 January 1966)

Some six years earlier, Lacan had devoted quite a few sessions of his seminar on the ethics of psychoanalysis to courtly love and the troubadours, insisting on the crucial significance of the female love-object's unattainability—if not in real life, at least in the songs and love poetry of the wandering singers (Lacan, 1992[1986], pp. 85–164). In extracting the jouissance from their songs, and concentrating on desire, the troubadours' *gai savoir* became, at least to Lacan, a more playful, less heavy, more truthful, and less petrified knowledge.

As we now know, in October 1967 and May 1971, Lacan said he was gay, but for all I know there was no further mention of *gai saber* during this period, until Friday, 14 July 1972. At the Crimean Astrophysical Observatory in the Ukraine, Lyudmila Vasilyevna Zhuravleva discovers asteroids #1959 Karbyshev and #2423 Ibarruri. France is celebrating its national holiday, and Lacan is making a contribution to the 50th anniversary of the establishment of the Henri-Rousselle hospital, which was effectively the first open psychiatric clinic in France—admitting patients without them necessarily having been sectioned. The text is called "L'étourdit" and although he does not explicitly say it—and I have no way of proving it—Lacan is rather gay in it, and so he conjures up the gay science:

Insofar as it is the language that is most propitious for the scientific discourse, mathematics is the science without conscience which has been promised to us by our dear old Rabelais; it is the science which can only remain blocked to a philosopher: the gay science [*la gaye science*] is rejoicing by presuming the ruin of the soul. (Lacan, 2001[1972], p. 453)

Eighteen months later, in *Television*, we know that Lacan was gay, because he himself said he had been a clown on it, if not *in* it. Much like he did when he delivered the closing speech at the conference on psychosis in October 1967, Lacan opposed gay science to sadness:

In contrast with sadness [*tristesse*] there is the Gay science [*gay sçavoir*], which is a virtue. A virtue absolves no one from sin—which is, as everyone knows, original. The virtue that I designate as the Gay science [*gay sçavoir*] exemplifies it, by showing clearly of what it consists: not understanding, not a poking into meaning, but a flying over it as low as possible without the meaning's gumming up this virtue, thus enjoying [*jouir*] the deciphering, which implies that the Gay science [*gay sçavoir*] cannot but meet in it the Fall, the return into sin. (Lacan, 1990[1974], p. 22, translation modified)

Gay Psychoanalysis

Only a handful of interpretations of Lacan's references to *gai saber* are available in French, and to the best of my knowledge no Lacan scholar in the English-speaking world has ever paid any serious attention to Lacan's gayness or to his reliance on the "gay science".[15] Yet, as Madeleine Chapsal observed when she first encountered the hirsute ginger Dr Lacan, the psychoanalyst was definitely a fantasist, and an extremely serious one at that.[16] Returning from Rome in September 1953, Lacan moved his weekly seminar to the Sainte-Anne hospital in Paris, and for the next 25 years or so he had a real blast, thoroughly enjoying himself with all kinds of things, from strange physical experiments to even stranger topological objects, indulging himself in recreational mathematics and performing more and more linguistic stunts as the years went by, whilst losing himself like a five-year-old boy in the endless twists and turns of a crazy little thing called the Borromean knot. Whether the people in his audience went through the same hilarious experience, I am not sure. Jacques-Alain Miller, the official editor of Lacan's seminars, could have included textual interpositions such as [*laughs*] whenever the audience laughed at something Lacan was saying or doing, but on that point the text of the seminars is silent and arid, and recordings of the seminars generally contain too much background noise for laughter in the audience to be clearly discernable. When asked about his encounters with Lacan, the French author Philippe Sollers, who attended Lacan's seminars throughout the late 1960s and 1970s, has always insisted on Lacan's great sense of humour (Sollers, 2005; 2011). In a 2011 interview, Jacques-Alain Miller stated that Lacan was "cheerful" until at least 1975–1976 and that a great many laughs were being had (Miller, 2020[2011], p. 141). What we do know is that the representatives of the psychoanalytic establishment and the guardians of the institutions at which Lacan was "performing" did not always think that the show was funny. The day is Monday, 7 November 1955. In the United States, the Supreme Court of Baltimore bans segregation in public recreational areas. In Vienna, at the neuropsychiatric clinic, Lacan is giving a lecture entitled "La chose freudienne" (The Freudian Thing), in which he proclaims "*Moi, la vérité je parle*" (I, truth, speak) (Lacan, 2006[1955b], p. 340). Viennese psychiatrists and psychoanalysts really do not like it when a French colleague says something like that.

But the tone was set at the beginning of his first public seminar at Sainte-Anne. "The closer we get to psychoanalysis being funny [*la psychanalyse amusante*]," Lacan said, "the more it is real psychoanalysis [*la véritable psychanalyse*]" (Lacan, 1988[1975], p. 77). Maybe his audience at the time—which was mainly made up of analysts-in-training—thought he was joking, but Lacan himself was entirely serious about the importance of having fun. The next year, he defined Hegel's concept of "absolute knowledge" (*savoir absolu*) as an "elaborated discourse" which is used as an instrument of power by self-identified masters, and he opposed it to the libidinal knowledge of the street-corner, produced by those who are having a good time in the local café listening to jazz music and dancing the night away. It is clear where his heart was (Lacan, 1988[1978], p. 72). Two years later, he said to his listeners that he was always trying to end a lecture on something that would amuse them (Lacan, 2020[1994], p. 325). And the year after, when focusing on the so-called "formations of the unconscious", he paid relatively little attention to dreams, bungled actions, and neurotic symptoms, but spent the entire first trimester talking about the "Freudian structures" of the joke (Lacan, 2017[1998], pp. 1–126).[17] At another point in this seminar, Lacan claimed that he was "not just amusing" himself by playing on words (*Je ne m'amuse pas à jouer sur les mots*) (Ibid., p. 324). I think he was joking. There are numerous other examples throughout the seminars and the written texts of things that Lacan finds funny and amusing: the optical installation of the inverted bouquet taken from Bouasse; Platonic dialogues; the works of Lévi-Strauss, Sade (!), and Kant (!!); topological structures, especially the cross-cap; a little story about a giant praying mantis; a book by Leopold de Saussure on Chinese astronomy; the golden section; T.S. Eliot's "The Waste Land"; the imagined jouissance of a plant. "I'm not giving any lectures here," he said to the crowd at his seminar on 9 February 1972. "As I have already said elsewhere, very seriously, I amuse myself. Serious or pleasant amusements" (Lacan, 2018[2011], p. 66, translation modified).[18]

At some point during his seminar of 1968–1969, Lacan revealed to his audience that he was having a particularly good time and a great deal of fun when being all on his own (Lacan, 2006a, p. 114). What on earth was he doing? The day is Friday, 30 June 2006. In Pasadena, CA, an MTA bus hits and kills a five-year-old girl riding a tricycle. In Paris, a public auction is being held at the Hôtel Marcel Dassault on the famous Champs-Elysées, during which 117 graphic designs and unpublished manuscripts by Dr Jacques Lacan are put up for sale. The collection belongs to Jean-Michel Vappereau, a psychoanalyst and mathematician who had worked with Lacan during the 1970s on the development of his knot theory, and it is being auctioned because Vappereau wants to buy an apartment in Paris to house a new archive of psychoanalytic texts. A funny-looking guy called Dany Nobus is in the audience, trying to secure a few items to satisfy his bibliophilic tendencies. Amongst the documents that are being sold, there are numerous sheets of paper with colourful drawings of highly intricate knots, which Lacan tended to refer to as his "*ronds de ficelle*" (rings of string) (Lacan, 1998[1975], pp. 118–131), as well as various undated handwritten texts. One of the most interesting ones starts with the line "*Je n'ai dit que des sottises*" (I've only ever said foolish things), and then goes on to show how Lacan is rewriting, in pseudo-Joycean fashion, the sentence and its constitutive parts in a newly invented language, which may still sound like French, but definitely no longer looks like French: "*jnédit kdessot'tise, kdesse ottise, jeûn'nez dit, jeun'nez dit quedès/quedesse*". The same process is subsequently applied to the next section of the text, or what now looks like the second stanza of a poem: "*La pensée* [thought], *ai-je une appensée?, Jnes padappe ansée, listerie, lister-ie, il faut que lister rie* [Lister laughs]. *Isteron est du même ordre. Boufonnerie.*" At the end of the text, the rules of French grammar are restored, and a question is being formulated: "*Qu'est-ce que l'utérin a affaire dans l'hystérie. Grossesse nerveuse. Et après.*" (What does the uterine have to do with hysteria. Nervous pregnancy. And afterwards).[19] Anyone who is taking these scribbles seriously is likely to react in one of two different ways, no doubt depending on the quality of the transference towards Lacan. The first reaction is to say that Lacan had finally lost it, that his writing, here, shows clear signs of a pathologically deteriorating mind which, although not necessarily representative of a florid psychosis, has driven the man and his ideas deeper and deeper into the darkest realms of a full-blown delusion. Lacan's writing, here, would come frightfully close, then, to the samples of "inspired writing" by psychotic patients he himself had studied so carefully as a psychiatrist during the 1930s.[20] The second reaction would start from the assumption that Lacan was actually entirely sane when he wrote the text, and then proceed to an in-depth investigation of the meaning of it all, as if the lines constitute an esoteric, hermetically locked set of words, whose real and true meaning can only be found if we manage to locate the right key for deciphering the document. I shall resist the temptation to pass judgment on Lacan's state of mind, but if we take the text not as the production of a madman, then the second, hermeneutic approach may in itself not be all that productive either. Regardless as to whether one finds the key to unlock the seal, the hermeneutic approach, which pokes at meaning and values the enjoyment of the deciphering that is associated with it—following Lacan's own assertions in and on *Television*—exemplifies how any type of "virtuous knowledge", even the most playful and joyous example, can be made to fall from grace and descend into sin, especially when it is taken too seriously.

Maybe it is just better to assume that as a gay psychoanalyst, Lacan was having fun, enjoying himself, and extolling the virtues of *gai saber*. Fantasist or not, he is bending over backwards to ensure that the knowledge he is producing remains light-hearted. When he is "demolishing" the French language—much like the surrealists were fond of doing, or like his younger literary contemporaries Philippe Sollers and Pierre Guyotat—enacting the content of the message (*je n'ai dit que des sottises*) through the style with which it is executed, he is bending the rules of grammar, turning syntax inside out, twisting words and sentences like he is working on yet another transformation of the Borromean knot. For Lacan, language and knowledge should be as flexible as a Möbius-strip, a Klein bottle, or a cross-cap. That is what he recognized and appreciated in the works of Rabelais, in the literary art of Baltasar Gracià, whose inimitable talent for generating maximum effect with minimum words was referred to as *agudeza*, or in the remarkable *Bigarrures* (variegations) of Etienne Tabourot, the Seigneur des Accords, and of course also in the books of James Joyce.[21] Yet in pursuing *gai saber*, and avoiding any kind of established, doctrinal knowledge production, Lacan was actually extremely serious about where the true value of psychoanalysis can be found, and what should become of knowledge when it enters the theory and practice of psychoanalysis. As his formula for the discourse of the analyst indicates, knowledge is held to operate on the place of truth, which does not mean that psychoanalytic knowledge, as it is employed by the analyst in his or her clinical practice, has to represent the truth, the whole truth and nothing but the truth, but paradoxically that the knowledge "in action" cannot be too serious, meaningful, and austere, so that it can *evoke* the truth—much like the medieval court jester would always speak the truth by never actually saying it.[22] And when, in *Television*, Lacan posited that the end of a psychoanalytic process is driven by the ethic of the "well-spoken" (*l'éthique du bien-dire*), what he had in mind was not that analysands at the end of their analysis would be more capable than before to articulate their thoughts and emotions in a serious and correct fashion, as though psychoanalytic treatment might constitute a lengthy elocution lesson, but rather that analysands would acquire the capacity to play on words, to put their life into perspective, to see the humour of it all (Lacan, 1990[1974], p. 22).[23] As such, *gai saber* is not just a theoretical flight of fancy for Lacan the fantasist, but also, and much more fundamentally, a clinical principle, which lies at the heart of psychoanalytic practice, psychoanalytic training and psychoanalytic epistemology. It is related to what Nicolas of Cusa—who was not a troubadour but a cardinal—designated as the *docta ignorantiae*, the wise ignorance (Cusanus, 1985[1440]), but it is also connected to the Freudian structure of the *Witz*, which much like any joke can be seen as a linguistic attempt at destabilizing an established set of expectations, or at steering existing mental and social structures in surprising, unanticipated directions (Freud, 1960[1905c]). As the anthropologist Mary Douglas put it: "A joke is a play upon form that affords an opportunity for realizing that an accepted pattern has no necessity" (Douglas, 1975, p. 96). It should not come as a complete surprise, then, that Lacan at one point also defined psychoanalytic interpretation as a *Witz*—not exactly a joke (and there is no evidence that Lacan ever told jokes when conducting his analyses) but a quip, a wittiness, a wordplay, a little piece of gay knowledge (Lacan, 2020[1974], p. 29). On another occasion, Lacan even went so far as to suggest that the procedure of the pass—a controversial arrangement for appointing new analysts—should be considered a *Witz*, or at least he used the structure of the *Witz*, which crucially relies on what Freud called *die Dritte Person* (*la troisième*, the third), in order to justify its precise structure (Lacan, 2001[1967a], p. 265). Lacan could only hope that his audience, and especially the psychoanalysts attending his seminars, would be as gay as he was, that they would not become bogged down in the pursuit of absolute knowledge and the quest for true meaning, that they would be able to listen to his words like they were coming from the sonorous mouth of a medieval troubadour, and that they would see the not-so-funny comedy of their own existence, as dedicated followers of Jacques the Fantasist. He could only hope.

The Episteme of Laughter

Given Lacan's lifelong commitment to *gai saber*, it would be inappropriate to employ his theory as a firmly established, doctrinal body of knowledge, and outright paradoxical to interpret his each and every word as a definitive statement. During the 1950s, Lacan criticized the representatives of ego-psychology not only for transforming Freud's invention into psycho-education and enlightened behaviourism, but also for systematizing and "straightening" Freud's ideas. Throughout his career, he remained profoundly skeptical of the scientific ideal of the integration of knowledge, truth and reality, and he consistently argued in favour of a knowledge economy that is based on the principles of uncertainty, undecidability, and incompletion. Instead of returning to Freud in order to generate a new, coherent, and consistent formalism, Lacan campaigned for psychoanalysis to be re-gay-ed—for it to re-establish itself as a new *gaya scienza*, for it to mellow its rigid concepts, structures, practices and procedures into a more light-hearted, open-ended, playful, and altogether amusing set of ideas, for it to become less scientific in the Teutonic sense, and more poetic in the Provençal sense, for it to stop worrying about social conventions and public respectability, for it to be intrinsically suspicious of customary practices, in short for it to have fun. As such, Lacan intended to contribute to the (re-) invention of psychoanalysis as a new episteme of laughter or, better still, as a laughing episteme—a sensual, passionate, "affected knowledge", which can be worn lightly, and whose playful permutations of words and ideas may generate unexpected new discoveries.

If there is an echo of Spinoza in all of this, then it is definitely not accidental. Whereas most teenagers would decorate the walls of their room with posters of their favourite pop stars, at the age of 16 Lacan preferred a self-designed diagram outlining the structure of Spinoza's *Ethics* (Roudinesco, 1997[1993], pp. 11, 53). For his doctoral thesis, he chose proposition 57 of the third book of the *Ethics* as an epigraph (Lacan, 1975[1932], p. 11). When, at the *Maison de la Chimie* and in *Television*, he opposed gaiety to sadness, he clearly alluded to Spinoza's two fundamental emotions of *laetitia* and *tristitia*. In addition, when Nietzsche started making notes for *Die Fröhliche Wissenschaft* in the summer of 1881, he wrote to his friend Franz Overbeck about his own indebtedness to the Dutch philosopher, and about the important task of "making knowledge the most *powerful affect*" (*die Erkenntniß zum* mächtigsten Affekt *zu machen*). However, by contrast with Spinoza, for whom knowledge is intrinsically joyful because it grants power over life, Nietzsche believed that knowledge is primarily painful, so that joyful knowledge is a philosophical assignment rather than an epistemic given (Nietzsche, 1996, p. 177; Spinoza, 1996[1677]).

Unlike Lacan, Freud never disclosed in public that he was "*fröhlich*", and although he admitted in his autobiographical study that Nietzsche's "guesses and intuitions [*Ahnungen und Einsichten*] often agree in the most astonishing way with the laborious findings of psycho-analysis", there is no evidence that Freud ever paid much attention to *The Gay Science* (Freud, 1959[1925*d*], p. 60).[24] Nonetheless, Freud was the first psychoanalyst, and for many years the only psychoanalyst, to give serious consideration to the structure and function of jokes, and in his works he often made use of irony and sarcasm to drive his points home. When, in 1926, the American writer Max Eastman visited Freud in Vienna, and the great man walked through the door to greet him, Eastman was surprised that "he was smaller" than expected, and "slender-limbed, and more feminine", and with a flatter nose than expected, and with a gentle voice. But Eastman particularly picked up on the fact that Freud smiled a lot, seemed quite amused a lot of the time, and would sometimes throw his head way back and laugh like a child (Eastman, 1942, pp. 261–273). It is not an image of Freud that one would ever get from the numerous "official" photographs of him that have entered the cultural domain over the years. Indeed, there is hardly a single photograph of Freud in which he can be seen laughing. For the later pictures, this may be explained with reference to the cancerous growth in his mouth and the cheek prosthesis he was forced to wear, but for all the others it may no doubt also be attributed to the public image of gravitas that he was expected (and to some extent also wanted) to maintain. In a sense, one could argue that the official photographs were meant to capture the serious-mindedness of the "institutional Freud", the Freud who approached the psychoanalytic study of the mind with authority, dignity, and respect, even if the results of his research were challenging, controversial, and scandalous.

It is precisely in this discrepancy between the private intellectual playfulness of one or more passionate, enthusiastic soul-searchers and the constant institutional quest for the public recognition of a firmly grounded doctrine that the problem of psychoanalytic knowledge needs to be situated. Were I to choose a psychoanalytic concept to "diagnose" the current and historical state of the knowledge operating within psychoanalytic institutions, it would have to be the good old Freudian notion of "disavowal" (*Verleugnung*), which he employed to characterize the attitude of the male fetishist towards castration, and which the French psychoanalyst Octave Mannoni brilliantly captured with the phrase "I know very well, but still ...." (*Je sais bien, mais quand même*) (Freud, 1961[1927e]; Mannoni, 2003[1969]). As a "gay psychoanalyst" Lacan too has to some extent been the unwilling victim of this type of institutional straightening, with its specific organizational epistemic disavowal. In a thought-provoking paper on the hugely problematic psychoanalytic concept of perversion, Tim Dean has demonstrated, for example, how Lacan's theoretical and practical celebration of division, fracture, and dehiscence, as well as his critical opposition to any form of subjective identity, which has effectively allowed for his ideas to be recuperated within the anti-identitarian configurations of queer theory, have regularly been re-adjusted into a set of formalistic normative categories and a hetero-centric logic of sexual identity (Dean, 2008, p. 108). In Rome, in 1974, and elsewhere Lacan was rather exasperated when he felt the need to remind people that he had been a clown on television. It is rather exasperating that Lacan's "I am gay"—although it could easily be dismissed as a passing remark, an insignificant punctuation, a momentary lapse of reason, or an extremely succinct para-textual digression—never seems to have been taken very seriously. I am not joking.

There is no evidence that Lacan ever read Nietzsche's *Fröhliche Wissenschaft*, but if he had, he would definitely have picked up on the following "aphorism":

> For most people, the intellect is an awkward, gloomy, creaking machine that is hard to start: when they want to work with this machine and think well, they call it 'taking the matter seriously'—oh, how taxing good thinking must be for them! The lovely human beast seems to lose its good mood when it thinks well; it becomes 'serious'! And 'where laughter and gaiety are found, thinking is good for nothing'—that is the prejudice of this serious beast against all 'gay science'. Well then, let us prove it a prejudice! (Nietzsche, 2011[1887], pp. 182–183)

The paragraph echoes something Nietzsche had already written in the introduction to his book:

> [Y]ou will never find someone who could completely mock you ... To laugh at oneself as one would have to laugh in order to laugh *from the whole truth*—for that, not even the best have had enough sense of truth, and the most gifted have had far too little genius! Perhaps even laughter still has a future—when the proposition 'The species is everything, an individual is always nothing' has become part of humanity and this ultimate liberation and irresponsibility is accessible to everyone at all times. Perhaps laughter will then have formed an alliance with wisdom; perhaps only 'gay science' will remain. (Ibid., pp. 27–28)

Not too long after writing these lines, Nietzsche collapsed physically and mentally, and never recovered his sanity. Sixty years later, Dr Jacques Lacan put on a hairy, ginger-coloured wig and invited a young woman to dance.

Notes

1 This chapter is based on an essay included in P. Gherovici and M. Steinkoler (Eds), *Lacan, Psychoanalysis, and Comedy* (Cambridge: Cambridge University Press, 2016), pp. 36–59. It is reproduced here with the permission of Cambridge University Press through PLS Clear.
2 The text of the interview was reprinted without the brief introduction, the sub-headings and the accompanying cartoons from the *New Yorker* in Chapsal's *Envoyez la petite musique* ... (Chapsal, 1984, pp. 42–54). In 1991, on the occasion of the tenth anniversary of Lacan's death, the text and the cartoons were also reprinted in the psychoanalytic magazine *l'Âne*, yet without reference to Chapsal, without the introduction, and with the original sub-headings replaced with a new and unattributed set of paragraph titles. A facsimile of the text was subsequently reprinted in 2000 in the psychoanalytic journal *la célibataire*, again without reference to Chapsal, yet with the acknowledgement of Françoise Giroud–the co-founder and editor of *L'express*–as the one who had made the interview possible. See Lacan (1991[1957]; 2000[1957]). An anonymous English translation of the interview as published in *l'Âne* can be accessed online: http://braungardt.trialectics.com/sciences/psychoanalysis/jacques-lacan/interview-jacques-lacan/.
3 The small volume entitled *Television* is effectively the edited text of two one-hour long "Lacan-shows" directed by Benoît Jacquot, which were aired during prime time on two consecutive Saturday evenings by France's main television channel ORTF, in March 1974, under the title *Psychanalyse I* and *Psychanalyse II*. In each of these, Lacan can be seen "acting out" a scenario he himself had written, in response to some questions by Jacques-Alain Miller, his son-in-law and intellectual heir. See Jacquot (2003; 2012).
4 It suffices to look at the name of the translator of the first translation mentioned here to know that this version is evidently vastly superior to the second, "officially sanctioned" version, if only because the first also comes with very detailed annotations, in a separate document (Nobus, 2013).
5 This is my own translation of the official French version of Lacan's seminar session (Lacan, 2006b, p. 120), verified against other, more literal transcriptions, such as the one that can be found at http://espace.freud.pagesperso-orange.fr/topos/psycha/psysem/semblan/semblan7.htm and a number of tape-recordings made by members of the audience, one of which can be found at http://www.valas.fr/IMG/mp3/7_semblant_12_5_71.mp3. For an excellent general introduction to Lacan's seminar, see Fink (2014a).
6 Indeed, in his unofficial English translation of Lacan's seminar session of 12 May 1971, Cormac Gallagher has rendered Lacan's "*je suis gai*" as "I am happy". See Lacan (1971b).
7 For a fascinating reconstruction of Nietzsche's alleged (suppressed) homosexuality, and its potential influence on the shaping of his ideas, see Köhler (2002[1989]).
8 Interestingly, for the new English edition of *The Complete Works of Friedrich Nietzsche*, which was launched by Stanford University Press in 1995 and which is based on the authoritative *Kritische Studienausgabe* by Colli-Montinari, the title of volume 6, whose publication date has not been announced yet, was originally

mentioned as *The Gay Science*, whereas the publisher's website subsequently had it listed as *The Joyful Science*, before deleting the title altogether. See the listings on Stanford University Press's website: http://www.sup.org/nietzsche/list/.
9 We know that Nietzsche re-read Emerson whilst he was working on *Die Fröhliche Wissenschaft* from a note he made during the Autumn of 1881: "In no other book [than Emerson's selected essays] have I ever felt so much at home and in my home—I can't praise it, it is just too close to me" (Nietzsche, 1988, p. 588). Emerson designated himself as a "Professor of the Joyous Science" in an early lecture entitled "Prospects", which was originally delivered at the Masonic Temple in Boston on 20 January 1842 (Emerson, 1972[1842], p. 368). He repeated the phrase 34 years later, in a lecture on "The Scholar", presented at the University of Virginia on 28 June 1876 (Emerson, 1888[1876], p. 250). Emerson specifically referred to "gai science" (*sic*) in the 1876 essay "Poetry and Imagination", which had started life as a lecture on "Poetry and English Poetry" from 1854 (Emerson, 1898[1836], p. 28). The literature on Nietzsche's intellectual indebtedness to Emerson is vast. For recent discussions, with a particular focus on *The Gay Science*, see Pippin (2011, pp. 33–34) and Grimstad (2013, pp. 33–36).
10 For more detailed elaborations of this point, see Ansell-Pearson (2012), Babich (2009), Higgins (2000), Langer (2010), and Janaway (2013).
11 Dragonetti taught at the University of Ghent from 1961 until 1968, when he accepted a chair at the University of Geneva. His 1961 book *Aux frontières du langage poétique* (Dragonetti, 1961) caught Lacan's attention, and Dragonetti and Lacan subsequently became good friends. Lacan also arranged for some of Dragonetti's books to be published in the collection he was editing at *Editions du Seuil*, and Dragonetti's own growing interest in Lacanian psychoanalysis, combined with his intellectual generosity towards his students, eventually resulted in the emergence of a small group of Lacanian medievalists, including Charles Méla, Henri Rey-Flaud, and Alexandre Leupin. A collection of letters between Dragonetti and Lacan is preserved at the Swiss Literary Archives in Bern. It is also worth noting, here, that the word *troubadour* is derived from the Occitan verb *trobar*, which means "to compose poetry", but also "to find" and "to invent" (Gaunt and Kay, 1999, p. 294).
12 As it happens, it was not until the late 19th century that scholars started to appreciate the humour and playfulness in troubadour poetry, but not until the 1960s, following the translation into English of Huizinga's *Homo Ludens*, that this type of appreciation in itself was taken seriously. See Huizinga (1949[1944]) and Monson (1999).
13 There are no references to Emerson in any of Lacan's written texts and seminars. As to Nietzsche, Lacan briefly referred to *The Birth of Tragedy*, *Thus Spoke Zarathustra*, and *On the Genealogy of Morality* in some of his seminars, but to the best of my knowledge he never mentioned *The Gay Science*. On two occasions, he did invoke the theme of the "death of God", which looms large over the third and fifth books of *The Gay Science*, but this in itself is no indication that he actually read Nietzsche's work in this respect. See Lacan (1965–1966, session of 25 May 1966; 1994[1973], p. 27).
14 For the full written text of Lacan's "Rome Discourse", see Lacan (2006[1953]). The reference to Rabelais appears on p. 230.
15 For sources in French, see Lebovits (2007), Vallois (2003), Cottet (1997), Lysy-Stevens (1993a; 1993b), and Kusnierek (1986). In her otherwise excellent study of how Lacan's theory of desire is crucially indebted to his reading of various medieval texts, Erin Felicia Labbie makes no mention whatsoever of the *gai saber* (Labbie, 2006). A book chapter by Joan Copjec raises high expectations, but does

not address Lacan's engagement with *gai saber* either (Copjec, 2005). It is also worth noting, here, that in 1969 Jean-Luc Godard released a film entitled *Le gai savoir*, which was re-titled *Joy of Learning* when it was distributed outside France. In the film, a young man and a young woman discuss language and the spoken word, which they designate as "the enemy", in the eerie space of an abandoned television studio. In a fine review of the film, the American film critic James Monaco described *Le gai savoir* as Godard's "ultimate effort at semioclasm" and the director's first "film d'role" (Monaco, 1975).

16 In 1993, an American PhD student was accorded a rare interview with Lacan's second wife, Sylvia Maklès, in which she described her husband as someone who was handsome without being droll, and someone who definitely could be funny when he ought to be. At the same time, she referred to Chapsal as a vulgar person, who was hardly a "great woman", although Lacan's wife would have had very good reasons for being dismissive of Chapsal ... See Hunt (1995, pp. 177, 180).

17 For all I know, this is the only seminar in which Lacan tells his audience a proper joke—a story of a student and an examiner, which he has borrowed from Raymond Queneau (Lacan, 2017[1998], p. 98).

18 The "elsewhere" refers to a series of talks (*entretiens*) Lacan was giving at the same time in the chapel of the Sainte-Anne Hospital, under the general title of "*Le savoir du psychanalyste*" (The knowledge of the psychoanalyst). See Lacan (2017[2011]).

19 For a facsimile reproduction and transcription of the document, see Lacan (2006c, p. 42).

20 See, for example, Lévy-Valensi, Migault, and Lacan (1975[1931]).

21 The reference to Tabourot appears late in Lacan's work, in the seminar *L'insu que sait de l'une-bévue s'aile à mourre*, of 1976–1977, and it shows, alongside the title of the Seminar, how Lacan, *pace* Miller, was still pretty gay at the time. See Lacan (1977–1979[1976–1977] 12/13, p. 15). For a brief presentation of the *Bigarrures*, see Vereecken (1987). For Lacan's 1975–1976 seminar on Joyce, see Lacan (2016[2005]).

22 On the discourse of the analyst, see Lacan (2007[1991]).

23 See also Miller (1998, pp. 12–13).

24 For detailed studies of Freud's indebtedness to Nietzsche and the Nietzschean themes in his work, see Assoun (2000[1980]), Gasser (1997), and Lehrer (1995).

Chapter 7

Once He Was a Poet: On Psychoanalysis as Poetry in Lacan's Clinical Paradigm

Introduction

To write about psychoanalysis as poetry is risky; it might even be considered inappropriate, reckless, and outright dangerous.[1] To be clear, I do not intend to write in this chapter about how psychoanalysis might be employed to interpret poetry, about how certain poets have taken inspiration from psychoanalysis, about the creative dialogue between psychoanalysts and poets, or about the (proto-psychoanalytic) healing power of poetry, but about how psychoanalytic theory and practice, and especially the Lacanian modality, are inflected and refracted by poetry. My argument is that in the Lacanian tradition, the psychoanalyst is expected to embrace the richly evocative playfulness of the *ars poetica*, which celebrates the polyphonic musicality of language whilst simultaneously adhering to specific formal structures and metrical patterns, in order to stay attuned to the uniquely human subjective truth from which the discipline derives its *raison d'être*.

Developing such an argument appears to be in flagrant violation of Freud's lifelong aspiration to secure the formal recognition of psychoanalysis as a proper science. In fact, it may even be perceived as jeopardizing contemporary attempts at rehabilitating the clinical practice of psychoanalysis as an effective, evidence-based treatment for various mental health problems. It will, no doubt, also play into the hands of all those who have been claiming for years that psychoanalysis firmly belongs in the arts and humanities, and that psychoanalysts (Freud included) are first and foremost creative writers, argonauts of the literary mind, dreamers with an eye for a show.

The danger is not imaginary; in fact, the risk is real. Nevertheless, it is my conviction that by ignoring the poetic dimension of their work, psychoanalysts stand to lose more than risking their scientific credibility or undermining their professional legitimacy. In failing to appreciate how much their discipline owes to literary craft and poetic artistry, they risk rendering psychoanalysis soulless. Moreover, to acknowledge the poetic quality of psychoanalysis does not *de facto* imply that the discipline becomes

DOI: 10.4324/9781003252276-8

completely devoid of scientific respectability. Even scientists bent on rigorous empirical verification occasionally admit that science and poetry are not strictly incompatible, that science contains poetic elements, and that unverified "poetic" theories may over time become validated scientific principles. For example, in *To Explain the World: The Discovery of Modern Science*, the Nobel Prize–winning physicist Steven Weinberg writes:

> There remains a poetic element in modern physics. We do not write in poetry; much of the writing of physicists barely reaches the level of prose. But we seek beauty in our theories, and use aesthetic judgments as a guide in our research. (Weinberg, 2015, p. 14)

Lacan's New Signifier

On 17 May 1977, at the very end of his 24th public seminar, which was delivered under the rather bizarre title of *L'insu que sait de l'une-bévue s'aile à mourre*, Lacan disclosed to his audience that he did not consider himself to be enough of a poet, to be "poet-enough". In the only version of this session of the seminar that is currently available in an official format, Lacan's words are transcribed as: "*Je ne suis pas assez poète. Je ne suis pas* poâte-assez" (I am not enough of a poet. I am not *poâte*-enough) (Lacan, 1977–1979[1976–1977]), 17/18, p. 22). Other, unofficial transcripts of the seminar mention the sentences in a number of alternative forms: "*Je ne suis pas assez poîte. Je ne suis pas poâte-assez*", "*Je ne suis pas assez poâte. Je ne suis pas poâtassé*", "*Je ne suis pas assez pohâte. Je ne suis pas pohâtassé*", "*Je ne suis pas assez pouate. Je ne suis pas pouate assez.*" The main reason as to why there are so many different textual versions of Lacan's words is that his pronunciation of the French word *poète* (poet) was distinctly odd, so much so that the sound of his signifier does not really allow for a single transcription that would do full justice to its composite sonority and strange resonances.[2] Phonetically, the signifier is pronounced by Lacan as *pwat*, which does not correspond to a single common word in French. Any transcription of Lacan's words, any reduction of the signifier to the letter, thus narrows down the semantic spectrum to one or more options, or indeed to a single neologism. In a sense, the issue of capturing meaning through writing, here, is exactly the opposite of what is required with James Joyce's *Finnegans Wake*, in which the writing requires the signifier for the text to become meaningful and legible. The most famous example of this, which Lacan quoted in his 1975 lecture on Joyce, is no doubt Joyce's sentence "Who ails tongue coddeau, aspace of dumbillsilly", which needs to be verbalized, in French, as "*Où est ton cadeau espèce d'imbécile*" (Where's your present, you imbecile?), for it to become comprehensible (Joyce, 1939, p. 15; Lacan, 2016[1975], p. 145).[3] However, Lacan's signifier *pwat* definitely deserves more detailed exploration, if only because he repeated it no less than ten times in the space of a few minutes, whilst his concurrent admission of failure—"I am not enough of a poet"—is also extremely evocative, to say the least.

What are we to make of Lacan's signifier, then? In 1923, the French poet and essayist Léon-Paul Fargue published a small collection of short, humorous poems entitled *Ludions* (Cartesian water devils), which were subsequently set to music by his friend Erik Satie. The shortest of the poems was entitled *Air du poète* (Poet's Tune) (Fargue, 1967[1923], p. 41). In it, Fargue played on the near homophony between the French word for poetry (*poésie*) and the French name of Papua New Guinea (*Papouasie-Nouvelle-Guinée*), in order to mock poor, mediocre, and silly poetry, whilst the form of this critique was also clearly poetic:

Air du poète
Au pays de Papouasie
J'ai caressé la Pouasie ...
La grâce que je vous souhaite
C'est de n'être pas Papouète.

Poet's Tune
In the land of Papua
I touched upon Papuatry ...
The grace I wish to you
Is that you shall not be Papoet[4]

Lacan was familiar with these verses, since he alluded to them in a "conversation" (*entretien*) at the chapel of the Sainte-Anne Hospital in Paris on 6 January 1972 (Lacan, 2017[2011], pp. 95–96). Exemplifying the lightheartedness (*gaieté*) with which he had always approached the foundations of psychoanalytic theory and practice, Lacan reminded his audience of a poem, by Antoine Tudal, that he had once chosen as an epigraph for the third section of his 1953 "Rome Discourse", and which he claimed to have culled from an almanac entitled *Paris en l'an 2000* (Paris in the Year 2000) (Lacan, 1966[1953], p. 289; 2006[1953], p. 239):

Entre l'homme et l'amour,
Il y a la femme.
Entre l'homme et la femme,
Il y a un monde.
Entre l'homme et le monde,
Il y a un mur.[5]

Between man and love,
There is woman.

> Between man and woman,
> There is a world.
> Between man and the world,
> There is a wall.

Thought-provoking as the content of these verses may be, as poetry they are of rather poor quality. At Sainte-Anne, Lacan stated that they were "not lacking in talent", but he nonetheless called them "*poésie proverbiale*" and "*vers de mirliton*", i.e., what would be designated in English as doggerel (Lacan, 2017[2011], p. 92).[6] It is, therefore, no coincidence that Lacan alluded to Fargue's *Air du poète* in the context of a discussion of the style, tone, and overall value of a mediocre poem taken from an almanac: "It's a matter now of seeing what will come next. How can it be written? What will there be between man, that is, him the pouet [*le pouète*]—the pouet of *Pouasie* as dear Léon-Paul Fargue once said—and love" (Ibid., pp. 95–96).[7] In addition, Fargue's *Pouasie*, and the sorry *Papouète* who produces it, reflect the poet's own humorous take on the pejorative French word *poâte*. Although this word is archaic and rare, it refers to a flawed lyrical poet, a peddler of mediocre verses, in short a rhymester, versifier, or poetaster, much like the inimitable William McGonagall or the equally famous bard Cacofonix in the comic books of Asterix and Obelix, who terrorizes the little village of indomitable Gauls with his unbearable musical drivel.[8] Lacan's signifier at the end of *Seminar XXIV* may thus be rendered more judiciously in writing as "*Je ne suis pas assez poâte. Je ne suis Papouète assez*".[9] Or, in accordance with some of the paranomasias that appeared in Lacan's paper "Lituraterre"—those familiar with the text will recall how he included the words *papeludun* (for *pas-plus-d'un*) and *hun-en-peluce* (for *un-en-plus*) (Lacan, 2013[1971a], p. 331)—I would even suggest that the signifiers in the last sentence are rendered more poetically, here, with the single word *papouètassé*.[10]

Although it does not seem to make immediate sense, "*Je ne suis papouètassé*", clearly incorporates an admission of failure—the failure being that Lacan considered himself to be not enough of a "mediocre poet", of the kind that produces doggerel. Of course, this admission is in itself quite ambiguous. If Lacan lamented the fact that he was not enough of a mediocre poet, does this imply that he effectively regarded himself as a highly accomplished poet? Or, does it merely mark his aspiration to be *more* of a mediocre poet, to become better and more prolific at producing mediocre poetry, and thus more successful at failing to be a good poet? If so, wouldn't a successful attempt at "failing more" still be a failure in its own right, despite the fact that the goal has been achieved? The paradox is similar to that of the student who is determined not to pass his exam: if he succeeds in failing, does this imply that he has properly failed, or rather that he has been successful after all? Even so, Lacan's admission of failure (of *insuccès*), here, constitutes the point where he inscribes himself in the title of his own seminar—*l'insu que sait* (the knowing unknown) is homophonic in French with *insuccès* (failure). At this point, Lacan thus allows the title of his seminar to become a placeholder for his own position, as a practicing psychoanalyst and a teacher of psychoanalysis. These clearly discernable overtones of failure (dissatisfaction, disappointment, and frustration) that characterize this last session of Lacan's *Seminar XXIV* are also reminiscent of the pessimism that pervaded Freud's late paper "Analysis Terminable and Interminable", in which the founder of psychoanalysis designated his own invention as an impossible profession, with the small comfort that the same applies to education and government (Freud, 1964[1937c], p. 248).

When Lacan confesses to "not being poetaster-enough", the pronouncement is as intriguing as it is surprising, as puzzling as it is provocative. As is so often the case with the "later Lacan", the statement is apodictic, declarative, and assertive, rather than the logical outcome of a carefully constructed argument. If there is an argument to support and justify the point, we are left with the task of having to construct it for ourselves. In what follows, then, I will demonstrate that, despite its fanciful, frivolous character, "not being poetaster-enough", reopens some fundamental issues concerning the "function of speech" and the "field of language" in psychoanalysis, and also raises important questions regarding the "function of interpretation" and the "field of meaning" in the direction of the treatment.

As a first approximation of this argument, it should be noted that Lacan's lament occurred as part of a series of reflections on how psychoanalysis operates—on the target, impact, and effect of psychoanalytic interpretations—and, more specifically, on how a psychoanalyst may escape spurious "effects of meaning" each time the patient is being offered an interpretation. This in itself indicates how Lacan's signifier *papouètassé* encapsulated a clinical and theoretical concern for the direction of the psychoanalytic treatment. It needs to be situated at the end of Lacan's lifelong quest for a type of psychoanalytic interpretation that might avoid the clinical pitfalls of a patient's being provided with additional, even alienating, sources of meaning. As he had already put it in *Seminar VIII*:

> [B]y interpreting, you [as a psychoanalyst] give the subject something speech can feed on ... Thus, every time you introduce metaphor ... you remain on the very path that gives the [patient's] symptom consistency. It is no doubt a more simplified symptom, but it is still a symptom, in relation, in any case, to the desire that must be brought out. (Lacan, 2015[2001], p. 208)

Whereas during the 1950s, Lacan had adhered to a conception of interpretation as decipherment, he had gradually come to the realization that this hermeneutic, "meaning-generating" approach merely replaced one system of meaning (the patient's) with another (the analyst's). As such, it did not succeed in moving beyond the boundaries of the symbolic network of signifiers in which the patient's symptoms were embedded. This had brought him to the formulation of an alternative modality of psychoanalytic interpretation, focusing on oracular or apophantic interventions, such as enigmas and citations, which would have the advantage of being non-suggestive, of not adding new meaning to the patient's discourse, and of reaching out towards what he called the Real—the point where all symbolization fails.[11]

In *Seminar XXIV*, Lacan at one stage reminds his audience of his definition of the signifier: the signifier represents the subject for another signifier. Lacan emphasizes that the subject (despite considering himself to be God, especially in his "scientific" pursuits) cannot actually justify why and how "signifier" is being produced, and even less why and how this signifier represents him for another signifier.[12] Yet, since all effects of meaning (*effets de sens*) have to pass through this process, it results in their being "blocked up" (*se bouchent*), which effectively constitutes an impasse. If this sounds obscure, then we should no doubt assume, here, that the effects of meaning become blocked up, because these effects endlessly proliferate as "fictional" corollaries of the symbolic, without ever succeeding in capturing the Real. Lacan continues by saying that man's shrewdness (*l'astuce de l'homme*) is to stuff all of this—the inherent deadlock of the effects of meaning—with poetry, which remains in itself an effect of meaning (*effet de sens*), but also an effect of the hole (*effet de trou*). "It is only poetry," he adds, "that allows for interpretation ... That's why in my technique I can no longer get it [interpretation] to hold up".[13] The point is that poetry does not just generate meaning, or that good poetry, apart from generating meaning, also makes space for meaning not to be reduced to one single strand of semantics. Put differently, any kind of meaning that is associated with (good) poetry is immediately undone by the fact that it should be balanced against other meanings, and against the musicality and the rhythm of language, so that poetry effectively creates a hole in the field of meaning, which allows for limitless semantic configurations and permutations to take place. In Lacan's late conception of psychoanalytic interpretation, poetry thus becomes a staple of the analytic act, and psychoanalysts are being given the duty and responsibility to safeguard the poetic quality of their words, as new signifiers that do not immediately enter a known symbolic circuit, and whose meaning is therefore not instantly recognizable. Does this imply that the best analyst is also a good poet? Why did Lacan say, then, that he was not enough of a poetaster, and that he no longer managed to get interpretation to hold up? Why, at this point, would he have expressed a desire to be more mediocre at producing poetry, assuming this is indeed what he intended to say?

A Born Poem

As I mentioned earlier, in conceding to being *papouètassé*, and thus admitting to his own failure, Lacan inscribed himself in the title of the seminar he was delivering, which was announced as a series of lessons on the failure of a blunder (*l'insuccès de l'une-bévue*), and which also conjured up the failure (and the knowing unknown) of the unconscious (*l'insu que sait de l'Unbewußte*).[14] Who or what is failing here? And what is the status of this failure, if its object is always already in itself some type of failed (disrupted and disruptive) accomplishment, be it the unconscious or, indeed, mediocre poetry? What does it mean for Lacan to have been a failed poetaster?

In 1933, the budding psychoanalyst—he had started his training analysis with Rudolph Loewenstein just the year before—published a sonnet entitled "Hiatus Irrationalis" in the final (double) issue of the short-lived and largely forgotten surrealist journal *Le Phare de Neuilly*, which was edited at the time by Lise Deharme (*née* Anne-Marie Hirtz), the mysterious lady with the sky-blue gloves in André Breton's *Nadja* (Breton, 1999[1928]; Lacan, 1933b). The poem in question, which Lacan sent to his friend Ferdinand Alquié, is dated August 1929, and would therefore have been composed around the time Lacan completed his clinical training in psychiatry at Gatian de Clérambault's *Infirmerie Spéciale de la Préfecture de Police*, and just before he embarked on a new two-year internship at the *Hôpital Henri-Rousselle*, which was attached to the Sainte-Anne Hospital in Paris.[15] A close reading of Lacan's poem reveals that, in all likelihood, the inspiration for it came from Alexandre Koyré's monumental 1929 treatise on the philosophy of Jacob Böhme (Koyré, 1929)—a German cordwainer *cum* Christian theologian and mystic, to whose theory of the "signature of things" (*signatura rerum*) Lacan would later return on a regular basis—and that it also adopted the style of the French writer and poet Pierre Jean Jouve, who was married to the psychoanalyst Blanche Reverchon at the time.[16]

Lacan does not seem to have referred to his youthful poetic production in any of his subsequent writings and seminars, despite the fact that its title as published, "Hiatus Irrationalis", may very well be regarded as an early anticipation of his later concept of the Real.[17] Insofar as the poem recalled Böhme's theory of signatures, in which the German theologian posited that the signature supersedes the sign as the decisive and superior operator of knowledge, it could even be argued that in his poem, Lacan attempted to convey the significance of symbolic representations for the revelation of the true meaning of "things"—a project which would keep him busy for 50 odd years. However, I am not particularly concerned, here, with the intellectual and artistic sources that could have prompted Lacan to compose his poem, even less with the meaning and importance of the poem for Lacan's subsequent theoretical and clinical trajectory. In a sense, the question that concerns me is much simpler, although no doubt much more difficult to answer than any question concerning sources of inspiration and intellectual significance. Was Lacan a good poet? Did he consider himself a good poet?[18]

In the summer of 1929, at the age of 28, Lacan wrote a poem which he sent to a dear friend yet which, for some reason, he did not decide to publish until four years later, and under a different title, when his psychiatric training was coming to an end, and his clinical training as a psychoanalyst had taken a start. In the summer of 1929, Lacan clearly believed he could be a poet, yet maybe not enough of a proper poet or too much of a mediocre poet (*papouète*) to push himself to release the poem into the public domain, only sending it to a friend and maybe sharing it with a loved one. In 1933, shortly after starting his analysis, when he submitted his poem to *Le Phare de Neuilly*, things had clearly changed, insofar as something prompted Lacan to stop keeping his poem to himself. He no longer considered himself enough of a mediocre poet, thought of himself as "not that bad a poet" or "not bad poet enough" (*papouètassé*) to publish his poem and expose it to external commentary and interpretation. Not being enough of a poetaster, not being poetaster enough, is thus, one could say, what encouraged Lacan to submit his poem to *Le Phare de Neuilly*. Once Lacan was a poet, once he considered himself a poet—a good enough poet to share his poem with others, notably the discerning readership of a trendy surrealist magazine. Yet over and above his own considerations regarding the artistic value of his verses, the question could be raised as to whether Lacan's poem actually constituted "good poetry". What, for that matter, is good poetry? Vice versa, when Lacan, in January 1972, referred to Antoine Tudal's verses as doggerel, what authorized him to make this claim? To all intents and purposes, Lacan's "Hiatus Irrationalis" is probably "not too bad", inasmuch as it was composed in proper alexandrines, with consistent metrical structures, in accordance with the Petrarchan, lyrical form of the sonnet (four stanzas, including two quatrains and two tercets), with careful attention to the musicality of the words, and with a perfect tail rhyme that even included his own surname. Compared to, say, the verses of William McGonagall, Lacan's poem is of a decent standard, but then again he was not a psychoanalyst yet, and he had not started bemoaning his failure to be a good poetaster.

Until roughly 15 years ago, I remained convinced that "Hiatus Irrationalis" was the only "philosophical" poem Lacan had ever committed to writing.[19] Yet on the 30th of June 2006, I was privileged to attend a public auction at the sumptuous Hôtel Marcel Dassault on the Champs-Elysées in Paris, during which 117 graphic designs and unpublished manuscripts by Lacan were put up for sale. The owner of this extraordinary cache of papers was Jean-Michel Vappereau, a psychoanalyst and mathematician with whom Lacan had worked during the 1970s on various intricate elaborations of his infamous knot theory. Amongst the documents sold was an undated and untitled hologram of 23 lines, written in violet ink, with corrections by

Lacan in black, and the caption "*A lire après*" (to be read afterwards).[20] The opening lines of the text read as follows:

> *Comme je suis 'né' poème et papouète, je dirai que le plus court étant le meilleur, il se dit: 'Etre où?' Ce qui s'écrit de plus d'une façon, à l'occasion: étrou. Le refuser pour que l'étrou vaille ..., tient le coup quoiqu'en suspens. C'est un poème signé: Là-quand ..., parce que ça a l'air d'y répondre, naturel ment.*

I shall hopefully be forgiven for not attempting a full translation of these lines here. Suffice it to say that the word *étrou*—although it exists in the dialect of the Anjou region in France, where it stands for an oarlock on the side of a rowing boat (Verrier and Orillon, 1908, p. 373)—does not correspond to any known French noun, and is another typically Lacanian paranomasia, in this case of the phrase "*être où*" (being where), which in itself contains a critical allusion to the French rendition of Heidegger's term *Dasein* (literally: being there), as "*être-là*", in Rudolf Boehm and Alphonse de Waelhens' seminal translation of the first section of Heidegger's *Sein und Zeit* (Heidegger, 1964[1927], p. 7, note 4).

For all I know, Lacan never actually read this text at his seminar, nor anywhere else for that matter, despite his own reminder at the top of the page. Maybe he changed his mind about it, maybe he gave the text to Vappereau (intentionally or accidentally) before reading it out and then forgot about it, maybe it was not intended to be read in public in the first place, but rather at a more intimate, private, and personal occasion.[21] Whatever the circumstances may be, the text is important for at least two reasons. First, Lacan's use of the term "*papouète*", here, indicates again that his wordplay on *poète* in the session of 17 May 1977 of his *Seminar XXIV* was not just a momentary flight of fancy, a sudden eruption of seemingly nonsensical lyricism, but indeed a deliberate evocation of the last line of Leon-Paul Fargue's "Air du poète", much like he had done at Sainte-Anne on 6 January 1972.[22] We need to be careful, therefore, not to immediately ascribe the status of neologism to words used by Lacan that do not always make "immediate sense", insofar as they are sometimes taken from specific literary sources (*papouète*) or the broader cultural realm of language (*poâte*). Second, in the unpublished manuscript which he gave to Jean-Michel Vappereau, Lacan describes himself not only as a *papouète*, but also, and quite crucially, as a *poem*: "... je suis "né" poème et papouète" (I am "born" a poem and not poet). Lacan may have decided to give the poem to Vappereau in response to his collaborator's own musings on poetry, mathematics, and topology, or in order to invite critical comments and stimulate further reflection, or simply as a present which he later seemed to have forgotten about—echoing Joyce, one might say "*Où est ton cadeau espèce d'imbécile?* (Where's your present, you imbecile?)—yet in the poem he also designates himself as a poem.

The statement, here, echoes a paragraph from Lacan's preface to the English edition of *Seminar XI*, which was dated 17 May 1976, roughly one week after Lacan delivered the last session of *Seminar XXIII*.[23] In French, the paragraph reads:

> *Quelle hiérarchie pourrait lui [l'analyste] confirmer d'être analyste, lui en donner le tampon? Ce qu'un Cht me disait, c'est que je l'étais, né. Je répudie ce certificat: je ne suis pas un poète, mais un poème. Et qui s'écrit, malgré qu'il ait l'air d'être sujet.* (Lacan, 2001[1976], p. 572)

In the English translation of *Seminar XI*, for which the preface was destined, Alan Sheridan renders these lines as:

> What hierarchy could confirm him as an analyst, give him the rubber-stamp? A certificate tells me that I was born. I repudiate this certificate: I am not a poet but a poem. A poem that is being written, even if it looks like a subject. (Lacan, 1994[1973], p. xl)

In the more recent, stand-alone re-translation of Lacan's preface by Russell Grigg, they read: "What hierarchy could confirm that he is an analyst, give him a rubber stamp? What a Sht told me is that I was born. I repudiate this certificate: I am not a poet but a poem. One that is being written, despite giving the appearance of being a subject" (Lacan, 2018[1976]), p. 25). Unfortunately, this new translation is equally flawed, and I would therefore suggest the following alternative:

> Which hierarchy could confirm to him [the analyst] that he is an analyst, could give him the seal of approval for it? What a Northener once told me, is that I always was one, born as such. I repudiate this certificate: I am not a poet but a poem. And which is being written, despite the fact that it looks like being a subject.[24]

Needless to say, even in a more accurate translation, these sentences remain rather cryptic, and therefore warrant an explanatory paraphrase. In short, Lacan argued that the psychoanalyst can now be counted (as a new professional position) amongst those who provide treatment. Without Freud, the psychoanalyst would have had no social status, because Freud is the one who invented the name "psychoanalyst". However, Lacan did not believe that anyone, or any professional body, should be exclusively entitled to nominate someone as "psychoanalyst". By way of an alternative, he proposed that psychoanalysts derive their authorization *qua* analysts exclusively from their own analysis, and therefore from themselves, regardless of the fact that this may subsequently be confirmed by a specific body within an institutional hierarchy, such as a training committee.[25] Disclosing how someone from the north of France had once told him that he was a "born analyst", Lacan explicitly rejected this kind of "certificate" on the grounds that he did not consider himself to be a born poet, but rather a poem—and a poem that is being written for that matter, however much it may give the impression that it is a subject.

What could it possibly mean for Lacan to claim, here, that he was not a born analyst *cum* poet, but rather a born poem? And doesn't this passage contradict the manuscript that ended up in the possession of Jean-Michel Vappereau, in which he wrote: *"je suis "né" poème et papouète"*? I think we need to read Lacan's *papouète* from *"A lire après"* as *"pas poète"*, and thus as born "not a poet", or indeed as born "not a proper poet"—perhaps born a mediocre poet, or a poetaster, but definitely not a poet who is truly deserving of that name. Furthermore, it is important to recognize that the statement *"je suis "né" poème et papouète"* in the Vappereau manuscript is in itself part of a poem, which probably would have gone unrecognized were it not for the fact that, much like an epigraph, Lacan placed it at the beginning of his text—thus setting it apart not only graphically, but also stylistically and semantically from the rest—and also explicitly identified it as such: *"C'est un poème ..."* (It's a poem). Hence, the *papouète* as it appears in the untitled poem which opens the untitled manuscript is Lacan's own poetic take on the *"pas poète"*, whereby he once again appropriated the word from Fargue's *Air du poète*. Yet whereas in Fargue's poem the *Papouète* is what the poet recognizes in exotic others, hoping that his reader will not commit any form of *Pouasie*, Lacan acknowledged the *papouète* in himself, which suggests that the untitled poem may not actually be a proper poem at all, or at least not a poem that is instantly recognizable, or even deserves to be recognized as such, and which may explain why Lacan felt the need to identify it as poetry himself. The matter is also made more complicated by the fact that we cannot reasonably assume that the *"je"* (the "I") in *"je suis "né" poème et papouète"*, i.e., the subject of the statement, coincides with the enunciating, or in this case the writing subject, i.e., Lacan. The "I" in the poem looks like it is, has the air of being the same subject as the one who writes the poem, yet one cannot be sure. We can only be sure that the poem is being written, or has been written, and that the subject is somewhere in the act of writing. What we cannot be sure of is whether the subject is equally present in the written text. For this reason, and also because of Lacan's own suggestion in the aforementioned paragraph of his introduction to the English edition of *Seminar XI*, and as a tribute to Léon-Paul Fargue, I propose to entitle the poem that features as the epigraph of the Vappereau manuscript as *Air d'être sujet*, which would then constitute—after "Hiatus Irrationalis"—a second "philosophical" poem stemming from the pen of Jacques Lacan.

> *Air d'être sujet*
> Comme je suis 'né' poème et papouète,
> je dirai que le plus court étant le meilleur, il se dit: 'Etre où?'
> Ce qui s'écrit de plus d'une façon, à l'occasion: étrou.
> Le refuser pour que l'étrou vaille ..., tient le coup quoiqu'en suspens
>
> *Là-quand*

> *Being Subject's Tune*
> Since I am 'born' a poem and not poet,
> I'll say that the shortest is the best, and called: 'Being where?'
> Which can be written in more than one way, on occasion: outhole
> To refuse it for the outhole to be valid ..., is holding on, although in suspense
>
> There-when

How are we supposed to interpret—in this poem, as well as in the distinctly unpoetic text of his introduction to the English edition of *Seminar XI*—Lacan's admission that he was not a born analyst *cum* poet, but rather a born poem? To answer this question, we need to focus on Lacan's signature—not so much the way in which he signed his letters in general, but on the peculiar play on the sound of his own name that he offered as a signature to the poem that from now on I will refer to as "*Air d'être sujet*". The subject writing the poem was born as Jacques Lacan—as it happens, he was born as Jacques-Marie Lacan—or, in short, Lacan. This Lacan does not feel very strongly about being called a born poet, let alone a born analyst, yet he believes he is a born poem, because the name (the proper name) does not make "immediate sense". It does not have an instantaneous "*effet de sens*", and if it elicits interpretation, this "reading" of the name will not contribute anything to a better understanding of it, let alone of the subject who carries it. This, for Lacan, is the key characteristic of (good) poetry: meaning is evacuated to the point where only "signification" remains. Put differently, (good) poetry is poetry whose meaning is not immediately clear, whose words evoke both more and less than what they mean in common parlance, and which therefore requires interpretation, although without this interpretative act generating a single meaning, however much interpretation is being exercised.[26] At that precise point, poetry coincides with the given name, the name one is given at birth. For if the given name is interpreted and recuperated within the symbolic structure of signifiers (as Lacan does by signing his poem *Là-quand*, i.e., literally "There-when"), this is a purely fictional attempt at "translation", which has no bearing on the Real of the subject who is covered by this name.

In "*Air d'être sujet*", it is written, then, that the shortest poem is the best, and that it is called: "*Etre où*" (Being where). This is followed by a wordplay, whereby the sound of "*Etre où*" is written down differently as *étrou*. It can be written in many different ways, the poem suggests, so *étrou* is but one amongst many options. Other alternatives may be *êtreou, êtrou*, or even *untrou*. *Étrou* does not mean anything as such in standard French, yet the preposition *é* generally refers to "taking out", "extracting", "allowing to be removed", as in *évacuer, évasion,* or *émigration,* etc. Were the verb to exist, *étrouer* could mean "carving out a hole". The play on words, here, resonates with what Lacan had averred earlier in the final session of *Seminar XXIV*, namely that poetry constitutes an effect of the hole, *un effet de trou*.

Conclusion

Towards the end of his career, Lacan did not consider himself enough of a poetaster to ensure that his psychoanalytic interpretations would remain effective. I do not think that this confession should be interpreted as an unequivocal expression of regret, that is to say as Lacan merely wishing that he had been *more* of a bad poet. On the contrary, as we saw with "Hiatus Irrationalis", and in a sense also with the poem he "donated" to Jean-Michel Vappereau, probably some time during the Spring/Summer of 1976, the fact that he considered himself "not enough of a bad poet" may have prompted him to share his verses with others, to release them into the public domain, or present them to a collaborator. Sharing a poem implies that the author does not regard oneself bad enough to keep the work to themselves. In the act of giving (to Vappereau), the object of the gift (the poem) would have been *de facto* turned into a "good object", especially if the gift-giving had occurred as an act of love—spontaneously, courageously, and riskily, like the morra game (*le jeu de la mourre*)—and if it had been driven by the "failure/knowing unknown" of the unconscious.[27] Indeed, Lacan's title of *Seminar XXIV* should be read, here, not as the unconscious having failed, but as failure (the knowing unknown) being the hallmark of the unconscious—of the unconscious being synonymous with failure, of failure being the name of the unconscious, and of this failure being the condition for love, in all its contingencies.

Bad poetry is poetry that does not require interpretation, because its meaning is obvious to anyone who reads it. Vice versa, the more the poetry is truly poetic, the more the interpretation will be challenging and limitless, to the point of it never resulting in any kind of fixed meaning. As Lacan said in *Seminar XXIV*, (good) poetry may have an effect of meaning, but it definitely also has a hole-effect, which implies that it does not provide the interpreter with any clear indication as to its signifieds, irrespective of the seductive play of the signifier. As such, the most radical poem would be the one which brings its reader to the conclusion that interpretation is futile, that the meaning of the poem will never become clear, that the poem's meaning is irrelevant compared to its other non-semantic aspects, i.e., its soundscape, its sonority, rhythm, metre, intonation, timbre, tempo, and musicality. At that particular point, the poem is indeed reduced to the quality of a personal name (and so Lacan referred to himself as a born poem) which, although it can carry a meaning (*Là quand*), is not to be read as a signifier representing the subject for another signifier, and thus generating effects of meaning.

What Lacan really complained about at the very end of his career, when he confessed to not being *papouètassé*, is that he had become too much of a professional bad poet. Partly owing to his public success, partly because of his firmly established reputation as a psychoanalyst, his words did not require interpretation anymore, because they had become saturated with meaning, so much so that as soon as he would say something his signifier would acquire a specific meaning. What Lacan complained about, as a teacher as well as a psychoanalyst, is that his words were no longer being questioned, probed, dismantled—neither by his audience nor by his patients. He had become the supreme interpreter of maladies, an intellectual sorcerer whose words served the exclusive purpose of turning nonsense into meaning, of making sense of gibberish, of unlocking hermetic seals. Paradoxically, this is precisely why he could claim that he no longer succeeded in making interpretation work. Lacan had spent his life looking for a psychoanalytic hermeneutics that would not just generate meaning, and here he felt trapped more than ever before in the realm of semantics. The upshot is that psychoanalytic interpretation should no longer be seen, here, as being situated exclusively on the side of the analyst. It is the analysand, as the recipient of the analyst's words, whose primary task it should be (and for which the analyst should create the circumstances) to interpret, to decipher, to explore meaning, and to balance one meaning against another. At the very end of his career, Lacan was therefore working towards the invention and articulation of a new, truly poetic signifier for psychoanalysis, a signifier approximating the Real, which no longer carried any meaning, but which was pure sonority, pure invocation, a polyphonic soundscape of infinite resonance—in short, a signifier of love. When Lacan considered the psychoanalyst's interpretations as "amateur good poetry", and "amateur good poetry" as the means to generate interpretation on the side of the analysand, it is because he did not wish for the psychoanalyst to become stuck in a self-absorbed, arrogant process of deciphering. Rather than being solely interpreting, he wanted the analyst's words to be interpreted in their own right.

Of course, if good poetry invites interpretation, and interpretation is always a form of translation, this process is most likely to generate loss, insofar as it could never do justice to the original, all the less so as the poetry celebrates the polyphony of language in its play on rhythm, intonation, resonance, etc. Something will always get lost in the act of interpretative translation. Yet what Lacan suggested in *Seminar XXIV* is for this loss itself to be elevated to the dignity of the Thing, for this Real to be regarded not as an obstacle, but as the most valuable, effective, and productive element of the equation—one that is initiated and maintained by the analyst during the course of an analytic treatment.[28] Poetry, as an interpretative act in Lacan's late clinical paradigm, needs to be re-evaluated in relation to the end of the psychoanalytic experience, as the patient's acceptance of the fundamental lack, loss, and uncertainty that governs the human condition.

Finally, in *Seminar XXIV*, Lacan moved from a new exploration of topological figures such as the torus towards the "invention of a new signifier", and thus from topology to poetics, with a view to advancing not just his own "linguis-tricks", but rather what I would call an idiosyncratic conception of "topo-linguistics". This new outlook was designed to turn language inside out, to explore the elasticity of the symbolic structure, much like topology explores the plasticity of space. Poetry added art to the science of topology, and the new hybrid form of "topo-linguistics" was there to shake the foundations of all epistemic structures, including those of language itself. This might also explain why, in his seminar of 1977–1978, Lacan moved towards psychoanalysis as a practice of babbling (*une pratique de bavardage*) (Lacan, 1979[1977]).[29] Needless to say, the cardinal question Lacan leaves us with—and it is a question that is never fully articulated, but which permeates each and every corner of the later seminars—is that of psychoanalytic training. How does one train a born poem, how does one train someone to become better, or good enough, at being an amateur good poet? How does one avoid someone becoming too much of a professional bad poet?

Notes

1 This chapter is based on an essay that was originally published under the title "Psychoanalysis as Poetry in Lacan's Clinical Paradigm" in A. Mukherjee (Ed.), *After Lacan: Literature, Theory, and Psychoanalysis in the 21st Century* (Cambridge: Cambridge University Press, 2018, pp. 74–92). It is reproduced here with the permission of Cambridge University Press through PLS Clear.

2 The reader can gauge the peculiar soundscape from a recording of the session that is available at http://www.valas.fr/IMG/mp3/12_insu17-05-77.mp3.

3 I should point out, here, that there are no less than three different texts by Lacan with the title "Joyce the Symptom", or a slight variant of it. The first text, in which his reading of Joyce's sentence "Who ails tongue coddeau, aspace of dumbillsilly" appears, is the transcript of Lacan's opening lecture at the fifth International James Joyce Symposium in Paris, on 16 June 1975, which is based on notes taken by Éric Laurent. This text was published in French on three separate occasions, with two different titles (Lacan 1982[1975]; 1987[1975]; 2005[1975]). It is available in English as an appendix to the English translation of Lacan's *Seminar XXIII* (Lacan, 2016[1975]). The second text is the essay Lacan submitted for inclusion in the proceedings of the fifth Joyce Symposium. Some overlap in argumentation aside, this text is totally different from the first and it was also published three times in French, again with two different titles (Lacan 1979; 1987[1979]; 2001[1979]). It was published in English with exactly the same

title as the first text in 2018 (Lacan, 2018[1979]). The third text is the transcript of a lecture Lacan delivered on 24 January 1976 at the Centre Universitaire Méditerranéen in Nice. This text, which has a title that is almost identical to the two others, is again totally different from the two previous ones and it was published for the first (and only) time in French in 2000, as the transcript of a tape-recording (Lacan, 2000[1976]). There is no official English translation of this text as yet. Even though I cannot conduct a comparative analysis of these three texts within the space of this chapter, it is fascinating to read them consecutively, in chronological order of composition (the "third text" mentioned above being placed between the two others), because this exercise offers a rare insight into the progress of Lacan's thinking on Joyce. Indeed, the first text was presented before the start of the yearlong seminar on Joyce (Lacan, 2016[2005]), whereas the third (Nice) text was delivered exactly halfway during this seminar, and the second text was in all likelihood written and/or rewritten after the seminar had ended.

4 To the best of my knowledge, there is no official English translation of the poem. Two English versions, one by Peter Low and one by Christopher Goldsack, are available on the internet, yet none of these captures Fargue's play on the near homophony between the French words for "not being a poet" (*pas poète*) and an inhabitant of Papua New Guinea (*Papouète*).

5 For the almanac from which Lacan took the poem, see Beucler and Masson (1949). Tudal's complete poem, which is entitled "Obstacles", can be found on p. 273. It is interesting to note, here, that when he quoted Tudal's poem in his conversation at Sainte-Anne, Lacan changed the first two lines to "*Entre l'homme et la femme,/Il y a l'amour./Entre l'homme et l'amour,/Il y a un monde*" (Lacan, 2017[2011], p. 92). Some small typographical errors aside, the lines included in the "Rome Discourse" match the original, and as tape-recordings of the conversation at Sainte-Anne evince, the text of the poem as included in the published versions of Lacan's conversation does not contain a transcription error. For an analysis of Lacan's poetic love-blunder, see Harari (1988) and Allouch (2009b, pp. 252–256). For a commentary on Lacan's engagement with Tudal, see Porret (2004).

6 At the bottom of the page in the almanac where the poem was reproduced it is stated that it was composed by Antoine Tudal when he was 14 years old.

7 Strictly speaking, Fargue did not use the word *pouète*, nor *pouète de Pouasie* for that matter, but only *Pouasie* and *Papouète*. Hence, *pouète de Pouasie* is Lacan's own take on Fargue's *pays de Papouasie*.

8 The word *poâte* appears, for instance, in the sixth short story (*Les voies de fait*) of Alphonse Daudet's *Les femmes d'artistes* (*Artists' Wives*). See Daudet (1874, p. 42). In this story, a certain Henri de B. writes a letter to his attorney Marestang about the fact that he has received news of his estranged wife Nina's return home: "For her, I was a poâte, the poâte one sees on the frontispieces of Renduel or Ladvocat, crowned with laurels, a lyre on his hips, and his short velvet-collared cloak blown aside by a Parnassian gust of wind. That was the husband she had promised her niece, and you may fancy how terribly my poor Nina must have been disappointed. Nevertheless, I admit that I was very bungling with the dear child. As you say, I wanted to go ahead too rapidly, I frightened her. It was my part gently to modify all that the rather narrowing and false education of the convent and the sentimental dreams of the Aunt had effected, leaving the provincial perfume time to evaporate. However all this can be repaired since she is returning. She is returning, my dear friend! This evening, I shall go and meet her at the station and we shall walk home arm in arm, reconciled and happy" (Daudet, 1892[1874], p. 119). Laura Ensor, the translator, has left the word poâte

untranslated, perhaps because she did not know what it meant, or could not think of a good English equivalent. Eugène Renduel and Pierre-François Ladvocat were famous 19th-century French publishers whose books were often adorned with engravings of romantic love scenes involving minstrels and troubadours. In his 1976 edition of a selection of Paul Verlaine's letters, Georges Zayed mentions that in a drawing by Ernest Delahaye the poet was represented at the offices of the journal *Courrier des Ardennes* (which never published any of his poems) as kneeled at the feet of its editor-in-chief Georges Thiébaud with a guitar strapped around his shoulder, handing over a copy of his collection of poetry *Sagesse*. The caption read: "Ceci (bien que très faiblard) c'est le poâte Pompe Verlard, s'anéantissant devant Thiébepompe Pacha, lui promet de ne plus faire de vers sans sa permission ..." (Verlaine, 1976, p. 93). In a similar context of derision, disdain, scorn, and mockery, the word "poâte" appears in Georges Bernanos's *Journal d'un curé de campagne* (Bernanos, 2019[1936]), and it was often used by the French surrealist poet Robert Desnos as a condescending designation for amateur, would-be poets.

9   In his intervention at the Rome Congress of the *École freudienne de Paris* (31 October 1974–3 November 1974), which was subsequently transcribed and published as "*La troisième*" (The Third), yet without the text having been verified by Lacan, he also seemed to have played on *poète*, *po(h)âte* and *pouète*, since the transcription (in both published versions) contains the following sentence, launched in response to the line "*Je ne me sentis plus guidé par les haleurs*" from Arthur Rimbaud's "*Bateau ivre*": "*Il n'y a aucun besoin de* rimbateau, *ni de* poâte *ni d'*Ethiopoâte ..." (Lacan, 1975[1974], p. 196; Lacan, 2011[1974], p. 26). In the English translation of the text, the lines have been rendered as "But there is no need for *rimboat*, *poâte* or *Éthiopoâte* ...", without any further explanation (Lacan, 2019[1974], p. 102).

10 For an excellent further exploration of Lacan's indebtedness to Fargue and the place of poetry in Lacan's work, see Rabaté (2019, pp. 27–53).

11 On interpretation as citation and enigma, see Lacan (2007[1991],, pp. 36–37). On the status of oracular speech, see Lacan (1998[1975]) p. 114; 2001[1973*b*]). On apophantic statements, see Lacan (2001[1972], pp. 479–483).

12 The French reads: "*Le sujet se prend pour Dieu, mais il est impuissant à justifier qu'il se produit du signifiant*". The expression "*qu'il se produit du signifiant*" is ambiguous and may also be rendered as "that he [the subject] is being produced by the signifier", or as "that signifier can be produced" (Lacan, 1977–1979[1976–1977], 17/18, p. 21).

13 The French "[*J*]*e n'arrive plus, dans ma technique, à ce qu'elle [l'interprétation] tienne*" could also be rendered as "In my technique, I no longer succeed in making interpretation work", or "In my technique, I am no longer successful at making effective interpretations" (Lacan, 1977–1979[1976–1977], 17/18, p. 22). As I explained in Chapter 1 of this book, Lacan used similar words ("*ça ne va pas tenir*") when he spoke to Derrida at the 1966 Baltimore conference about his concern over the fact that his *Écrits* might fall apart.

14 Freud's German term *Unbewußte* is always translated in English as "the unconscious", yet given the fact that *wußte* is derived from the verb *wissen* (to know), it would not be far-fetched to consider the alternative, more literal option of "the unbeknownst".

15 The published poem differs in a number of places from the manuscript of it that Lacan sent to Alquié. First of all, the title of the original poem was not "Hiatus Irrationalis", but "Πάντα ῥεῖ" ("Everything flows", the key principle of Heraclitus's philosophy). Second, the original poem ended with the mark

"Melancholiae Tibi Bellae. Hardelot. 6 août 29", which was exchanged for "H.-P., août 29." in the published version. The Latin words literally mean "your war-melancholy", yet the initials M. T. B. also invoke the name of Marie-Thérèse Bergerot, who was Lacan's partner in 1929, and from whom he had separated by the time the poem was published in 1933. Hardelot is abbreviated to H.-P. for Hardelot-Plage in *"Le Phare de Neuilly"*. Third, the original poem ends with Lacan's signature, whereas the published version has his printed name. On Lise Deharme and *Le Phare de Neuilly*, see Barnet (2003). The manuscript of the poem as sent to Ferdinand Alquié is in the archives of the *Bibliothèque municipale de Carcassonne*, 60817-AL QMS 34. Lacan's poem was reprinted in "*Le magazine littéraire*" in 1977, yet apart from the fact that in this version the word "*dense*" is replaced with "*doux*" in the third line of the first quatrain, the reprint also completely omits the fourth line of the second quatrain, so that the structure of the sonnet is no longer identifiable. See Lacan (1977[1933]).

16 For a detailed commentary and analysis of the poem, see Allaigre-Duny (2001). For a discussion of Lacan's sources of inspiration for it, see also Dufour (1998). Böhme's theory of signatures, in which the German theologian argued that the signature supersedes the sign as the decisive and superior operator of knowledge, i.e., that which makes the world intelligible, was in itself based on Book 9 of Paracelsus' treatise *De natura rerum* (On the Nature of Things), entitled *De signatura rerum naturalium* (Concerning the Signature of Natural Things). See, in this respect, the terrific study by Agamben (2009[2008]). A new, historical-critical edition of the complete works of Böhme in 30 volumes is currently under way with the German publisher Frommann-Holzboog.

17 The notion of "*hiatus irrationalis*" was coined in 1804 by the German idealist philosopher Fichte to capture the transcendental abyss, the irreducible and un-bridgeable gap that separates thought from reality. See Fichte (1986[1804], p. 217).

18 It is rarely mentioned that Sigmund Freud too once tried his hand at poetry. On 29 December 1899, he saluted the arrival of Wilhelm Fliess' second son, and the imminent new century, by sending his friend a poem with the title "Hail" (Masson, 1985, pp. 393–394). Unlike Lacan's poem, Freud's was never published during his lifetime and only entered the public domain when his letters to Wilhelm Fliess were released. Unlike Lacan's, we may reasonably assume, Freud's was a so-called "occasional poem", written for or on a special occasion. Unlike Lacan's, Freud's poem was not signed, although we could of course accept the date of the letter, its address, provenance, and handwriting as a signature. Since Freud did not decide to submit his poem for publication, we could say that he did not consider it to be good enough for public consumption, or that he considered himself to be not enough of a proper poet and thus too much of a mediocre poet to extract it from the private letter, yet the fact that the poem was literally addressed to a single private person (Wilhelm Fliess) may also have stopped Freud from releasing it into the public domain. Indeed, the fact that it was written for, addressed to, and sent to his friend may in itself be regarded as enough proof that Freud considered himself not enough of a mediocre poet to stop himself from following his muse and sharing his verses with his friend in Berlin. Not being enough of a bad poet, not being bad poet enough (*papouètassé*), is thus also what emboldened Freud to put pen to paper and surprise Fliess with his lyrical salute on 29 December 1899.

19 I am discounting, here, the last three lines of Lacan's essay "The Freudian Thing", because they are not set apart from the rest of the text and are not explicitly identified by Lacan as a poem. However, one could reasonably argue that they constitute a poem on account of their rhythm, tone and perfect rhyme.

The reader should also note that, in the English translation of *Écrits*, these lines, which start with "Actaeon, too guilty …", have not been rendered as a poem by Bruce Fink, because neither the metre nor the rhyme has been preserved. See Lacan (2006[1955b], pp. 362–363). I am also discounting various love poems Lacan included in a large number of letters he sent to Madeleine Chapsal between 1955 and 1974 (see also Chapter 6 of this book).

20 For a facsimile, see Lacan (2006c, p. 48).

21 Lacan's instruction at the top of the page is in black ink, and thus forms part of his later corrections to the text, and it is also preceded by a large Roman letter 2 (II), yet this in itself does not prove that he himself intended to read the revised version at his seminar, or at the end of a conference talk. If "*à lire après*" is clear as an instruction—but to whom exactly?—one is still left with the question "*Après quoi?*". After the first part of a presentation? After dinner? After Lacan's death?

22 As a matter of fact, the manuscript sold at auction in Paris contains the only written trace that I have been able to find of Lacan literally employing Fargue's word *papouète*, all the other texts being transcriptions of oral presentations, and therefore open to error.

23 The unpublished manuscript "*A lire après*"—as good a title as any that Lacan could have given it—may therefore have been composed around the same time, and may have served as a coda to *Seminar XXIII*.

24 Lest I am being accused of poor scholarship, I should draw the reader's attention, here, to the fact that in the Spring 2019 issue of "The Lacanian Review", which followed the issue in which Grigg's re-translation of Lacan's preface to the English edition of *Seminar XI* had been published, a correction by Grigg was included at the very end of the volume (and not included in the Table of Contents as such), in which he stated that a line in his own previous translation should be changed to "What a Cht told me is that I was one [an analyst], a born one" (Grigg, 2019). The correction thus relates to the second sentence in the quoted paragraph from Lacan's preface. Justifying his correction, Grigg refers to an online essay by a certain Réginald Blanchet (member of the New Lacanian School), in which said authority had demonstrated that the "Cht" in Lacan's sentence refers to Sacha Nacht (Blanchet, 2019). However, looking at Blanchet's little note, it is quite extraordinary to see how he had arrived at this conclusion, although it is even more baffling that Grigg would uncritically adopt it as definitive proof of "Cht" indeed being Sacha Nacht. In short, Blanchet indicated (I am reluctant to use the word "argued") that Lacan had fallen out with Sacha Nacht during the time of the first split in the French psychoanalytic movement in the Spring of 1953 (so far so good) and that Lacan subsequently never ever referred to Nacht by his name again (so further so good too), and that the Cht was therefore, "without a shadow of a doubt", Lacan's idiosyncratic way of conjuring up his formal rival. Now, the latter point is evidently a complete and utter *non sequitur,* which any person with a modicum of intelligence should be able to expose. However, let us assume, for a moment, that in 1976 Lacan had indeed decided to refer to Nacht with the three last letters of his surname. In this case, he would have probably referred to him not as "un Cht", but simply as "cht", or as "a certain cht", or even as "someone called cht". Irrespective of the fact that there would have been no good reason for Lacan to write the first letter of the signifier "cht" with a capital C, given that it was the third letter of Nacht's surname, the simple grammatical sequence in French does not in any way suggest a specific person, unless there would be all kinds of people called Cht, but even then. Even so, in justifying his conclusion with the point that Lacan had never referred to

Nacht by name anymore after their disagreements in 1953, the honourable Blanchet (member of the New Lacanian School) unwittingly offers an argument as to why "Cht" *would not*, or *could not* be Nacht. For if Lacan had categorically refused to mention Nacht's name for more than twenty years, why on earth would he suddenly decide to do otherwise, even if "otherwise" means restricting the name to the last three letters of the surname? None of Blanchet's "demonstration" makes any sense whatsoever and it really does not require great acumen to see this. In order to get to the bottom of the matter, we need to start with the observation that Lacan's preface was originally commissioned by M. Masud R. Khan, who was the editor of the series in which the English edition of *Seminar XI* would be published. In a 1982 review of a selection of papers from analysts in Lacan's "École freudienne de Paris", Khan disclosed that he had asked Lacan for a new preface to the book, and that Lacan's text had disappointed him (and understandably so), because he felt that it would only fuel people's perception of Lacan's work as a load of impenetrable nonsense (Khan, 1982, p. 96). In this respect, Khan definitely had a reason to be angry, because in his preface to *Seminar XI* Lacan talks about many different things, but not at all about *Seminar XI*, neither about its contents, nor about the circumstances under which it was delivered. This probably also explains why Khan did not commission a new introduction from Lacan to the English edition of his selected *Écrits*. However, Khan scrutinized Lacan's new preface to *Seminar XI* before sending it to the translator (Alan Sheridan) and asked Lacan for specific clarifications, including a gloss on the strange word "Cht". Lacan responded in writing and indicated to Khan that "Cht" is the way French people refer to those living in the North of the country, and whose language, which is also called "Cht", is markedly different from standard French (Lacan, 1976b). Why Khan did not relay this information to Sheridan, I do not know, because in the end Sheridan translated "Cht" as certificate, but it is clear from Lacan's letter that "un Cht" was intended as a demonym, similar to "un Parisien" or "un Bordelais" (someone from the region of Bordeaux). The fact that people from the north of France generally refer to themselves (and their language) as *Ch'ti*, *Chti* or *Chtimi* probably says more about Lacan's own lack of knowledge about how to write the word exactly than about anything else, yet in any case the puzzling "Cht" thus merely refers to a (French) Northener, which also explains why the word is capitalized in the text. All of this could easily be perceived as a matter of largely irrelevant detail, were it not for the fact that other French commentators (outside the New Lacanian School) on Lacan's 1976 preface to *Seminar XI* have immediately understood "Cht" as Northener, without having had access to Lacan's letter to Khan, but without their commentary being taken seriously. I can refer, for example, to Bousseyroux (2011, p. 300), who is not a "Cht", but a Toulousian ('un Toulousain'), and who has even gone so far as to speculate that the "Cht" in question could have been Pierre Bastin or Élie Doumit, both practicing Lacanian psychoanalysts from Lille. In other words, the fact that Grigg agreed to correct his own translation on the basis of a fundamentally flawed non-argument and did not even bother to verify alternative interpretations (outside the New Lacanian School) demonstrates the tragedy of doctrinal, institutionalized knowledge. If the only true knowledge is the knowledge that is being produced within the confines of a School, in this case the New Lacanian School, (psychoanalytic) knowledge itself becomes void, empty, and vacuous, precisely because it is regarded as definitive. For the record, I should also mention that, in the spirit of scholarly exchange, I sent a friendly message to Russell Grigg on 20 October 2018, i.e., before his re-translation of Lacan's preface was published, about his ongoing work on the text, and in particular about its quandaries around poetry. I attached a copy of the essay on which this chapter is based to the e-mail, including my reasons for interpretating "Cht" as "Northener", yet I never received even a token acknowledgement, let alone an offer of discussion. For some reason, it reminded me of the time when, as a non-member of the New Lacanian School, I attended a conference of the New Lacanian School and how, in the midst of me making a critical remark about the Lacanian movement, the chair of the panel promptly decided to turn off my microphone ....

25 On the controversial, and often misunderstood, principle that psychoanalysts derive their professional authorization only from themselves, see Lacan (1995[1967], p. 1; 2001[1973a]).
26 Lacan's perspective on poetry was clearly indebted, here, to Geoffrey Hartman's deconstructionist views, which could have been transmitted to him through the work of Tzvetan Todorov, although Lacan also met Hartman in person at Yale in November 1975. See Lacan (1976[1975b]) and Todorov (1978).
27 The second part of the title of Lacan's *Seminar XXIV*, "*s'aile à mourre*" is homophonic with "*c'est l'amour*" (is love), and invokes the ancient morra game (*jeu de la mourre*), in an equivocation reminiscent of Apollinaire's poem "*l'Ermite*": "*Les humains savent tant de jeux l'amour la mourre ...*" (Apollinaire, 2009[1913], p. 49).
28 In *Seminar VII*, Lacan defined sublimation as what "raises an object ... to the dignity of the Thing", with the caveat that the Thing is the quality of the object that can never be reached (Lacan, 1992[1986], p. 112). For a detailed discussion of this formula, see Chapter 8 of this book.
29 Lacan would have known something about babbling from the works of his friend, Roman Jakobson. See Jakobson (1968[1940–1942]) and Heller-Roazen (2008, pp. 9–12).

Chapter 8

Lacan's Clinical Artistry: On Sublimation, Sublation, and the Sublime

Introduction

Sometime during the spring of 1934, Mária Thomán, an acclaimed concert violinist who was the daughter of István Thomán, distinguished professor of musicology at the Royal Hungarian Academy of Music in Budapest (Slonimsky, 1984, p. 891), wrote a letter to Sigmund Freud. Since the original has never been found, we do not know its exact content, nor Thomán's specific reason for writing. Was she interested in starting an analysis with Freud, either for personal reasons or because she wanted to train as a psychoanalyst herself? Did she want Freud's advice because she or one of her musical friends had already started analysis in Hungary, and there had been some concern over how it might impact upon the artistic inspiration? Or did she simply want to ask "Herr Professor" about a troubling issue, hoping to extract some precious wisdom from him or, better still, alerting him to an unresolved matter in his psychoanalytic explorations of art and culture? We can only speculate about what prompted Thomán to seek Freud's counsel, yet Freud himself must have been sufficiently charmed and captivated by the young woman's letter, since he wrote back to her on 27 June 1934 with the following words:

> It is not out of the question that an analysis results in its being impossible to continue an artistic activity. Then, however, it is not the fault of the analysis; it would have happened in any case and it is only an advantage to learn that in good time. When, on the other hand, the artistic impulse [*der Trieb zur Kunst*] is stronger than the internal resistances, analysis will heighten, not diminish, the capacity for achievement [*so wird die Leistungsfähigkeit durch die Analyse nur gesteigert, nie erniedrigt*].
>
> (cited in Jones, 1957, p. 416)[1]

Freud's statement, here, has always intrigued me, although I simultaneously feel that I have never fully fathomed its precise meaning and its concrete

DOI: 10.4324/9781003252276-9

implications. Freud's biographer, Ernest Jones, quoted the letter at the very end of a chapter devoted to Freud's attitude towards art, with a view to emphasizing the liberating effects of a psychoanalytic treatment process on the artistic inspiration, yet I have never been convinced by the purportedly uplifting tone of Freud's response to Thomán. For one, Freud seems to be insinuating that a psychoanalytic process is unable to turn someone into an artist if the artistic, creative impulse is not already present from the start, and in a sufficiently powerful capacity to oppose and conquer the forces operating against it. However, psychoanalysis may very well contribute to the fuller expression of this creative impulse, because it can help destroy, or at least soften up, the pockets of resistance that preclude its full deployment. Yet if psychoanalysis may enhance a strong artistic drive that is already present—stimulating, we may assume, the artist to become more productive, or to become better at producing works of art—following Freud it is nonetheless incapable of protecting this drive against its own extinction. If the flame of inspiration is withering, there is nothing psychoanalysis can do to prevent it from dying out altogether. As such, psychoanalysis would seem doomed to follow—in the sense of "being merely responsive to"—the self-sufficient, autonomous mechanism of the creative impulse. If ever an amateur artist were elated by the alluring prospect of his or her craftsmanship being purified and elevated at the hands of a psychoanalyst, I do not think Freud's words would sound very encouraging. And if ever a high-brow creative genius were to think that she or he could find new inspiration in the psychoanalytic exploration of the darkest recesses of the mind, Freud's words would probably not come as a great relief either.

Perhaps Freud's little note to Thomán is highly overdetermined, given that it was written at a moment when he himself was afflicted by one of the most pessimistic moods in his entire career. Ominous socio-political circumstances, fuelled by Hitler's unstoppable rise to power in Germany, had followed upon painful professional crises (Sándor Ferenczi, a close personal friend and a highly valued member of Freud's inner circle, had recently died of pernicious anemia, after progressively taking his distance from the established psychoanalytic approach), and had made devastating personal ailments (Freud's cancer of the jaw was advancing rapidly) all the more tangible and intractable.[2] Even then, the pessimistic overtones of Freud's letter to Thomán may have also reflected a deeper intellectual scepticism as to the use of psychoanalysis for the enhancement of the creative impulse, or even for the installation of any kind of mental equilibrium that would bring emotional tranquillity and lasting peace of mind. As Freud had already suggested in "Civilization and Its Discontents", as a theory psychoanalysis may shed some light on how the "sublimation of the instincts" [*Sublimierung der Triebe*]—i.e., "shifting the instinctual aims in such a way that they cannot come up against frustration from the external world", and thus induce "finer and higher" satisfactions—can help assuage the multifarious sources of human suffering, yet the psychoanalytic treatment process has little or nothing to contribute when it comes to initiating, consolidating or sustaining these particular displacements of the libido (Freud, 1964[1930a], pp. 79–80). And as he would later admit in the posthumously published expository text "An Outline of Psycho-Analysis", "God is on the side of the big battalions" but by no means always on the side of psychoanalysis, at least not when it is engaged in the treatment of neurotic conflicts. Of the three factors that might help the psychoanalyst win the war—the patient's "capacity for sublimating his instincts", his "capacity for rising above the crude life of the instincts" and "the relative power of his intellectual functions"—none are directly receptive or amenable to psychoanalytic intervention (Freud, 1964[1940a], pp. 181–182). If anyone was ever expecting something sublime to occur at the end of a psychoanalytic treatment process, then it was not just the outcome, but even the process of sublimation leading up to it that was beyond Freud's control, since the latter was allegedly rooted in a particular disposition which, much like the creative impulse itself, obstinately followed its own solipsistic path.[3]

In this chapter, I want to critically reexamine the dual tension that runs through Freud's conception of the creative process, in order to interrogate Lacan's prolonged engagement with the questions of sublimation and the sublime during his 1959–1960 seminar on the ethics of psychoanalysis (Lacan, 1992[1986], pp. 85–164) and some related texts. In doing so, I intend to arrive at a conclusion with a fresh reading of the nature and place of the sublime, both in relation to the conceptual status of sublimation, whose qualitative transformation of the sexual drive into a de-sexualised, higher socio-cultural object continues to puzzle scholars and practitioners of psychoanalysis, and in relation to the dynamic interface between the artistic and the psychoanalytic creative process.

The first tension stages the ostensible disparity between Freud's mechanism of sublimation, which he generally presented as the purification and re-direction (elevation) of libidinal energy towards a "higher" socio-cultural aim (Freud, 1957[1910a], pp. 53–54), and the profoundly ambiguous status of its outcome.[4] Irrespective of largely unresolved debates pertaining to the exact nature of Freud's proto-Jungian vision of a de-sexualised libido, not to mention the contentious convergence between sublimation, repression and reaction-formation, sublimation lies at the heart of the Freudian creative process. Yet whilst sublimation is held responsible for "our highest cultural successes" (Freud, 1957[1910a], p. 54), the latter are consistently held to contain very little, almost nothing truly innovative or inventive. Culturally successful or artistically sublime as the results of the redirection of the libidinal energy towards a de-sexualised aim and object may be, they would always conceal the Nietzschean cycle of eternal recurrence under their appealing mask of creativity. In other words, the first tension puts the great creative force of sublimation fundamentally at odds with the invariably derivative character of its products—sublimely successful as they may appear. What is the meaning of creative sublimation, then, if it only ever leads to a repetition of the same? How can anything still be called sublime if it only ever constitutes a disguised permutation of the subliminal?

If this first tension may easily come across, and could even be dismissed as purely conceptual, meta-psychological or transcendental, the second tension should take away any doubt as to the practical, empirical significance of Freud's intermittent disquisitions on the creative process. Whether dispensing advice to young musicians, or reflecting upon the rampant discontents in civilization, Freud was not just interested in applying and extrapolating his psychoanalytic knowledge to socio-cultural issues. On each and every occasion he invoked the questions of creation and creativity it was also the clinical effectiveness of the psychoanalytic treatment paradigm that was at stake. Hence, the second tension concerns the dynamic connection between the act of artistic creation and the creative potential of the psychoanalytic experience. Theoretical problems aside, this may be the principal reason as to why so many psychoanalysts have deplored, and continue to expose the painful "lack of a coherent theory of sublimation" in Freud's work (Laplanche and Pontalis, 1973[1967], p. 433).[5] If sublimation is not merely the psychic mechanism underpinning artistic creation, i.e., the driving force behind the emergence of works of art and other cultural objects, but also a key factor in the transformational change that is effectuated by a clinical psychoanalytic intervention, then how should the psychoanalyst operate with or upon this force? What does it mean for a patient to substitute sublimation for repression? How can the endgame of a psychoanalytic treatment process be conceived in terms of the sublime if the patient is not an artist, or does not engage in any type of conventional artistic activity? And if the transformational change on the side of the psychoanalytic patient is sublimely artistic, does this imply that the metamorphic labour on the side of the creative artist may also legitimately be conceived as sublimely psychoanalytic?

First Tension: Sublimation as Creative Destruction

Quite a few years before he would become the assigned leader of the French surrealist movement, André Breton already expressed great enthusiasm for Freud's discoveries—as early as 1916 in fact, when he was deployed as a young military doctor at the neuro-psychiatric centre of Saint-Dizier (Bonnet, 1992). With none of Freud's works being available in French translation yet, and him being unable to read German, Breton was forced to rely on secondary source materials to indulge in his intellectual curiosity, but that did not stop him from sharing copious notes and reflections with his friend, Théodore Fraenkel (Rémy, 1991, pp. 5–8). In one of these, he summarized what he had understood about the practice of psychoanalysis as follows:

Depending on the case, the doctor calls upon the subject's adult established reason to destroy the effects of an anterior, infantile judgement, and employs the energy of the repressed complex by exchanging it for behavioural motives, or superior non-sexual thoughts (sublimation, *Sublimierung*), or finally allows the subject to freely accept a well understood sexual hygiene.

(cited in Bonnet, 1992, p. 127)

Were Freud to have read this sentence, he would probably have disagreed with Breton's rather simplistic depiction of the psychoanalytic treatment process, but it nonetheless shows that, by 1916, the mechanism of sublimation was already sufficiently well-known in psychoanalytic circles for it to be commonly regarded as an indispensable cornerstone of the new Viennese clinical science.

Deeply imbued with the creative spirit of the Dada movement, yet still intellectually preoccupied with Freud's ingenious method of dream interpretation and the supporting technique of free association, Breton secured a visit to Freud's residence at Berggasse 19 on 10 October 1921 (Esman, 2011, p. 174; Scheidhauer, 2010, pp. 33–36). Undoubtedly expecting a warm welcome, the 26-year-old Frenchman was sat instead amongst Freud's patients in the waiting room until Herr Professor was ready for him. And when he was finally admitted into the master's chambers, it was not exactly the start of a stimulating dialogue, let alone a close friendship. Desperately trying to pique his host's interest by lacing the conversation with the names of the great French clinicians, Breton was soon back in the local café with nothing but vague compliments, a small pocket full of theoretical generalities, and a bitter sense of disappointment (Breton, 1990[1922]; Polizzotti, 2009, p. 146). Throughout the 1920s, Freud's theory continued to have a major impact on the surrealist practice of automatic writing, and many of its key proponents in a wide range of artistic idioms drew inspiration from it (Alexandrian, 1974; Lomas, 2000). But the *Sublimierung* Breton had originally highlighted as an essential psychoanalytic tool eventually became a major obstacle. In *Les Vases Communicants*, Breton called Freud "a relatively unlearned philosophic mind" and he reproached him "for having sacrificed all that he could have drawn from this [the importance of sexuality in unconscious life]... to commonplace self-interested motives" (Breton, 1997[1932], p. 22). When, in December 1932, Breton sent Freud a copy of his little volume, he received no less than three written responses, Freud first promising his interlocutor that he would read the book carefully, then defending himself against the accusation that he had omitted an important source in *The Interpretation of Dreams* (Freud, 1953[1900a]), and finally finishing off the exchange with a peculiar admission:

Although I receive so much evidence of the interest which you and your friends show toward my research, for myself I am not in the position to explain what Surrealism is and what it is after. It could be that I am not in any way made to understand it; I am at such a distant position from art. (cited in Davis, 1973, p. 131)[6]

As an excuse or a disclaimer, the final sentence cannot but strike as emphatically disingenuous, if only because Freud was known to invest vast amounts of money in his ever-expanding collection of Graeco-Roman and Egyptian statuettes, a small selection of which occupying a prominent place on his desk (Armstrong, 2005; Burke, 2006; Gamwell and Wells, 1989).[7] He may have kept his distance from modern art, yet he kept himself as close as he could to his beloved antiquities. In addition, by the early 1930s, Freud had publicly professed the greatest admiration for the sublime artistic achievements of Michelangelo, Leonardo da Vinci, Shakespeare, Goethe, and Dostoevsky. If he felt rather underwhelmed by the surrealists' confident embrace of psychoanalysis as a perfect technique for releasing the creative spirit, it was no doubt less because of his distance from and insensitivity to art, but due to his fundamental disbelief in the creative potential of psychoanalysis itself, and by extension in the creative potential of the human mind in general, *pace* the mechanism of sublimation.

Numerous examples can be advanced of how Freud time and again reduced the ostensible emergence of the new to the surreptitious return of the old. In Freud's view, the appearance of something previously unseen or unheard was always no more than a cunning simulacrum, concealing the recurrence of something thought to be lost and forgotten. For instance, towards the end of his *Three Essays on the Theory of Sexuality*, he claimed that the finding of an object, which can be used here as a generic phrase for what is conventionally designated as "dating" and "mating", is always but the repetition of an anterior phenomenon: "The finding of an object is in fact a refinding of it [*Die Objektfindung is eigentlich eine Wiederfindung*]" (Freud, 1953[1905d], p. 222). Although it commonly presents itself in the form of something entirely new, the object either reinforces templates from early childhood (*frühinfantilen Vorbilder*), or constitutes in narcissistic fashion an avatar of the subject's own ego.[8] Outside the realm of sexuality, Freud adopted the same modus operandi (of substituting the old for the new) in order to dispute Gustave Le Bon's claim that groups are capable of eliciting new behaviours in their members:

> [I]n a group the individual is brought under conditions which allow him to throw off the repressions of his unconscious instinctual impulses [*Triebregungen*]. The *apparently new characteristics* which he then displays are in fact the manifestations of this unconscious, in which all that is evil in the human mind is contained as a predisposition. (Freud, 1955[1921c], p. 74 emphasis added)

Most significant for the issues of sublimation and the sublime is Freud's recourse to a virtually identical strategy in his 1919 essay "The 'Uncanny'", in which he refuted the idea—adduced previously by the German psychiatrist Ernst Jentsch—that the subjective experience of the uncanny is rooted in persistent psychic uncertainty and a human being's visceral misoneism (Freud, 1955[1919*h*], pp. 226–233; Jentsch, 1997[1906]).[9] For Freud, the uncanny has nothing to do with any kind of anxiety that may be felt as a result of mental indecision or vacillation, or owing to an ineluctable exposure to the new, but epitomizes instead the anxiety experienced in confrontation with what "ought to have remained secret and hidden but has come to light", most notably the infantile castration complex (Freud, 1955[1919*h*], pp. 225, 230–231). Why is this relevant for our understanding of sublimation and the sublime? Jentsch's concept of "intellectual uncertainty", which he employed to account for the subjective sensation of uncanniness, clearly echoes Kant's explanation of the sublime (*das Erhabene*), as a struggle between reason and imagination, as what frustrates rational orientation, and as a disruption of judgement by what exceeds the boundaries of comprehension (Kant, 2007[1790], pp. 75–164).[10] Freud's contemporary, the German theologian Rudolf Otto, accordingly averred that *das Erhabene*, which he preferred to render as the "numinous", embodies exactly the same *sui generis* conjunction of mystery and fascination as the uncanny (Otto, 1958[1917], p. 40), an idea that would subsequently be recuperated by Carl Gustav Jung, Mircea Eliade, C. S. Lewis, Aldous Huxley, and many others.[11] The close affinity between the uncanny and the sublime (or the numinous) subsequently prompted scholars to argue that the uncanny is nothing but the secular sublime (Prawer, 1963), or the post-Enlightenment, literary "negative" sublime (Bloom, 1982, pp. 101, 108). Owing to this historical, phenomenological, and philological confluence between the uncanny and the sublime, Harold Bloom even went so far as to say that Freud's essay on the uncanny is "the only major contribution that the 20th century has made to the aesthetics of the Sublime" (Ibid., p. 101).[12]

By contrast with Otto's conception, the Freudian uncanny (and its sensuo-spiritual counterpart of the sublime) is not at all *sui generis*. If there is one thing that stands out from Freud's essay, it is his obstinate refusal to accept that the uncanny is *de facto* unrepresentable, unknowable, and inexplicable, both in its emergence as a subjective sensation and in terms of the object to which it is attached.[13] As Derrida has suggested, in a characteristically inspired note to his 1970 essay "The Double Session": in "The 'Uncanny'", Freud's relentless objections to undecidable ambivalence (as conveyed, for instance, by Jentsch's intellectual uncertainty) invariably give way to "the process of interminable substitution", one after the other (literary) figuration of the uncanny being "explained" as a (fictional) replacement for an old, and supposedly forgotten, unconscious (psychic) conflict (Derrida, 1981[1970], p. 268, note 67). As I pointed out in the introduction to this chapter, Freud's assiduous urge to locate and identify the archaic sources of cultural products—be it those that appear with the affective quality, or under the guise of the uncanny and the sublime—forcibly minimizes the creative power of sublimation, as the combined diversion of the object and the aim of the sexual drive towards "higher" socio-cultural accomplishments. Freud's proposed antagonism between sublimation and direct sexual satisfaction, here, is not distinctly problematic just because it assumes that artists have somehow "learnt" how to postpone direct sexual gratification (or to exchange sex for something more culturally respected), or because it encapsulates a surreptitious value judgment on the advantages of sexual abstinence—in a sagacious amalgamation of the Stoic *sustine et abstine*, the protestant work ethic, and the good old Communist principle of *переключение* (switching) (Zalkind, 2001[1929])—but because the outcome of the libidinal transformation is constantly shown to fail at the very point of its allegedly higher, new creative value. For all of Freud's emphasis on the transformational power of sublimation, in his unmitigated appreciation of its inherently repetitive outcomes (from the uncanny to the sublime), he consistently demonstrated his fervent espousal of what can deservedly be termed a "catastrophe theory of creativity" (Bloom, 1982), which not only reduces the (artistic) quality of the newly created object and its associated (socio-cultural) goal, but also radically destabilizes the psychic process leading up to it, whereby the latter becomes a troublesome contest between the "pull of the new" and the "push of the old"—a "secular psychomachia" as Jack Spector once called it (Spector, 1972, p. 145).

How did Lacan address this first major tension in Freud's work?[14] When returning to the questions of sublimation and the sublime in his 1959–1960 seminar *The Ethics of Psychoanalysis*, Lacan first implicitly reminded his audience of how, at the very end of his previous seminar, on *Desire and its Interpretation*, he had outlined the dialectical relationship between the social system, as predicated upon a symbolic law, and cultural achievements, which are simultaneously within the system and exceeding its boundaries (Lacan, 2019[2013], p. 483).[15] For Lacan, a subject who identifies with and abides by the rules and regulations of the social fabric in which she or he is embedded may simultaneously protest against the various restrictions imposed by the symbolic system, by virtue of opening up of a realm of activity beyond their sphere of influence. It is precisely this subjective act of concurrent compliance with and radical transcendence of the socio-symbolic limits that Lacan initially designated as sublimation (Ibid., p. 484). In *Seminar VII*, he elaborated on this idea, arguing that the most general formula of sublimation is that "it raises an object… to the dignity of the Thing [*elle élève un objet… à la dignité de la Chose*]" (Lacan, 1992[1986], p. 112). In typically Lacanian fashion, this formula defies easy understanding, yet it is immediately clear that whereas Freud had defined sublimation, in his *Three Essays on the Theory of Sexuality* and elsewhere, as a psychic process through which the sexual goal of the drive is exchanged for a "higher", non-sexual goal (Freud, 1953[1905*d*], pp. 238–239; 1964[1930*a*], p. 79), Lacan recalibrated sublimation by situating it primarily with reference to the object. Furthermore, whereas Freud had argued that sublimation entails a diversion, or a re-direction of sexual energy away from its "natural" course (as leading to the realization of the sexual goal)—which also explains his intermittent designation of sublimation as a means of fixating "preliminary" sexual goals, such as looking and touching—Lacan, for his part, did not regard sublimation as a process which bars access to the (sexual) object, but which, on the contrary, clears the path for its being refashioned into something else. In other words, the mechanism of sublimation and its projected object of the sublime are collapsed, here, into a single transformational process. In Freud's take on the matter, the object is displaced as a result of the sublimatory diversion of the drive's goal; in Lacan's reworking, the transformation of the object coincides with the alteration of the goal.

Whilst Lacan did not directly refer to Hegel's dialectic when he articulated the most general formula of sublimation in *Seminar VII*, the term "elevation" (raising) should undoubtedly be acknowledged here in its Hegelian connotations of *Aufhebung*: a process through which something is being lifted onto a higher level, and thereby simultaneously annihilated and preserved (Hegel, 2018[1807]).[16] Looking at Lacan's formula through a Hegelian lens, and taking account of the standard English translation of *Aufhebung* as "sublation", one could thus posit that, in Lacan's reading, sublimation sublates the object onto the dignity of the Thing, whereby the object is at once destroyed (in its previous, original state) and lifted up onto a higher level of functioning.[17] Drawing on a different idiom, one might say that sublimation emerges here as the psychoanalytic equivalent of Schumpeter's gale (1976[1942]): it is the mechanism of creative destruction by which an object is simultaneously abolished and maintained. This conception clearly alleviates the first major tension emanating from Freud's theory of sublimation, because the underlying process is no longer conceived or interpreted as strictly creative, and its anticipated outcome is unequivocally ascertained as partially destructive.

How are we to understand the difference, then, between what Lacan termed "an object", underscoring the *in*definite article, and "the Thing", as distinctively presented with the definite article? Merely based on the way in which Lacan constructed his formula of sublimation, it can already be inferred that the main difference between "an object" and "the Thing" is a difference in value, since Lacan proclaimed that sublimation elevates an object to the "dignity" of the Thing. Of course, Freud too had argued that the diversion of sexual energy in the direction of an artistic or intellectual goal (rather than a sexual one) constituted a "superior" achievement, compared to the "inferior" sexual act. Yet it remains unclear whether Lacan's term "dignity" should really be taken at face value. It might very well be ironic, especially in light of the fact that, just before he pronounced the phrase "the dignity of the Thing" (*la dignité de la Chose*), he told his audience that, in finishing his formula, he would have recourse to some wordplay: "I don't mind the suggestion of a play on words in the term I use [*Je ne me refuserai pas aux résonances de calembour qu'il peut y avoir dans l'usage du terme que je vais amener*]" (Lacan, 1992[1986], p. 112). The amusing resonances are effectively twofold. First, during the early stages of the seminar, Lacan had spent two sessions on the observation that, unlike the French (and the English), the German language has two words for "thing": "*das Ding*" and "*die Sache*" (Ibid., pp. 43–70), whereby he had associated "*das Ding*" with an inaccessible, unknowable emptiness, in an implicit reformulation of Kant's transcendental "*Ding an Sich*" (thing-in-itself), i.e., a noumenon which can enter reason, and which is therefore thinkable, but which cannot be empirically experienced, let alone known (Kant, 1997[1788], pp. 47–49).[18] In referring to the dignity of the Thing, he thus first of all played on the near-homophony between dignity and "*Ding*". However, the French word "*la Chose*" (the Thing) also sounds exactly like "*l'a-chose*" (the un-thing, or the no-thing), and later in his work Lacan would often write "*la Chose*" precisely as "*l'a-chose*" or "*l'achose*" (Lacan, 2001[1970], p. 404; 2006b, p. 77; 2013[1971a], p. 331). More importantly, the French word "*la Chose*" is routinely used to designate trivial non-descript things, comparably to how in English people would refer to an insignificant, forgotten, or forgettable thing with words such as "thingumajig", "thinga-mabob", or even "whatnot". Given these connotations of "*la Chose*", Lacan's term "dignity" acquires a rather different tone, then, which might indicate that the dignity in question has nothing to do with the inherent quality of "the thing". "The thing" may very well be an abject, useless "piece of shit"—more of a non-object than an object in and of itself. Put differently, on the surface there might not be any difference whatsoever between "an object" and "the Thing", yet what makes "the Thing" different from "an object" is the fact that the former has passed through a process of subl(im)ation, and therefore occupies a certain liminal place vis-à-vis the socio-symbolic structures in which it is immersed. Perhaps creative artists will already begin to recognize certain elements, here, of how objects come to be appreciated (or despised) as sublime works of art: what constitutes sublime art has nothing to do with the intrinsic quality (the natural beauty, the underlying craftsmanship, or the moral-ideological value) of an object, but with the transformational work that has given rise to its emergence, its fundamental negation of any kind of use-value that would have been attached to the object, and its particular place within and vis-à-vis the socio-symbolic networks and narratives surrounding it.[19]

An object operates strictly within the confines of the symbolic order, the realm of socially established discursive practices of language and the law. In this order, it is born, evolves, is being exchanged and transmitted, may become lost and subsequently be found back—not unlike Freud's aforementioned comment on the object as something that is always already refound. The Thing, on the other hand, exceeds the limits of the symbolic order; it defies the socially sanctioned norms and values with a view to opening up a "real" space, to which the accepted rules and regulations no longer apply. Whereas the circuit of objects operates in conformity with the regulatory mechanisms that are endorsed and imposed by a given discourse, the Thing is radically non-conformist, and situates itself as the antipode of symbolic compliance with an ideological code.

We can now understand how sublimation, in the Lacanian sense, may contribute to the production of (sublime) works of art. What characterizes a work of art is that it interrogates and potentially undermines the normative models of reasoning that keep the hegemonic symbolic structures alive. The work of art is therefore by definition "transgressive", because it refuses to abide by the moral and legal principles maintaining the social fabric. As "the Thing", the work of art is also intrinsically "uncanny", and therefore always already containing within itself the potentiality of the sublime, precisely because it confronts us with the instability of our most cherished worldviews, and offers us an opportunity to escape the symbolic constraints that simultaneously make possible and delineate our mental operations and social interactions. The work of art shows us the threshold of liberty, gives us a view of the edge, and this potentiality is simultaneously fascinating, mysterious, and terrifying, including in the Jungian sense of the alchemical *mysterium coniunctionis* (Jung, 1970[1963]).

As Lacan proposed in *Seminar VII*, this process (of the synthesis of the opposites) takes place as a sublation of an object, or a set of objects, that is available within the socio-symbolic landscape, but the "artistic" quality of the product of this subl(im)ation concerns the process rather than the outcome. Some artists have gone very far in trying to demonstrate how art has nothing to do with the nature of the object, but crucially relies on this underlying transformational mechanism. I could refer here to Marcel Duchamp's famous urinal, Jackson Pollock's "Number 26A 'Black and White'", or Mark Rothko's "Reds". The classic philistine response to these objects—'This is unacceptable, stupid and offensive'—is in a sense precisely what "the Thing" is designed to provoke. It is unacceptable from within the boundaries of an accepted social discourse. It offends those who cherish the norms and values of a socially sanctioned ideology. Yet it only has these effects, because an object (a urinal, the intercourse of black and white, shades of red) has been taken outside these ideological boundaries, and placed within a supra- or trans-ideological space of artistic freedom.

In this way, the work of art simultaneously attaches itself to the hegemonic social strategies (by operating with and upon objects that exist within them), and transcends these strategies in the act of subl(im)ation. Or, to look at it from the perspective of the artist, when sublating an object to the dignity of the Thing, the artist operates within a given socio-symbolic code, selects an object within this code, and subsequently transcends the code by sublating the codified objects and placing them as "the Thing" within a transgressive sphere. With these Lacanian developments, we can also solve the persistent Freudian problem of the distinction between sublimation and repression.[20] By situating sublimation as a process involving the transgression of the symbolic law, Lacan implicitly clarified how it needs to be distinguished from repression, which epitomizes a radical compliance with the symbolic law. For Lacan, the Freudian mechanism of repression coincides with the subject's assimilation of the symbolic rules of language and the law; it follows the subject's identification with the signifiers of the Other. Subl(im)ation, however, is rooted in an act of protest against the identificatory mechanisms that maintain subjective compliance. In an act of subl(im)ation, the subject ventures to escape from the alienating clutches of the assimilated social contract, and endeavours to separate itself from the Other by opening up a new space of artistic, creative freedom.

When Lacan first broached the issue of sublimation, at the end of his seminar *Desire and its Interpretation*, he did not hesitate to associate it with perversion and criminality, because "the pervert" also entertains a dialectical relationship with the law—complying with it in order to manipulate it, control it, and "pervert" it (Lacan, 2019[2013], pp. 482–485). However, in *The Ethics of Psychoanalysis*, Lacan suggested a distinction between sublimation and perversion/criminality on the basis of a structural criterion that involves the relationship between the subject and the object. In short, Lacan argued that the difference between sublimation and perversion/criminality relates to what comes to occupy the place *beyond* the symbolic order. In an act of sublimation, this place "beyond the law" is occupied by the object or, to put it more precisely, by the elevated, sublated, and "Thingified" object, in which we can indeed recognize the work of art. But the subject remains firmly situated "on the side" of the law; it is from a position within the symbolic order that the artist manages to carve out a space beyond it for "the Thing" that is his or her work of art. When the perverse criminal transgresses the symbolic order, the place beyond the law is occupied by the subject him- or herself, from which she or he then attempts to transform the subjects "on the side" of the law into the new object of his or her "perverse" law. Whereas the subl(im)ating artist lets his or her object "challenge" the law whilst maintaining a law-abiding position as subject, the perverse criminal (or criminal pervert) challenges the law *qua* subject, thus employing it from a position of presumed mastery, as a tool for objectifying indiscriminately all those who continue to function within its radius.

Lacan illustrated the latter principle with the celebrated 1957 novel by Roger Vailland entitled *La loi* (Vailland, 2008[1957]; Lacan, 1992[1986], p. 73). The story is set in a village in southern Italy, where it is no longer possible to distinguish between the "legal law" and the "illegal law", insofar as "enforcing the law" has become the standard phrase used by organised criminals to terrorize and subdue the local population. The inextricable mixture of the social order and criminal practices has even led to the development of a game, appropriately called "the law", in which the winner is allowed to "enforce the law" and tell the losers to do whatever he or she believes is necessary, which eventually comes down to telling them when and how to speak. For Lacan, this fictional narrative exemplifies how the perverse criminal follows an alternative law, starting from a subjective position outside the "legal law". The subl(im)ating artist, by contrast, only goes so far as allowing this "illegal" or "illegitimate" position to be occupied by the artistic object.

Second Tension: The Sublime and Psychoanalytic Creativity

With Lacan's outlook on sublimation, as a process of creative destruction leading to the uncanny sublimity of the conceivable yet unknowable Thing, we are thus able to separate sublimation from repression, and offer a structural distinction between sublimation and perversion. The latter differentiation is important, because Freud too struggled with the issue. Witness the following passage, again from the *Three Essays on the Theory of Sexuality*:

> It is perhaps in connection precisely with the most repulsive perversions that the mental factor must be regarded as playing its largest part in the transformation of the sexual instinct. It is impossible to deny that in their case a piece of mental work has been performed which, in spite of its horrifying result, is the equivalent of *an idealization of the instinct* [*den Wert einer Idealisierung des Triebes nicht absprechen kann*]. (Freud, 1953[1905*d*], p. 161, italics added)

Freud is unequivocally referring, here, to the intrinsic creative aspect of the perverse psychic mechanism, which was subsequently taken up again by post-Freudian psychoanalysts such as Joyce McDougall (1995) and Janine Chasseguet-Smirgel (1985), who both argued that perversion incorporates a dimension of radical creativity.

Nonetheless, despite its advantages over Freud's account of sublimation, Lacan's theory still does not explain the vexed relationship—which I have designated in my introduction as the "second tension"—between the artistic impulse, sublimation, and the psychoanalytic treatment process, although he himself was very much aware of it. For example, in 1971, when alluding to the fact that James Joyce had at one point been instructed by his patron Edith Rockefeller to commence an analysis with Jung (Ellmann, 1983, p. 466), Lacan averred: "One will recall that a lady "Maecenas" [*messe-haine*], in wanting to help him [Joyce], offered him a psychoanalysis, as one might offer someone a shower. And with Jung of all people... In the game I am alluding to [Lacan referred to Joyce's project of "littering" the letter], he would have gained nothing there, going straight in it to the best one may expect from psychoanalysis at its end" (Lacan, 2013[1971a], p. 327). Lacan himself thus entertained the idea that the composition of a work of art, in this case the book entitled *Finnegans Wake* (Joyce, 1939), may epitomize the "best one may expect" from a psychoanalytic treatment process. However, much like Freud in his response to Thomán, he did not elaborate on his statement, and also failed to explain how exactly the two processes might be linked. The other extant problem with Lacan's theory of sublimation is that it somehow appears to de-sexualize the entire mechanism. For Freud, sublimation is essentially linked to a diversion of sexual energy away from the realization of the "normal" sexual goal. Yet when Lacan argued that the most general formula of sublimation is the sublation of an object to the dignity of the Thing, one feels entitled to wonder, despite Lacan's endorsement of all the connotations associated with the notion of "Thing", what has happened to the sexual dimension highlighted by Freud. Moreover, Lacan can hardly be accused, like Jung at one point was, of de-sexualizing Freudian theory, in favour of a pseudo-mystical system of trans-historical and cross-generational archetypes. The answer to both questions—the relationship between the artistic impulse and the psychoanalytic process, and the sexual dimension of sublimation—is to be found, I believe, in the operative mechanism of the fantasy, which Lacan, quite surprisingly, did not re-introduce when discussing the issue of sublimation, even though within his theory the fantasy is the primary psychic factor that modulates the relation between the subject and the object.

The fantasy intermittently surfaced in Freud's discussions of sublimation, yet it is seldom clear which precise role Freud attributed to it. In the final paragraph of his 23rd introductory lecture on psychoanalysis, which notably deals with the paths to symptom formation, Freud alerted his audience to what he described as "a side of the life of phantasy [*sic*] which deserves the most general interest" (Freud, 1963[1916–1917], p. 375). The side Freud had in mind "leads back from phantasy to reality" and concerns "the path of art" (Ibid., pp. 375–376). After conceding that the artist may suffer from neurotic inhibitions as much as any other "unsatisfied" individual, and may consequently turn his back on reality in order to indulge in the "wishful constructions" of phantasy life, Freud detailed how artists may still succeed in solving the conflict between their "instinctual needs" and their neurotic failure to find satisfaction in life. Rather than summarizing or paraphrasing Freud's words, I prefer to quote them at length:

> Their [the artists'] constitution probably includes a strong capacity for sublimation and a certain degree of laxity in the repressions which are decisive for a conflict. An artist, however, finds a path back to reality in

the following manner. To be sure, he is not the only one who leads a life of phantasy. Access to the half-way region of phantasy is permitted by the universal assent of mankind, and everyone suffering from privation [*jeder Entbehrende*] expects to derive alleviation and consolation from it. But for those who are not artists the yield of pleasure [*Lustgewinn*] to be derived from the sources of phantasy is very limited. The ruthlessness of their repressions forces them to be content with such meagre day-dreams as are allowed to become conscious. A man who is a true artist has more at his disposal. In the first place, he understands how to work over his day-dreams in such a way as to make them lose what is too personal about them and repels strangers, and to make it possible for others to share in the enjoyment [*mitgenießbar*] of them. He understands, too, how to tone them down so that they do not easily betray their origin from proscribed sources. Furthermore, he possesses the mysterious power of shaping some particular material until it has become a faithful image of his phantasy; and he knows, moreover, how to link so large a yield of pleasure [*Lustgewinn*] to this representation of his unconscious phantasy that, for the time being at least, repressions are outweighed and lifted by it [*aufgehoben werden*]. If he is able to accomplish all this, he makes it possible for other people once more to derive consolation and alleviation from their own sources of pleasure in their unconscious which have become inaccessible to them; he earns their gratitude and admiration and he has thus achieved *through* his phantasy what originally he had achieved only *in* his phantasy—honour, power and the love of women. (Ibid., pp. 376–377)[21]

Irrespective of Freud's rather condescending description of what artists desire, his explanation of their idiosyncratic strategy for avoiding the neurotic solution to internal conflicts deserves closer attention, if only because it includes an additional gloss on the mechanism of sublimation. In short, Freud argued that artists, unlike "mainstream" neurotic people, manage to accord some kind of universal value to their daydreams, so that they lose their self-centred particularities and may start to command universal appreciation. Moreover, artists know how to transform their daydreams in such a way that they can generate uncensored pleasure. In other words, artists can enjoy their daydreams with impunity, similar to how the dreamer fulfils his or her unconscious wishes through the transformation of the forbidden (latent) dream thoughts into a more acceptable (manifest) dream content. Thirdly, and perhaps most crucially, artists know how to create objects that constitute a crystallization of their fantasy or, to reiterate Freud's own words: artists possess "the mysterious power of shaping some particular material until it has become a faithful image" of their phantasy (Ibid., p. 377). Each of these three points undoubtedly warrants detailed investigation, yet within the context of this chapter, and my current examination of the "second tension", I merely wish to draw attention to how Freud linked sublimation and the creative process, here, to an activity that essentially takes place at the level of the fantasy (and its derivatives, the conscious daydreams).

Apart from this passage, which is no more than an addendum to a lecture which effectively deals with something else (the pathways to symptom formation), there is at least one other text by Freud in which the connection between the fantasy and the artistic/creative impulse is made, i.e., the short essay "Creative Writers and Day-dreaming" (Freud, 1959[1908e]). As Freud mentioned in the very first sentence of this paper, the main issue he intended to address in it concerns the question as to where, from which source, artists (in this case creative writers) obtain their materials. All creative activity, Freud argued, needs to be situated in children's play, which serves the purpose of structuring and mastering reality.[22] Unlike the child, adolescents and adults relinquish recourse to the structures of reality, and seek to satisfy their (unsatisfied, and largely unsatisfiable) wishes by indulging in fantasies. Apart from the fact that adults tend to be much more ashamed and embarrassed by their fantasies than children about their play, there are several other characteristics of fantasizing which Freud highlighted here. First, a fantasy is a type of wish-fulfilment, especially of ambitious (emulative) and erotic wishes. Two, a fantasy connects the present, the past, and the future in one continuous sequence: it takes advantage of an event in the present to rekindle an event in the past during which the wish was fulfilled, with a view to creating an event in the future which also displays the fulfilment of the wish.

How do creative writers use fantasies, then, as a basis for their creations? Freud's answer was remarkably simple: the protagonist-hero of the novel is an avatar of the ego, which always occupies the spotlight in the fantasy. As in the concluding paragraph of his 23rd lecture, Freud eventually also broached the issue as to how the creative writer succeeds in giving pleasure to his readership by indulging in the expression of his own fantasies. And Freud's answer was almost identical to that which he offered in his introductory lectures: creative writers tone down the egotistical qualities of their daydreams, and the aesthetic expression of their artwork functions as an incentive-bonus (*Verlockungsprämie*), or a type of fore-pleasure (*Vorlust*)—an aesthetic "yield of pleasure" (*ästhetischen Lustgewinn*) that is capable of triggering larger quantities of unconscious pleasure in the reader, who can then enjoy this newfound pleasure without shame or self-reproach.[23]

By integrating the notion of the fantasy into the theory of subl(im)ation and the creative process, we can both preserve the sexual element in the act of subl(im)ation, and enhance our understanding of the relationship between the subject and the object (including the specific position of "the Thing") in Lacan's theory of sublimation. From a Lacanian perspective, the fantasy epitomizes the formal mechanism of desire, so much so that Lacan even went so far as to define the fantasy as "desire for/of" (*désir de*) (Lacan, 2006[1962], p. 653; 2014[2004], p. 100; 2015[2001], p. 315), and as the structure which modulates every "object-relation" (Lacan, 2019[2013], p. 366). As such, the fantasy is not only the place where the subject finds his or her objects of desire, that is to say where his or her desires are being fulfilled, but also the point at which the subject maintains his or her desire, precisely because the fantasy represents desire as "un-realized", as something which has not found its realization in reality (just yet). As a structure that modulates and fluctuates between the subject and the object, the fantasy should not be regarded as something that is controlled and monitored by the subject. The subject does not assimilate the fantasy, in order to use it subsequently as a template for (re)finding certain objects. This is where the Lacanian perspective differs from the Freudian viewpoint. Freud remained convinced that the fantasy is the most basic template from which other activities, and especially the creative process, proceed. For Freud, the artist's work is a secondary formation which originates in the primary structure of the fantasy. For Lacan, by contrast, the fantasy is a specific relationship between the subject and the object that follows its autonomous path, which is neither controlled by the subject nor the object.

How does the fantasy affect the transformational act, process, or mechanism of subl(im)ation? In Lacan's most general formula of sublimation—the sublation of an object to the dignity of the Thing—the Thing is situated beyond the boundaries of the symbolic order, in a sublime, transcendental, transgressive space. I believe that this act of protest, which lies at the root of the creative impulse, and which constitutes a form of creative destruction, effectively puts the object in a highly privileged position—hence the term "dignity"—from which it acquires unprecedented power over the symbolic order buttressing and underpinning the fantasy. It seems to me, here, that in its subl(im)ation to the level of "the Thing", the object not only challenges the cherished principles of the symbolic order, but also serves the (re)construction of the fantasy as such. To put it more provocatively, in the process of subl(im) ation that leads to the emergence of a (potentially sublime) work of art, it is not the fantasy that constructs the work of art, *pace* Freud, but the work of art that constructs the fantasy. And this may in turn explain, then, why artists are incapable of revealing the source and origin of their work. The work of art is in itself the source and origin of a creative act, which contributes to the (re) construction of the fundamental fantasy.

However, the key issue permeating the "second tension" concerns the relationship between the creative act and the psychoanalytic treatment process. And so the question remains as to how all of the above may be applied to psychoanalytic clinical practice. As Lacan pointed out towards the very end of his *Seminar XI*, on *The Four Fundamental Concepts of Psychoanalysis*, the construction (and subsequent traversal) of the fantasy, which involves a prolonged labour of "working-through" (Freud, 1958[1914g]) on the side of the patient, can be regarded as the most advanced goal of a psychoanalytic process (Lacan, 1994[1973], pp. 273–274). Art and psychoanalysis thus share the same teleological principle, that of the construction and traversal of the fantasy.[24] This, it seems to me, is precisely why Lacan could say that Joyce would not have gained anything from his analytic treatment with Jung that he had not already achieved in his writing, even before the publication of *Finnegans Wake*. This is also, I believe, why Freud, in his letter to Thomán, refused to situate psychoanalysis beyond the artistic impulse, as some kind of meta-artistic discourse that might be capable of releasing and/or taming the vicissitudes of creative power. Rather than a discourse which might be able to master the mainspring of fine art, psychoanalysis is rather to be conceived as a fine art in itself. However, its fine art would not consist of explaining away the creative impulse—as Freud pointed out to Thomán, psychoanalysis can neither prevent the artistic impulse from dying out, nor its being expressed more vehemently, if it does not already have a power of its own—but in mapping out its terrain as a highly delicate, clinical process of subl(im)ation, which is simultaneously transformational, transgressive, and traversive. Away from the analytic couch, artists may achieve subl(im)ation and the installation of the sublime "Thing" via the intense process of making, re-making, and un-making objects, doing, re-doing, and un-doing letters, notes, paint, and clay; within the clinical setting, the patient arrives at the symbolic equivalent of "the Thing", which Lacan also designated as S(A), via an arduous working and re-working, a laborious locating and dislocating of the signifier.[25]

Conclusion

For Freud, there is no such thing as *creatio ex nihilo*. The product of a creative process is never irreducible, since it can always be traced back to a constellation of anterior factors presiding over its realization, be it the materials derived from creative writers' daydreams. It should not come as a surprise, then, that Freud was rather pessimistic concerning the creative potential of psychoanalysis, all the more so as his life's work developed and his working life entered its final stages. As he suggested in "Analysis Terminable and Interminable", psychoanalysis cannot completely overrule, cancel out, or disable unconscious mental processes (Freud, 1964[1937c]). At best, it can reorganize these processes in such a way that the subject is less "subjected" to them, or feels less troubled by their intractable pressures. Or, as he already put it during the mid 1890s, in the final paragraph of the *Studies on Hysteria*: psychoanalysis can probably do no more than transform hysterical misery into the unhappiness of everyday life (Breuer and Freud, 1955[1895d], p. 305).

Freud did not believe in "creationism"—as the production of something out of nothing, the emergence of a new fullness from an empty nothingness—

and it is precisely because he did not believe in it that he believed he could offer an explanatory framework for it. In this respect, he generally avoided employing the term "creation" altogether—the German nouns "*Schöpfung*" or "*Schaffung*" do not even feature in the index to his complete works—and preferred to talk about "productive processes", or the "capacity for achievement" (*Leistungsfähigkeit*), as he did in his 1934 letter to Mária Thomán. The fundamental question then is: how are we to conceive psychoanalytically of these processes, and of the works (of art) that they generate? Starting from Freud's letter to Thomán, I have supplemented this foundational question with a series of others invoking the relationship between sublimation and the sublime, and inscribing the interface between the "artistic/creative impulse", the realization of the work of art, and the process and goals of a psychoanalytic treatment. How does the artistic impulse lead to the crystallization of an artwork? Does the mechanism operate beyond the boundaries of language and rationality, or is it strictly controlled by a symbolic machinery? And if a psychoanalytic process can only "follow" the artistic impulse in its autonomous, self-regulatory functioning, without being able to affect it directly, what does this parallelism reveal about the operative mechanisms within the treatment?

Returning to the letter of Freud's statements on sublimation, I have endeavoured to answer these questions by identifying two constitutive tensions running through his work. The first, largely theoretical tension concerns the antinomy between the ostensibly creative power of sublimation and the invariably derivative nature of the sublime to which it gives rise. The second, distinctly clinical tension questions the practical significance of sublimation within the psychoanalytic treatment, as a key transformational process that lies at the heart of analytic (or therapeutic) effectiveness. Without wanting to go so far as to say that Lacan's explorations of sublimation (and the sublime) in his seminar on *The Ethics of Psychoanalysis* encapsulate the only possible operation to alleviate these tensions, and resolve the aforementioned questions, I have demonstrated how Lacan's reconsideration of sublimation as the sublation of an object to the level (and the dignity) of the Thing presents sublimation as a process of creative destruction. Insofar as the Hegelian dialectical operator of sublation (*Aufhebung*) involves both a cancelling out and a preservation of the object on a new, higher level of functioning, it indeed allows us to think of sublimation as a process that is not unequivocally creative, and to consider the sublime as an outcome that is not strictly derivative. Inasmuch as Lacan defined the (sublime) outcome as the dignity of the Thing, we may also acquire a new understanding of how sublimation generates another type of object, which is conceivable without being fully knowable, and which has lost its practical use-value on account of its positioning outside the socio-symbolic rules and regulations of an established order.

With regard to the second tension, I have argued that the conceptual bridge between the artistic work of sublimation and its clinical equivalent in the psychoanalytic treatment is to be found in the psychic structure of the fantasy, which represents a space of desire, and which modulates the relationship between subject and object. However, when inserting this term in the equation between sublimation, sublation, and the sublime, it is important to acknowledge that the fantasy does not (re-)construct the Thing, but that the Thing (re-)constructs the fantasy. Lacan's assertion that the end of analysis coincides with a traversal of the fantasy is therefore crucially predicated upon the articulation, location, and identification of the Thing. At this point, I have drawn a parallel between the sublimatory work of the artist, which may be ascertained in the writer's littering of the letter, or the painter's pasting of the paint, and the sublimatory working-through of the psychoanalytic patient, which may be acknowledged in his or her protracted shedding of the signifier.

We may never know what Thomán's concrete request to Freud was, when she wrote her letter to him in the spring of 1934. Yet despite the inconsistencies and infelicities of his response, he was undoubtedly right when he resisted the temptation to recommend to her that she start an analysis with him, or with one of his colleagues. For as an acclaimed violinist, she was already deeply immersed, and probably on a daily basis, in the working and re-working of notes, chords, keys, and scales. She would not become the Anne-Sophie Mutter of her generation, yet (paraphrasing Lacan) in the game I am alluding to, she would have gained nothing from a psychoanalytic treatment with Freud or anyone else, going straight in it to the best one may expect from psychoanalysis at its end.

Notes

1 Freud's original letter to Thomán is preserved in the Sigmund Freud Papers at the Library of Congress in Washington, DC, and can now also be accessed online via the Library's website: www.loc.gov. Full transcriptions of the letter can be found in Rauchfleisch (1990, p. 1124) and Widmaier-Haag (1999, p. 34).

2 After his appointment as Chancellor of Germany, at the end of January 1933, Hitler gradually tightened his political grip, culminating in the infamous "Night of the Long Knives" of 30 June 1934, i.e., three days after Freud's letter to Thomán. Sándor Ferenczi had died on 22 May 1933, at the age of 59. In his obituary, Freud had written: "From unexhausted springs of emotion the conviction was borne in upon him that one could effect far more with one's patients if one gave them enough of the love which they had longed for as children… Wherever it may have been that the road he had started along would have led him, he could not pursue it to the end… It is impossible to believe that the history of our science will ever forget him" (Freud, 1960[1933c], p. 229). As to Freud's deteriorating health, a letter to Marie Bonaparte of 2 May 1934 contained the following admission: "I am not writing anything. For this one does need a certain measure of physical well-being which I can no longer muster up, and also a friendlier attitude to the world than it is possible to have at this time" (cited in Schur, 1972, p. 454). For an excellent discussion of the impact of Hitler's rise to

power and the Nazi annexation of Austria on Freud and psychoanalysis, see Edmundson (2007).
3 It goes without saying that I am not suggesting, here, that all theories of the sublime *de facto* pre-suppose a psychic mechanism of sublimation, even in the most general sense of the term—as a particular transformation of matter, form, or energy. In fact, apart from Nietzsche and (to a lesser extent) Schopenhauer (2017[1851]), none of the most important pre-Freudian scholars and theorists of the sublime, such as Longinus (1995), Boileau (1965[1674]), Silvain (1732), Burke (2015[1757]), Mendelssohn (1997[1761]), Kant 2007[1790]; 2011[1764]), Schiller (1998[1793]), and Hegel (1998[1835]), consider its occurrence relative to a specific psychic mechanism called sublimation. Even Freud himself may not have interpreted all instances of the sublime as the result of a psychic process of sublimation, although whenever the issue of sublimation arose, he habitually described its outcome in terms of "higher" artistic, moral or socio-cultural aims (see, for example, Freud, 1953[1905*d*], p. 157; 1964[1930*a*], p. 79). Purely with reference to Freud, we thus already need to guard ourselves against the fallacy of the *non distributio medii*: if all sublimation gives rise to a form of the sublime, all forms of the sublime may not necessarily be due to sublimation. For excellent general surveys of the notion of the sublime, see Russo (1987) and Saint Girons (1993; 2005).
4 In their definitive philological account of sublimation, the subliminal and the sublime, Cohn and Miles posited that Freud had borrowed the term sublimation (*Sublimierung*) from "a chemical-scientific vocabulary", although they also noted how Freud consistently wrote the word in *Sperrschrift*, which was the German publishers' equivalent of the current practice of italicization, generally suggesting either a specific emphasis or the use of a neologism (Cohn and Miles, 1977, p. 301). However, in a letter to Jung of 10 January 1912, Freud commented on an essay by Lou Andreas-Salomé as follows: "We ought not in principle to decline [the paper's publication], provided she contents herself with sublimation [*Sublimierung*] and leaves sublimates [*Sublimation*] to the chemists" (McGuire, 1974, p. 480). In other words, Freud was (understandably) fully conversant with the chemical-scientific vocabulary of his era, but explicitly distanced himself from it, in opting to designate his newly coined psychic mechanism as *Sublimierung* instead of *Sublimation*. Of course, this does not solve the question as to whether Freud had silently "borrowed" the term from Nietzsche, who uses *Sublimirung* (*sic*) or its cognates regularly in *Human, All Too Human* (1996[1878]), *Daybreak* (1997[1881]), and occasionally in *Beyond Good and Evil* (Nietzsche, 2002[1886], p. 79) and *On the Genealogy of Morals* (Nietzsche, 1998[1887], p. 49). For a painstakingly detailed, historical and semantic analysis of sublimation in Freud and Nietzsche, see Gasser (1997, pp. 313–365). For more accessible, critical discussions of the matter, see Kaufmann (2013[1950], pp. 211–256), Lehrer (1995), and Gemes (2009).
5 The numerous lucunae and inconsistencies in Freud's theory of sublimation, which he himself never failed to acknowledge (Freud, 1955[1923*a*], p. 256; 1964[1930*a*], p. 79; Jones, 1957, p. 464), were already highlighted by the early Freudians, and have resulted in countless post-Freudian revisions of the concept and its psychoanalytic significance. For early criticisms of Freud's ideas on sublimation, see Bernfeld (1922), Sterba (1930), Glover (1931), Deri (1939), and Levey (1939). For critical surveys of the various passages on sublimation in Freud's work, see Flournoy (1967), Laplanche (1980), Gay (1992), Vergote (1997), de Mijolla-Mellor (2012), Goebel (2012[2009], pp. 107–155), and Rath (2019, pp. 19–140). Shortly after the outbreak of World War I, Freud started

work on 12 interconnected essays for a book provisionally titled *Zur Vorbereitung der Metapsychologie* (In Preparation for the Metapsychology) (Paskauskas, 1993, p. 312), yet the volume never materialized and only five of the essays were ever published as separate texts during Freud's lifetime, the other seven disappearing without a trace, apart from the final one, which was discovered by accident in 1983, in a cache of documents Sándor Ferenczi had left to his Hungarian pupil Michael Balint (Grubrich-Simitis, 1987). In his editor's introduction to Freud's papers on metapsychology for the *Standard Edition* of Freud's work, James Strachey opined that at least one of the vanished essays dealt with the question of sublimation (Strachey, 1957, p. 106), yet this proposition cannot be supported on the basis of clear documentary or other evidence.

6 The whereabouts of Freud's copy of Breton's book remain unknown. In 1938, faced with the dire prospect of imminent emigration, Freud decided to leave part of his substantive personal library in the hands of his friend Paul Sonnenfeld, who in turn sold the books to the antiquarian bookdealer Heinrich Hinterberger. Most of the books in this collection were eventually bought by the New York State Psychiatric Institute, and arrived in the United States in September 1939. Among these books, there was a copy of Breton's *Second manifeste du surréalisme* (Breton, 1930), which is now at Columbia University, and an uncut dedicated copy of Breton and Éluard's *L'immaculée conception* (Breton and Éluard, 1930), which is now held at the Library of Congress. The dedication on the title page of the latter volume reads: "*Exemplaire du Professeur Freud | notre véritable père | André Breton | Paul Éluard*". See Eissler (1979, p. 40).

7 For an illustrated guide to all the art objects Freud kept right in front of him on his desk, see Spankie (2015). For a different reading of Freud's final letters to Breton, see Rabaté (2014, pp. 96–98).

8 Between 1905 and 1925, the *Three Essays* went through six, sometimes extensively revised editions, yet the quoted sentence was already included in the very first edition and remained unaltered throughout the book's life-cycle. For excellent critical analyses of the various editions of the *Three Essays*, see Van Haute and Westerink (2017; 2021).

9 The reader will find more detailed discussions of Freud's critique of Jentsch in Nobus (1993), Morlock (1997), Royle (2003, pp. 39–50), and Masschelein (2011).

10 For synthetic expositions of Kant's views on the sublime, see Crowther (1989), Crockett (2001, pp. 9–22), Clewis (2009, pp. 32–145), Doran (2015, pp. 171–285), and Shaw (2017, pp. 93–115).

11 Even though Otto's seminal volume on the holy was published in 1917, i.e., around the time Freud would have been considering the notion of the uncanny, he did not refer to it, neither in the essay itself nor in any of his other published works. Cohn and Miles (1977, p. 301) indicated that Freud did use the word *Erhabene* in "The 'Uncanny'", yet this is factually incorrect. Whereas Strachey's English translation of the essay does refer to the sublime (Freud, 1955[1919*h*], p. 219), the original German text has the word *anziehenden*, which could have been more accurately rendered as "the attractive".

12 Other scholars who have since drawn attention to the convergence of the uncanny and the sublime include Lehmann (1989), Ellison (2001, pp. 52–84), González Moreno (2007), and Hertz (2009[1985], pp. 113–134).

13 "Inexplicable" is also the title of a short story by L. G. Moberly, to which Freud alluded in "The 'Uncanny'", without mentioning this title or its author (Freud, 1955[1919*h*], pp. 244–245; Moberly 1917). In a terrific essay on the way in which Freud's paper on the uncanny was profoundly shaped by the turbulent times of World War I and its traumatic aftermath, John Zilcosky has claimed that

Moberly's story has been almost completely neglected in the voluminous scholarship on "The 'Uncanny'" (Zilcosky, 2018, p. 172 note 20). However, back in 1992, I already published a French translation of this story alongside a detailed critical commentary, which was followed the year after by a Dutch translation of both the story and the commentary. See Moberly (1992[1917]; 1993[1917]) and Quackelbeen and Nobus (1992; 1993).

14 Restrictions of space will prevent me from doing justice to each and every aspect of Lacan's theory of sublimation. The secondary literature on the topic is extensive, yet readers wishing to investigate the matter further will benefit from Moyaert (1994), Crockett (2007, pp. 51–67), De Kesel (2009[2001], pp. 163–203; 2019), Porge (2018), Rath (2019, pp. 48–52, 141–152), and various essays in Adams (2003).

15 Curiously, Jacques-Alain Miller, the general editor of Lacan's seminars, has placed the final session of *Seminar VI* under the double heading of "Conclusion and Overture", and "Toward Sublimation" (Lacan, 2019[2013], pp. 469–471). Lacan's decision to devote no less than six sessions of his seminar on the ethics of psychoanalysis to a careful unpacking of the problem of sublimation may seem equally strange, were it not for the fact that, in a strictly Freudian sense, sublimation already invokes the origin of "higher", moral systems of thought, i.e., Kant's famous "pure practical reason" (Kant, 1997[1788]). In addition, from the very start of his seminar, Lacan also made it clear that he would utilise the phrase "ethics of psychoanalysis" as a generic name for the aims and objectives, the goals and direction of the psychoanalytic treatment, to which sublimation has always been linked.

16 Hegel uses the noun *Aufhebung*, or the verb *aufheben*, in numerous passages of *The Phenomenology of Spirit* as well as in subsequent works, but one of his clearest definitions of it occurs in the second section of the first part of the *Phenomenology*, on consciousness: "The *sublation* [*Das Aufheben*] exhibits its truly doubled meaning, something which we already have seen in the negative; it is now a *negating* [*ein Negieren*] and at the same time a *preserving* [*ein Aufbewahren*]" (Hegel, 2018[1807], p. 69). It should also be noted that in Hegel's *Aesthetics*, instances of the sublime (*das Erhabene*) are consistently attributed to the dialectical movement of *Aufhebung*. See, for example, Hegel (1998[1835], pp. 362–365). In one of his annotations to Lacan's *Seminar XXIII*, Jacques-Alain Miller asserts that the "elevatory means of sublimation as an upward operation was often named by Lacan using the well-known Hegelian term *Aufhebung*", yet there is no solid evidence for this (Lacan, 2016[2005], p. 185).

17 The noun "sublation" and its various cognates were first introduced by the Scottish philosopher James Hutchison Stirling in his hugely influential 1865 volume *The Secret of Hegel* (Stirling, 1972[1865]).

18 Lacan extracted the notion of *das Ding* from Freud's posthumously published *Project for a Scientific Psychology* (Freud, 1966[1950a]), yet his theoretical explorations of it were also indebted to Heidegger's eponymous 1950 lecture on the topic (Heidegger, 1954[1950]). This lecture was included in the 1954 collection *Vorträge und Aufsätze* (Heidegger, 1954), from which Lacan had already translated the essay "Logos" for the first issue of "La psychanalyse" (Heidegger, 1954[1951]; 1956[1951]). Of course, Lacan's conception of the Thing also echoes Hegel's definition of the sublime: "The sublime in general is the attempt to express the infinite, without finding in the sphere of phenomena an object that proves adequate for this representation. Precisely because the infinite is set apart from the entire complex of objectivity as explicitly an invisible meaning devoid of

shape and is made inner, it remains, in accordance with its infinity, unutterable, and sublime above any expression through the finite (Hegel, 1998[1835], p. 363)
19 "Use-value" must be understood, here, in the sense of functional, or instrumental worth, or as serving a practical purpose. Hence, I do not want to go so far as suggesting that art is inherently devoid of uses and effects, yet these artistic powers need to be considered outside the sphere of concrete functionalism, in terms of the transmission or the deconstruction of meaning. For an excellent discussion of the semantic usage of (symbolist) art, and its relation to counter-empiricist movements in mathematics and logic, see Pop (2019).
20 Freud never provided a satisfactory answer to the question concerning the difference between sublimation and repression, unless he resolved the issue in one of his lost metapsychological essays. One possible solution to the problem might proceed from a differential appreciation of the outcome. For whenever Freud referred to the result of a process of sublimation, he mentioned intellectual work and works of art, reserving the term "symptom" for more clinically based phenomena such as obsessional ideas, bodily ailments, etc. Yet it seems rather gratuitous to use the status of the outcome as a criterion for assessing and differentiating between the nature of the mechanisms responsible for it. Furthermore, there is no good reason to believe that all intellectual work is by definition non-symptomatic, never driven by an "obsessive" structure, or never reducing the quality of life. Alternatively, were we to add "social value" to the distinction, and say that the products of sublimation are always socially valued, whereas those stemming from repression are not, we may run the risk of employing an arbitrary ideological criterion for separating between two distinct psychic mechanisms.
21 The italics appear in Strachey's translation, but do not feature in the original text.
22 Throughout his text, Freud was at great pains to point out that the opposite of play is not "seriousness", because the child takes its play very seriously, but rather "reality", because a child knows how to distinguish between play and reality, and takes the templates for its play from reality.
23 When read in conjunction with the last paragraph of Lecture 23, Freud's text clearly offers additional insights into the origins of the creative process (and, as can be inferred from Lecture 23, Freud later extended his ideas to the artist in general), yet it also seems to contain two major inconsistencies. First, if creative writers derive their material from the activity of their daydreams, why is it then that, as Freud himself stated at the beginning of his paper, "the writer himself gives us no explanation, or none that is satisfactory" (Freud, 1959[1908e], p. 143). Second, if the novel's protagonist is modelled after the writer's ego, and this can be justified by virtue of those writers Freud described as "the less pretentious authors of novels, romances and short stories, who nevertheless have the widest and most eager circle of readers of both sexes" (Ibid., p. 149), it seems exceptionally difficult to understand how this aspect of "mimesis" could possibly operate outside the realm of literature—in abstract art and non-representative idioms, such as music. Perhaps these inconsistencies could be alleviated by minimizing the impact of conscious day-dreams, and emphasizing the significance of the formal structure of the fantasy, which not only operates at the level of the unconscious (and thus requires reconstruction, owing to its inaccessibility to consciousness), but which is also quite far removed from direct representations of the fantasizing individual's ego, as Freud demonstrated in "A Child is Being Beaten" (Freud, 1955[1919e]). However, neither in "Creative Writers and Day-Dreaming" nor elsewhere did Freud consider this option.

24 It remains an open question whether this fantasy ought to be reserved for the subject of the artist, or might also be extended to the subject who reads, looks at, or listens to works of art. In addition, when Lacan referred to the traversal (*la traversée*) of the fantasy, what he had in mind was not a reduction, let alone an abolition of the fantasy, but rather a subjective (criss-) crossing of the fantasy, leading to its acquiring more versatile, less petrified characteristics.

25 In "The Subversion of the Subject and the Dialectic of Desire", Lacan defined S(A̶) as "a line that is drawn from its circle without being able to be counted in it. This can be symbolized by the inherence of a (-1) in the set of signifiers. It is, as such, unpronounceable ..." (Lacan, 2006[1960], p. 694). The difficulty of rendering S(A̶), much like "the Thing", in a meaningful way expresses precisely what the term itself is meant to convey. S(A̶) epitomizes the symbolic representation (S) of a lack in the symbolic order (A); it constitutes, by way of an algebraic notation, the signifier (or better, the trait) for what does not exist as a complete entity, for the place where the Other reaches its limit, for the point where the power of the Other ends. In other words, S(A̶) represents the un-representable, and accounts for the epistemic point where knowledge meets and newly becomes ignorance. This clearly resonates with Hegel's definition of the sublime as "the attempt to express the infinite, without finding in the sphere of phenomena an object which proves adequate for this representation" (Hegel, 1998[1835], p. 362). For a more detailed discussion of how S(A̶) plays out in the analytic discourse and the endgame of psychoanalysis, see Nobus (2017a). I have also extended the argument of painting as a labour of creative destruction, in the context of a reconsideration of the artistic practice of Francis Bacon (Nobus, 2019).

Chapter 9

Lacan with Antigone: On Tragedy and Desire in the Ethics of Psychoanalysis

Introduction

The original French text of Lacan's 1959–1960 seminar at Sainte-Anne Hospital in Paris was first published in September 1986 as *L'éthique de la psychanalyse* (Lacan, 1986). At that time, some 35 years ago, I was sufficiently close to the *École de la cause freudienne* in Paris and Brussels to sense the wave of excitement that was being unleashed upon the Lacanian community. *Séminaire VII*, or "*L'éthique*" as we called it back then, was the first book in the series of Lacan seminars to be published in five years, the first to have been prepared after Lacan's death, and the first to which Lacan himself had not contributed in any way by commenting on and approving the transcription of his lecture course. Until then, Jacques-Alain Miller, Lacan's son-in-law and the designated official editor of the seminars, had always been able to rely on Lacan's assistance for verifying names, words, and passages that had remained unclear in the stenography and the copious notes taken by various participants (Miller, 2018, p. 142; 1985, p. 26).[1] Now, after Lacan's death, Miller remained solely responsible for the creation and publication of a text that would become the standard, definitive, and authoritative record of what Lacan had said. In 1986, those attending Miller's own weekly seminars and private reading groups in Paris had known for more than three years that the release of *Seminar VII* was under way, yet to many of us Miller's choice had nonetheless been surprising and unexpected, because it was felt that it would have been more logical to continue the series with *Seminar IV*, now that the first three books had already been published.

Miller clearly realized that his decision would elicit questions as to his reasons for breaking the sequence and so he justified his choice in his own seminar, *Du symptôme au fantasme, et retour* of 1982–1983, on three separate grounds. First, Miller reminded his audience that *Seminar VII* had always occupied a special place in Lacan's work, so much so that it was the only lecture course he ever considered turning into a full-fledged monograph—the fact that he never realized his ambition merely being conditioned by Lacan's persistent belief that he could (or should) say something more about the issues included therein (Lacan, 1998[1975], pp. 1, 53). In other words, Miller stated that he had taken on the challenge of transcribing and editing *Seminar VII* before any of the others, not despite, but precisely by virtue of Lacan's explicit wish to publish it himself (Miller, 1985, p. 33; 2018, p. 144). Second, Miller argued that Lacan's seminar on ethics constitutes a radical turning point in his oeuvre, because it is the lecture course in which "the "other Lacan" truly begins" (Miller, 2018, p. 146). Throughout the 1950s, Miller posited, Lacan had been mainly exploring the relation between the subject and the signifier (the symbolic order, the Other), without therefore losing track of its clinical import and the technical challenges this relation poses to practicing psychoanalysts. Now, on the cusp of a new decade, Lacan had moved away from the signifier, towards the much more intractable register of the Real, with the caveat that it would take him at least another four years to come up with a solid, workable definition of this most implacable dimension of the human lived experience (Miller, 2018, pp. 146–147). As Lacan himself had put it in the opening lesson of *Seminar VII*: whilst the vast majority of ethical systems had revolved around the formulation of a set of ideals for the governance of human desire, his own outlook on the subject matter would "proceed instead from the other direction by going more deeply into the notion of the real" (Lacan, 1992[1986], p. 11). Third, in light of the still young and emerging *École de la cause freudienne*, Miller intimated that having the printed text of its founder on the question of ethics would offer the necessary foundation upon which all the other aspects of psychoanalytic work within the school could be constructed, a set of key ethical precepts which had always been lacking within the International Psycho-Analytic Association (IPA), as a result of which they had continued to lose themselves in endless debates around one or the other technical rule (Miller, 2018, p. 21). *Seminar VII* would pitch the ethical rigour of the *École de la cause freudienne* against the technical rigidity of the IPA, promote formalization over the IPA's formalisms and formalities, and prepare the ground for the development of new theoretical principles and institutional structures against the palpably sterile, rusty, musty, and crusty practices of the psychoanalytic establishment.[2] Accordingly, the publication of *Seminar VII* may not have been the most logical option for Miller to take, but it was definitely a calculated, strategic decision, whose repercussions had been as carefully considered as they were eagerly anticipated. In many ways, the release of *L'éthique de la psychanalyse* was an ethical act in its own right.

I cannot remember when I first read *Séminaire VII* from cover to cover, but I do recall checking the Table of Contents at the back of the volume, skimming through the 375 pages of text, reading the extract from the 15th lesson on the back cover, admiring the glorious reproduction of Man Ray's 1938 "*Portrait imaginaire de D.A.F. de Sade*" on the front cover, reading the titles and subheadings of the various lectures (all of which invented by

Miller), and being simultaneously fascinated and intimidated by Lacan's choice of source materials. I also recall how my preliminary encounter with the text already generated a panoply of questions around the contents and structure of Lacan's seminar, and how my first approach of *Seminar VII* stretched my own elementary instruction in Lacanian psychoanalysis towards previously ignored or unexplored philosophical horizons whose concrete clinical or practical significance was everything but clear.

Since this chapter is strictly confined to Lacan's reading of Sophocles' *Antigone* in *Seminar VII*, I thought my own questions at the time pertaining to this particular part of the text might still offer the best guide for structuring my line of reasoning.[3] Even though I was not a complete novice when I first laid hands on Lacan's "*Ethics*", I feel that my questions back then are still sufficiently pertinent and naïve for them to be rekindled as the constitutive links of what is meant to be a coherent explanation and critical analysis of what Lacan intended to accomplish with his analysis of the ancient Greek tragedy. Without being so presumptuous as to think that all new readers of *Seminar VII* will raise exactly the same questions, here is what I asked myself. What place do *Antigone* and its tragic heroine occupy in a discussion on the ethics of psychoanalysis? What could have prompted Lacan, towards the end of his seminar, to devote no less than three entire lectures to the study of this particular tragedy? What could an interpretation of *Antigone* contribute to the (formulation of an) ethics of psychoanalysis? How did Lacan approach Sophocles' text? What interpretative models or methodologies did he employ when he analyzed and presented *Antigone* to his audience, which mainly consisted of psychoanalytic trainees?[4] Which conceptual tools did Lacan rely on when demonstrating the meaning and relevance of *Antigone* for (the ethics of) psychoanalysis? Which conclusions did Lacan arrive at? How do these conclusions affect (the ethics of) psychoanalysis? What did *Antigone* and Antigone teach Lacan about (the ethics of) psychoanalysis? If psychoanalytic clinical practice requires an ethical framework and *Antigone* may help establish this framework, how does a practicing psychoanalyst stand to benefit from Lacan's reading of it? At which points does *Antigone* connect with the clinical concerns of psychoanalytic practitioners?

When Lacan announced to his audience, on 18 May 1960, that he would pursue his enquiry into what human beings desire, and what they defend themselves against, with a reading of *Antigone* (Lacan, 1992[1986], p. 240), he was evidently in a very different position than me when I picked up a copy of *Séminaire VII* in September 1986. As I will demonstrate, Lacan was far from naïve when it came to the question of ethics and already exceptionally well-informed as regards the interpretative traditions that had crystallized around Sophocles' tragedy. In principle, this should not have stopped him from articulating all or some of the aforementioned questions, yet it simply was not in Lacan's nature to do so. Although I have no doubt that Lacan already knew everything he intended to say about *Antigone* before he broached the subject, his style of exposition was rarely didactic, linear, and systematic, but more often than not characterized by lengthy diversions, lyrical asides, and ostensibly irrelevant digressions.

Nonetheless, in what follows, I shall keep to the chronology of Lacan's three lectures on *Antigone* instead of attempting a retroactive reconstruction of its arguments, because this is undoubtedly how most readers will access the text, starting with Lecture 19 and ending with Lecture 21 of *Seminar VII*. Some of the questions above will inevitably force me to refer to previous and subsequent sessions of the Seminar, and indeed to previous and subsequent Lacan seminars, yet this does not imply that I would expect the reader to assimilate all of these as well. In addition, since the publication of *Seminar VII* was deliberately stripped of any kind of scholarly apparatus, despite Lacan's numerous implicit references and allusions, I also considered it my (ethical) duty to provide the reader with detailed clarifications of Lacan's own "scholarship" and to offer suggestions for further reading, because these may assist the understanding, appreciation, and study of Lacan's conclusions.[5] Finally, this chapter will unavoidably be more than a mere description and explanation of Lacan's commentary on *Antigone*, because the nature and style of his work require a high degree of interpretation in order to generate a coherent and consistent narrative. Were Lacan's lectures to be fully transparent, my own presentation would be utterly superfluous. Since they are not crystal-clear and readily accessible, one needs to have recourse to occasionally extensive (and therefore debatable) interpretations to separate the wheat from the chaff. Hence, what follows constitutes an interpretation of a commentary that is in itself an interpretation of a tragedy, which is also an interpretation of an ancient Greek myth. I shall leave it to others to decide whether my own interpretation is justified and correct, yet as far as Lacan's interpretation is concerned, I believe it definitely necessitates interpretation but not necessarily criticism—*pace* the factual, transcription, and translation errors that mar the text and which I shall highlight whenever necessary—because it is essentially a reading of a work of art, perhaps the most magnificent tragedy ever produced, and thus the outcome of a specific, subjective encounter, which is as valid as the result of any other interpretative act. In the process, one should of course also be mindful of how, in this case, interpretation is crucially predicated upon translation, from the ancient Greek into French, and from the ancient Greek and French into English.

Background and Context

At the risk of relieving the reader from the task of reading Sophocles' *Antigone* before delving into Lacan's protracted commentary on the play, it might be useful to give a succinct outline of its mythical background and central plot.[6] After Antigone's father, Oedipus, discovered that he had unwittingly fulfilled the oracle's prophecy according to which he would kill his father and marry his mother, he blinded himself and abdicated the throne of Thebes, his wife *cum* mother, Jocasta, taking her own life as self-punishment for her heinous involvement in the disastrous events. However, before leaving the city, Oedipus ordered that his two sons, Eteocles and Polynices, should share the throne by alternating power between them and replacing each other at the end of every full year of governance. During the first year of Eteocles' rule, Polynices decided to go into exile and was welcomed into the rival city of Argos, where he married the king's daughter. When it was Polynices' turn to rule Thebes, Eteocles refused to make room for his brother, which resulted in Polynices launching an attack on the city alongside six other warriors. In one of the battles before the gates of Thebes, Eteocles and Polynices killed one another, which placed Creon—Jocasta's brother—on the throne. This is where Sophocles' *Antigone* begins.

In his first act as the new ruler, Creon decrees that Eteocles should be awarded proper burial rites, whereas the corpse of his brother, the traitor Polynices, should be left to rot. Antigone is angered by this injunction and, after having failed to persuade her sister, Ismene, to jointly defy Creon's orders, she takes it upon herself to honour the dead body of Polynices. When she is caught red-handed and brought before Creon, the latter decides that she should be buried alive by way of punishment for her having deliberately broken the laws of the city. After Antigone has been taken away, the prophet Tiresias informs the ruler of Thebes that his death sentence will bring further evil upon the city, which makes Creon change his mind. Yet when he arrives at the cave in which Antigone has been entombed, he realizes that he is too late. Much like her mother before her, Antigone has already taken her own life. In a violent struggle in front of the cave between Creon and his son, Haemon, who is Antigone's betrothed, Haemon also kills himself. Overwhelmed by sorrow, grief, and despair, Creon returns to Thebes, only to hear that his wife, Eurydice, has now also committed suicide, but not before first cursing her wretched husband for the terrible misery he has brought upon his family and the city. This is where the tragedy ends.

It is rather odd, given the centrality of the Oedipus saga and the eponymous complex throughout Freud's theory of psychoanalysis, but when Lacan started relaying his views on *Antigone*—in the 19th session of *Seminar VII*, on 25 May 1960—he was the first psychoanalyst in history to express a serious interest in it.[7] At the end of the previous week's lecture, Lacan had announced that he would pursue his enquiries into ethics by focusing on a tragedy in which the "underlying structure" (*la sous-structure*) of the "morality of happiness" (*la morale du bonheur*) is presented on the surface, in full view, whereby he insinuated that this tragic revelation of the hidden structure of human happiness in *Antigone* also constitutes the main reason why it had preoccupied so many people over the centuries, including some of the world's greatest minds.[8] To grasp Lacan's point, here, I need to provide the reader with a brief summary of his arguments in *The Ethics of Psychoanalysis* until then, if only because the lessons on *Antigone* cannot be separated from a series of questions and issues Lacan had been advancing since the start of his seminar.

From the very beginning of *Seminar VII*, Lacan was adamant that any serious critical analysis of human desire, which he himself had conducted in *Seminar VI*, on *Desire and Its Interpretation* (Lacan, 2019[2013]), inevitably leads to the question of ethics, as the consideration of what human desire is aimed at, what it is hoping and expected to achieve, what it is geared towards. Hence, much like Aristotle had suggested in the opening lines of his *Nicomachean Ethics*, Lacan conceived the question of ethics as an investigation into the goals, aims, and objectives of human desire (Aristotle, 1934). Concurrent with a philosophical tradition going as far back as Plato, he also acknowledged that an investigation into the goal of human desire would not only generate questions about ethics, but also invoke the field of aesthetics, since the "morally good" had consistently been associated with the "beautiful".[9] Hence, to Lacan, the term "ethics" pertained to questions concerning the goal of human desire, and these questions would not only be important for the development of a proper understanding of the human condition, but also for the conception of the psychoanalytic treatment, on at least three distinct levels. First, insofar as it is the patient's suffering that brings her or him to see a psychoanalyst, to what extent is this suffering fundamentally related to a certain disparity between the (aims of the) patient's desire and what he or she has, or has not, accomplished? Second, assuming that it is indeed a disparity between desire and its aims that has induced the suffering, what can a patient hope for in terms of the outcome of the treatment process? And third, since the treatment process is facilitated by the psychoanalyst, how should the latter's own desire be conceptualized as a professional clinical force that is aimed at the realization of a certain outcome? For Lacan, "the ethics of psychoanalysis" should thus be understood in the subjective as well as the objective sense of the genitive: it is a psychoanalytic consideration *of* ethics (a psychoanalytic perspective *on* ethics) that leads to the formulation of an ethics *for* psychoanalysis. It needs to be underscored, here, that Lacan was in no way concerned with the development of a deontology, a regulatory framework, or a list of do's and don'ts that could serve as a manual for psychoanalytic practitioners. The question of the ethics of psychoanalysis refers to what the psychoanalytic treatment process—the patient going through it and the psychoanalyst directing it—is aimed at, and as such to requisite reflections upon the end, the termination, and the finality of the treatment.

In the opening session of *Seminar VII*, Lacan conceded that he was by no means the first to think about the preferred outcome of a psychoanalytic treatment. However, most of his predecessors had defined this outcome—much like the philosophers before them—as a set of ideals, such as genital love, authenticity, and independence (Lacan, 1992[1986], pp. 8–10). The problem with these ideals is not only that they are exactly that—ideal, and therefore unattainable goals—but also that they are generally more indicative of ideological norms and moral values than of what concrete human beings want, and what is most likely to make them happy (Ibid., p. 302). On this basis, Lacan set out to articulate a radically different take on psychoanalytic ethics, which not only challenged firmly established views on treatment outcomes, such as the sublimation (and concurrent de-sexualization) of the patient's drives, but also integrated the numerous, often controversial, contributions Freud had made to our understanding of the human condition: the seemingly irreducible impact of the death drive (Freud, 1955[1920g]), the insistent human discontents in civilization (Freud, 1964[1930a]), the recurrent problem of masochism (finding pleasure in one's own pain and misery) (Freud, 1961[1924c]), etc. Considering these classic Freudian observations, Lacan questioned how anyone could still advance an ethical doctrine that is exclusively predicated on the principle that the highest moral good is not only achievable, but also desirable? Given these Freudian principles, how could anyone continue to believe that human happiness is conditioned by the desire for, or the realization of, a concrete state of perfection, which would be as good as it is beautiful, and which should orient, regulate, and direct all aspects of our human existence? How could an analyst still think that the ultimate confluence of moral goodness and spiritual beauty is what patients want, what could make them happy, and what they themselves, as clinical "facilitators", could deliver?

At this point in his disquisition, Lacan resolved to be led by *Antigone* and Antigone, in order to demonstrate: 1. how the object (goal, aim) of human desire does not coincide with the perfect realization of a sovereign good, because it is impossible to know exactly what this sovereign good entails; 2. how human happiness does not stem from the ultimate fulfilment (satisfaction) of desire; 3. how the radical emancipation of human desire from all of its socio-symbolic constraints is an unequivocal recipe for disaster. These three axes frame the tragic "underlying structure" of the "morality of happiness", and they basically show how this "morality of happiness" is hopelessly fraught with countless inconsistencies. In revealing this dialectical, "underlying structure" of desire, Lacan argued that Sophocles' *Antigone*—the play that Hegel had designated as "the most perfect" tragedy, although, in Lacan's opinion, "for the worst reasons" (Lacan, 1992[1986], p. 240, translation modified)—does not only expose the fallacies of the "morality of happiness", but also paints a more accurate picture of the trials and tribulations of human desire, from which the theory and practice of psychoanalysis can take their lead.[10]

The Cathartic Effect of Antigone's Brilliance

Initially, Lacan's audience may have wondered why he decided to commence his commentary on *Antigone* with a lengthy reflection upon the purpose of tragedy in general. Even so, the first lecture in Lacan's own trilogy already offered, in no uncertain terms, the fundamental thesis to which his meticulous reading of Sophocles' play had led him. I shall unpack it in all its idiosyncratic features below, yet it can be captured in a single sentence: as the central figure of the tragedy, Antigone comes to represent a focal point of exceptional brilliance, which is both the main source of the play's cathartic effects upon the audience and the problematic place where human desire finds its ultimate fulfilment. Lacan constructed this thesis upon the resonances of two separate small passages in *Antigone*: a few lines spoken by Antigone shortly before she is led away to the cave in which she will be buried alive (909–912), and one verse sung by the chorus just before Antigone is brought before Creon for the last time (795–797).[11] Lacan highlighted Antigone's own words at the end of his first lecture, whereas for the chorus's song his audience would have to wait until the following session. In relying on these fragments, Lacan explicitly distanced himself from Hegel's interpretations of the play, whilst simultaneously endorsing the authenticity of verses that many scholars had considered unworthy of Sophocles, and conceivably as interpolations by another playwright, since the early 19th century.

During the first part of his lecture, Lacan recalled how *Antigone* constitutes a tragedy (as opposed to a comedy) and how ancient Greek tragedy had not only proven to be important for psychoanalysis owing to Freud's extraction of the Oedipus-complex from Sophocles' *Oedipus the King*, but also because of Freud's reliance on the defining purpose (aim, objective) of all ancient Greek tragedies for his conceptualization of the goal of clinical interventions, even before his adoption of psychoanalytic treatment principles. As Aristotle had put it in the sixth section of his *Poetics*, the purpose of tragedy is the catharsis of emotions, which is being accomplished δι' ἐλέου καὶ φόβου, "through pity and fear" (Aristotle, 1999, pp. 47–48).[12] Since this particular part of Aristotle's book does not include a definition of catharsis—maybe because Aristotle deferred his explanation of it to other chapters of the *Poetics*, those that have not survived—it is impossible to gauge from the *Poetics* what Aristotle meant by catharsis. However, the philosopher was quite explicit about the nature of catharsis at the very end of his *Politics*, where he stated that it involves "a pleasant feeling of purgation and relief" (Aristotle, 1962, p. 314). In other words, catharsis coincides with pleasure, which made Lacan wonder aloud about the nature of "this pleasure to which one returns after a crisis that occurs in another dimension, a crisis that sometimes threatens pleasure" (Lacan, 1992[1986], p. 246).

When Breuer and Freud adopted the term *catharsis* in their 1893 "Preliminary Communication" to the *Studies on Hysteria*, they translated it as "*Abreagiren*", a process they described as the patient's putting into actions or words of the troublesome affective quantities that are attached to repressed memories (Breuer and Freud, 1955[1893a], p. 8). This process of purgation and purification, whose name James Strachey translated as "abreaction", thus coincides with the point in the treatment when the patient succeeds in liberating the affect from its unconscious representations and proceeds to discharging it verbally (or otherwise), which then results in an alleviation of the clinical symptoms.[13] Ancient Greek tragedy, of which *Antigone* is one of the best examples, is therefore closely related to the psychoanalytic treatment, because Breuer and Freud inscribed its purpose literally into their account of how the treatment unfolds. Catharsis, as the characteristic purpose of tragedy, reappears in the endgame of psychoanalytic clinical practice, and it is therefore intimately related to the ethics (the aims and objectives) of the treatment. It is important to note, here, that over the years Freud came to think rather differently about what a psychoanalytic treatment should be aimed at, yet he never went so far as to discard catharsis completely as an erroneous, misguided, or insufficient goal (see, for example, Freud, 1959[1926d], p. 167). When reconstructing these connections, Lacan emphasized that, at least in principle, Breuer and Freud had replaced the original ethical and aesthetic connotations of catharsis with a strictly medical meaning, by which they had taken advantage of a long tradition of classical and other scholarship, in which Aristotle's original notion had been extrapolated to include ideas pertaining to the palpably therapeutic impact of the purification of the psyche.[14]

So where does catharsis emanate from in *Antigone*? Which part(s) of the play render it possible? Where is it to be situated? Here, Lacan argued that it is to be found specifically in the distinctive place Antigone occupies at the end of her final appearance, before she is taken away. This argument is first of all based on Lacan's conviction that Antigone is the undisputed protagonist of the play. This may strike the reader as an emphatically trivial point, yet in rendering his own position explicit in this way, Lacan not only showed once again that he had familiarized himself with the scholarly literature and the associated debates on the tragedy, but also that he was prepared to take a stand against all those who had claimed that the central figure of *Antigone* is Creon and that any discussion of the play's ethical dimensions should therefore be focused on the new ruler of Thebes rather than on his niece, Antigone.[15] Putting Antigone at the heart of *Antigone*, Lacan averred that, at the high point of her presence, she epitomizes the target (*le point de visée*) of desire, notably that which desire is aimed at.[16] For Lacan, it is by virtue of what Antigone incarnates and represents, at the culmination of her involvement in the dramatic action, just before her punishment is implemented, that *Antigone* succeeds in producing catharsis. In other words, insofar as catharsis is the overall aim and the defining feature of tragedy, this effect is generated by how Antigone herself appears, in her final moment on stage, as the prototypical personification of what commands fear and pity. This, for Lacan, is the place where the ethical truth of the tragedy is to be located.

The heart of *Antigone* having been identified as such, Lacan then approached it from a wide range of different angles, offering various descriptions of this ethical truth along the way. First and foremost, he designated it as Antigone's "unbearable brilliance" (*éclat insupportable*), a source of high-intensity luminosity that is not at all intolerable to herself, but hugely insufferable to everyone who is confronted with it (Lacan, 1992[1986], p. 247).[17] It is important to reiterate, here, that Lacan was not interested in the meaning of *Antigone*, let alone the function Antigone serves at that particular point in the play, but rather in what the place she occupies represents for the nature and structure of human desire. Finding alternative designations for it, he suggested that it is a place of sublime beauty, which is simultaneously fascinating and horrifying, and which does not appease the senses but induces a complex admixture of captivation and trembling, terror and enchantment, pity and fear. It is a place of turmoil (*émoi*), the place which the fictional Pope Pius VI—one of the libertines in Marquis de Sade's *Juliette*—could have explained as the point of the "second death", where the natural cycle of the endless regeneration of life is itself radically abolished after the "first death" of an individual's living substance.[18] Implicitly employing Heideggerian terminology, Lacan also pointed to this locus of unbearable brilliance as "the place where the metamorphoses of 'that which is' [*das Seiende*] are being separated from the [naked, pure] 'position of being' [*das Sein*]", so that the latter stands out in the full advent of its unfathomable presence (Lacan, 1992[1986], p. 248, translation modified).[19] Additionally, drawing on Kant's transcendental philosophy of pure reason (Kant, 1998[1781]) and Freud's posthumously published "Project for a Scientific Psychology" (Freud, 1966[1950a]), he referred to it as an existential twilight zone, where the only factor coming into play is the perfectly thinkable, but radically unknowable Thing (Lacan, 1992[1986], p. 253).

As I indicated at the beginning of this section, Lacan derived the textual evidence in support of his argument from two small passages in *Antigone*: a tiny part of Antigone's final lament and an even tinier invocation from one of the chorus's songs. The lines (909–912) spoken by Antigone run as follows:

πόσις μὲν ἄν μοι κατθανόντος ἄλλος ἦν,
καὶ παῖς ἀπ' ἄλλου φωτός, εἰ τοῦδ' ἤμπλακον,
μητρὸς δ' ἐν Ἅιδου καὶ πατρὸς κεκευθότοιν
οὐκ ἔστ' ἀδελφὸς ὅστις ἂν βλάστοι ποτέ.

In the English translation of *Antigone* by Hugh Lloyd-Jones, they are rendered as: "If my husband had died, I could have had another, and a child by another man, if I had lost the first, but with my mother and my father in

Hades below, I could never have another brother" (Sophocles, 1998, p. 87).[20] The context in which this sentence appears is worth recalling, here, because it adds poignancy to the tone and significance of Antigone's words. Antigone is brought before Creon one last time and she is both reflecting upon her fate and contemplating her reasons for defying Creon's injunction that Polynices must not be buried. Whereas previously Antigone had explained her "criminal act" with reference to the unwritten, divine law that elevates kinship far above the written rules and regulations of the city, now she justifies her decision to honour her dead brother in a different way. Whereas earlier she had exposed Creon's order as a decree running counter to the laws of Hades (Sophocles, 1998, p. 51)—putting herself in the position of a dutiful, compliant servant of the gods—now she acknowledges another law. She is no longer speaking to Creon, nor to anyone else for that matter but, as Bernard Knox has put it, she is engaging in a "lonely, brooding introspection, a last-minute assessment of her motives, on which the imminence of death confers a merciless clarity" (Knox, 1984, p. 46). And when she has finished articulating the true motive of her act, she addresses herself directly to the dead body of Polynices: "Such was the law for whose sake I did you [Polynices] special honour, but to Creon I seemed to do wrong and to show shocking recklessness, O my own brother" (Sophocles, 1998, pp. 88–89). Whatever the divine laws may have encouraged her to do, in the final instance Antigone concedes that she decided to perform funerary rites for her dead brother, and sacrifice herself in the process of doing so, because he is quite simply irreplaceable. Faced with death, she suddenly sees that she relinquished her own life for Polynices owing to his absolute, incommensurable uniqueness.

I shall elaborate on Lacan's reasons for situating Antigone's "unbearable brilliance" at this particular point of the play in the next section of this chapter, yet for now it should already be clear that the source of Antigone's most advanced rationale for breaking Creon's law is exceptionally difficult to describe. Making abstraction of her outspoken reliance on the unwritten, divine laws, it is much easier to encapsulate and render intelligible her antagonistic "No" to Creon than to pinpoint the root source of her "Yes". What exactly is it that drives Antigone to remain steadfast in her conviction that Polynices is fully deserving of the same ceremonial rites as anyone else? She firmly believes that Creon's edict is unjustifiable and should be opposed, but on what grounds? What exactly is it that Antigone believes in and that she is willing to die for? In fact, the immense challenge of trying to make sense of Antigone's words at 909–912 has prompted numerous scholars since the early 19th century to consider them interpolated, and in his seminar Lacan demonstrated that he was very much aware of the debate they had sparked (Lacan, 1992[1986], pp. 254–256).

In a sense, it had all started in 1821, with a classical philologist called August Ludwig Jacob, who argued, in the first volume of a massive compilation of "Sophoclean questions", that "Antigone, as she is called, is so apt in claiming that her brother is irreplaceable, that she becomes utterly ridiculous" (Jacob, 1821, p. 366).[21] In subsequent years, scholars such as August Böckh and Hermann Hinrichs categorically opposed Jacob's arguments, whereby they (sometimes implicitly) rekindled Hegel's famous analysis of *Antigone* in *The Phenomenology of Spirit*, in which 909–912 are mentioned without any suspicion concerning their genuineness being raised (Böckh, 1824; 1828; Hegel, 2018[1807], p. 264; Hinrichs, 1827). However, serious doubts remained and continue to linger until this day.[22] On Wednesday, 28 March 1827, none other than Johann Wolfgang von Goethe, the greatest mind of his generation, confessed to his friend Johann Peter Eckermann: "There is a passage in *Antigone* [909–912] which I always look upon as a blemish, and I would give a great deal for an apt philologist to prove that it is interpolated and spurious", because it is "quite unworthy" and "almost borders on the comic"; "when placed into the mouth of a heroine going to her death, [it] disturbs the tragic tone" (Eckermann, 2012[1836–1848], pp. 371–372).

From Lacan's detailed presentation of the controversy, it can be inferred that he knew very well how 909–912 had appeared in nearly identical form in the *Histories* by Sophocles' contemporary Herodotus—with the proviso that in this episode the "chosen brother" is still alive (Herodotus, 2014, p. 243)—but also that he fully endorsed the main argument against the hypothesis according to which verses 909–912 must be spurious: Aristotle (mis)quoted 911–912 in his *Rhetoric* without questioning their authenticity, even though the philosopher indicated that in this case Antigone's argument is quite "hard to believe" (ἄπιστον) (Aristotle, 2020, pp. 446–447, translation modified).[23] Erudition aside, the fact that Lacan discovered the truth of *Antigone* in verses whose genuineness was highly disputed is already highly instructive with regard to his methodology.

Having told his audience that, as psychoanalysts, they would be expected to pay attention to the circulations of the signifier, whether in the words of a patient or the written text of a document, rather than applying one or the other key concept as an "intellectual talisman", he proceeded to focus not on the most outstanding, thematically prominent signifiers, but on those emerging in the margins of the play—disruptive and disturbing signifiers, words that do not seem to fit into the overall picture of the narrative tone and dramatic action, verses so strange and unusual that a plethora of eminent scholars had concluded that they must be inauthentic.[24] In doing so, he implicitly embraced a classic Freudian *modus operandi*, which I have designated elsewhere as the "Zadig-Morelli method" (Nobus, 2000, p. 58). In his 1914 essay "The Moses of Michelangelo", Freud had compared psychoanalytic technique to the innovative method for establishing the authorship (and authenticity) of a painting which had been introduced by the Italian art critic Giovanni

Morelli during the late 19th century: rather than looking at the central composition of the work, one needs to pay careful attention to the smallest of details, because this is where the true identity of the artist would reveal itself. Psychoanalysis too, Freud wrote, "is accustomed to divine secret concealed things from despised or unnoticed features, from the rubbish-heap, as it were, of our observations [*Auch diese ist gewohnt, aus gering geschätzten oder nicht beachteten Zügen, aus dem Abhub—dem "refuse"—der Beobachtung, Geheimes und Verborgenes zu erraten*]" (Freud, 1958[1914*b*], p. 222). As to the act of psychoanalytic "divination" itself, this would generally adopt the format of what Thomas Huxley dubbed a "retrospective prophecy", an *ex post facto* hypothesis which explains how, on balance of probability, the rubbish-heap had come to pass, and for which Voltaire's fictional character Zadig provides the paradigmatic illustration (Huxley, 1894[1880]; Voltaire, 1964[1747]). In singling out verses 909–912, Lacan quite literally took the "despised features" of *Antigone* as one of his starting points for developing a psychoanalytic interpretation of Sophocles' tragedy. Of course, Lacan's assertion that the truth of the entire play is to be situated in just a few easily overlooked, barely noticeable, or deliberately discarded verses is also methodologically reminiscent of Heidegger's approach to *Antigone* in his 1935 lecture course *Introduction to Metaphysics* (Heidegger, 2000[1953], pp. 112–126) and, more poignantly, in his 1942 lectures on Hölderlin's hymn "The Ister" (Heidegger, 1996[1984], pp. 51–122), in which he concentrated almost exclusively on just a few words in the first and especially the second choral odes of the play (332–333).[25]

Before I move on to a discussion of Lacan's arguments in the two other sessions he devoted to *Antigone*, I should also comment briefly on his recurrent criticism of Hegel's interpretation of the tragedy. In all likelihood, Lacan first encountered Hegel's analysis of *Antigone* when attending Alexandre Kojève's lectures on *The Phenomenology of Spirit* (Hegel, 2018[1807]) during the 1930s in Paris. Although the transcription of Kojève's courses is incomplete, we know that he addressed the sixth chapter of *The Phenomenology of Spirit*—in which the ethical dimensions of *Antigone* are being discussed (Hegel, 2018[1807], pp. 253–267)—during the academic year 1935–1936 (Kojève, 2017[1947], pp. 122–123).[26] In sum, Hegel's entire conception of the tragedy revolves around the dialectical opposition between the law of the state, as represented by Creon, and the law of the family, as embodied by Antigone, which reaches its climax in the emergence of "equality by *justice*", which is "the simple spirit of he who has suffered wrong" (Hegel, 2018[1807], p. 266). As Hegel put it in his *Aesthetics*:

> Everything in this tragedy is logical; the public law of the state is set in conflict over against inner family love and duty to a brother; the

woman, Antigone, has the family interest as her "pathos", Creon, the man, has the welfare of the community as his. (Hegel, 1975[1820–1829], p. 464)[27]

Throughout his discussion of *Antigone*, Lacan expressed his disagreement with Hegel on two separate matters. First, he argued that Hegel's portrayal of Creon and Antigone as two opposing polarities is too uni-dimensional (Lacan, 1992[1986], p. 254). In other words, Lacan criticized Hegel for failing to appreciate the intrinsically conflicted nature of both Creon and Antigone—their insecurities, their fragility and, ultimately, their self-doubt. Second, Lacan distanced himself from Hegel, because he felt that neither *Antigone* nor *Oedipus at Colonus* culminate in some form of reconciliation between the opposing forces (Lacan, 1992[1986], pp. 249–250).[28] To Lacan, the dialectical drama of the two antagonistic principles is not resolved in a higher synthesis, but left wide open, which is exactly why *Antigone* is a sublime tragedy. Whether these criticisms are entirely justified is a question that would require a separate investigation, yet I think it is fair to say that Hegel was much more subtle in his analysis of *Antigone* than Lacan's disparaging remarks intimate. In addition, as I shall show below, there is at least one point where Hegel's critique reconnects with Lacan's interpretation, so that Lacan was perhaps more Hegelian in his reading than he would have wanted his audience to believe.

Beyond Desire and What Antigone Found There

In this section, I shall present a combined reading of lessons 20 and 21 of Lacan's *Seminar VII*, partly because Lacan himself announced that the second of these lessons would be an in-depth continuation of the first (Lacan, 1992[1986], p. 269), partly because the two lessons revolve around the same set of questions. I shall also include some observations derived from the so-called "Supplementary Note" (Lacan, 1992[1986], pp. 284–287), which should have been included into the transcription of the seminar as a stand-alone lesson, and thus as lesson 22, because it concerns a completely separate session.[29]

In his first lesson on *Antigone* (Lesson 19), Lacan had argued that, at the high point of the play, the heroine occupies a place of "unbearable brilliance", from which she commands pity and fear, and elicits the tragic effect of catharsis. Delving deeper into the "articulations" of Sophocles' work, which should be understood here both as its "formulations" and its "joints", Lacan now set out to substantiate Antigone's ultimate locus of luminosity with reference to another part of the tragedy, whilst providing further glosses on how this place—which also attests to the target of human desire—should be understood, especially in light of the disputed verses 909–912. In addition, he endeavoured to explain how Antigone had succeeded in reaching this place. By virtue of which precise actions and motives did she accomplish the realization of her desire? What exactly had driven her to enter this highly charged location from which the catharsis would flow? In answering these questions, Lacan continuously emphasized the multi-faceted nature of the tragedy's two main characters (Creon and Antigone)—thus countering what he regarded as the uni-dimensionality of the opposing polarities in Hegel's reading of *Antigone*—whilst also highlighting "the theme [*motif*] or true axis on which the whole tragedy turns" (Lacan, 1992[1986], p. 283). For Lacan, this pivot is to be found in a single word: ἄτη.

Let me start with Lacan's key statement that Antigone comes to inhabit a place of "unbearable brilliance". How does she get there? Lacan's answer was exceedingly simple: she manages to reach her destination by crossing a certain line, exceeding a limit, breaking a rule, transgressing a boundary. However, in order to understand what this limit consists of, it needs to be approached from two different angles: from the viewpoint of Creon and from the perspective of Antigone herself. Indeed, the limit Antigone crosses is not the same for Creon as it is for her. Even though the end point is identical, the perception of the actions and motives that lead up to it differs depending on the character defining the limit that has been exceeded. If we approach the transgression from Creon's point of view, the limit is as inflexible as it is unequivocal: the dead body of the traitor Polynices shall not be honoured with funerary rites. Accordingly, in Creon's opinion, Antigone has become *persona non grata* because she has dared to disobey his orders—not once, but twice.[30] In the eyes of Creon, the fact that she did what he had formally prohibited makes her a criminal and fully warrants her receiving the death penalty. However, Lacan argued that, for Antigone herself, there is much more at stake than breaking an official edict. Much as she despises Creon's law because she believes it ignores the unwritten laws of the gods, Antigone takes advantage of the opportunity presented to her (to break the law and commit a criminal act) in order to cross another limit. For Lacan, Antigone antagonizing Creon by burying Polynices is just a means to another, much more important objective, notably her breaking the dreadful spell that has brought innumerable misfortunes upon her family (the House of Labdakos), ever since the days the Delphic oracle had told her grandfather, Laius, that under no circumstances he should father a child. It is by virtue of transgressing Creon's law that Antigone believes she can cross another limit, by which she can then relieve her family, for once and for all, of the terrible grief, shame, and disgrace that have befallen it since time out of mind. Whereas Creon's limit is the law that Polynices must not be buried, Antigone's limit is the law that has brought horrendous suffering upon her family. The former law is a written policy of the city; the latter law is an unwritten malediction called ἄτη.

The term ἄτη is exceptionally difficult to translate in any modern language and Lacan did not even venture to suggest a concise French equivalent (Lacan, 1992[1986], pp. 262–263). Over the years, English translators of *Antigone* have tried to capture ἄτη with a cornucopia of different words, ranging from madness, fantasy, and delusion to bewilderment, chaos, ruin, and disaster, all of which being context-dependent and relaying slightly different aspects of the term, depending on the nature and style of the discourse in which it features. Because this chapter is not intended as a philological study of *Antigone*, and at the risk of attracting the wrath of various classicists and Hellenists, I shall render it as "curse".[31] Hence, for Lacan, Antigone reaches the place of "unbearable brilliance" not merely on account of her having defied Creon's law, but also because she has broken the curse that has devastated the House of Labdakos for so long.

In his seminar, Lacan drew his audience's attention to the fact that ἄτη is easily overlooked, even though it is mentioned in various parts of the tragedy (Lacan, 1992[1986], p. 262). And indeed, he could have stated, for instance, that it is brought into play from the very beginning, because it already appears in the second sentence of Antigone's opening words to her sister, Ismene (4–6):

οὐδὲν γὰρ οὔτ' ἀλγεινὸν οὔτ' ἄτης γέμον
οὔτ' αἰσχρὸν οὔτ' ἄτιμόν ἐσθ', ὁποῖον οὐ
τῶν σῶν τε κἀμῶν οὐκ ὄπωπ' ἐγὼ κακῶν.

Hugh Lloyd-Jones translates these three verses as: "No, there is nothing painful or laden with destruction or shameful or dishonouring among your sorrows [ἄτης] and mine that I have not witnessed (Sophocles, 1998, p. 5). However, of all the occurrences of ἄτη in the play, the one that Lacan was most interested in is at the very end of the second strophe in the third choral ode, which constitutes the bridge between Antigone's taking sole responsibility for her crime in front of Creon, and Creon being confronted by his son, Haemon, who tries to convince his father that he needs to reconsider his orders, if only because they do not accord with the will of the people. Reflecting upon the curse that has thrown the House of Labdakos into disarray, the chorus sings about the unfathomable, omnipotent power of the gods, compared to which the will of earthly mortals must remain forever diminutive and insignificant. Enthralled by its grandiose encomium, the chorus then proclaims its own law (611–614):

τό τ' ἔπειτα καὶ τὸ μέλλον
καὶ τὸ πρὶν ἐπαρκέσει
νόμος ὅδ'' οὐδὲν ἕρπει
θνατῶν βιότῳ πάμπολύ γ' ἐκτὸς ἄτας.

In Lloyd-Jones's translation: "For present, future and past this law shall suffice: to none among mortals shall great wealth come without disaster [ἐκτὸς ἄτας]" (Sophocles, 1998, p. 61).³² The conventional reading of this law suggests that disaster (ἄτη) is inevitable if ordinary mortals aspire to great wealth. Yet Lacan's interpretation was markedly different, insofar as he considered ἐκτὸς ἄτας not as signifying "without" or "in the absence of" disaster, but rather as connoting "outside", "beyond", or "on the other side of" disaster. To Lacan, the chorus's law therefore conveys another sense, and another injunction: no mortals shall ever acquire great riches unless they succeed in going beyond disaster. And since ἄτη is precisely the limit Antigone wants to cross, ἐκτὸς ἄτας is the point at which her desire is directed (Lacan, 1992[1986], p. 263).

Lacan thus intimated that Antigone reaches this "otherworldly" place, "beyond the curse", as soon as she has broken Creon's law, but that Creon himself remains ignorant of Antigone's true purpose. In the eyes of Creon, his niece has committed a heinous crime, yet to Antigone herself she has only done something that is morally good. As Lacan put it: "something beyond the limits of *Atè* [sic] has become Antigone's good" (Lacan, 1992[1986], p. 270).³³ What Creon is expecting to hear as an explanation of his niece's crime thus enters Antigone's speech as a justification of her welldoing. What Antigone is hearing in Creon's defence of his own ordinance is not the explanation of a just law, but the motive of a criminal act in its own right. What both Creon and Antigone are seeing in one another is an irreconcilable outlook on what is right and what is wrong, which precludes any kind of reconciliation between the two parties.

At this particular point of the perilous juncture between Creon and Antigone—whereby the latter has not only broken the former's law, but also the curse of the House of Labdakos, yet without Creon being aware of this second transgression—Lacan detected the multi-dimensionality, the trials and tribulations, the dilemmas, and the internal conflicts of the play's two principal characters. At first, Creon defends his decree on the basis of an entirely reasonable principle, which could have only been appreciated by the theatregoers as a fair and just decision: murderous traitors who are intent on destroying both their own city and their kin do not deserve any kind of honours when they perish on the battlefield, because they have become enemies of the state. In considering this principle, Lacan went so far as to say that its purportedly universal, unconditional validity would make it fit rather well as a classic, paradigmatic example of a Kantian categorical imperative (Kant, 1997[1788], p. 28; Lacan, 1992[1986], p. 259). Yet it is not in Creon's act of formulating this law that his ἁμαρτία—the "error of judgement" which Aristotle designated as the cardinal trait of all tragic heroes (Aristotle, 1999, pp. 70–71)—needs to be situated.³⁴ If Creon epitomizes ἁμαρτία, it is because he involuntarily allows his law to become contaminated with at least four kinds of lethal poison, and it is through these confusions and aberrations that his weakness of character transpires. Lacan did not mention each and every source of contamination, and one could undoubtedly write an entire essay on why he "forgot" to include some of them, yet they can be summarized as follows. First, Creon erroneously believes that the written law he has passed is *de facto* in accordance with the unwritten laws of the gods, and that his sense of justice (δίκη) is synonymous with the gods' spirit of moral order and fair judgement (162–210) (Lacan, 1992[1986], pp. 276–277; Sophocles, 1998, pp. 19–23). Second, whereas Creon has ruled that all those who break his law shall be put to death by public stoning (29–36), when he discovers that Antigone is the perpetrator, he abandons his own "fixed penalty" in favour of a much harsher punishment, so that her suffering can be prolonged—sustained and extended for as long as possible (773–780) (Lacan, 1992[1986], pp. 260–262; Sophocles, 1998, p. 77).[35] Third, when Creon hears from his son, Haemon, that Antigone's death sentence does not represent the will of the people, he does not hesitate to reaffirm his decision on the basis of a self-proclaimed autocratic position: the city belongs to the ruler and I, Creon, can do whatever I want (736–738) (Sophocles, 1998, p. 71). Finally, Creon states on two occasions that he is not prepared to compromise, let alone pardon the perpetrator, because he cannot accept his sovereign masculinity to become unsettled through the actions of a woman (525, 680) (Sophocles, 1998, pp. 51, 65).[36] Only after his eyes have been opened by the blind prophet Tiresias, and he himself is consumed by pity, fear, and self-doubt, does Creon realize that he has made a tragic mistake, but at that point the damage has already been done: Antigone is dead; Haemon will follow her to Hades; and so will Creon's wife, Eurydice.

As far as Antigone is concerned, she too is conflicted, but for completely different reasons than Creon. Lacan conceded that, unlike Creon, Antigone experiences neither pity nor fear until the very end. In fact, he argued that it is precisely because she never gives in to pity and fear that she commands pity and fear in the audience and that her ultimate appearance is cathartic (Lacan, 1992[1986], p. 258).[37] But she is torn in another way, which may not be emblematic of ἁμαρτία, but which nonetheless leaves her in a state of turmoil and self-doubt. Lacan insinuated that Antigone's own conflicted state of mind comes to the fore most strongly when she stops saying "No" to Creon, relinquishes her attempts to justify her "criminal act" in front of the ruler of Thebes, and goes in search of answers to the question of her own transgression, that of the trans-generational ἄτη. As long as Antigone is immersed in her defence vis-à-vis Creon, she remains headstrong, but when she distances herself from this defence (and from Creon), towards an exploration of what has prompted her to say "Yes" to her own desire to break the curse, she becomes unsteady and unsure, hesitant and tentative, so much so that her words are verging on the irrational. It is in this moment, which Lacan located in the disputed verses 909–912 and which, to him, constitute the true core of the play (as opposed to a spurious interpolation), that Antigone acquires her "unbearable brilliance", because she is no longer interested in revolting against a written law, but fully taken up by the mystery of her own acquiescence, the motive behind her desperate desire to break the curse.[38]

Lacan thus differentiated between Antigone's uncompromising allegiance to the unwritten laws of the gods—as what motivated her "crime"—and her sudden moment of "lonely, brooding introspection" (Knox, 1984. p. 46), in which she searches for an answer to her own question about the source of her desire to break the curse. Both parts of Antigone's oration are equally important—and so the second part should by no means be considered as totally unworthy of the tragic heroine, as Goethe and others had done—but they contrast radically in contents, style, and tone, because they refer to completely different psycho-social registers. In the first register, Antigone is being interrogated by the ruler of Thebes about how she could have gone so far as to give up her own life for the burial of a dead traitor. In this sphere, Antigone keeps repeating that she merely acted in accordance with the divine laws, and Lacan did not hesitate to attribute her fearless self-sacrifice to her spiritual membership of the divine contingent of Ares, which Socrates explains in Plato's *Phaedrus* as a state of mind that can easily drive someone who is enamoured (with another human being or with the gods) to commit murder or self-sacrifice (Lacan, 1992[1986], p. 260; Plato, 2005, p. 33 [252c5]).[39] In the second register, Antigone moves away from Creon and interrogates herself about her motives for crossing the limit of ἄτη. And here the answers do not flow freely, nor do they come across as rational, understandable, and acceptable. The only thing Antigone can think of, the only thing that occurs to her, is that Polynices was irreplaceable, yet this reveals much less about her brother than about the fact that their parents are dead and therefore cannot produce another brother for her. As such, Polynices is neither less nor more irreplaceable than Antigone's other siblings—the dead Eteocles and the living Ismene. Antigone's argument falters and to Lacan it could not have been otherwise, because she is desperately trying to describe the core of her own desire, for which no words will ever suffice. What she is attempting to say is that, ultimately, she did what she did because she loved her brother deeply. However, she cannot bring herself to find the right words, as if they might actually exist.[40] In this particular instance, Lacan's reading of *Antigone* does chime with Hegel's interpretation of the play, because in his *Aesthetics*, Hegel, too, asserted that in verses 909–912, Antigone is animated by "her holy love for her brother" (Hegel, 1975[1820–1829], p. 221).[41]

In any case, because Antigone struggles to articulate the motive behind her desire to break the curse, what she is left with is a state of confusion, uncertainty, and self-doubt. And so the firm ethical stance that she adopted vis-à-vis Creon dissipates and transmutes into an episode of sublime beauty, which is greatly intensified by the fact that Antigone also realizes that she will only learn afterwards, i.e., after her own death, whether her actions were in keeping with the gods' will:

> [B]y acting piously, I have been convicted of impiety. Well, if this conviction is approved among the gods, I should forgive them for what I have suffered, since I have done wrong; but if they [Creon and the state] are the wrong-doers, may they suffer nothing worse than all the evils they have unjustly inflicted upon me! [925–928]. (Sophocles, 1998, p. 89, translation modified)

Antigone's "unbearable brilliance" is therefore concurrent with the (rather awkward and altogether failed) expression of the source and origin of her deepest desire. She is transformed into a dazzling point of high-powered luminosity, because the inexpressible force of her own desire suddenly erupts onto the stage in all its blazing purity.

However, Lacan identified another moment in the tragedy when Antigone becomes one with the birthplace of her desire. In this case, the moment is not part of Antigone's own discourse, but included in the fourth choral ode, which follows the end of Haemon's futile attempt at changing his father's mind. After the famous opening strophe in which the chorus pays tribute to the invincibility of romantic love (Ἔρως ἀνίκατε μάχαν, 781), they pursue the antistrophe with a paean to Antigone herself (795–800):

> νικᾷ δ' ἐναργὴς βλεφάρων
> ἵμερος εὐλέκτρου
> νύμφας, τῶν μεγάλων
> πάρεδρος ἐν ἀρχαῖς
> θεσμῶν ἄμαχος γὰρ ἐμ-
> παίζει θεὸς, Ἀφροδίτα.

Lloyd-Jones translates these verses as: "Victory goes to the visible desire [ἵμερος ἐναργὴς] that comes from the eyes of the beautiful bride, desire that has its throne beside those of the mighty laws; for irresistible in her sporting is the goddess Aphrodite" (Sophocles, 1998, p. 79). In this sentence, the words that mattered the most to Lacan are ἵμερος ἐναργὴς, because they indicate how Antigone's desire has become clearly discernible, distinctly perceptible—in no uncertain terms, in all its immediacy, naked in the pure presence of its implacable being (Lacan, 1992[1986], pp. 268, 281). Lacan also deservedly emphasized, here, how Sophocles did not employ the more common ancient Greek word for desire (ἐπιθυμία), but the word ἵμερος, which has less pejorative connotations than ἐπιθυμία, and which quite literally refers to elements that flow together in a stream of longing, craving, or yearning, as Socrates again explains in Plato's *Phaedrus* (Lacan, 1992[1986], p. 268; Plato, 2005, p. 32).[42]

For Lacan, ἔστ' ἀδελφὸς ὅστις ἂν βλάστοι ποτέ (912), which conjures up the irreplaceability of Polynices, and ἵμερος ἐναργὴς (795–796), which renders Antigone's desire visible, thus constitute the essence of the place beyond ἄτη, where nothing is left of Antigone, other than the immaculate presence of the core of the desire that has taken her to the other side. However, even though the leader of the chorus praises Antigone for having gone there "by virtue of her own law" (αὐτόνομος, 820) (Sophocles, 1998, p. 81, translation modified), Lacan was not particularly keen to ascertain in the tragic heroine a paragon of free will (Lacan, 1992[1986], p. 282). Likewise, he remained rather sceptical about the idea that Sophocles' tragedy exemplifies the basic principles of humanism: the emancipatory value of self-determination, the liberating force of freedom of thought, the inexhaustible resource of human willpower, the strength of the human spirit to realize its full potential in conscious, confident acts of self-assertion.[43] In Lacan's reading, Antigone's being called αὐτόνομος does not mean that she is the sole author of the law that drives her. As the theory of human desire Lacan had constructed over the years would suggest, Antigone's desire to take advantage of Creon's edict, in order to break the curse of the House of Labdakos, had probably already been mediated by another desire, yet here Lacan did not go any further than obliquely designating it as the desire of the Other, whilst insinuating that this "Other desire" may in fact find its origin in the desire of Antigone's mother, Jocasta (Lacan, 1992[1986], pp. 282–283).[44]

Before I bring this chapter to a close, there are two other matters that deserve some attention—one interpretative, the other methodological. As far as Lacan's interpretation of Antigone's desire goes, the place beyond ἄτη she comes to occupy after having broken both Creon's decree and the curse of the House of Labdakos is not a grand realm of unsullied, "prelapsarian" bliss. Antigone's life ἐκτὸς ἄτας is everything but cheerful and tranquil, even though she would have had every reason to feel completely satisfied, given how she has succeeded in fulfilling her deepest desire. Instead of eliciting an experience of limitless joy, the satisfaction of Antigone's desire, for which she herself takes full responsibility, results in torment, isolation, rejection, and profound self-doubt. In short, just because Antigone has accomplished what she originally set out to do does not mean that she is happy; quite the contrary. One could argue, of course, that she would not have ended up in this state of turmoil had it not been for Creon's unwillingness to compromise and his obstinate refusal to pardon her for performing funerary rites on the body of Polynices. Yet this is counterfactual history and moreover Antigone already knew before she did the deed that she would probably be punished harshly for it. Antigone's state of mind ἐκτὸς ἄτας is a place of profound solitude, where she is morally disconnected from her only surviving sibling (Ismene) and cannot even find solace in the arms of her beloved Haemon.[45] On two separate occasions, Lacan described Antigone in her insular space ἐκτὸς ἄτας as "running on empty" (*à-bout-de-course*): she takes full responsibility for the consequences of her act, yet she is struggling to find meaning in her newfound freedom and is forced to acknowledge that she cannot even be entirely sure that the "moral good" she endeavoured to achieve is as significant and valuable as she thought it was.[46] Paraphrasing the title of one of Lacan's earlier essays, one might say that, once she is outside ἄτη, Antigone exists in a state of "anticipated certainty" (Lacan, 2006[1945]), because only after her death will it be revealed whether she was right or wrong. Only after she herself has entered Hades will she know the truth (see verses 925–928 above) (Sophocles, 1998, p. 89). Finally, as if all of this was not enough, Antigone also concedes that the nature of her death sentence has put her in a highly troublesome "ontological position" (850–852):

ἰὼ δύστανος, βροτοῖς
οὔτε νεκρὸς νεκροῖσιν
μέτοικος οὐ ζῶσιν, οὐ θανοῦσιν.

In Lloyd-Jones's translation these verses read: "Ah, unhappy one, living neither among mortals nor as a shade among the shades, neither with the living nor with the dead!" (Sophocles, 1998, p. 83). Here and later on, in her final lament (916–920), Antigone refers to herself explicitly as the "unhappy one" (δύστανος), because she is now dead amongst the living and will soon be alive amongst the dead.[47] In his seminar, Lacan referred to Antigone's state of mind as "being shut up or suspended in the zone between life and death" (Lacan, 1992[1986], p. 280), and subsequently one of the participants would suggest the term "between-two-deaths", which Lacan gladly adopted.[48]

As regards Lacan's methodology, then, it is interesting to see that throughout the period of his commentary on *Antigone*, he engaged in a conversation with Claude Lévi-Strauss, whose structuralist method for interpreting myths is mentioned on various occasions in the course of the seminar. Engaging in a conversation should be taken literally, here, because every so often Lacan would tell his audience about Lévi-Strauss's views on one or the other aspect of the tragedy (Lacan, 1992[1986], p. 274), and at one point he even took credit for persuading his interlocutor to re-read Sophocles' work (Lacan, 1992[1986], pp. 282, 285). The motive for Lacan's personal discussions on *Antigone* with Lévi-Strauss should probably not be attributed here to the mere fact that Lévi-Strauss and Lacan entertained a close friendship, and were in the habit of spending time together at Lacan's country-house in Guitrancourt (Lévi-Strauss and Eribon, 1991[1988], pp. 66, 109).[49] I think the motive is rather to be found in the contents of Lévi-Strauss's 1955 essay "The Structural Study of Myth" (Lévi-Strauss, 1955), a French translation of which had been included in *Anthropologie Structurale* (Lévi-Strauss, 1958[1955]), a generous collection of papers released in 1958, just a year before Lacan started his seminar *The Ethics of Psychoanalysis*. In that essay, Lévi-Strauss had presented an innovative, structuralist reading of the Oedipus-myth, in which it was situated within a much broader mythological framework, reorganized in its orthogonal diachronic and synchronic dimensions, and reduced to a set of structurally invariant units (mythemes) (Lévi-Strauss, 1963[1955], pp. 213–217).[50] In Lévi-Strauss's interpretation, Antigone's decision to bury the body of her dead brother, Polynices, appeared as a diachronic transmutation of Oedipus marrying his mother, Jocasta, and, higher up the mythological ladder, Cadmos going in search of his sister, Europa (Ibid., p. 214).

When Lacan disclosed to the participants at his seminar that Lévi-Strauss had told him personally that Antigone represents a place of synchrony in opposition to the diachronical position of Creon (Lacan, 1992[1986], p. 285), it was thus Lévi-Strauss's methodology and terminology from "The Structural Study of Myth" that had been extended to inform a closer look at *Antigone*. However, despite his unmistakable enthusiasm for Lévi-Strauss's interest in *Antigone*, Lacan's own reading of the tragedy does not fit into the structural(ist) study of myth, if only because Lacan approached the play primarily as a work of art rather than the transfiguration of an ancient Greek myth. Yet in addition to this, he was not particularly interested in extracting from *Antigone* the elementary symbolic schemes that contribute to the construction of subjective positions and which underpin the binary dialectical oppositions within and between psycho-social relations of property and exchange, as he had done with great success a few years earlier in his seminal reading of Edgar Allan Poe's "The Purloined Letter" (Lacan, 2006[1957a]). For all the exceptional value of kinship in the tragedy's unfolding intrigue—as the driving force behind Creon's decree and Antigone's defiance of it—Lacan was not particularly interested in extracting its elementary structures. In fact, the only time he allowed himself a little foray into the structural study of the Antigone-myth was when he considered the mystery of Antigone's death at her own hands. "Antigone hanging in her own tomb evokes something very different from an act of suicide", Lacan posited, "since there are all kinds of myths of hanged heroines... [O]ne finds there a whole ritual and mythical background, which may be brought back to resituate in its religious harmony all that is produced on the stage" (Lacan, 1992[1986], p. 286).[51]

Conclusion

Let me return now to the questions I posed in the introduction to this chapter and endeavour to formulate some answers. Lacan resolved to devote his 1959–1960 seminar to the age-old query as to what human desire is geared towards, and to how these goals, aims, and objectives of desire play out within the space of a clinical psychoanalytic encounter. This project would have followed naturally from his having spent an entire year investigating the meaning and function of desire, both in the human mind and in the act of psychoanalytic interpretation. Lacan intended his investigation of the aims of desire to be theoretical as well as practical, and for it to be of direct relevance to the psychoanalytic trainees attending his seminar. Accordingly, *The Ethics of Psychoanalysis* would not only be a seminar on the aims of desire, in the broadest sense of the word, but also on the aims (goals, direction, finality) of the psychoanalytic treatment, insofar as the latter is conceived as a particular "therapy" of (the patient's) desire. When broaching the question of the aims of desire, Lacan also knew that, at least since the ancient Greeks, it had been consistently addressed within the context of philosophical reflections on ethics—a discipline which not only revolves around the challenge of identifying and defining robust criteria for differentiating between right and wrong, but also around in-depth examinations of the particular relationship (and the essential or contingent discrepancies) between human desire and various (socio-political) ideals of concrete outcomes and deliverables that are representative of the highest moral good. Considered in this light, it should not come as a surprise at all that Lacan entitled his seminar *The Ethics of Psychoanalysis*, which invoked both a psychoanalytic interpretation of ethics and the formulation of an ethical system that is attuned to the highly specific circumstances of the psychoanalytic setting.

As always, Lacan would have had to make strategic choices when it came to deciding which topics to include under this heading, even though he had a whole year to expose his views. I do not know when exactly he came to the conclusion that it would be a good idea to include a detailed critical analysis of Sophocles' *Antigone* in his seminar, yet the fact that he reserved a substantial portion of it to a discussion of ancient Greek tragedy was justified on two grounds. First, the goal of ancient Greek tragedy, which had been designated since Aristotle as catharsis (Aristotle, 1999, pp. 47–48)—a purification or cleansing of the psyche—featured explicitly in Breuer and Freud's *Studies on Hysteria* as the overall aim of their treatment paradigm, whereby they had defined it as the patient's process of releasing (through words or concrete actions) the disruptive affects that are attached to repressed unconscious representations (Breuer and Freud, 1955[1893a], p. 8). After Freud abandoned the hypno-cathartic method of treatment in favour of an approach he termed psychoanalysis, which no longer relied on hypnotic techniques, he did not simultaneously relinquish catharsis as a suitable designation for the goal of the treatment, even though he would subsequently entertain alternative notions, such as "working-through" (Freud, 1958[1914g]). Second, in the final session of his seminar, Lacan offered another reason as to why ancient Greek tragedy deserves to feature in a research programme on the ethics of psychoanalysis:

> The ethics of analysis has nothing to do with speculation about prescriptions for, or the regulation of what I have called the service of the goods. Strictly speaking, the ethics of analysis implies the dimension that is expressed in what is called the tragic experience of life. (Lacan, 1992[1986], p. 313, translation modified)[52]

I shall return to this second reason below, yet over and above the confluence of the goal of ancient Greek tragedy and the aim of psychoanalysis, Lacan thus averred that the study of ancient Greek tragedy could be highly instructive for practicing psychoanalysts, because the clinical psychoanalytic experience constitutes in itself a real-life confrontation with the tragedy of human existence.

Innumerable ancient Greek tragedies have not survived the passing of time, yet Lacan would still have been spoilt for choice when it came to deciding which tragedy to focus on in his seminar. If he settled on Sophocles' *Antigone*, I believe it is not so much because it follows in the wake of *Oedipus Rex*—the tragedy from which Freud had derived the Oedipus complex, one of the conceptual cornerstones of psychoanalysis—but because *Antigone*, perhaps more than any other tragedy, stages precisely the tragic impact of human desire. If Lacan was looking for an ancient Greek tragedy in order to substantiate his arguments on ethics and desire, he would not need to look further than *Antigone*, because in this tragedy Sophocles had organized the entire ethical conflict around the quandaries of desire. Whether or not one agrees with Hegel's judgement that *Antigone* is one of the most sublime works of art of all time (Hegel, 1975[1820–1829], p. 464), the (chronologically) third instalment of Sophocles' Theban trilogy showcases the tragedy of conflicting desires, between as well as within the characters of Creon and Antigone, and it also raises fundamental questions about the existential gains and losses that are associated with the fulfilment of desire. In sum, if Lacan's seminar, *The Ethics of Psychoanalysis,* would focus on the ethical question concerning the aim of desire, Sophocles' *Antigone* had already focused—profoundly, poignantly, and most magnificently—on the ethical conflicts resulting from the insistence of desire and the realization of its aim. When I first leafed through the pages of *The Ethics of Psychoanalysis*, I was undeniably puzzled as to why Lacan would have wanted to spend three (or four) sessions on Sophocles' *Antigone*, yet with the benefit of hindsight (and some personal reflection) his resolution now occurs to me as glaringly obvious.

When the time arrived for Lacan to commence his interpretation of *Antigone*, he would have also had to consider which methodology to employ, i.e., which interpretative techniques to use in order to distill the central contributions of *Antigone* and Antigone to the development of an ethics for psychoanalysis. In this respect, it is quite remarkable—although to the best of my knowledge no commentators on Lacan's reading of *Antigone* have ever highlighted it—that, when it came to analyzing Sophocles' text, Lacan's conceptual toolkit was almost entirely empty. At the end of the 1950s, Lacan's own theory of psychoanalysis was sufficiently well advanced for him to rely on it with great confidence for teasing out the intricacies of an ancient Greek tragedy. In 1959–1960, Lacan was not only the intellectual figurehead of the *Société française de psychanalyse*, one of the most fervent readers of Freud's oeuvre, and a tireless critic of the prevalent traditions in contemporary psychoanalysis (ego-psychology and the object-relations movement), but also a relentless conceptual innovator, who had already demonstrated the value of structural linguistics for psychoanalysis and who was in the process of promoting a topological perspective on key psychoanalytic questions.

It is nothing short of astonishing, then, to observe that throughout his three (or four) lessons on *Antigone*, Lacan did not refer a single time to his famous triad of the Real, the Symbolic, and the Imaginary, nor to any of the other concepts for which he had already gained a certain notoriety: jouissance, the fantasy, the signifying chain, the phallus, and the object *a*. Likewise, with the exception of one cursory mention of the death drive (Lacan, 1992[1986], p. 281), he did not bring out any of the classic Freudian notions that could have served a good interpretative purpose: the Oedipus complex, the superego, castration, penis envy, the pleasure principle, etc. Even more noteworthy, perhaps, especially in light of an established practice within the field of applied psychoanalysis, or psychoanalytic interpretations of literature, is that Lacan completely shied away from attempting a certain diagnosis (and a concurrent pathologization) of the characters in *Antigone*. At no given point did Lacan intimate, even in the vaguest of terms, that Antigone, Creon, or some of the other characters in the tragedy could be understood as literary exemplifications of hysteria, obsessional neurosis, or psychosis. The only concept that is constantly present throughout Lacan's discussion of *Antigone* is desire. Yet whilst this notion was at least as important in Lacan's theory of psychoanalysis as the other terms mentioned above—and it should not be forgotten, here, that he had devoted an entire seminar to it in 1958–1959—desire is of course also the key issue around which the tragedy of *Antigone* itself unfolds. It would therefore be an exaggeration to claim that Lacan injected desire into *Antigone*, or that he reorganized the entire tragedy around (the ethics of) desire, because (the ethics of) desire is already the main theme of the play. It may not be coincidental that Lacan situated one of the most significant messages of *Antigone* in a verse in which the chorus glorifies the visibility of the young woman's desire, yet he would not have had to work hard to argue his point, because the word desire (ἵμερος) is already present, literally and distinctively, at the level of the text.

As I have attempted to demonstrate previously, when interpreting *Antigone*, Lacan also generally avoided Lévi-Strauss's structuralist study of myth, with which he would have been deeply familiar, in favour of an implicit reliance on what I have called the "Zadig-Morelli method", which

Freud himself had singled out as the art-historical equivalent of psychoanalytic technique (Freud, 1958[1914*b*], p. 222). In doing so, he followed the example of Heidegger's interpretation of *Antigone* in his *Introduction to Metaphysics* (Heidegger, 2000[1953], pp. 156–176) and in his lecture course on Hölderlin's "The Ister" (Heidegger, 1996[1984], pp. 51–122), yet much as I would be surprised if Heidegger knew about Zadig and Morelli, I do not think that Lacan had an in-depth knowledge of Heidegger's methods of reading in this particular instance. Most important, however, is that Lacan himself instructed his audience not to use conceptual tools as a magic talisman that would reveal the secrets of a text, but rather to trust the internal logic of the fictional space and follow its leads (Lacan, 1992[1986], pp. 251–252). This is also why I preferred not to place this chapter under the title "Lacan's Antigone", because I would feel very hard-pressed to concede that Lacan appropriated *Antigone* and/or Antigone. It is undoubtedly the case that he did not perform a purely inductive reading—as if this would even be possible—yet at the same time I do not think one could proffer the thesis that Lacan integrated or incorporated *Antigone* into a pre-fabricated or pre-established psychoanalytic framework. The *Antigone* that emerges out of Lacan's interpretation is distinctly unique and, as such, definitely Lacan's own *Antigone* and his *Antigone* alone, yet this does not imply that he went so far as to take ownership of Sophocles' intentions, the dramatic structure of the tragedy, or the conflictual dialectics of desire that are being staged therein. Between 25 May and 15 June 1960, Lacan went on an intellectual journey "with" *Antigone*, whereby he seemed more than happy to allow its eponymous heroine to take the reins.[53]

What did Lacan's interpretation of *Antigone* contribute, then, to the formulation of an ethics for psychoanalysis? Insofar as "ethical system" refers to aims and objectives, how could the finality of psychoanalysis be (re-)conceptualized on the basis of what Sophocles' tragedy teaches us? In this context, I should first of all draw attention to one of the most tenacious (and arguably tragic) misreadings in the history of Lacanian thought.[54] Since the early 1980s, i.e., from the years before *Seminar VII* was even officially released in French, countless scholars of Lacanian theory and self-identified Lacanians have reduced the ethics of psychoanalysis to a single imperative: Do not give up on your desire![55] From Badiou to Žižek and Zupančič, and a pleiad of eager followers of Lacan in between, "Do not give up on your desire!" has become the single most important ethical mantra to be derived from *Seminar VII*.[56] This precept, which has sometimes been rephrased as "the ethics of the Real" (Zupančič, 2000), or "the ethics of jouissance" (Zupančič, 2002), and for which Antigone would then be put forward as the principal literary prototype, has become so prominent and widespread as Lacan's most advanced formulation of a psychoanalytic ethics that the entire seminar on *The Ethics of Psychoanalysis* has occasionally been presented as driven by, or steered towards, the explicit articulation of this one ethical maxim.[57]

The first problem with this interpretation of Lacan's *Seminar VII*, and Lacan's reading of *Antigone* within it, is that it cannot be substantiated on the basis of any kind of textual evidence. Not a single time during his entire lecture course did Lacan even come close to suggesting that "Do not give up on your desire!" should become the ethical motto of psychoanalytic practice, and that the figure of Antigone could, in one form or another, be hailed as its most sublime incarnation. Even though it is true that Antigone never gives up on her desire (to perform funerary rites on the dead body of her brother, Polynices), this does not mean that she should therefore be elevated to the status of patron saint or fairy godmother of psychoanalytic ethics. The only time Lacan mentioned *"céder sur son désir"* (giving up on one's desire) in his seminar was in the final session. He never employed the expression with a negative—as in *"ne pas céder sur son désir"* (not giving up on one's desire)—and it never took the form of an imperative, let alone an ethical precept, even less an ethical axiom for psychoanalysis (Lacan, 1992[1986], pp. 319–321).[58] As to "giving up on one's desire", Lacan only proposed that, quite paradoxically, it may be the most fundamental thing (neurotic) human beings tend to feel guilty about, because the thought of "having given up" on something routinely occurs alongside an impression of (self-)betrayal (Lacan, 1992[1986], pp. 319–321).[59]

Needless to say, advocates of the adage "Do not give up on your desire!" may argue that it was always already implicit in Lacan's discourse, or that, as a concise extrapolation of his words, it might still serve as a foundational principle for psychoanalytic practice. Unfortunately, this argument does not hold water and could only be formulated by someone who has never had any clinical psychoanalytic experience, or whose professional and/or personal interests are extremely far removed from what is at stake in the psychoanalytic treatment of patients. Were a psychoanalyst to operate with the ethical precept that patients should consistently, if not always explicitly, be brought to the point where they can accept that the source of their happiness is always to be found in "not giving up on their desire", she or he would not only run the risk of aiding and abetting the patient to commit various (criminal) transgressions, but much more problematically he or she would also be acting upon the illusion that happiness coincides with the fulfilment (satisfaction or gratification) of desire. Were "Do not give up on your desire!" to be framed in gold above the psychoanalytic couch, the patient would not only be spending money on learning how to exchange a life of suffering for that of a criminal, but the analyst would effectively be joining the reprehensible ranks of all those *faux* experts who cunningly take advantage of someone's else's problems in order to enrich themselves through the sale of false hope and empty promises.[60]

What Antigone teaches Lacan, during the four weeks they go on a journey together, is that the realization of one's desire does not by definition lead to happiness. Here is what Antigone tells Lacan after she has finally succeeded in going beyond ἄτη. Strange as it may seem, Dr Lacan, now that I have buried the body of Polynices, I am still not sure whether I have satisfied my desire to break the curse. For that uncertainty, which creates a great deal of mental turmoil, to go away, I shall have to wait until some kind of final judgement, yet when this moment comes, I shall no longer be alive to reap the fruits of my own act, should it indeed be decided that it was in accordance with my desire and that my desire was justified. Strange as it may seem, Dr Lacan, now that I have broken Creon's law, and taken the opportunity presented to me by it, in order to also break the curse that has brought so much misery upon my family, I still feel miserable, because I do not know whether the satisfaction of my desire, as I see it, will indeed have the desired effect. Strange as it may seem, Dr Lacan, now that I have ostensibly liberated my desire from any kind of constraint and I should have every reason to feel happy, I am not happy at all, because the price I have had to pay for my act seems extraordinarily high. It is not just that I have now been condemned to death, and that I shall be forced to take my own life in order to deprive Creon of the pleasure of knowing that I will suffer tremendously until I finally starve to death. It is rather that I am now no longer sure whether I was right in taking it upon myself to break the curse. In fact, I am no longer sure whether there really was a curse in the first place, because it may have just been my imagination. In any case, Dr Lacan, I cannot find the words to describe the source of my desire, as if my own being is not strong or resourceful enough to render it clear to myself. Strange as it may seem, I definitely do not know whether the realization of my desire has resulted in something good, whether for myself, or for all those who shall come after me.

This is what Antigone tells Lacan during the time they spend together, but it is not what a psychoanalyst would expect to hear from a patient at the end of a psychoanalytic treatment. Much like Antigone, patients will always in some way be confronted with the fundamental tragedy of the human condition—the inevitability of death, the persistent elusiveness of (self-)knowledge, the desperate yet endless search for meaning—but, unlike Antigone, they are not expected to experience this tragedy as a result of the realization of their desire, and even less to experience it as an irreversible *fait accompli*. In effect, contrary to what the aforementioned motto prescribes, one cannot not give up on one's desire, because being a (more or less) respectable, law-abiding citizen ineluctably requires compromise, and therefore a certain degree of (self-)betrayal. In order to ensure that patients do not, or no longer fall to pieces when they are confronted with the tragedy of human existence, the analyst may facilitate a process in which the relationships between desire and the law, the pleasure principle and the reality principle, are thoroughly examined and gradually taken towards an acceptable state of equilibrium. In the final instance, this will not only require patients to explore the fantasy that is sustaining their desire and all the illusory images of eternal bliss that might stem from its satisfaction. It will also require them to acknowledge and assume the tragic reality of the human condition, notably that the very "fact of being" shall always remain insufficient to lead one's life successfully, properly, and happily. It will require them to acknowledge the tragedy of intrinsic human vulnerability, in order to find the pathways to some form of (transient) goodness and (momentary) happiness. Here, the finality of the psychoanalytic treatment reconnects with the conclusions of Martha Nussbaum in her influential book, *The Fragility of Goodness*: a well-lived life is predicated upon the acceptance that living well cannot be divorced from the impossibility of always being well (Nussbaum, 2001). In the final instance, this ethical dimension of the finality of the psychoanalytic treatment will require analysts themselves to adopt a certain desire. However, in order to formalize this "desire of the analyst" (Lacan, 1992[1986], p. 300)—as the non-negotiable foundation of the ethics of psychoanalysis—Lacan would need another ten years and quite a few additional psychoanalytic encounters with fictional and other heroines.

Notes

1 Jacques-Alain Miller's own seminars from 1981 until 2011 have only been published in Spanish translation, yet the reader will find the original French text without difficulty online, for example at http://jonathanleroy.be/2016/02/orientation-lacanienne-jacques-alain-miller/
2 In this respect, see also Miller's programmatic paper "Pas de clinique sans éthique" (Miller, 1983).
3 Throughout my essay, I shall refer to Sophocles' play as *Antigone* and to its eponymous heroine as Antigone.
4 Much like all the other seminars Lacan delivered between 1953 and 1963, *L'éthique de la psychanalyse* was presented as part of the psychoanalytic training programme of the *Société française de psychanalyse*. However, this did not prevent other people from attending. For instance, in the opening session of *Seminar VII* Lacan explicitly saluted the presence of the linguist Roman Jakobson (Lacan, 1992[1986], p. 12).
5 I should nonetheless emphasize, here, that I shall restrict myself to an explication of Lacan's commentary, and that the suggestions for further reading will be primarily confined to materials in which one or the other point in the text is explored in more detail. As such, I shall engage only tangentially with the secondary literature on Lacan's interpretation of *Antigone*, which is quite substantial, especially in the Anglophone world. Readers wishing to assemble a list of secondary sources should at least include Irigarary (1985[1974]), Kowsar (1990), Lee (1990, pp. 122–132), Lacoue-Labarthe (1991), Guyomard (1991; 1992), Loraux (1986; 1991), Jacobs (1996), Chanter (1998), Van Haute (1998), Butler (2000), Sauverzac (2000, pp. 175–199), Rabaté (2001, pp. 69–84), Copjec (2002), Leonard (2003; 2005, pp. 101–130; 2006), Zupančič (2000; 2002; 2003), Sjöholm (2004, pp. 101–110; 2014), Weber (2004), Griffith (2005; 2010), Miller (2007a), Hurst (2008, pp. 318–347), Shepherdson (2008b), De Kesel (2009[2001], pp. 205–248; 2015; 2018), Marder (2009), Eagleton (2010), Jaramillo (2010), Morel (2010), Söderbäck (2010), Meltzer (2011), Naveau (2011), Neill (2011, pp. 211–235), Clemens (2013, pp. 63–83), Freeland (2013), Honig (2013), Lauret

(2014, pp. 80–86), Roudinesco (2014[2011], pp. 129–139), Themi (2014, pp. 41–63), Ruti (2015, pp. 99–118; 2017, pp. 46–56), Žižek (2016), Finkelde (2017), Harris (2017, pp. 125–162), Balaska (2018), Zafiropoulos (2019, pp. 85–113), and Luepnitz (2020).

6 What follows is not an outline of the Antigone myth, but of Sophocles' *Antigone*, which is but one theatrical dramatization amongst many of the ancient Greek myth. For example, in Euripides' *Phoenician Women*, with which Lacan was also familiar (Lacan, 2006[1955a], p. 279; 1992[1986], p. 264), Oedipus and Antigone leave Thebes and go into exile together after the death of Eteocles, Polynices, and Jocasta (Euripides, 2005, pp. 55–57). Readers looking for general introductions to Sophocles' *Antigone*, its mythological background, historical context, and diverse reception over the centuries, will benefit hugely from Cairns (2016) and Stuttard (2018).

7 During the first half of the 20th century, psychoanalysis spread to the four corners of the globe and the psychoanalytic literature expanded accordingly, yet the only source materials in which *Antigone* received some psychoanalytic attention are Chandler (1913), van der Sterren (1948, pp. 109–126; 1952), Fromm (1959[1948]), and Kanzer (1950). Of these five studies, van der Sterren's 1948 monograph offers by far the most comprehensive reading of Sophocles' Theban trilogy—*Antigone*, *Oedipus the King,* and *Oedipus at Colonus*—but his emphasis is still predominantly on Oedipus rather than Antigone. Freud himself had known Sophocles' Theban trilogy since his secondary school days, but he never ventured beyond the central intrigue of *Oedipus the King* (Rudnytsky, 1987, pp. 11–12, 318). Also, after he had been diagnosed with jawbone cancer in 1923, Freud tended to refer to his youngest daughter and closest companion Anna as his Antigone, thereby invoking Antigone's unconditional love for her incapacitated father during the last years of his life in *Oedipus at Colonus*. See Falzeder, Brabant, and Giampieri-Deutsch (2000, p. 352) and E. L. Freud (1970, p. 106). For a wide-ranging discussion of Anna Freud as the Antigone of psychoanalysis, see Stewart-Steinberg (2011, pp. 96–143).

8 For some reason, the English translator of *Séminaire VII* did not translate a sentence in the original text in which Lacan asserted that there is actually no field in ancient Greece where the horizon has remained closed to its underlying structure: "… *d'ailleurs il n'y a pas chez les Grecs de champ où l'horizon soit resté fermé à la sous-structure*" (Lacan, 1986, p. 281).

9 For the best critical survey of how ancient Greek ethical systems generally revolved around an examination of the aims of human desire, which then resulted in philosophy becoming the medicine of the psyche, see Nussbaum (1994). For the historical confluence between the morally good and the beautiful, see for instance Plato (2007, p. 247[520c]). The number in square brackets, here, refers to the so-called Stephanus pagination of Plato's texts, which is reproduced in most editions of his work. In his *Critique of Judgement*, Kant reiterated that "the beautiful is the symbol of the morally good" (Kant, 2007[1790], p. 180). It would seem that Hegel was the first to propose a radical distinction between the good and the beautiful, yet the convergence of the two notions continued to flourish during the Romantic period and even informed Wittgenstein's 1921 *Tractatus*, albeit as a parenthetical remark (Wittgenstein, 1961[1921], p. 86). See, in this respect, Walker (2012). For a comprehensive critical study of the intersection between ethics and aesthetics, and its influence on European literary traditions, see Ellison (2001).

10 In his *Lectures on the History of Philosophy*, Hegel referred to Sophocles' heroine as "the heavenly Antigone, that noblest of figures that ever appeared on earth"

(Hegel, 1955[1819–1830], p. 441), whereas in his *Aesthetics* he designated *Antigone* as "one of the most sublime and in every respect most excellent works of art of all time" (Hegel, 1975[1820–1829], p. 464). In the documents that have survived, Hegel mentioned *Antigone* for the very first time in a handwritten marginal note to a sentence from a 1796 manuscript that is generally known by its incipit *Jedes Volk*…. The sentence in question is worth mentioning, because it shows how Hegel invoked *Antigone* as the paradigmatic illustration of the autonomous power of the human spirit, in a distinctly humanistic take on the state of the human condition: a human being's "will is free and only obeys to its own law; it does not know any divine commands, or when it refers to the moral law of a divine command, this law is nowhere to be found. It does not exist in writing, but rules invisibly" (Hegel, 1989[1796], p. 368). We also know that during his adolescent years, Hegel translated various parts of *Antigone* in German, endeavouring to capture the original metre of the verses in an ongoing dialogue with Hölderlin, yet the text of these translations has not survived (Rosenkranz, 1844, p. 11). During the 19th century, Hegel was by no means alone in having recourse to superlatives when describing the tragedy (Steiner, 1984, p. 4) and Lacan himself intermittently echoed Hegel's judgement, although for quite different reasons. Also, whilst Lacan had very specific (psychoanalytic) motives for including a reading of *Antigone* in his seminar on ethics, it probably would not come as a surprise to any classicist or philosopher that *Antigone* is given a place in a lecture series on ethics, since the tragedy unfolds around a plethora of ethical conflicts. Needless to say, this does not imply that the tragic events of *Antigone* only revolve around an ethical conflict, because the play also elicits political, aesthetic, and genealogical (kinship) questions, as well as the hugely contentious issues of gender roles, gendered positions of power, and the gendering of social relations.

11 The numbers refer to the verse numbering in the original text of the play, which has been reproduced in most English translations of *Antigone*, although the reader needs to be aware that some English versions, such as the translation by Fagles (Sophocles, 1984), have adopted a different numbering. Whereas Lacan primarily relied on the 1947 bilingual Greek-French edition by Pignarre and published by Garnier (Lacan, 1992[1986], pp. 254, 270; Sophocle, 1947), I shall use the 1998 English translation by Lloyd-Jones (Sophocles, 1998), providing alternative renditions of the Greek when useful or required.

12 In *Seminar VII*, Lacan initially argued that it is *by means of* pity and fear that catharsis is accomplished (Lacan, 1992[1986], pp. 247–248), yet later on he posited that fear and pity need to be superseded in themselves for catharsis to happen (Lacan, 1992[1986], p. 323), reiterating this statement one year later, in *Seminar VIII*, on *Transference* (Lacan, 2015[2001], p. 279). The reader should note that in the English text of the latter seminar, Aristotle's words have been reproduced incorrectly.

13 For an insightful reflection upon the intersections of trauma, abreaction, and catharsis in Breuer and Freud's work, see Starobinski (2003[1999], pp. 174–197).

14 Without providing a detailed overview of this historical extrapolation of catharsis into the medical domain, Lacan indicated that one can find traces of it in Molière's 1666 farce *Le médecin malgré lui* (*A Doctor in Spite of Himself*), in which the fake doctor Sganarelle explains to the father of a young girl who has lost her ability to speak that her disease could be alleviated by the purgation of her "morbid humours" (Molière, 1959[1666], p. 186). More interestingly, Lacan also suggested that Freud could have come across the medical meaning of catharsis in the works of the eminent classicist Jacob Bernays, his wife's uncle,

who had written a seminal essay in 1857 on Aristotle and ancient Greek tragedy, in which he had argued that catharsis should be interpreted primarily in a therapeutic sense (Bernays, 1857; 1880). Since he had only verified the historical significance of Jacob Bernays in the first volume of Jones' biography of Freud (Jones, 1953, p. 101), Lacan formulated his remarks very tentatively, yet it has now been persuasively demonstrated that Freud would definitely have been familiar with Bernays' work (Funke, 1996). Lacan also wondered why Bernays' essay had been published first in Breslau, yet we now know that in 1853 he had been appointed there as professor of classical philology at the *Jüdisch-Theologische Seminar* (Bollack, 1998, p. 107). For a fascinating discussion of Bernays' ideas on catharsis, see Porter (2015).

15 For the argument that *Antigone* is less about Antigone and more about Creon, i.e., that Creon rather than Antigone is the protagonist of the play, and the textual evidence upon which this argument rests, see for example Frey (1878), Kitto (1956, pp. 138–178), Calder (1971), and Groot (2015).

16 In the English version of the seminar, Porter has translated "*point de visée*" as "line of sight", which completely misses the point and renders Lacan's argument incomprehensible (Lacan, 1992[1986], p. 247).

17 Porter has translated *éclat* as "splendour" (Lacan, 1992[1986], p. 247), a term that has been adopted uncritically in many Anglophone studies of Lacan's seminar, such as Freeland (2013), yet Lacan is not underscoring the grandeur of Antigone's appearance, but the blinding light that radiates from her presence. *Éclat* should be rendered as brilliance or radiance.

18 For the principle of the "second death" in *Juliette*, see Sade (1968[1797], pp. 769–772) and Nobus (2017b, pp. 61–67). With regard to *émoi*, the English translation is again inaccurate and confusing, because the translator has opted to render the word as "excitement" (Lacan, 1992[1986], p. 249). Precisely in order to prevent his audience from interpreting the term as some form of emotion, Lacan adduced its etymological roots, emphasizing that *émoi* is neither an emotion nor an unequivocally positive, uplifting experience. It definitely has nothing to do with "excitement", as the English translation suggests. In the absence of a clear English equivalent, one could have recourse to a circumlocution such as "being beside oneself", which would come very close to the literal sense of *émoi*. If I have chosen the term "turmoil", it is because this notion at least captures the strong connotations of "mental instability" in *émoi*, but also because this is how Adrian R. Price has rendered it in his translation of Lacan's *Seminar X*, in which it is included within the matrix of anxiety. See Lacan (2014[2004], pp. 12–13).

19 Here, the English translation, which reads "the point where the false metaphors of being (*l'étant*) can be distinguished from the position of Being (*l'être*) itself" (Lacan, 1992[1986], p. 248), is totally nonsensical, partly because Porter has failed to realize that there is a rather embarrassing transcription error in the original French text—"*métaphores fausses*" (false metaphors) should have been "*métamorphoses*" (metamorphoses)—and partly because he has completely ignored the Heideggerian terminology (*l'étant, das Seiende* vs *l'être, das Sein*) and thus also the conventional English translations of these concepts ("that which is" vs "being").

20 It would seem that Lacan only quoted the last two verses of this four-verse sentence, so that Antigone's lament is reduced to "with my mother and father in Hades below, I could never have another brother" (Lacan, 1992[1986], p. 255; Sophocles, 1998, p. 87).

21 I think that Jacob drew attention to Antigone's name in his sub-clause "as she is called", because the name Antigone literally means "against heritage" or "against

family", whereby the word "against" should not only be interpreted as "standing in opposition to", but also as "leaning against" or "relying on". Compare the English phrase: "She was leaning against the wall".

22 For more detailed reflections on the nature and implications of the debate surrounding the authenticity of 909–912 and the entire passage of 904–920 in which the words feature, see Pischel (1893), Jebb (1900, pp. 258–260), Schadewaldt (1929, pp. 82–99), Agard (1937), Wycherley (1947), van der Sterren (1948, pp. 110–118), Kirkwood (1994[1958], pp. 88–89, 163–169), Kaufmann (1979[1968], pp. 219–225), Szlezák (1981), Murnaghan (1986), Sourvinou-Inwood (1989), Neuburg (1990), Foley (1995), Cropp (1997), Benardete (1999[1975], pp. 110–114), and Honig (2013, pp. 123–140).

23 Whereas Sophocles wrote κεκευθότοιν ("are concealed in") in verse 911, Aristotle reproduced the word as βεβηκότων ("have gone to"), probably because he quoted from memory rather than from a written source document. See Sophocles (1998, p. 86) and Aristotle (2020, p. 446).

24 At this point, the English translation is infuriatingly flawed, because when Lacan said to his listeners "*aucun [des termes que j'aurai poussés devant vous] ne pourra jamais, de mon fait, servir à quiconque de gri-gri intellectuel*", Porter made Lacan proclaim that "none of the terms will in the end enable anyone of you to turn into an intellectual cricket on my account" (Lacan, 1992[1986], p. 252). The word "*gri-gri*", which is more commonly written as "*gris-gris*", refers to a talisman, an amulet, i.e., an object endowed with magical powers. Unless Porter thought that the word "*gri-gri*" was an idiosyncratic onomatopoeia, it is a mystery to me how he arrived at the conclusion that it should be rendered as "cricket". And what on earth would it mean for someone to turn into an "intellectual cricket"?!

25 Around Easter in 1955, Lacan went to see Heidegger in Freiburg im Breisgau, and later that year he entertained Heidegger and his wife for a number of days at his Summer house in Guitrancourt, before Heidegger went to the major, nine-day conference on his work that was held at Cerisy-la-Salle from 27 August until 4 September 1955. However, there is no record of the two men having discussed *Antigone* during these periods (Roudinesco, 1997[1993], pp. 224–231). In fact, according to the Greek-French philosopher Kostas Axelos, who acted as the main interpreter throughout Heidegger's stay in France during the late summer of 1955, Lacan and Heidegger mainly talked about trivial matters rather than philosophy and psychoanalysis (Janicaud, 2001, p. 12). In the spring of 1960, when Lacan embarked upon his own reading of *Antigone*, Heidegger's *Introduction to Metaphysics* had already been released in German and Lacan owned a copy of the book, which he asked Heidegger to sign when he was at Guitrancourt, yet the book does not contain any annotations in Lacan's hand, so I cannot prove that Lacan had read it. Heidegger's 1942 lecture course on Hölderlin's "The Ister" was not published in German until after Lacan's death, so he could have had no knowledge of it, unless Heidegger had told him about it in a personal conversation. Over and above the methodological confluence between Lacan's and Heidegger's interpretative strategies of *Antigone*, it is also remarkable how their conceptual developments converge upon an instance of "the formidable", which Lacan situated in the sublimity of Antigone's "unbearable brilliance" and Heidegger recognized in the uncanniness (δεινόν, terrible wonder) that the chorus invokes in verse 332 as the defining characteristic of all human beings (Heidegger, 1996[1984], pp. 63–64). In his commentary on *Antigone*, Lacan also referred on two separate occasions to the verses that had caught Heidegger's attention, going so far as quoting them in full the second time, yet without mentioning Heidegger's name. See Lacan (1992[1986], pp. 267,

274), where the verses have been misprinted. During his discussion of *Antigone*, Lacan equally referred to "Logos", the essay by Heidegger he had translated into French, yet without mentioning Heidegger's reading of the play (Heidegger, 1956[1951]; Lacan, 1992[1986], p. 276). For excellent critical analyses of Heidegger's views on *Antigone*, see Pearson Geiman (2001) and Fleming (2015).

26 The notes of the lectures in which Kojève commented on the sixth chapter of *The Phenomenology of Spirit* have not been retained in the heavily abridged English edition of Kojève's lecture course (Kojève, 1969[1947]).

27 For detailed analyses of Hegel's discussions of *Antigone* in the context of his overall conception of tragedy, see Jagentowicz Mills (1986), Donough (1989), Berthold-Bond (1994), Chanter (1995, pp. 80–126), Conklin (1997), De Boer (2008), Burke (2013), and Vuillerod (2020). The most incisive commentary of Hegel's interpretation of *Antigone* is undoubtedly that performed by Derrida in the left column of *Glas* (Derrida, 2021[1974], pp. 164–214).

28 With regard to *Oedipus at Colonus*, Lacan substantiated his point with reference to the famous words μὴ φῦναι ("not to be born"), as sung by the chorus in a gripping reflection upon Oedipus's inescapable fate (Sophocles, 1998, p. 547), yet he wrongly designated them as the final words of Oedipus (Lacan, 1992[1986], pp. 250, 305, 313). Lacan commented on these words on numerous occasions. See Lacan (1988[1978], p. 233; 1993[1981], p. 244; 2006[1962], p. 657; 2015[2001], p. 301).

29 If Miller decided not to do so, it is clearly because the text of Lacan's words on 15 June 1960 was considered too short, which was in itself due to the fact that for that day Lacan had asked Pierre Kaufmann to give a lecture on beauty and the sublime in Kant's work. As Miller had done with the previous editions of Lacan's seminars, all major contributions by participants, such as this one, were consistently omitted from the transcription.

30 In effect, Antigone "buries" Polynices twice. The first time, she is not caught by the men keeping watch over the dead body, and so the messenger can only report to Creon that an unidentified person has contravened his orders (Sophocles, 1998, p. 27). Yet after Creon's guards have removed the dust that had been sprinkled over Polynices' body, Antigone performs her act again, and only then is she caught in the act (Sophocles, 1998, pp. 37–39).

31 When he first introduced ἄτη, Lacan claimed that it is also the root of the French word "*atroce*" (atrocious) (Lacan, 1992[1986], p. 263), yet this is factually incorrect, because the etymology of "*atroce*" and "atrocious" is the Latin word "*atrox*" (sombre, cruel), which is itself derived from "*ater*" (black). In the following year's lecture course (*Seminar VIII, Transference*), Lacan recapitulated his interpretation of *Antigone* in the context of a protracted discussion of Paul Claudel's Coûfontaine-trilogy. At that point, he simply referred to ἄτη as "destiny" (*destin*), which does not really capture the subtlety of the word, but which nonetheless suggests that ἄτη is Antigone's inexorable fate. This new interpretation also seems to overturn Lacan's own argument in *Seminar VII* that Antigone's primary goal is to go beyond ἄτη. In fact, it is not the only place where Lacan's subsequent summary of his reading of Sophocles' tragedy contradicts his original interpretation. For example, in *Seminar VIII*, Lacan referred to Antigone's appearance in verses 909–912 and verses 795–796—I shall explain the latter further on in this chapter—as a "phenomenon of beauty", which is qualitatively different from how he described it in *Seminar VII*, notably as an instance of "unbearable brilliance". See Lacan (1992[1986], p. 247; 2015[2001], p. 276).

32 Of these four verses, the general meaning of 613–614 remains disputed, if only because the word πάμπολύ does not really make sense. The sentence after the colon is supposed to suggest "great riches" or "enormous wealth", yet this is not

conveyed by the semantic spectrum of the Greek word. See Sophocles (1999, pp. 228–229). The point is arguably philological, yet it is not at all insignificant, here, because one could say that Lacan's interpretation of the phrase is as good as any other.

33 Both here, as well as in numerous other places in the French and the English editions of Lacan's seminar, the Greek contains a misspelling. Most, yet by no means all of these errors have been listed in Bergounioux (2005, pp. 67–86).

34 Classicists have argued for decades whether ἁμαρτία is meant to indicate a "tragic fault" or a "tragic flaw", the first option suggesting an "accidental mistake" and the second referring to a "character defect". See, for instance, Hyde (1963) and Golden (1978). Outside the *Poetics*, the word also appears five times in Aristotle's *Nicomachean Ethics* (Aristotle, 1934). For an excellent discussion of these mentions, see van Braam (1912). In his seminar, Lacan opted to translate ἁμαρτία as "mistake", "blunder", or "stupidity" (*bêtise*), whilst simultaneously disagreeing with Aristotle that this "error" always typifies the tragic hero, because he felt that, at least in *Antigone*, it only defines the "counter- or secondary hero", i.e., Creon (Lacan, 1992[1986], pp. 258–259, 277).

35 When reflecting upon Creon's excessive punishment, Lacan reminded his audience of how one of the libertines in Sade's *Juliette* also fantasizes about the possibility of making his victims suffer forever, even after they have been tortured to death. In this context, he again invoked the "second death" in the system of Pope Pius VI, rather than the more directly relevant fantasy of everlasting torment in the discourse of the libertine Saint-Fond, although the two perspectives are evidently related. See Lacan (1992[1986], p. 260) and Sade (1968[1797], p. 369). See also Lacan (2006[1962], p. 655) and Nobus (2017b, p. 61). However, rather than its being an unequivocal index of Creon's excessive cruelty towards his niece, there is an alternative reading of his decision to bury Antigone alive. By killing a relative, Creon would run the risk of attracting the wrath of the gods and calling down divine punishment upon Thebes and himself, so instead of "actively" killing her, walling her up in a cave would be a specious solution to ensure that his hands remain clean and the community stays safe. See, for example, Sophocles (1998, p. 87), where Creon states: "We are guiltless where this girl is concerned". I am grateful to Armand d'Angour for drawing my attention to this passage and highlighting Creon's cunning strategy to avoid further divine retribution.

36 Much like the previous "contamination", Lacan did not mention this one either, yet he did draw attention to the fact that in the discourses of the guards, the chorus, and Creon himself, Antigone is consistently referred to in condescending terms as ἡ παῖς (literally, "the child", but in this context "the girl" or "the young woman"). See, for example, verses 423 and 654 (Lacan, 1992[1986], p. 250; Sophocles, 1998, pp. 40–41, 64–65).

37 It goes without saying that, in considering the presence of pity and fear within the play and its characters, Lacan moved away from the conception of catharsis advanced by Aristotle, for whom the effect is situated exclusively in the audience.

38 I am fully aware that my interpretation, here, differs radically from that of De Kesel (2009[2001], pp. 205–248; 2015), who argues that Antigone's beauty resides in her saying "No" to Creon. In my reading, Antigone's "No" to Creon is as attractive as any socio-political uprising or rebellion—admirable, courageous, and inspiring, but not particularly beautiful. Antigone's defiance of Creon may very well be ethical, then, but it is not exactly aesthetic. I think that the source of Antigone's beauty, which spills over into the sublime and the uncanny, does not lie in her "No" to Creon at all, but rather in her "Yes" to transcending the curse,

which she only manages to explain as motivated by her unconditional love for an irreplaceable brother.
39 For a more detailed explanation of Socrates' point about the attendants of Ares, see Plato (2011, p. 156).
40 Guyomard (1992) has posited that Antigone's intense love for Polynices is in itself a continuation of the incestuous desire that has brought misfortune upon her family, yet there is no textual evidence in Sophocles' tragedy that Antigone's love for her brother is passionate, romantic, or sexual, so the argument is rather loose and impossible to substantiate on the basis of an in-depth reading of the play. The only time Eros is invoked in Sophocles' tragedy is when the chorus sings about Haemon's vehement defence of his betrothed (781) (Sophocles, 1998, p. 77).
41 Over the years, a number of scholars have indeed argued, although not always as an extrapolation of Hegel's assertion, that Antigone's spurious logic is but an indication of her unconditional love for Polynices. For instance, in his 1944 volume *Sophoclean Tragedy*, the influential British classicist Cecil Maurice Bowra wrote: "It is the strangeness [of Antigone's words] that counts. Antigone is no ordinary woman, and she breaks ordinary rules for a remarkable reason. But the reason is real to her and in the end quite simple. She is moved by an intense love for her brother, a feeling that her relation to him is unique and demands a special loyalty. So she explains herself in this unsophisticated, even primitive way.... She could have neglected her brother and lived safely with Haemon. She has chosen otherwise, to satisfy her love for her brother at the cost of her life. If we take her words as they come, they are deeply touching and perfectly natural" (Bowra, 1944, p. 95). Likewise, the great British-American classicist Bernard Knox conceded: Antigone's "speech is not logical; it is an almost hysterically hyperbolic expression of her love for the brother who in death, as in life, has every man's hand against him; the references to husband and child are not to be understood as a logical scheme of values but as an evocation of that life as wife and mother which she has sacrificed in order to bury her brother's body" (Knox, 1979[1968], p. 180). Lacan could have been familiar with Bowra's work, yet I have not found any evidence to support this.
42 For a detailed discussion of the differences between ἐπιθυμία, ἵμερος, πόθος and other ancient Greek words for desire, see Plato (1998, p. 61[419*e*-420*b*]) and Sedley (2003).
43 Lacan claimed that *Sophocle, c'est l'humanisme* (*Sophocles is Humanism*) was redolent of "the name of one of the many works" he had consulted (Lacan, 1992[1986], p. 273). In all likelihood, the book Lacan had in mind here was the 1951 monograph on Sophocles by the American classicist Cedric Whitman, who was also an ardent defender of the thesis that verses 909–912 are an interpolation: "A more disillusioning passage could scarcely be imagined, but fortunately it can be safely expunged as spurious. No more glaring example of an actor's interpolation exists in ancient tragedy, and it is only the fact that the reasoning here resembles a passage in Herodotus that has prevented scholars from rejecting it unanimously" (Whitman, 1951, pp. 92–93). Beyond the confines of Whitman's volume, it is worth noting that the idea according to which Sophocles' tragic representation embodies all the cardinal humanist values—in *Antigone* as well as Antigone—dates back to at least the 16th century. See, for example, the successful 1580 adaptation of the play by Robert Garnier (2000[1580]). Lacan's outspoken opposition to the humanist dimensions of the play is yet another reason why the word "*éclat*" in lesson 19 should not be translated as "splendour", because the latter term can easily be interpreted as being representative of the

grandiose victories of the indomitable human spirit. For a thorough discussion of αὐτόνομος in *Antigone*, which constitutes the first recorded instance of the word, see McNeill (2011).

44 Neither in *Seminar VII* nor elsewhere did Lacan develop this hypothesis further, and it remains difficult to justify, partly because Jocasta did act upon her incestuous desire for Oedipus, partly because the curse of the House of Labdakos did not come to an end with Jocasta's suicide. Lacan's theory of desire, which was partly inspired by Kojève's reading of Hegel's *Phenomenology of Spirit* (Hegel, 2018[1807]; Kojève, 1969[1947]), was built upon three main pillars: 1. Desire is always conditioned by another desire, which remains opaque and can only be approached via a fantasy; 2. There is only a subject of desire in the sense that the subject is possessed by (subjected to) it, and so the subject does not control desire; 3. The object of desire can never be fully apprehended and therefore causes rather than satisfies desire. I should also remind the reader, here, that Lacan had devoted a year-long seminar to the study of desire just before embarking upon the project of formulating the ethics of psychoanalysis (Lacan, 2019[2013]).

45 We do not know what happened after Antigone was locked up in the cave, yet Sophocles' text insinuates that Haemon managed to gain access to her "burial chamber", found her lifeless body hanging in the cave, released her from the noose, and held her in his arms until his loving embrace was disturbed by the arrival of his father. When developing the point about Antigone's psycho-social isolation ἐκτὸς ἄτας, Lacan explicitly relied on the work of the influential German Hellenist Karl Reinhardt (Lacan, 1992[1986], p. 271; Reinhardt, 1979[1933]). Reinhardt's book on Sophocles was not translated into French until 1971, so he would have had to consult the original 1933 German edition.

46 Porter has translated Lacan's "*à-bout-de-course*" as "a stance of the-race-is-run" (Lacan, 1992[1986], pp. 272, 279), yet this literal translation suggests that Antigone eventually becomes defeatist and fatalistic, which could not be further from the truth. Outside ἄτη, Antigone remains as defiant and courageous as she has always been, even though she has to admit that whatever is left of her life is pretty miserable, that she may not have the resources at her disposal to justify her actions to herself, and that she cannot even be sure that it was all worth it. In the words of Simone Weil, who was often called Antigone by her parents and who regularly employed the moniker in the letters she wrote to them: Antigone is a typical Sophoclean heroine and therefore someone who obstinately "holds on and never lets [herself] be corrupted by misfortune" (Weil, 1998[1936], p. 19).

47 The word Antigone uses to describe herself in her final lament is δύσμορος (919). It literally means "ill-fated", but Lloyd-Jones has also rendered it as "unhappy" (Sophocles, 1998, p. 89).

48 The expression "between-two-deaths" was only offered to Lacan *after* he had finished his commentary on *Antigone* and it remains unclear which of the seminar participants coined it. Miller's title "Antigone between-two-deaths" for lesson 21 is therefore misleading, because it suggests that the term was already employed at that point in the seminar, whereas it was only produced afterwards, as is clear from lesson 24 (Lacan, 1992[1986], p. 320). The fact that Lacan liked the expression can be inferred from his essay "Kant with Sade", in which he employed it with reference to the status of the victims in the fantasy of absolute destruction of Sade's libertine heroes (Lacan, 2006[1962], pp. 654–655), and from the opening session of *Seminar VIII*, in which he rather bizarrely situated it "in the adventure of *Oedipus Rex*" (Lacan, 2015[2001], p. 7).

49 In a remark following Pierre Kaufmann's presentation on 15 June 1960 (see note 29 above), Lacan also referred to Lévi-Strauss's inaugural lecture at the *Collège de*

France, which took place on Tuesday 5 January 1960. In the absence of a publicly accessible Lacan-archive, I cannot prove that Lacan's comment, here, was based on his having attended the ceremonial event, rather than on a mere reading of the text, which was published around the time of Lacan's own lectures on *Antigone* (Lévi-Strauss, 1960), yet I would not be surprised if he had indeed been in the audience on 5 January 1960. For English translations of Lévi-Strauss's lecture, see Lévi-Strauss (1967[1960]) and Lévi-Strauss (1983[1960]). In the latter translation, the date of the lecture has been misstated as 6 January 1960.

50 The term "mytheme" did not appear in the original English version of Lévi-Strauss's paper (Lévi-Strauss, 1955), but was added by him when he re-translated the text into French for the collection *Anthropologie Structurale*, which was published in July 1958 (Lévi-Strauss, 1958[1955], p. 233). As such, it also featured in the subsequent English translation of this book (Lévi-Strauss, 1963[1955], p. 211).

51 Lacan returned briefly to this mythical background of Antigone's death towards the end of lesson 22, where the influence of Lévi-Strauss's structural study of myth is again clearly noticeable (Lacan, 1992[1986], p. 299).

52 In a sense, Lacan had already suggested this idea in his second lesson on *Antigone*, in which he stated: "[T]he structure of the ethic of tragedy... is also that of psychoanalysis (Lacan, 1992[1986], p. 258).

53 It is interesting to see, in this respect, that Lacan himself spent some time talking about the significance of the word "with" in the tragedy itself. See Lacan (1992[1986], p. 265). Without referring to Lacan's methodology, George Steiner wrote in his *Antigones* that "Sophocles' *Antigone* will not suffer from Lacan", whereby he intimated that the original work is sufficiently resilient to stand up to any adaptation or interpretative act (Steiner, 1984, p. 297). In a review of Steiner's book, Bernard Knox was clearly pleased with this affirmation, so much so that he even felt the need to reinforce the point: "That Sophocles' *Antigone* will not suffer from Lacan is something about which I have no doubt whatever—for the simple reason that Lacan is unreadable even now and will be forgotten tomorrow" (Knox, 1989[1984], p. 130). Thirty-five years after these words were written, it is probably fair to say that Lacan is still unreadable, even now, but he definitely has not been forgotten.... To appreciate the subtlety of Lacan's approach, one may also want to contrast his reading with a prototypical example of the conventional, reductionist psychoanalytic interpretation of the text, such as that offered by the American psychiatrist and "theatre expert" Philip Weissman, who argued that Antigone's fierce determination to bury Polynices is purely conditioned by her fundamental "neurotic virginity", which culminates in a "climactic portrayal of [her] psychosexual development toward old maidenhood, her preoedipal attachments, [and] her devaluation and incapacity for a finalizing heterosexual relationship and having her own child" (Weissman, 1964, pp. 34–35).

54 To the best of my knowledge, the only scholar who has exposed this misreading in all its logical inconsistencies and fallacious repercussions is De Kesel (2018).

55 I can state this date with confidence, because on 26 January 1983, Jacques-Alain Miller devoted an entire session of his seminar to this particular misinterpretation, whereby he argued vehemently, yet evidently to no avail, against the promotion of "Do not give up on your desire!" to the status of a Lacanian ethical axiom. See Miller (2018, pp. 193–204).

56 See, for instance, Badiou (2001[1998], p. 47), Žižek (1989, p. 3; 1994, p. 70), and Zupančič (2000, pp. 250–251).

57 In fairness to Žižek, I should nonetheless point out that he did not repeat the precept in the introduction to his own, rather well-crafted adaptation of *Antigone*

(Žižek, 2016). For recent instances of the reduction of Lacan's ethics of psychoanalyis to the single precept that one should not give up on one's desire, see for example Ruti (2012, p. 71), Critchley (2019, p. 130), and Luepnitz (2020, p. 355).

58 Porter has translated the phrase "*céder sur son désir*" rather clumsily as "having given ground relative to one's desire" (Lacan, 1992[1986], pp. 319–321).

59 The reason why Lacan emphasized the paradoxical nature of his proposition is that guilt is conventionally attributed to the opposite of "having given up on something". Giving up on something implies that one does not do what one thinks one is supposed to do, yet guilt is much more commonly associated with having done what one thinks one is *not* supposed to do.

60 For a painfully sinister example of how "Do not give up on your desire!" could easily be turned into a justification for criminal acts, I can refer the reader to the case of Yerodia Abdoulaye Ndombasi, a rather charming, jovial, and altogether amicable man who was Lacan's personal butler for almost 15 years—from the late 1960s until Lacan's death in 1981—and who I had the pleasure of meeting in person during the early 1990s. During the mid-1990s, Yerodia (or "Abdoul" as he was commonly known) moved back to the Congo in order to serve as a minister in the government of Laurent-Désiré Kabila. In 1998, he could be heard on the Congolese radio encouraging the genocide of millions of Congolese Tutsis, an act for which the International War Crimes Tribunal in The Hague subsequently issued an arrest warrant. Abdoul was never tried, but when asked about his motives, he did not hesitate to quote his master, Jacques Lacan, as having stated that one should never give up on one's desire.... See, in this respect, Hendrickx (2001) and Nobus (2016).

Bibliography

Abraham, K. (1954[1924]). A Short Study of the Development of the Libido, Viewed in the Light of Mental Disorders. In *Selected Papers on Psychoanalysis* (pp. 418–501). D. Bryan and A. Strachey (Trans.). New York, NY: Basic Books.

Adams, P. (Ed.) (2003). *Art: Sublimation or Symptom*. London-New York, NY: Karnac Books.

Agamben, G. (2009[2008]). Theory of Signatures. In *The Signature of All Things: On Method* (pp. 33–80). L. D'Isanto and K. Attell (Trans.). New York, NY: Zone Books.

Agard, W. R. (1937). Antigone 904-20. *Classical Philology*, 32(3): 263–265.

Alexandrian, S. (1974). *Le surréalisme et le rêve*. Paris: Gallimard.

Alfandary, I. (2016). *Derrida—Lacan. L'écriture entre psychanalyse et déconstruction*. Paris: Hermann.

Allaigre-Duny, A. (2001). À propos du sonnet de Lacan. *L'Unebévue*, 17: 27–48.

Allouch, J. (2009a). *Les impromptus de Lacan*. Paris: Mille et une nuits.

Allouch, J. (2009b). *L'amour Lacan*. Paris: EPEL.

American Psychiatric Association (Ed.) (2013). *Diagnostic and Statistical Manual of Mental Disorders, Fifth Edition—DSM-5*. Washington DC: American Psychiatric Association.

Anderson, M. M. (2006). Thy Word in Me: On the Prayer of Union in St. Teresa of Avila's Interior Castle. *Harvard Theological Review*, 99(3): 329–354.

André, S. (1985). Jouissance psychotique, jouissance féminine, jouissance sexuelle. *Quarto*, 18: 46–59.

André, S. (1999[1986]). Jouissances. In *What Does a Woman Want?* S. Fairfield (Trans.). (pp. 227–249). New York NY: Other Press.

Anglade, J. (Ed.) (1919–1920). *Las Leys d'Amors. Manuscrit de l'Académie des Jeux Floraux*. Toulouse: Privat.

Anglade, J. (1930). La doctrine grammaticale et poétique du Gai Savoir. In J. D. Fitz-Gerald and P. Taylor (Eds), *Todd Memorial Volumes: Philological Studies*, vol. 1 (pp. 47–58). New York NY: Columbia University Press.

Anonymous (1976[1670]). Constantine Brought to the Pillory. G. C. Bauer (Trans.). In G. C. Bauer (Ed.), *Bernini in Perspective* (pp. 46–53). Englewood Cliffs, NJ: Prentice-Hall, Inc.

Ansell-Pearson, K. (2012). The Gay Science. In P. Bishop (Ed.), *A Companion to Friedrich Nietzsche: Life and Works* (pp. 167–192). Rochester, NY: Camden House.

Apollinaire, G. (2009[1913]). l'Ermite. In *Alcools* (p. 49). Paris: Gallimard.
Aristotle (1934). *Nicomachean Ethics*. H. Rackham (Trans.). Cambridge MA-London: Harvard University Press.
Aristotle (1962). *The Politics*. J. A. Sinclair (Trans.). Harmondsworth: Penguin Books.
Aristotle (1999). *Poetics*. S. Halliwell (Trans.). Cambridge, MA-London: Harvard University Press.
Aristotle (2020). *Art of Rhetoric*. J. H. Freese and G. Striker (Trans.). Cambridge, MA-London: Harvard University Press.
Armstrong, R. H. (2005). *A Compulsion for Antiquity: Freud and the Ancient World*. Ithaca, NY-London: Cornell University Press.
Arnaud, G. (1999). Quelques considérations sur la fonction symbolique de l'argent pour la psychanalyse. *Revue internationale de psycho-sociologie*, 13: 37–49.
Arnaud, G. (2002). The Organization and the Symbolic: Organizational Dynamics Viewed from a Lacanian Perspective. *Human Relations*, 55: 691–716.
Arnaud, G. (2003a). Money as Signifier: A Lacanian Insight into the Monetary Order. *Free Associations*, 10: 25–43.
Arnaud, G. (2003b). A Coach or a Couch? A Lacanian Perspective on Executive Coaching and Consulting. *Human Relations*, 56: 1131–1154.
Arnaud, G. and Vanheule, S. (2007). The Division of the Subject and the Organization: A Lacanian Approach to Subjectivity at Work. *Journal of Organizational Change Management*, 20: 359–369.
Arnoux, D., Berrebi, E., Boudet, M. and Germond, J. (Eds) (2016). *Lacan 66. Réception des Écrits*. Paris: EPEL.
Assoun, P.-L. (2000[1980]). *Freud and Nietzsche*. R. L. Collier Jr. (Trans.). London: Athlone Books.
Atkins, P. (1995). Science as Truth. *History of the Human Sciences*, 8(2): 97–102.
Attié, J. (1983). Sur la traversée du fantasme. *La lettre mensuelle*, 21: 3–4.
Avery, Ch. (2006). *Bernini: Genius of the Baroque*. London: Thames and Hudson.
Ávila, Teresa of (1957[1588]). *The Life of Saint Teresa of Ávila by Herself*. J. M. Cohen (Trans). Harmondsworth: Penguin.
Ávila, Teresa of (1961[1588]). *Interior Castle*. E. A. Peers (Ed. and Trans.). New York NY: Doubleday.
Babich, B. E. (2009). Nietzsche's 'Gay' Science. In K. Ansell Pearson (Ed.), *A Companion to Nietzsche* (pp. 97–114). Malden, MA-London: Wiley-Blackwell.
Backès, J.-L. (1968). Le gai saber. *Critique*, 251: 347–367.
Badiou, A. (2001[1998]). *Ethics: An Essay on the Understanding of Evil*. P. Hallward (Trans.). London-New York, NY: Verso.
Balaska, M. (2018). Can There Be Happiness in Psychoanalysis? Creon and Antigone in Lacan's *Seminar VII*. *College Literature: A Journal of Critical Literary Studies*, 45(2): 308–329.
Barcham, W. (1993). Some New Documents on Federico Cornaro's Two Chapels in Rome. *The Burlington Magazine*, 135(1089): 821–822.
Barcham, W. (2001). *Grand in Design: The Life and Career of Federico Cornaro. Prince of the Church, Patriarch of Venice and Patron of the Arts*. Venezia: Istituto Veneto di Scienze, Lettere ed Arti.

Barnet, M.-C. (2003). To Lise Deharme's Lighthouse: *Le Phare de Neuilly*, a Forgotten Surrealist Review. *French Studies*, 57: 323–334.
Barthes, R. (1987[1966]). *Criticism and Truth*. K. Pilcher (Trans.). London: The Athlone Press.
Barzilai, S. (1999). *Lacan and the Matter of Origins*. Stanford, CA-London: Stanford University Press.
Bataille, G. (2001[1957]). *Eroticism*. M. Dalwood (Trans.). London: Penguin.
Beattie, T. (2013). *Theology after Postmodernity: Divining the Void – A Lacanian Reading of Thomas Aquinas*. Oxford-New York, NY: Oxford University Press.
Beiser, F. C. (2001). *German Idealism: The Struggle Against Subjectivism, 1781–1801*. Cambridge, MA-London: Harvard University Press.
Benardete, S. (1999[1975]). *Sacred Transgressions: A Reading of Sophocles'* Antigone. South Bend, IN: St. Augustine's Press.
Berger, B. and Newman, S. (Eds) (2012). *Money Talks, in Therapy, Society, and Life*. New York, NY-London: Routledge.
Bergounioux, G. (2005). *Lacan débarbouillé*. Paris: Max Milo.
Bernanos, G. (2019[1936]). *Journal d'un curé de campagne*. Paris: Flammarion.
Bernays, J. (1857). Grundzüge der verlorenen Abhandlung des Aristoteles über Wirkung der Tragödie. *Abhandlungen der historisch-philosophischen Gesellschaft in Breslau*, 1: 35–122.
Bernays, J. (1880). *Zwei Abhandlungen über die Aristotelische Theorie des Dramas*. Berlin: Hertz.
Bernfeld, S. (1922). Bemerkungen über 'Sublimierung'. *Imago: Zeitschrift für die Anwendung der Psychoanalyse auf die Geisteswissenschaften*, 8(3): 333–344.
Berthold-Bond, D. (1994). Hegel on Madness and Tragedy. *History of Philosophy Quarterly*, 11(1): 71–99.
Beucler, A. and Masson, J. (Eds) (1949). *Almanach de Paris. An 2000*. Paris: Paul Dupont.
Bicknell, M. and Liefooghe, A. (2010). Enjoy your Stress! Using Lacan to Enrich Transactional Models of Stress. *Organization*, 17: 317–330.
Bion, W. R. (1946). Leaderless Group Project. *Bulletin of the Menninger Clinic*, 10: 77–81.
Bion, W. R. (1961[1948-1951]). Experiences in Groups. In *Experiences in Groups and Other Papers* (pp. 27–137). London: Routledge.
Bion, W. R. (1961[1952]). Group Dynamics. In *Experiences in Groups and Other Papers* (pp. 139–191). London: Routledge.
Bion, W. R. and Rickman, J. (1961[1943]). Intra-group Tensions in Therapy: Their Study as the Task of the Group. In W. R. Bion, *Experiences in Groups and Other Papers* (pp. 11–26). London: Routledge.
Blanchet, R. (2019). What is Concealed by the So-Called 'Cht' and Why? Ph. Dravers (Trans.). https://www.nlscongress2019.com/new-blog/what-is-concealed-by-the-so-called-cht-and-why. Accessed on 3 June 2021.
Bloom, H. (1982). Freud and the Sublime: A Catastrophe Theory of Creativity. In *Agon: Towards a Theory of Revisionism* (pp. 91–118). Oxford: Oxford University Press.
Bloom, P. and Cederström, C. (2009). The Sky's the Limit: Fantasy in the Age of Market Rationality. *Journal of Organizational Change Management*, 22: 159–180.

Böckh, A. (1824). Über die *Antigone* des Sophokles. *Abhandlungen der historisch-philologischen Klasse der königlichen Akademie der Wissenschaften zu Berlin aus dem Jahre 1824*, 1: 41–88.
Böckh, A. (1828). Über die *Antigone* des Sophokles. *Abhandlungen der historisch-philologischen Klasse der königlichen Akademie der Wissenschaften zu Berlin aus dem Jahre 1828*, 1: 49–112.
Boileau, N. (1965[1674]). Preface to the Translation of Longinus on the Sublime. In *Selected Criticism* (pp. 43–52). E. Dilworth (Ed. and Trans.). Indianapolis IN: Irvington.
Bollack, J. (1998). *Jacob Bernays: un homme entre deux mondes.* Villeneuve-d'Ascq: Presses Universitaires du Septentrion.
Bollas, C. (1987). *The Shadow of the Object.* London: Free Association Books.
Bonaparte, M. (1948). De l'essentielle ambivalence d'Eros. *Revue française de psychanalyse*, 12(2): 167–212.
Bonnet, M. (1992). La rencontre d'André Breton avec la folie: Saint-Dizier, août-novembre 1916. In F. Hulak (Ed.). *Folie et psychanalyse dans l'expérience surréaliste* (pp. 115–135). Nice: Z'éditions.
Borch-Jacobsen, M. (1988[1982]). *The Freudian Subject.* C. Porter (Trans.). Stanford, CA: Stanford University Press.
Borch-Jacobsen, M. (1991[1990]). *Lacan: The Absolute Master.* D. Brick (Trans.). Stanford, CA: Stanford University Press.
Borch-Jacobsen, M. (1993[1991]). The Freudian Subject: From Politics to Ethics. In *The Emotional Tie: Psychoanalysis, Mimesis, and Affect.* D. Brick (Trans.). (pp. 15–35). Stanford, CA: Stanford University Press.
Boucher, B. (1998). *Italian Baroque Sculpture.* London: Thames and Hudson.
Bousseyroux, M. (2011). *Au risque de la topologie et de la poésie. Élargir la psychanalyse.* Toulouse: Érès.
Boussidan, G. (2009). La jouissance sexuelle. In J.-M. Jadin and M. Ritter (Eds). *La jouissance au fil de l'enseignement de Lacan* (pp. 369–390). Toulouse: Érès.
Bowra, C. M. (1944). *Sophoclean Tragedy.* Oxford: Clarendon Press.
Breton, A. (1930). *Second manifeste du surréalisme.* Paris: Kra.
Breton, A. (1990[1922]). Interview du Professeur Freud. In *Les pas perdus* (pp. 94–95). Paris: Gallimard.
Breton, A. (1997[1932]). *Communicating Vessels.* M. A. Caws and G. T. Harris (Trans.). Lincoln, NE-London: University of Nebraska Press.
Breton, A. (1999[1928]). *Nadja.* R. Howard (Trans.). London: Penguin Books.
Breton, A. and Éluard, P. (1930). *L'immaculée conception.* Paris: Éditions surréalistes.
Breuer, J. and Freud, S. (1955[1893*a*]). Preliminary Communication. In J. Strachey (Ed. and Trans.), *The Standard Edition of the Complete Psychological Works of Sigmund Freud*, vol. 2. (pp. 1–17). London: The Hogarth Press and the Institute of Psycho-Analysis.
Breuer, J. and Freud, S. (1955[1895*d*]). Studies on Hysteria. In J. Strachey (Ed. and Trans.), *The Standard Edition of the Complete Psychological Works of Sigmund Freud*, vol. 2. (pp. 1–305). London: The Hogarth Press and the Institute of Psycho-Analysis.
Brosses, Ch. de (1986). *Lettres d'Italie 1739-1740*, Tôme 2. Paris: Mercure de France.
Buekens, F. (2005). *Jacques Lacan. Proefvlucht in het luchtledige.* Leuven-Amersfoort: Acco.

Bulletin of the IPA (1937). Bulletin of the International Psycho-Analytical Association. *The International Journal of Psycho-Analysis*, 18(1): 78.
Bulletin of the IPA (1949). Bulletin of the International Psycho-Analytical Association. *The International Journal of Psycho-Analysis*, 30(1): 203.
Burckhardt, J. (1855). *Der Cicerone. Eine Anleitung zum Genuß der Kunstwerke Italiens*. Basel: Schweighauser'sche Verlagsbuchhandlung.
Burke, E. (2015[1757]). *A Philosophical Enquiry into the Sublime and the Beautiful*. Oxford: Oxford University Press.
Burke, J. (2006). *The Sphinx on the Table: Sigmund Freud's Art Collection and the Development of Psychoanalysis*. New York, NY: Walker & Company.
Burke, V. I. (2013). The Substance of Ethical Recognition: Hegel's Antigone and the Irreplaceability of the Brother. *New German Critique*, 40(1): 1–27.
Burrell, G. (1988). Modernism, Post-modernism and Organizational Analysis 2: The Contribution of Michel Foucault. *Organization Studies*, 9: 221–235.
Butler, J. (1997). *The Psychic Life of Power. Theories in Subjection*. Stanford, CA: Stanford University Press.
Butler, J. (2000). *Antigone's Claim: Kinship Between Life and Death*. New York, NY: Columbia University Press.
Cairns, D. (2016). *Sophocles: Antigone*. London-New York, NY: Bloomsbury.
Calder, W. M. (1971). The Protagonist of Sophocles' 'Antigone'. *Arethusa*, 4(1): 49–52.
Careri, G. (1995). *Bernini: Flights of Love, the Art of Devotion*. L. Lappin (Trans.). Chicago, IL-London: The University of Chicago Press.
Carrington, A. (2016). Money Matters: Lacanian Clarifications on the Functions of Money in the Psychic Economy. *Jcfar: Journal of the Centre for Freudian Analysis and Research*, 27: 90–110.
Carter, P. and Jackson, N. (2004). Gilles Deleuze and Felix Guattari. In S. Linstead (Ed.). *Organization Theory and Postmodern Thought* (pp. 105–126). London-Thousand Oaks, CA-New Delhi: Sage.
Cassin, B. (2020[2012]). *Jacques the Sophist: Lacan, Logos, and Psychoanalysis*. M. Syrotinski (Trans.). New York, NY: Fordham University Press.
Cassin, B. (Ed.) (2014). *Dictionary of Untranslatables: A Philosophical Lexicon*. S. Rendall, C. Hubert, J. Mehlman, N. Stein and M. Syrotinski (Trans.). Princeton, NJ-Oxford: Princeton University Press.
Caudill, D. S. (1997). *Lacan and the Subject of Law: Toward a Psychoanalytic Critical Legal Theory*. Atlantic Highlands, NJ: Humanities Press.
Caws, M. A. (1999). *The Surrealist Look: An Erotics of Encounter*. Cambridge, MA-London: The MIT Press.
Cederström, C. and Hoedemaekers, C. (Eds) (2010). Preface. In *Lacan and Organization*. (pp. xiii–xviii). London: MayFly Books.
Chandler, A. R. (1913). Tragic Effect in Sophocles. Analyzed According to the Freudian Method. *The Monist*, 23(1): 59–89.
Chanter, T. (1995). *Ethics of Eros: Irigaray's Rewriting of the Philosophers*. New York, NY-London: Routledge.
Chanter, T. (1998). Tragic Dislocations: Antigone's Modern Theatrics. *Differences*, 10(1): 75–97.

Chapsal, M. (1984). Jacques Lacan. In *Envoyez la petite musique* ... (pp. 29–54). Paris: Grasset.
Charcot, J.-M. (1897). *La foi qui guérit*. Paris: Félix Alcan.
Chasseguet-Smirgel, J. (1985). *Creativity and Perversion*. New York, NY: W. W. Norton & Company.
Chiesa, L. (2014). Woman and the Number of God. In C. Davis, M. Pound and C. Crockett (Eds). *Theology After Lacan: The Passion for the Real* (pp. 166–191). Eugene, OR: Wipf and Stock.
Cho, K. D. (2009). *Psychopedagogy: Freud, Lacan, and the Psychoanalytic Theory of Education*. Basingstoke-New York, NY: Palgrave Macmillan.
Clavreul, J. (1977[1964]). Exposé introductif—Réunion GEP. In J.-A. Miller (Ed.), *L'excommunication. La communauté psychanalytique en France—2* (pp. 138–148). Paris: Navarin.
Clavreul, J. (2001). Entretien avec Jean Clavreul. In A. Didier-Weill, E. Weiss and F. Gravas (Eds). *Quartier Lacan. Témoignages sur Jacques Lacan* (pp. 23–32). Paris: Denoël.
Clavreul, J. (2007). Questions à Jean Clavreul. In A. Didier-Weill and M. Safouan (Eds). *Travailler avec Lacan* (pp. 19–29). Paris: Aubier.
Clemens, J. (2013). *Psychoanalysis Is an Antiphilosophy*. Edinburgh: Edinburgh University Press.
Clewis, R. R. (2009). *The Kantian Sublime and the Revelation of Freedom*. Cambridge: Cambridge University Press.
Cohn, J. and Miles, T. H. (1977). The Sublime: In Alchemy, Aesthetics and Psychoanalysis. *Modern Philology*, 74(3): 289–304.
Conklin, W. (1997). Hegel, the Author and Authority in Sophocles' *Antigone*. In L. G. Rubin (Ed.). *Justice vs. Law in Greek Political Thought* (pp. 129–151). New York, NY-Oxford: Rowman & Littlefield.
Contu, A., Driver, M. and Jones, C. (2010). Jacques Lacan with Organization Studies. *Organization*, 17: 307–315.
Cook, M. (1999). The Missionary Position: A Reading of the Mystic Woman in Lacan's Seminar XX. *Tessera*, 27: 82–89.
Cooper, R. (1989). Modernism, Post Modernism and Organizational Analysis 3: The Contribution of Jacques Derrida. *Organization Studies*, 10: 479–502.
Copjec, J. (2002). The Tomb of Perseverance: On *Antigone*. In *Imagine There's No Woman: Ethics and Sublimation* (pp. 12–47). Cambridge, MA-London: The MIT Press.
Copjec, J. (2005). Gai Savoir Sera: The Science of Love and the Insolence of Chance. In G. Riera (Ed.), *Alain Badiou: Philosophy and its Conditions* (pp. 119–135). Albany, NY: State University of New York Press.
Costas, J. and Taheri, A. (2012). The Return of the Primal Father in Postmodernity? A Lacanian Analysis of Authentic Leadership. *Organization Studies*, 33: 1195–1216.
Cottet, S. (1997). Gai savoir et triste vérité. *La cause freudienne. Revue de Psychanalyse*, 35: 33–36.
Cowles, H. M. (2020). *The Scientific Method: An Evolution of Thinking from Darwin to Dewey*. Cambridge, MA-London: Harvard University Press.
Critchley, S. (2019). *Tragedy, the Greeks and Us*. London: Profile Books.

Crockett, C. (2001). *A Theology of the Sublime*. London-New York, NY: Routledge.
Crockett, C. (2007). *Interstices of the Sublime: Theology and Psychoanalytic Theory*. New York, NY: Fordham University Press.
Cropp, M. (1997). Antigone's Final Speech (Sophocles, *Antigone* 891–928). *Greece & Rome*, 44(2): 137–160.
Crowther, P. (1989). *The Kantian Sublime: From Morality to Art*. Oxford-New York, NY: Oxford University Press.
Cusanus, N. (1985[1440]). *On Learned Ignorance*. J. Hopkins (Trans.). Minneapolis, MN: Arthur J. Banning Press.
Danto, E. A. (2005). *Freud's Free Clinics: Psychoanalysis and Social Justice, 1918–1938*. New York, NY-London: Columbia University Press.
Daudet, A. (1874). *Les femmes d'artistes*. Paris: Alphonse Lemerre.
Daudet, A. (1892[1874]). *Artists' Wives*. L. Ensor (Trans.). London: George Routledge & Sons.
Davis, C. (2010). *Critical Excess: Overreading in Derrida, Deleuze, Levinas, Žižek and Cavell*. Stanford, CA-London: Stanford University Press.
Davis, F. (1973). Three Letters from Sigmund Freud to André Breton. *Journal of the American Psychoanalytic Association*, 21(1): 127–134.
Dean, T. (2008). The Frozen Countenance of the Perversions. *Parallax*, 14 (2): 93–114.
de Beauvoir, S. (1990[1950–1951]). Must We Burn Sade? A. Michelson (Trans.). In Marquis de Sade, *The 120 Days of Sodom and Other Writings* (pp. 3–64). London: Arrow Books
de Beauvoir, S. (1997[1949]) *The Second Sex*. H. M. Parshley (Trans.). London: Vintage Books.
De Boer, K. (2008). Hegel's *Antigone* and the Tragedy of Cultural Difference. *Mosaic: An Interdisciplinary Journal*, 41(3): 31–45.
de Frutos Salvador, Á. (1994). *Los Escritos de Jacques Lacan. Variantes textuales*. Madrid: Siglo XXI.
De Kesel, M. (2009[2001]). *Eros and Ethics: Reading Jacques Lacan's Seminar VII*. S. Jöttkandt (Trans.). Albany, NY: State University of New York Press.
De Kesel, M. (2015). De ethiek van een mooi nee. Lacans interpretatie van Antigone. In M. De Kesel and B. Schomakers (Eds). *De schoonheid van het nee. Essays over Antigone* (pp. 151–181). Amsterdam: Sjibbolet.
De Kesel, M. (2018). The Real of Ethics: On a Widespread Misconception. In B. W. Becker, J. P. Manoussakis and D. M. Goodman (Eds). *Unconscious Incarnations: Psychoanalytic and Philosophical Perspectives on the Body* (pp. 76–93). Abingdon-New York, NY: Routledge.
De Kesel, M. (2019). Sublimatie en perversie. Hoe psychoanalyse onze moderne ethiek heroriënteert. In *Het Münchhausen Paradigma. Waarom Freud en Lacan ertoe doen* (pp. 83–100). Nijmegen: Vantilt.
de Maré, P. B. (1985). Major Bion. In M. Pines (Ed.). *Bion and Group Psychotherapy* (pp. 108–113). London: Routledge & Kegan.
de Mijolla, A. (2010). *Freud et la France (1885–1945)*. Paris: Presses Universitaires de France.
de Mijolla, A. (2012). *La France et Freud. Tôme 1: Une pénible renaissance (1946–1953)*. Paris: Presses Universitaires de France.

de Mijolla-Mellor, S. (Ed.) (2012). *Traité de la sublimation*. Paris: Presses Universitaires de France.
Depoortere, F. (2005). Jouissance féminine? Lacan on Bernini's *The Ecstasy of Saint Teresa* vs Slavoj Žižek on Lars von Trier's *Breaking the Waves*. In L. Boeve, H. Geybels and S. Van den Bossche (Eds). *Encountering Transcendence: Contributions to a Theology of Christian Religious Experience* (pp. 21–37). Leuven: Peeters.
Deri, F. (1939). On Sublimation. *The Psychoanalytic Quarterly*, 8(3): 325–334.
Derrida, J. (1981[1970]). The Double Session. In *Dissemination*. B. Johnson (Trans.) (pp. 187–316). Chicago, IL-London: The University of Chicago Press.
Derrida, J. (1987[1975]). Le facteur de la vérité. In *The Post Card: From Socrates to Freud and Beyond* (pp. 411–496). A. Bass (Trans.). Chicago, IL-London: The University of Chicago Press.
Derrida, J. (1998[1996]). *Resistances of Psychoanalysis*. P. Kamuf, P.-A. Brault and M. Naas (Trans.). Stanford, CA: Stanford University Press.
Derrida, J. (2021[1974]). *Clang*. G. Bennington and D. Wills (Trans.). Minneapolis, MN-London: University of Minnesota Press.
Descartes, R. (1985[1637]). Discourse on the Method. In *The Philosophical Writings of Descartes*, vol. 1. (pp. 111–151). J. Cottingham, R. Stoothoff and D. Murdoch (Trans.). Cambridge: Cambridge University Press.
Devereux, G. (1968). *From Anxiety to Method in the Behavioral Sciences*. The Hague: Mouton.
Donougho (1989). The Woman in White: On the Reception of Hegel's Antigone. *The Owl of Minerva*, 21(1): 65–89.
Doran, R. (2015). *The Theory of the Sublime: From Longinus to Kant*. Cambridge: Cambridge University Press.
Dosse, F. (1998[1991]). *History of Structuralism. Vol. 1: The Rising Sign (1945-1966)*. D. Glassman (Trans.). Minneapolis, MN-London: University of Minnesota Press.
Douglas, M. (1975). *Implicit Meanings: Essays in Anthropology*. London-New York, NY: Routledge.
Dragonetti, R. (1961). *Aux frontières du langage poétique. Études sur Dante, Mallarmé, Valéry*. Gand: Romanica Gandensia.
Dragonetti, R. (1965). Dante et Narcisse ou les faux-monnayeurs de l'image. *Revue des Études Italiennes*, 102: 85–146.
Dragonetti, R. (1982). *Le gai savoir dans la rhétorique courtoise. Flamenca et Joufroi de Poitiers*. Paris: du Seuil.
Driver, M. (2009a). From Loss to Lack: Stories of Organizational Change as Encounters with Failed Fantasies of Self, Work and Organization. *Organization*, 16: 353–369.
Driver, M. (2009b). Struggling with Lack: A Lacanian Perspective on Organizational Identity. *Organization Studies*, 30: 55–72.
Driver, M. (2009c). Encountering the Arugula Leaf: The Failure of the Imaginary and Its Implications for Research on Identity in Organizations. *Organization*, 16: 487–504.
Driver, M. (2014). The Stressed Subject: Lack, Empowerment and Liberation. *Organization*, 21: 90–105.
Dufour, D.-R. (1998). *Lacan et le miroir sophianique de Boehme*. Paris: E.P.E.L.

Eagleton, T. (2010). Lacan's Antigone. In S. E. Wilmer and A. Žukauskaitė (Eds). *Interrogating Antigone in Postmodern Philosophy and Criticism* (pp. 101–109). Oxford: Oxford University Press.
Earlie, P. (2021). *Derrida and the Legacy of Psychoanalysis.* Oxford: Oxford University Press.
Eastman, M. (1942). Visit in Vienna: The Crotchety Greatness of Sigmund Freud. In *Heroes I Have Known: Twelve who Lived Great Lives* (pp. 261–273). New York, NY: Simon & Schuster.
Eckermann, J. P. (2012[1836–1848]). *Conversations of Goethe with Eckermann and Soret*, Vol. 1. J. Oxenford (Trans.). Cambridge: Cambridge University Press.
Edmundson, M. (2007). *The Death of Sigmund Freud: Fascism, Psychoanalysis and the Rise of Fundamentalism.* London: Bloomsbury.
Egan, G. (1982). *The Skilled Helper: Model, Skills, and Methods for Effective Helping.* 2nd Edition. Pacific Grove, CA: Brooks/Cole Publishing.
Egginton, W. (2007). *The Philosopher's Desire: Psychoanalysis, Interpretation, and Truth.* Stanford, CA: Stanford University Press.
Eire, C. (2019). *The Life of Saint Teresa of Ávila: A Biography.* Princeton, NJ-Oxford: Princeton University Press.
Eissler, K. R. (1974). On Some Theoretical and Technical Problems Regarding the Payment of Fees for Psychoanalytic Treatment. *International Review of Psychoanalysis*, 1(1): 73–101.
Eissler, K. R. (1979). Bericht über die sich in den Vereinigten Staaten befindenden Bücher aus S. Freuds Bibliothek. *Jahrbuch der Psychoanalyse: Beiträge zur Theorie und Praxis*, 11: 10–50.
Eissler R. S. (Ed.) (1954). 106th Bulletin of the International Psycho-Analytical Association. *International Journal of Psychoanalysis*, 35(1): 267–290.
Ellison, D. (2001). *Ethics and Aesthetics in European Modernist Literature: From the Sublime to the Uncanny.* Cambridge: Cambridge University Press.
Ellmann, R. (1983). *James Joyce.* New and Revised Edition. Oxford-New York, NY: Oxford University Press.
Emerson, R. W. (1888[1876]). The Scholar. In *Complete Works. Vol. X: Lectures and Biographical Sketches* (pp. 261–290). Boston, MA: Houghton Miflin & Co.
Emerson, R. W. (1898[1836]). Poetry and Imagination. In *Letters and Social Aims* (pp. 1–58). London: Macmillan and Co.
Emerson, R. W. (1972[1842]). Prospects. In R. E. Spiller and W. E. Williams (Eds). *The Early Lectures of Ralph Waldo Emerson. Vol. III: 1838-1842* (pp. 366–382). Cambridge, MA-London: The Belknap Press of Harvard University Press.
Ensor, J. (1950). *Écrits.* Bruxelles: Sélection.
Esman, A. H. (2011). Psychoanalysis and Surrealism: André Breton and Sigmund Freud. *Journal of the American Psychoanalytic Association*, 59(1): 173–181.
Etchegoyen, R. H. and Miller, J.-A. (1996). *Silence brisé. Entretien sur le mouvement psychanalytique.* Paris: Agalma.
Euripides (2005). Phoenician Women. In *The Bacchae and Other Plays* (pp. 1–57). J. Davie (Trans.). London: Penguin Books.
Eyers, T. (2012). *Lacan and the Concept of the 'Real'.* Basingstoke: Palgrave Macmillan.
Falzeder, E., Brabant, E. and Giampieri-Deutsch, P. (Eds) (2000). *The Correspondence of Sigmund Freud and Sándor Ferenczi, Vol. 3: 1920-1933.* P. T.

Hoffer (Trans.). Cambridge, MA-London: The Belknap Press of Harvard University Press.

Fargue, L.-P. (1967[1923]). Ludions. In *Poésies—Tancrède. Ludions. Poëmes. Pour la musique* (pp. 39–54). Paris: Gallimard.

Ferenczi, S. (1964[1927]). Das Problem der Beendigung der Analysen. In *Bausteine zur Psychoanalyse. Band III: Arbeiten aus den Jahren 1908-1933* (pp. 367–379). Bern-Stuttgart: Verlag Hans Huber.

Fichte, J. G. (1986[1804]). *Die Wissenschaftslehre. Zweiter Vortrag im Jahre 1804*. Hamburg: Felix Meiner Verlag.

Fink, B. (1990). Alienation and Separation: Logical Moments of Lacan's Dialectic of Desire. *Newsletter of the Freudian Field*, 4(1/2): 78–119.

Fink, B. (1995). *The Lacanian Subject: Between Language and Jouissance*. Princeton, NJ-London: Princeton University Press.

Fink, B. (2002). Knowledge and Jouissance. In S. Barnard and B. Fink (Ed.). *Reading Seminar XX: Lacan's Major Work on Love, Knowledge, and Feminine Sexuality* (pp. 21–45). Albany, NY: State University of New York Press.

Fink, B. (2004). The Lacanian Phallus and the Square Root of Negative One. In *Lacan to the Letter: Reading* Écrits *Closely* (pp. 129–140). Minneapolis, MN-London: University of Minnesota Press.

Fink, B. (2012). Analysis and Analyst in the Global Economy, or Why Anyone in their Right Mind Would Pay for an Analysis. In D. Bennett (Ed.), *Loaded Subjects: Psychoanalysis, Money and the Global Financial Crisis* (pp. 52–66). London: Lawrence & Wishart.

Fink, B. (2014a). An Introduction to Lacan's *Seminar XVIII*. In *Against Understanding. Vol.2: Cases and Commentary in a Lacanian Key* (pp. 71–91). London-New York, NY: Routledge.

Fink, B. (2014b). An Introduction to 'Kant with Sade'. In *Against Understanding. Vol. 2: Cases and Commentary in a Lacanian Key* (pp. 105–130). London-New York, NY: Routledge.

Finkelde, D. (2017). *Excessive Subjectivity: Kant, Hegel, Lacan, and the Foundations of Ethics*. New York, NY: Columbia University Press.

Fleming, K. (2015). Heidegger's *Antigone*: Ethics and Politics. In J. Billings and M. Leonard (Eds), *Tragedy and the Idea of Modernity* (pp. 178–193). Oxford: Oxford University Press.

Flournoy, O. (1967). La sublimation. *Revue française de psychanalyse* 31(1): 59–93.

Foley, H. P. (1995). Tragedy and Democratic Ideology: The Case of Sophocles' *Antigone*. In B. Goff (Ed.), *History, Tragedy, Theory: Dialogues on Athenian Drama* (pp. 131–150). Austin, TX: The University of Texas Press.

Forrester, J. (1990). *The Seductions of Psychoanalysis: Freud, Lacan and Derrida*. Cambridge: Cambridge University Press.

Forrester, J. (1997). Gift, Money, and Debt. In *Truth Games: Lies, Money, and Psychoanalysis* (pp. 110–171). Cambridge, MA-London: Harvard University Press.

Fotaki, M. (2009). Maintaining the Illusion of a Free Health Service in Post-socialism: A Lacanian Analysis of Transition from Planned to Market Economy. *Journal of Organizational Change Management*, 22: 141–158.

Foucault, M. (1970[1966]). *The Order of Things: An Archaeology of the Human Sciences*. A. Sheridan (Trans.). London: Tavistock.

Foucault, M. (1978[1976]). *The History of Sexuality. Vol. 1: An Introduction*. R. Hurley (Trans.). New York, NY: Random House.

Freeland, Ch. (2013). *Antigone, in Her Unbearable Splendor: New Essays on Jacques Lacan's* The Ethics of Psychoanalysis. Albany, NY: State University of New York Press.

Freud, E. L. (Ed.) (1970). *The Letters of Sigmund Freud and Arnold Zweig*. New York, NY: Harcourt, Brace & World, Inc.

Freud, S. (1953[1900*a*]). The Interpretation of Dreams. In J. Strachey (Ed. and Trans.), *The Standard Edition of the Complete Psychological Works of Sigmund Freud*, vols 4/5. London: The Hogarth Press and the Institute of Psycho-Analysis.

Freud, S. (1953[1905*d*]). Three Essays on the Theory of Sexuality. In J. Strachey (Ed. and Trans.), *The Standard Edition of the Complete Psychological Works of Sigmund Freud*, vol. 7 (pp. 123–245). London: The Hogarth Press and the Institute of Psycho-Analysis.

Freud, S. (1953[1905*e*]). Fragment of an Analysis of a Case of Hysteria. In J. Strachey (Ed. and Trans.), *The Standard Edition of the Complete Psychological Works of Sigmund Freud*, vol. 7 (pp. 7–122). London: The Hogarth Press and the Institute of Psycho-Analysis.

Freud, S. (1955[1909*d*]). Notes Upon a Case of Obsessional Neurosis. In J. Strachey (Ed. and Trans.), *The Standard Edition of the Complete Psychological Works of Sigmund Freud*, vol. 10 (pp. 151–249). London: The Hogarth Press and the Institute of Psycho-Analysis.

Freud, S. (1955[1917*a*]). A Difficulty in the Path of Psycho-analysis. In J. Strachey (Ed. and Trans.), *The Standard Edition of the Complete Psychological Works of Sigmund Freud*, vol. 17 (pp. 135–144). London: The Hogarth Press and the Institute of Psycho-Analysis.

Freud, S. (1955[1918*b*]). From the History of an Infantile Neurosis. In J. Strachey (Ed. and Trans.), *The Standard Edition of the Complete Psychological Works of Sigmund Freud*, vol. 17 (pp. 1–122). London: The Hogarth Press and the Institute of Psycho-Analysis.

Freud, S. (1955[1919*a*]). Lines of Advance in Psycho-analytic Therapy. In J. Strachey (Ed. and Trans.), *The Standard Edition of the Complete Psychological Works of Sigmund Freud*, vol. 17 (pp. 157–168). London: The Hogarth Press and the Institute of Psycho-Analysis.

Freud, S. (1955[1919*e*]). 'A Child is Being Beaten': A Contribution to the Study of the Origin of Sexual Perversions. In J. Strachey (Ed. and Trans.), *The Standard Edition of the Complete Psychological Works of Sigmund Freud*, vol. 17 (pp. 175–204). London: The Hogarth Press and the Institute of Psycho-Analysis.

Freud, S. (1955[1919*h*]). The 'Uncanny'. In J. Strachey (Ed. and Trans.), *The Standard Edition of the Complete Psychological Works of Sigmund Freud*, vol. 17 (pp. 217–256). London: The Hogarth Press and the Institute of Psycho-Analysis.

Freud, S. (1955[1920*a*]). The Psychogenesis of a Case of Homosexuality in a Woman. In J. Strachey (Ed. and Trans.), *The Standard Edition of the Complete Psychological Works of Sigmund Freud*, vol. 18 (pp. 145–172). London: The Hogarth Press and the Institute of Psycho-Analysis.

Freud, S. (1955[1920g]). Beyond the Pleasure Principle. In J. Strachey (Ed. and Trans.), *The Standard Edition of the Complete Psychological Works of Sigmund Freud*, vol. 18 (pp. 1–64). London: The Hogarth Press and the Institute of Psycho-Analysis.

Freud, S. (1955[1921c]). Group Psychology and the Analysis of the Ego. In J. Strachey (Ed. and Trans.), *The Standard Edition of the Complete Psychological Works of Sigmund Freud*, vol. 18 (pp. 65–143). London: The Hogarth Press and the Institute of Psycho-Analysis.

Freud, S. (1955[1923a]). Two Encyclopaedia Articles. In J. Strachey (Ed. and Trans.), *The Standard Edition of the Complete Psychological Works of Sigmund Freud*, vol. 18 (pp. 233–259). London: The Hogarth Press and the Institute of Psycho-Analysis.

Freud, S. (1957[1910a]). Five Lectures on Psycho-Analysis. In J. Strachey (Ed. and Trans.), *The Standard Edition of the Complete Psychological Works of Sigmund Freud*, vol. 11 (pp. 7–55). London: The Hogarth Press and the Institute of Psycho-Analysis.

Freud, S. (1957[1914c]). On Narcissism: An Introduction. In J. Strachey (Ed. and Trans.), *The Standard Edition of the Complete Psychological Works of Sigmund Freud*, vol. 14 (pp. 67–102). London: The Hogarth Press and the Institute of Psycho-Analysis.

Freud, S. (1957[1915c]). Instincts and their Vicissitudes. In J. Strachey (Ed. and Trans.), *The Standard Edition of the Complete Psychological Works of Sigmund Freud*, vol. 14 (pp. 109–140). London: The Hogarth Press and the Institute of Psycho-Analysis.

Freud, S. (1957[1915d]). Repression. In J. Strachey (Ed. and Trans.), *The Standard Edition of the Complete Psychological Works of Sigmund Freud*, vol. 14 (pp. 141–158). London: The Hogarth Press and the Institute of Psycho-Analysis.

Freud, S. (1957[1915e]). The Unconscious. In J. Strachey (Ed. and Trans.), *The Standard Edition of the Complete Psychological Works of Sigmund Freud*, vol. 14 (pp. 159–215). London: The Hogarth Press and the Institute of Psycho-Analysis.

Freud, S. (1957[1917e]). Mourning and Melancholia. In J. Strachey (Ed. and Trans.), *The Standard Edition of the Complete Psychological Works of Sigmund Freud*, vol. 14 (pp. 237–258). London: The Hogarth Press and the Institute of Psycho-Analysis.

Freud, S. (1958[1911c]). Psycho-Analytic Notes on an Autobiographical Account of a Case of Paranoia (Dementia Paranoides). In J. Strachey (Ed. and Trans.), *The Standard Edition of the Complete Psychological Works of Sigmund Freud*, vol. 12 (pp. 1–82). London: The Hogarth Press and the Institute of Psycho-Analysis.

Freud, S. (1958[1912b]). The Dynamics of Transference. In J. Strachey (Ed. and Trans.), *The Standard Edition of the Complete Psychological Works of Sigmund Freud*, vol. 12 (pp. 97–108). London: The Hogarth Press and the Institute of Psycho-Analysis.

Freud, S. (1958[1912e]). Recommendations to Physicians Practising Psycho-Analysis. In J. Strachey (Ed. and Trans.), *The Standard Edition of the Complete Psychological Works of Sigmund Freud*, vol. 12 (pp. 109–120). London: The Hogarth Press and the Institute of Psycho-Analysis.

Freud, S. (1958[1913c]). On Beginning the Treatment (Further Recommendations on the Technique of Psycho-Analysis I). In J. Strachey (Ed. and Trans.), *The*

Standard Edition of the Complete Psychological Works of Sigmund Freud, vol. 12 (pp. 121–144). London: The Hogarth Press and the Institute of Psycho-Analysis.

Freud, S. (1958[1914*b*]). The Moses of Michelangelo. In J. Strachey (Ed. and Trans.), *The Standard Edition of the Complete Psychological Works of Sigmund Freud*, vol. 13 (pp. 209–237). London: The Hogarth Press and the Institute of Psycho-Analysis.

Freud, S. (1958[1914*g*]). Remembering, Repeating and Working-Through (Further Recommendations on the Technique of Psycho-Analysis II). In J. Strachey (Ed. and Trans.), *The Standard Edition of the Complete Psychological Works of Sigmund Freud*, vol. 12 (pp. 145–156). London: The Hogarth Press and the Institute of Psycho-Analysis.

Freud, S. (1958[1915*a*]). Observations on Transference-Love (Further Recommendations on the Technique of Psycho-Analysis III). In J. Strachey (Ed. and Trans.), *The Standard Edition of the Complete Psychological Works of Sigmund Freud*, vol. 12 (pp. 157–171). London: The Hogarth Press and the Institute of Psycho-Analysis.

Freud, S. (1959[1908*b*]). Character and Anal Erotism. In J. Strachey (Ed. and Trans.), *The Standard Edition of the Complete Psychological Works of Sigmund Freud*, vol. 9 (pp. 167–175). London: The Hogarth Press and the Institute of Psycho-Analysis.

Freud, S. (1959[1908*e*]). Creative Writers and Day-Dreaming. In J. Strachey (Ed. and Trans.), *The Standard Edition of the Complete Psychological Works of Sigmund Freud*, vol. 9 (pp. 141–153). London: The Hogarth Press and the Institute of Psycho-Analysis.

Freud, S. (1959[1925*d*]). An Autobiographical Study. In J. Strachey (Ed. and Trans.), *The Standard Edition of the Complete Psychological Works of Sigmund Freud*, vol. 20 (pp. 1–70). London: The Hogarth Press and the Institute of Psycho-Analysis.

Freud, S. (1959[1926*d*]). Inhibitions, Symptoms and Anxiety. In J. Strachey (Ed. and Trans.), *The Standard Edition of the Complete Psychological Works of Sigmund Freud*, vol. 20 (pp. 75–174). London: The Hogarth Press and the Institute of Psycho-Analysis.

Freud, S. (1960[1901*b*]). The Psychopathology of Everyday Life. In J. Strachey (Ed. and Trans.), *The Standard Edition of the Complete Psychological Works of Sigmund Freud*, vol. 6. London: The Hogarth Press and the Institute of Psycho-Analysis.

Freud, S. (1960[1905*c*]). Jokes and their Relation to the Unconscious. In J. Strachey (Ed. and Trans.), *The Standard Edition of the Complete Psychological Works of Sigmund Freud*, vol. 8. London: The Hogarth Press and the Institute of Psycho-Analysis.

Freud, S. (1960[1933*c*]). Sándor Ferenczi. In J. Strachey (Ed. and Trans.), *The Standard Edition of the Complete Psychological Works of Sigmund Freud*, vol. 22 (pp. 225–229). London: The Hogarth Press and the Institute of Psycho-Analysis.

Freud, S. (1961[1923*b*]). The Ego and the Id. In J. Strachey (Ed. and Trans.), *The Standard Edition of the Complete Psychological Works of Sigmund Freud*, vol. 19 (pp. 1–66). London: The Hogarth Press and the Institute of Psycho-Analysis.

Freud, S. (1961[1924*c*]). The Economic Problem of Masochism. In J. Strachey (Ed. and Trans.), *The Standard Edition of the Complete Psychological Works of*

Sigmund Freud, vol. 19 (pp. 155–170). London: The Hogarth Press and the Institute of Psycho-Analysis.

Freud, S. (1961[1925*h*]). Negation. In J. Strachey (Ed. and Trans.), *The Standard Edition of the Complete Psychological Works of Sigmund Freud*, vol. 19 (pp. 235–239). London: The Hogarth Press and the Institute of Psycho-Analysis.

Freud, S. (1961[1925*j*]). Some Psychical Consequences of the Anatomical Distinction Between the Sexes. In *The Standard Edition of the Complete Psychological Works of Sigmund Freud*, vol. 19 (pp. 241–258). London: The Hogarth Press and the Institute of Psycho-Analysis.

Freud, S. (1961[1927*e*]). Fetishism. In J. Strachey (Ed. and Trans.), *The Standard Edition of the Complete Psychological Works of Sigmund Freud*, vol. 21 (pp. 147–157). London: The Hogarth Press and the Institute of Psycho-Analysis.

Freud, S. (1962[1894*a*]). The Neuro-Psychoses of Defence. In *The Standard Edition of the Complete Psychological Works of Sigmund Freud*, vol. 3 (pp. 41–61). London: The Hogarth Press and the Institute of Psycho-Analysis.

Freud, S. (1962[1898*a*]). Sexuality in the Aetiology of the Neuroses. In J. Strachey (Ed. and Trans.), *The Standard Edition of the Complete Psychological Works of Sigmund Freud*, vol. 3 (pp. 261–285). London: The Hogarth Press and the Institute of Psycho-Analysis.

Freud, S. (1963[1916–1917]). Introductory Lectures on Psycho-Analysis. In J. Strachey (Ed. and Trans.), *The Standard Edition of the Complete Psychological Works of Sigmund Freud*, vols 15/16. London: The Hogarth Press and the Institute of Psycho-Analysis.

Freud, S. (1964[1930*a*]). Civilization and its Discontents. In J. Strachey (Ed. and Trans.), *The Standard Edition of the Complete Psychological Works of Sigmund Freud*, Vol. 21 (pp. 57–145). London: The Hogarth Press and the Institute of Psycho-Analysis.

Freud, S. (1964[1933*a*]). New Introductory Lectures on Psycho-Analysis. In J. Strachey (Ed. and Trans.), *The Standard Edition of the Complete Psychological Works of Sigmund Freud*, vol. 22 (pp. 1–182). London: The Hogarth Press and the Institute of Psycho-Analysis.

Freud, S. (1964[1937*c*]). Analysis Terminable and Interminable. In J. Strachey (Ed. and Trans.), *The Standard Edition of the Complete Psychological Works of Sigmund Freud*, vol. 23 (pp. 209–253). London: The Hogarth Press and the Institute of Psycho-Analysis.

Freud, S. (1964[1939*a*]). Moses and Monotheism. In J. Strachey (Ed. and Trans.), *The Standard Edition of the Complete Psychological Works of Sigmund Freud*, vol. 23 (pp. 1–137). London: The Hogarth Press and the Institute of Psycho-Analysis.

Freud, S. (1964[1940*a*]). An Outline of Psycho-Analysis. In J. Strachey (Ed. and Trans.), *The Standard Edition of the Complete Psychological Works of Sigmund Freud*, vol. 23 (pp. 139–207). London: The Hogarth Press and the Institute of Psycho-Analysis.

Freud, S. (1964[1940*e*]). Splitting of the Ego in the Process of Defence. In J. Strachey (Ed. and Trans.), *The Standard Edition of the Complete Psychological Works of Sigmund Freud*, vol. 23 (pp. 271–278). London: The Hogarth Press and the Institute of Psycho-Analysis.

Freud, S. (1966[1950*a*]). Project for a Scientific Psychology. In J. Strachey (Ed. and Trans.), *The Standard Edition of the Complete Psychological Works of Sigmund*

Freud, vol. 1 (pp. 281–397). London: The Hogarth Press and the Institute of Psycho-Analysis.
Frey, K. (1878). Der Protagonist in der Antigone des Sophokles. *Neue Jahrbücher—Abteilung 1*, 117: 460–464.
Fromm, E. (1959[1948]). The Oedipus Complex and the Oedipus Myth. In R. N. Anshen (Ed.), *The Family: Its Function and Destiny*, revised edition (pp. 334–358). New York, NY: Harper & Brothers.
Fuechtner, V. (2011). *Berlin Psychoanalytic: Psychoanalysis and Culture in Weimar Republic Germany and Beyond*. Berkeley/Los Angeles, CA-London: University of California Press.
Funke, H. (1996). Bernays und die Aristotelische Poetik. In J. Glucker and A. Laks (Eds), *Jacob Bernays. Un philologue juif* (pp. 59–75). Villeneuve-d'Ascq: Presses Universitaires du Septentrion.
Furedi, F. (2003). *Therapy Culture: Cultivating Vulnerability in an Uncertain Age*. London-New York, NY: Routledge.
Gallop, J. (1982). *The Daughter's Seduction: Feminism and Psychoanalysis*. Ithaca, NY-London: Cornell University Press.
Gamwell, L. and Wells, R. (Eds) (1989). *Sigmund Freud and Art: His Personal Collection of Antiquities*. New York, NY: Abrams.
Garnier, R. (2000[1580]). *Antigone ou la piété. Tragédie humaniste*. J.-D. Beaudin (Ed.). Paris: Honoré Champion.
Gasser, R. (1997). *Nietzsche und Freud*. Berlin-New York, NY: Walter de Gruyter.
Gaunt, S. and Kay, S. (Eds) (1999). *The Troubadours: An Introduction*. Cambridge: Cambridge University Press.
Gay, V. P. (1992). *Freud on Sublimation: Reconsiderations*. Albany, NY: State University of New York Press.
Geblesco, E. (2008). *Un amour de transfert. Journal de mon contrôle avec Lacan (1974–1981)*. Paris: EPEL.
Gemes. K. (2009). Freud and Nietzsche on Sublimation. *Journal of Nietzsche Studies*, 38(1): 38–59.
Genette, G. (1966). *Figures*. Paris: du Seuil.
Gherovici, P. and Steinkoler, M. (2020). The Situation of Psychoanalysis and the Training of Psychoanalysts in 1956. In D. Hook, C. Neill and S. Vanheule (Eds), *Reading Lacan's* Écrits: *From 'The Freudian Thing' to 'Remarks on Daniel Lagache'* (pp. 104–130). London-New York, NY: Routledge.
Gibeault, A (1989). Symbolique de l'argent et psychanalyse. *Communications*, 50: 51–79.
Giroud, F. (1990). *Leçons particulières*. Paris: Fayard.
Glover, E. (1931). Sublimation, Substitution and Social Anxiety. *The International Journal of Psycho-Analysis*, 12(3): 263–297.
Glynos, J. (2011). On the Ideological and Political Significance of Fantasy in the Organization of Work. *Psychoanalysis, Culture and Society*, 16: 373–393.
Godin, J.-G. (1990). *Jacques Lacan, 5 rue de Lille*. Paris: du Seuil.
Goebel, E. (2012[2009]). *Beyond Discontent: 'Sublimation' from Goethe to Lacan*. J. C. Wagner (Trans.). London: Continuum.
Golden, L. (1978). Hamartia, Ate, and Oedipus. *The Classical World*, 72(1): 3–12.

González Moreno, B. (2007). *Lo sublime, lo gótico y lo romántico: La experiencia estética en el romanticismo inglés*. Cuenca: Ediciones de la Universidad de Castilla-La Mancha.
Goux, J.-J. (1990[1973–1978]). *Symbolic Economies. After Marx and Freud*. J. Curtiss Gage (Trans.). Ithaca, NY-London: Cornell University Press.
Greimas, A. J. (1983[1966]). *Structural Semantics: An Attempt at a Method*. D. McDowell, R. Schleifer and A. Velie (Trans.). Lincoln NE-London: The University of Nebraska Press.
Griffith, M. (2005). The Subject of Desire in Sophocles' *Antigone*. In V. Pedrick and S. M. Oberhelman (Eds), *The Soul of Tragedy: Essays on Athenian Drama* (pp. 91–135). Chicago, IL-London: The University of Chicago Press.
Griffith, M. (2010). Psychoanalysing Antigone. In S. E. Wilmer & A. Žukauskaitė (Eds), *Interrogating Antigone in Postmodern Philosophy and Criticism* (pp. 110–134). Oxford: Oxford University Press.
Grigg, R. (2019). Corrections. *The Lacanian Review: Journal of the New Lacanian School and the World Association of Psychoanalysis*, 7: 237.
Grimstad, P. (2013). *Experience and Experimental Writing: Literary Pragmatism from Emerson to the Jameses*. New York, NY-Oxford: Oxford University Press.
Groot, G. (2015). Anti-Antigone. In M. De Kesel and B. Schomakers (Eds), *De schoonheid van het nee. Essays over Antigone* (pp. 69–89). Amsterdam: Sjibbolet.
Grubrich-Simitis, I. (Ed.) (1987). *Sigmund Freud. A Phylogenetic Fantasy: Overview of the Transference Neuroses*. A. Hoffer and P. T. Hoffer (Trans.). Cambridge MA-London: The Belknap Press of Harvard University Press.
Grünbaum, A. (1984). *The Foundations of Psychoanalysis: A Philosophical Critique*. Berkeley/Los Angeles, CA-London: The University of California Press.
Guéguen, P.-G. (2012). *Etre en analyse: la séance courte, l'argent et la vérité*. https://www.causefreudienne.net/etre-en-analyse-la-seance-courte-largent-et-la-verite/ accessed on 12 May 2021.
Guyomard, P. (1991). Sur l'éclat d'Antigone. In M. Cardot, Y. Duroux, P. Guyomard, Ph. Lacoue-Labarthe and R. Major (Eds), *Lacan avec les philosophes* (pp. 61–66). Paris: Albin Michel.
Guyomard, P. (1992). *La jouissance du tragique. Antigone, Lacan et le désir de l'analyste*. Paris: Aubier-Flammarion.
Haddad, G. (2002). *Le jour où Lacan m'a adopté*. Paris: Grasset.
Hahn, G. (1883). *Les phénomènes hystériques et les révélations de Sainte Thérèse*. Bruxelles: Alfred Vromant.
Harari, R. (1988). Un doble lapsus de Lacan. *Revista de Psicoterapia psicoanalítica*, 2: 417–430.
Harding, N. (2007). On Lacan and the Becoming-ness of Organizations/Selves. *Organization Studies*, 28: 1761–1773.
Harmand, C. (1993). La traversée du fantasme. *Letterina—Bulletin de l'ACF Normandie*, 5: 21–27.
Harris, O. (2017). *Lacan's Return to Antiquity: Between Nature and the Gods*. London-New York, NY: Routledge.
Harrison, T. (2000). *Bion, Rickman, Foulkes and the Northfield Experiments: Advancing on a Different Front*. London: Jessica Kingsley.

Harvey, R. (1999). Courtly Culture in Medieval Occitania. In S. Gaunt and S. Kay (Eds), *The Troubadours: An Introduction* (pp. 8–27). Cambridge: Cambridge University Press.

Hayes, T. (1999). A Jouissance Beyond the Phallus: Juno, Saint Teresa, Bernini, Lacan. *American Imago*, 56(4): 331–355.

Heath, S. (1978–1979). Difference. *Screen*, 19(3): 51–112.

Hegel, G. W. F. (1955[1819–1830]). *Lectures on the History of Philosophy*, vol. 1. E. S. Haldane (Trans.). London: Routledge & Kegan Paul.

Hegel, G. W. F. (1975[1820–1829]). *Aesthetics: Lectures on Fine Art*. vol. 1. T. M. Knox (Trans.). Oxford: Clarendon Press.

Hegel, G. W. F. (1989[1796]). Jedes Volk ... In *Gesammelte Werke. Vol. 1: Frühe Schriften* (pp. 359–378). F. Nicolin and G. Schüler (Eds). Hamburg: Felix Meiner Verlag.

Hegel, G. W. F. (1998[1835]). Symbolism of the Sublime. In *Aesthetics: Lectures on Fine Art*. vol. 1. (pp. 362–377). T. M. Knox (Trans.). Oxford: Clarendon Press.

Hegel, G. W. F. (2018[1807]). *The Phenomenology of Spirit*. T. Pinkard (Trans.). Cambridge: Cambridge University Press.

Heidegger, M. (1954). *Vorträge und Aufsätze*. Pfullingen: Günther Neske.

Heidegger, M. (1954[1950]). Das Ding. In *Vorträge und Aufsätze* (pp. 163–181). Pfullingen: Günther Neske.

Heidegger, M. (1954[1951]). Logos. In *Vorträge und Aufsätze* (pp. 207–229). Pfullingen: Günther Neske.

Heidegger, M. (1956[1951]). Logos. J. Lacan (Trans.). *La psychanalyse* 1: 59–79.

Heidegger, M. (1964[1927]). *L'Être et le temps*. R. Boehm and A. de Waelhens (Trans.). Paris: Gallimard.

Heidegger, M. (1968[1954]). *What Is Called Thinking?*. F. D. Wieck and J. G. Gray (Trans.). New York, NY-London: Harper & Row.

Heidegger, M. (1996[1984]). *Hölderlin's Hymn "The Ister"*. W. McNeill and J. David (Trans.). Bloomington/Indianapolis, IN-London: Indiana University Press.

Heidegger, M. (2000[1953]). *Introduction to Metaphysics*. G. Fried and R. Polt (Trans.). New Haven, CT-London: Yale University Press.

Heidegger, M. (2002[1954]). *Was heißt Denken?. Gesamtausgabe. I. Abteilung: Veröffentlichte Schriften 1910-1976. Band 8*. Frankfurt am Main: Vittorio Klostermann.

Heller-Roazen, D. (2008). *Echolalias: On the Forgetting of Language*. New York, NY: Zone Books.

Hendrickx, W. (2001). Kuifje in Congo (1): Oog in oog met het monster. *Humo*, 27 February: 42–47.

Hendrix, J. S. (2006). *Architecture and Psychoanalysis: Peter Eisenman and Jacques Lacan*. New York, NY: Peter Lang.

Herodotus (2014). *The Histories*. T. Holland (Trans.). London: Penguin Books.

Herron, W. G. and Rouslin Welt, S. (1992). *Money Matters: The Fee in Psychotherapy and Psychoanalysis*. New York, NY-London: The Guilford Press.

Hertz, N. (2009[1985]). *The End of the Line: Essays on Psychoanalysis and the Sublime*. 2nd Expanded Edition. Aurora, CO: The Davies Group Publishers.

Hibbard, H. (1965). *Bernini*. London: Pelican Books.

Higgins, K. M. (2000). *Comic Relief: Nietzsche's Gay Science*. New York, NY-Oxford: Oxford University Press.

Hinrichs, H. F. W. (1827). *Das Wesen der antiken Tragödie in ästhetischen Vorlesungen*. Halle: Friedrich Ruff.

Hobson, J. A. (2002). *Dreaming: An Introduction to the Science of Sleep*. Oxford-New York: Oxford University Press.

Hobson, J. A. (2011). *Dream Life: An Experimental Memoir*. Cambridge, MA-London: The MIT Press.

Hobson, J. A. and McCarley, R. W. (1977). The Brain as a Dream State Generator: An Activation-Synthesis Hypothesis of the Dream Process. *American Journal of Psychiatry*, 134: 1335–1348.

Hollywood, A. (2002). *Sensible Ecstasy: Mysticism, Sexual Difference, and the Demands of History*. Chicago, IL-London: The University of Chicago Press.

Homer, S. (2005). *Jacques Lacan*. London-New York, NY: Routledge.

Honig, B. (2013). *Antigone, Interrupted.* Cambridge: Cambridge University Press.

Houbbalah, A. (2007). Contrôle avec Lacan. In A. Didier-Weill and M. Safouan (Eds), *Travailler avec Lacan* (pp. 49–56). Paris: Aubier.

Hugo, V. (2002). *Écrits politiques*. Paris: Le livre de poche.

Huizinga, J. (1949[1944]). *Homo Ludens: A Study of the Play-Element in Culture*. London: Routledge and Kegan Paul.

Hunt, J. (1995). *Absence to Presence: The Life History of Sylvia [Bataille] Lacan*. Doctoral Dissertation, Rice University.

Hunt, J. (1998). The Mirrored Stage: Reflections on the Presence of Sylvia [Bataille] Lacan. In P. Phelan and J. Lane (Eds), *The Ends of Performance* (pp. 236–246). New York, NY-London: New York University Press.

Hurst, A. (2008). *Derrida vis-à-vis Lacan: Interweaving Deconstruction and Psychoanalysis*. New York, NY: Fordham University Press.

Huxley, T. H. (1894[1880]). On the Method of Zadig. In *Science and Hebrew Tradition: Essays* (pp. 1–23). New York, NY: D. Appleton & Company.

Hyde, I. (1963). The Tragic Flaw: Is It a Tragic Error? *Modern Language Review*, 58(3): 321–325.

Hyppolite, J. (1956). Commentaire parlé sur la *Verneinung* de Freud. *La psychanalyse*, 1: 29–40.

Hyppolite, J. (1971[1956]). Commentaire parlé sur la *Verneinung* de Freud. In *Figures de la pensée philosophique. Écrits 1931-1968*. Tôme 1 (pp. 385–396). Paris: Presses Universitaires de France.

Hyppolite, J. (1988[1956]). A Spoken Commentary on Freud's *Verneinung*. In J. Lacan, *The Seminar. Book I: Freud's Papers on Technique (1953-'54)* (pp. 289–297). J.-A. Miller (Ed.). J. Forrester (Trans.). Cambridge: Cambridge University Press.

Hyppolite, J. (2006[1956]). Appendix I: A Spoken Commentary on Freud's 'Verneinung' by Jean Hyppolite. In J. Lacan, *Écrits* (pp. 746–754). B. Fink (Trans.). New York, NY-London: W. W. Norton & Company.

Irigaray, L. (1976). Così Fan Tutti. In A. Verdiglione (Ed.), *La jouissance et la loi* (pp. 219–238). Paris: Union Générale d'Éditions.

Irigaray, L. (1977[1976]). Così Fan Tutti. In *Ce sexe qui n'en est pas un* (pp. 83–101). Paris: Minuit.

Irigarary, L. (1985[1974]). The Eternal Irony of the Community. In *Speculum of the Other Woman* (pp. 214–226). G. G. Gill (Trans). Ithaca, NY-London: Cornell University Press.

Irigarary, L. (1985[1976]). Così Fan Tutti. In *This Sex Which is Not One* (pp. 86–105). C. Porter and C. Burke (Trans.). Ithaca, NY-London: Cornell University Press.

Jacob, A. L. G. (1821). *Sophocleae Quaestiones. Praemittuntur Disputationes de Tragoediae Origine et de Tragicorum Graecorum cum Republica Necessitudine.* Volumen Primum. Varsaviae: Impensis Auctoris.

Jacobs, C. (1996). Dusting Antigone. *MLN*, 111(5): 889–917.

Jacquot, B. (2003). Television. B. P. Fulks and J. Jauregui (Trans.). *Lacanian Ink*, 21: 86–89.

Jacquot, B. (2012). How Lacan. A. Alvarez (Trans.). *Lacanian Ink*, 39: 66–77.

Jagentowicz Mills, P. (1986). Hegel's Antigone. *The Owl of Minerva*, 17(2): 131–152.

jagodzinski, j. (2005). *Music in Youth Culture: A Lacanian Approach*. Basingstoke-New York, NY: Palgrave Macmillan.

Jagose, A. (2013). *Orgasmology*. Durham, NC-London: Duke University Press.

Jakobson, R. (1968[1940–1942]). *Child Language, Aphasia, and Phonological Universals.* A. R. Keiler (Trans.). The Hague: Mouton.

Janáček, L. (2009). *Écrits*. Paris: Fayard.

Janaway, C. (2013). The Gay Science. In K. Gemes and J. Richardson (Eds), *The Oxford Handbook of Nietzsche* (pp. 252–271). Oxford-New York, NY: Oxford University Press.

Janicaud, D. (2001). *Heidegger en France. II: Entretiens*. Paris: Albin Michel.

Jaques, E. (1951). *The Changing Culture of a Factory*. London: Tavistock Publications.

Jaramillo, J. I. (2010). La Antígona de Lacan: Comentario al apartado 'La esencia de la tragedia' del Seminario 7, La ética del psicoanálisis. *Affectio Societatis*, 7(12): 1–15.

Jebb, R. C. (1900). Appendix. In *Sophocles. The Plays and Fragments. Part 3. The Antigone* (pp. 258–265). R. C. Jebb (Trans.). Cambridge: Cambridge University Press.

Jentsch, E. (1997[1906]). On the Psychology of the Uncanny. R. Sellars (Trans.). *Angelaki: Journal of the Theoretical Humanities*, 2(1): 7–16.

Johnsen, R. and Gudmand-Høyer, M. (2010). Lacan and the Lack of Humanity in HRM. *Organization*, 17: 331–344.

Jones, C. and Spicer, A. (2005). The Sublime Object of Entrepreneurship. *Organization*, 12: 223–246.

Jones, E. (1953). *The Life and Work of Sigmund Freud. Vol. 1: The Formative Years and the Great Discoveries (1856-1900)*. New York, NY: Basic Books.

Jones, E. (1957). *The Life and Work of Sigmund Freud. Vol. 3: The Last Phase (1919-1939)*. New York, NY: Basic Books.

Joyce, J. (1939). *Finnegans Wake*. London: Faber & Faber.

Jung, C. G. (1970[1963]). Mysterium Coniunctionis: An Inquiry into the Separation and Synthesis of Psychic Opposites in Alchemy. G. Adler and R. F. C. Hull (Trans.). In *The Collected Works of C. G. Jung.* vol. 14. Princeton, NJ: Princeton University Press.

Kant, I. (1997[1788]). *Critique of Practical Reason.* M. Gregor (Trans). Cambridge: Cambridge University Press.
Kant, I. (1998[1781]). *Critique of Pure Reason.* P. Guyer and A. W. Wood (Trans.). Cambridge: Cambridge University Press.
Kant, I. (2007[1790]). *Critique of Judgement.* N. Walker (Ed.). J. Creed Meredith (Trans.). Oxford: Oxford University Press.
Kant, I. (2011[1764]). Observations on the Feeling of the Beautiful and Sublime. P. Guyer (Trans.). In *Observations on the Feeling of the Beautiful and Sublime and Other Writings* (pp. 9–62). P. Frierson and P. Guyer (Eds). Cambridge: Cambridge University Press.
Kanzer, M. (1950). The Oedipus Trilogy. *The Psychoanalytic Quarterly*, 19(4): 561–572.
Kaufmann, W. (2013[1950]). *Nietzsche: Philosopher, Psychologist, Antichrist.* Princeton, NJ-Oxford: Princeton University Press.
Kaufmann, W. (1974). Translator's Introduction. In F. Nietzsche, *The Gay Science, With a Prelude in Rhymes and an Appendix of Songs* (pp. 3–26). W. Kaufmann (Trans.). New York, NY: Vintage.
Kaufmann, W. (1979[1968]). *Tragedy and Philosophy.* Princeton, NJ-London: Princeton University Press.
Kenny, K. (2009). Heeding the Stains: Lacan and Organizational Change. *Journal of Organizational Change Management*, 22: 214–228.
Khan, M. M. R. (1982). Returning to Freud: Clinical Psychoanalysis in the School of Lacan: Selections Edited and Translated by Stuart Schneiderman. New Haven: Yale University Press. 1980. Pp. 265. (Book Review). *The International Journal of Psycho-Analysis*, 63(1): 95–96.
King, P. (2003). Introduction: The Rediscovery of John Rickman and His Work. In *No Ordinary Psychoanalyst: The Exceptional Contributions of John Rickman* (pp. 1–68). P. King (Ed.). London-New York, NY: Karnac Books.
Kirkwood, G. M. (1994[1958]). *A Study of Sophoclean Drama.* New Edition. Ithaca, NY: Cornell University Press.
Kitto, H. D. F. (1956). *Form and Meaning in Drama: A Study of Six Greek Plays and of* Hamlet. London: Methuen.
Klein, M. (1993[1957]). Envy and Gratitude. In *Envy and Gratitude and Other Works 1946-1963* (pp. 176–235). London: Karnac Books and the Institute of Psycho-Analysis.
Knox, B. (1979[1968]). Review: Sophokles, *Antigone*. In *Word and Action: Essays on the Ancient Theater* (pp. 165–182). Baltimore, MD-London: The Johns Hopkins University Press.
Knox, B. (1984). Antigone—Introduction. In Sophocles, *The Three Theban Plays: Antigone, Oedipus the King, Oedipus at Colonus* (pp. 35–53). R. Fagles (Trans.). London: Penguin Books.
Knox, B. (1989[1984]). The Life of a Legend. In *Essays Ancient & Modern* (pp. 129–136). Baltimore, MD: The Johns Hopkins University Press.
Köhler, J. (2002[1989]). *Zarathustra's Secret: The Interior Life of Friedrich Nietzsche.* R. Taylor (Trans.). New Haven, CT-London: Yale University Press.

Kojève, A. (1969[1947]). *Introduction to the Reading of Hegel: Lectures on the Phenomenology of Spirit*. A. Bloom (Ed.). J. H. Nichols, Jr. (Trans.). Ithaca, NY-London: Cornell University Press.

Kojève, A. (2017[1947]). *Introduction à la lecture de Hegel*. R. Queneau (Ed.). Paris: Gallimard.

Kosmala, K. and Herrbach, O. (2006). The Ambivalence of Professional Identity: On Cynicism and Jouissance in Audit Firms. *Human Relations*, 59: 1393–1428.

Kowsar, M. (1990). Lacan's *Antigone*: A Case Study in Psychoanalytical Ethics. *Theatre Journal*, 42(1): 94–103.

Koyré, A. (1929). *La philosophie de Jacob Boehme*. Paris: J. Vrin.

Kripal, J. (1995). *Kali's Child: The Mystical and the Erotic in the Life and Teachings of Ramakrishna*. Chicago, IL-London: The University of Chicago Press.

Krueger, D. W. (Ed.) (1986). *The Last Taboo: Money as Symbol and Reality in Psychotherapy and Psychoanalysis*. New York, NY: Brunner/Mazel.

Kusnierek, M. (1986). Le gay sçavoir, un affect lacanien? *Quarto*, 25: 3.

Labbie, E. F. (2006). *Lacan's Medievalism*. Minneapolis, MN-London: University of Minnesota Press.

Lacan, J. (1931). Structure des psychoses paranoïaques. *La semaine des hôpitaux de Paris*, 14(7 juillet): 437–445.

Lacan, J. (1933a). Sur le problème des hallucinations. *L'encéphale*, 8: 686–695.

Lacan, J. (1933b). Hiatus Irrationalis. *Le Phare de Neuilly*, 3-4: 37.

Lacan, J. (1947). La psychiatrie anglaise et la guerre. *L'évolution psychiatrique*, 1: 293-42.

Lacan, J. (1949). Intervention sur l'exposé de F. Pasche: 'La délinquance névrotique'. *Revue française de psychanalyse*, 13(2): 315.

Lacan, J. (1957). Clefs pour la psychanalyse. *L'express*, 310(31 mai): 20–22.

Lacan, J. (1961–1962). *Le Séminaire IX: L'identification*. unpublished.

Lacan, J. (1965–1966). *Le Séminaire XIII: L'objet de la psychanalyse*. unpublished.

Lacan, J. (1966a). *Écrits*. Paris: du Seuil.

Lacan, J. (1966b). *Écrits*. Paris: du Seuil, copy dedicated to Jean Beaufret, private collection.

Lacan, J. (1966c). *Écrits*. Paris: du Seuil, copy dedicated to Maud and Dominique-Octave Mannoni, private collection.

Lacan, J. (1966[1953]). Fonction et champ de la parole et du langage en psychanalyse. In *Écrits* (pp. 237–322). Paris: du Seuil.

Lacan, J. (1966–1967). *Le Séminaire XIV: La logique du fantasme*. unpublished.

Lacan, J. (1967–1968). *Le Séminaire XV: L'acte psychanalytique*. unpublished.

Lacan, J. (1968). Discours de clôture des Journées sur les psychoses chez l'enfant. *Recherches*, 8: 143–152.

Lacan, J. (1970). *Écrits I*. Paris: du Seuil.

Lacan, J. (1971a). *Écrits II*. Paris: du Seuil.

Lacan, J. (1971b). *The Seminar. Book XVIII: On a Discourse That Might Not Be a Semblance*. C. Gallagher (Trans.). privately printed.

Lacan, J. (1972). Interventions sur l'exposé de P. Mathis, 'Remarques sur la fonction de l'argent dans la technique analytique' au Congrès de l'École freudienne de Paris sur La technique psychanalytique (Aix-en-Provence). *Lettres de l'École freudienne. Bulletin intérieur de l'École freudienne de Paris*, 9: 195–205.

Lacan, J. (1972[1956]). Seminar on 'The Purloined Letter'. J. Mehlman (Trans.). *Yale French Studies*, 48: 38–72.
Lacan, J. (1973). *Le Séminaire. Livre XI: Les quatre concepts fondamentaux de la psychanalyse (1964)*. J.-A. Miller (Ed.). Paris: du Seuil.
Lacan, J. (1973–1974). *Le Séminaire XXI: Les non-dupes errent*. unpublished.
Lacan, J. (1973–1980). *Schriften* I-III. N. Haas (Ed.). Ch. Creusot, W. Fietkau, N. Haas, H.-J. Rheinberger and S. M. Weber (Trans.). Olten-Freiburg: Walter Verlag.
Lacan, J. (1974[1966]). *Scritti*. G. B. Contri (Trans.). Torino: Einaudi.
Lacan, J. (1975a). *Le Séminaire. Livre XX: Encore*. J.-A. Miller (Ed.). Paris: du Seuil.
Lacan, J. (1975b). Le Séminaire XXII: R. S. I. Leçon de 11 mars 1975. *Ornicar?*, 5: 16–28.
Lacan (1975[1932]). De la psychose paranoïaque dans ses rapports avec la personnalité. In *De la psychose paranoïaque dans ses rapports avec la personnalité, suivi de Premiers écrits sur la paranoïa* (pp. 1–362). Paris: du Seuil.
Lacan, J. (1975[1933]). Le problème du style et la conception psychiatrique des formes paranoïaques de l'expérience. In *De la psychose paranoïaque dans ses rapports avec la personnalité, suivi de Premiers écrits sur la paranoïa* (pp. 383–388). Paris: du Seuil.
Lacan, J. (1975[1974]). La troisième. *Lettres de l'École freudienne. Bulletin intérieur de l'École freudienne de Paris*, 16: 177–203.
Lacan, J. (1976a). Letter to M. Masud R. Khan of 14 March 1976. Masud Khan Papers. Archives of the British Psycho-Analytic Society. Now destroyed.
Lacan, J. (1976b). Letter to M. Masud R. Khan of 15 August 1976. Masud Khan Papers. Archives of the British Psycho-Analytic Society. Now destroyed.
Lacan, J. (1976[1975*a*]). Interventions dans la séance de travail sur 'Du plus une'. *Lettres de l'École freudienne. Bulletin intérieur de l'École freudienne de Paris*, 18: 219–229.
Lacan, J. (1976[1949]). Règlement et doctrine de la commission de l'enseignement. In J.-A. Miller (Ed.). *La scission de 1953. La communauté psychanalytique en France—1* (pp. 29–36). Paris: Navarin.
Lacan, J. (1976[1975*b*]). Conférences et entretiens dans des universités nord-américaines. Yale University—Kanzer Seminar. 24 novembre 1975. *Scilicet*, 6/7: 7–31.
Lacan, J. (1977). *Écrits: A Selection*. A. Sheridan (Trans.). London: Tavistock.
Lacan, J. (1977[1933]). Hiatus Irrationalis. *Le magazine littéraire*, 121: 11.
Lacan, J. (1977[1973]). *The Four Fundamental Concepts of Psycho-Analysis*. J.-A. Miller (Ed.). A. Sheridan (Trans.). London: The Hogarth Press and the Institute of Psycho-Analysis.
Lacan, J. (1977–1979[1976–1977]). Le Séminaire. Livre XXIV: L'insu que sait de l'une-bévue s'aile à mourre. *Ornicar?*, 12/13: 4–16; 14: 4-9; 15: 5-9; 16: 7-13; 17/18: 7–23.
Lacan, J. (1979). Joyce le symptôme. In J. Aubert and M. Jolas (Eds), *Joyce & Paris 1902... 1920–1940...1975. Actes du Cinquième Symposium International James Joyce. Paris 16-20 juin 1975* (pp. 13–17). Lille-Paris: Publications de l'Université Lille 3-Éditions du CNRS.

Lacan, J. (1979[1953]). The Neurotic's Individual Myth. M. N. Evans (Trans.). *The Psychoanalytic Quarterly*, 48(3): 405–425.
Lacan, J. (1979[1977]). Le moment de conclure. *Ornicar?*, 19: 5–9.
Lacan, J. (1979[1978]). Conclusions. *Lettres de l'École freudienne. Bulletin intérieur de l'École freudienne de Paris*, 25: 219–220.
Lacan, J. (1981[1972]). La mort est du domaine de la foi. *Quarto*, 3: 5–20.
Lacan, J. (1981[1980]). The Seminar, Caracas, July 12th 1980. O. Zentner (Trans.). *Papers of the Freudian School of Melbourne*, 2: 103–106.
Lacan, J. (1982). *Feminine Sexuality: Jacques Lacan and the école freudienne*. J. Mitchell and J. Rose (Eds). J. Rose (Trans.). New York, NY-London: W. W. Norton & Company.
Lacan, J. (1982[1972]). Jacques Lacan à l'Ecole belge de psychanalyse, le 14 octobre 1972. *Quarto*, 5: 4–23.
Lacan, J. (1982[1975]). Joyce le symptôme. J.-A. Miller (Ed.). *L'Âne: Le magazine freudien*, 6: 3–5.
Lacan, J. (1982[1980]). D'écolage. *École de la cause freudienne—Annuaire et textes statutaires* (pp. 14–16). Paris: ECF.
Lacan, J. (1982–1983[1961]). Merleau-Ponty: In Memoriam. W. Ver Eecke and D. De Schutter (Trans.). *Review of Existential Psychology and Psychiatry*, 18(1-3): 73–81.
Lacan, J. (1984[1938]). *Les complexes familiaux dans la formation de l'individu. Essai d'analyse d'une fonction en psychologie*. Paris: Navarin.
Lacan, J. (1986). *Le Séminaire. Livre VII: L'éthique de la psychanalyse (1959-'60)*. J.-A. Miller (Ed.). Paris: du Seuil.
Lacan, J. (1986[1947]). La psychiatrie anglaise et la guerre. In R. Gori, J.-A. Miller and R. Wartel (Eds). *La querelle des diagnostics* (pp. 15–42). Paris: Navarin.
Lacan, J. (1987[1947]). La psychiatrie anglaise et la guerre. *Bulletin de l'Association freudienne*, 22: 9–16.
Lacan, J. (1987[1965]). Homage to Marguerite Duras, on *Le ravissement de Lol V. Stein*. P. Connor (Trans.). In M. Duras, *Marguerite Duras* (pp. 122–129). San Francisco, CA: City Lights Books.
Lacan, J. (1987[1975]). Joyce le symptôme I. In J. Aubert (Ed.), *Joyce avec Lacan* (pp. 21–29). Paris: Navarin.
Lacan, J. (1987[1979]). Joyce le symptôme II. In J. Aubert (Ed.), *Joyce avec Lacan* (pp. 31–36). Paris: Navarin.
Lacan, J. (1988[1975]). *The Seminar. Book I: Freud's Papers on Technique (1953-'54)*. J.-A. Miller (Ed.). J. Forrester (Trans.). Cambridge: Cambridge University Press.
Lacan, J. (1988[1978]). *The Seminar. Book II: The Ego in Freud's Theory and in the Technique of Psychoanalysis (1954-'55)*. J.-A. Miller (Ed.). S. Tomaselli (Trans.). Cambridge: Cambridge University Press.
Lacan, J. (1989[1962]). Kant with Sade. J. B. Swenson, Jr. (Trans.). *October*, 51: 55–75.
Lacan, J. (1990). *Television/A Challenge to the Psychoanalytic Establishment*. J. Copjec (Ed.). D. Hollier, R. Krauss, A. Michelson and J. Mehlman (Trans.). New York, NY-London: W.W. Norton & Company.
Lacan, J. (1990[1960]). Letter to D. W. Winnicott. J. Mehlman (Trans.). In J. Lacan, *Television/A Challenge to the Psychoanalytic Establishment* (pp. 75–77). J. Copjec

(Ed.). D. Hollier, R. Kraus, A. Michelson and J. Mehlman (Trans.). New York, NY-London: W. W. Norton & Company.

Lacan, J. (1990[1963]). Introduction to the Names-of-the-Father Seminar. J. Mehlman (Trans.). In *Television/A Challenge to the Psychoanalytic Establishment* (pp. 81–95). J. Copjec (Ed.). D. Hollier, R. Kraus, A. Michelson and J. Mehlman (Trans.). New York, NY: W. W. Norton & Company.

Lacan, J. (1990[1964]). Founding Act. J. Mehlman (Trans.). In *Television/A Challenge to the Psychoanalytic Establishment* (pp. 97–106). J. Copjec (Ed.). D. Hollier, R. Kraus, A. Michelson and J. Mehlman (Trans.). New York, NY: W. W. Norton & Company.

Lacan, J. (1990[1974]). Television. D. Hollier, R. Krauss and A. Michelson (Trans.). In *Television/A Challenge to the Psychoanalytic Establishment* (pp. 1–46). J. Copjec (Ed.) D. Hollier, R. Kraus, A. Michelson and J. Mehlman (Trans.). New York, NY-London: W.W. Norton & Company.

Lacan, J. (1990[1980]). Letter of Dissolution. J. Mehlman (Trans.). In *Television/A Challenge to the Psychoanalytic Establishment* (pp. 129–131). J. Copjec (Ed.). D. Hollier, R. Kraus, A. Michelson and J. Mehlman (Trans.). New York, NY: W. W. Norton & Company.

Lacan, J. (1991[1957]). Entretien avec Jacques Lacan. *l'Âne* 48: 28–33.

Lacan, J. (1992[1986]). *The Seminar. Book VII: The Ethics of Psychoanalysis (1959-'60)*. J.-A. Miller (Ed.). D. Porter (Trans.). New York, NY-London: W. W. Norton & Company.

Lacan, J. (1993[1981]). *The Seminar. Book III: The Psychoses (1955-'56)*. J.-A. Miller (Ed.). R. Grigg (Trans.). New York, NY-London: W. W. Norton & Company.

Lacan, J. (1994[1973]). *The Seminar. Book XI: The Four Fundamental Concepts of Psychoanalysis (1964)*. J-A. Miller (Ed.). A. Sheridan (Trans.). Harmondsworth: Penguin.

Lacan, J. (1994[1976]). Preface to the English-Language Edition. In *The Four Fundamental Concepts of Psycho-Analysis (1964)* (pp. xxxix–xli). A. Sheridan (Trans.). Harmondsworth: Penguin.

Lacan, J. (1995[1967]). Proposition of 9 October 1967 on the Psychoanalyst of the School. R. Grigg (Trans.). *analysis*, 6: 1–13.

Lacan, J. (1996[1966]). Presentation of the *Memoirs* of President Schreber in French Translation. A. J. Lewis (Trans.). *analysis*, 7: 1–4.

Lacan, J. (1998[1975]). *The Seminar. Book XX: On Feminine Sexuality, the Limits of Love and Knowledge (Encore) (1972-'73)*. J.-A. Miller (Ed.). B. Fink (Trans.). New York, NY: W. W. Norton & Company.

Lacan, J. (2000[1947]). British Psychiatry and the War. Ph. Dravers and V. Voruz (Trans.). *Psychoanalytical Notebooks of the London Circle*, 4: 9–33.

Lacan, J. (2000[1957]). Les clefs de la psychanalyse. *la célibataire*, 4: 99–104.

Lacan, J. (2000[1976]). De James Joyce comme symptôme. *Le croquant: Sciences humaines, Art, Littérature*, 28: 29–36.

Lacan, J. (2001[1938]). Les complexes familiaux dans la formation de l'individu. Essai d'analyse d'une fonction en psychologie. In *Autres Écrits* (pp. 23–84). Paris: du Seuil.

Lacan, J. (2001[1945–1946]). Le nombre treize et la forme logique de la suspicion. In *Autres Écrits* (pp. 85–99). Paris: du Seuil.
Lacan, J. (2001[1947]). La psychiatrie anglaise et la guerre. In *Autres Écrits* (pp. 101–120). Paris: du Seuil.
Lacan, J. (2001[1953]). Discours de Rome. In *Autres Écrits* (pp. 133–164). Paris: du Seuil.
Lacan, J. (2001[1967a]). Discours à l'École freudienne de Paris. In *Autres Écrits* (pp. 261–281). Paris: du Seuil.
Lacan, J. (2001[1967b]). La méprise du sujet supposé savoir. In *Autres Écrits* (pp. 329–339). Paris: du Seuil.
Lacan, J. (2001[1968]). La psychanalyse. Raison d'un échec. In *Autres Écrits* (pp. 341–349). Paris: du Seuil.
Lacan, J. (2001[1970]). Radiophonie. In *Autres Écrits* (pp. 403–447). Paris: du Seuil.
Lacan, J. (2001[1971]). Lituraterre. In *Autres Écrits* (pp. 11–20). Paris: du Seuil.
Lacan, J. (2001[1972]). L'étourdit. In *Autres Écrits* (pp. 449–495). Paris: du Seuil.
Lacan, J. (2001[1973a]). Note italienne. In *Autres Écrits* (pp. 307–311). Paris: du Seuil.
Lacan, J. (2001[1973b]). Introduction à l'édition allemande d'un premier volume des *Écrits*. In *Autres Écrits* (pp. 553–559). Paris: du Seuil.
Lacan, J. (2001[1976]). Préface à l'édition anglaise du *Séminaire XI*. In *Autres Écrits* (pp. 571–573). Paris: du Seuil.
Lacan, J. (2001[1979]). Joyce le Symptôme. In *Autres Écrits* (pp. 565–570). Paris: du Seuil.
Lacan, J. (2004[1951]). Some Reflections on the Ego. *Journal for Lacanian Studies*, 2(2): 306–317.
Lacan, J. (2005[1975]). Joyce le symptôme. In *Le Séminaire. Livre XXIII: Le sinthome (1975-'76)* (pp. 161–169). J.-A. Miller (Ed.). Paris: du Seuil.
Lacan, J. (2006a). *Le Séminaire. Livre XVI: D'un Autre à l'autre (1968-'69)*. J.-A. Miller (Ed.). Paris: du Seuil.
Lacan, J. (2006b). *Le Séminaire. Livre XVIII: D'un discours qui ne serait pas du semblant (1971)*. J.-A. Miller (Ed.). Paris: du Seuil.
Lacan, J. (2006c). *Œuvres graphiques et manuscrits*. Paris: Artcurial Briest.
Lacan, J. (2006[1936]). Beyond the 'Reality Principle'. In *Écrits* (pp. 58–74). B. Fink (Trans.). New York, NY-London: W. W. Norton & Company.
Lacan, J. (2006[1945]). Logical Time and the Assertion of Anticipated Certainty: A New Sophism. In *Écrits* (pp. 161–175). B. Fink (Trans.). New York, NY-London: W. W. Norton & Company.
Lacan, J. (2006[1946]). Presentation on Psychical Causality. In *Écrits* (pp. 123–158). B. Fink (Trans.). New York, NY-London: W. W. Norton & Company.
Lacan, J. (2006[1949]). The Mirror Stage as Formative of the *I* Function as Revealed in Psychoanalytic Experience. In *Écrits* (pp. 75–81). B. Fink (Trans.). New York, NY-London: W. W. Norton & Company.
Lacan, J. (2006[1951]). Presentation on Transference. In *Écrits* (pp. 176–185). B. Fink (Trans.). New York, NY-London: W. W. Norton & Company.
Lacan, J. (2006[1953]). The Function and Field of Speech and Language in Psychoanalysis. In *Écrits* (pp. 197–268). B. Fink (Trans.). New York, NY: W.W. Norton & Company.

Lacan, J. (2006[1954]). Response to Jean Hyppolite's Commentary on Freud's 'Verneinung'. In *Écrits* (pp. 318–333). B. Fink (Trans.). New York, NY: W. W. Norton & Company.

Lacan, J. (2006[1955a]). Variations on the Standard Treatment. In *Écrits* (pp. 269–302). B. Fink (Trans.). New York, NY: W.W. Norton & Company.

Lacan, J. (2006[1955b]). The Freudian Thing, or the Meaning of the Return to Freud in Psychoanalysis. In *Écrits* (pp. 334–363). B. Fink (Trans.). New York, NY: W. W. Norton & Company.

Lacan, J. (2006[1956]). The Situation of Psychoanalysis and the Training of Psychoanalysts in 1956. In *Écrits* (pp. 384–411). B. Fink (Trans.). New York, NY-London: W. W. Norton & Company.

Lacan, J. (2006[1957a]). Seminar on 'The Purloined Letter'. In *Écrits* (pp. 6–48). B. Fink (Trans.). New York, NY-London: W. W. Norton & Company.

Lacan, J. (2006[1957b]). Psychoanalysis and Its Teaching. In *Écrits* (pp. 364–383). B. Fink (Trans.). New York, NY-London: W. W. Norton & Company

Lacan, J. (2006[1957c]). The Instance of the Letter in the Unconscious, or Reason Since Freud. In *Écrits* (pp. 412–441). B. Fink (Trans.). New York, NY-London: W. W. Norton & Company.

Lacan, J. (2006[1958a]). The Direction of the Treatment and the Principles of its Power. In *Écrits* (pp. 489–542). B. Fink (Trans.). New York, NY: W. W. Norton & Company.

Lacan, J. (2006[1958b]). The Signification of the Phallus. In *Écrits* (pp. 575–584). B. Fink (Trans.). New York, NY-London: W. W. Norton & Company.

Lacan, J. (2006[1959]). On a Question Prior to Any Possible Treatment of Psychosis. In *Écrits* (pp. 445–488). B. Fink (Trans.). New York, NY-London: W. W. Norton & Company.

Lacan, J. (2006[1960]). The Subversion of the Subject and the Dialectic of Desire in the Freudian Unconscious. In *Écrits* (pp. 671–702). B. Fink (Trans.). New York, NY-London: W. W. Norton & Company.

Lacan, J. (2006[1961]). Appendix II: Metaphor of the Subject. In *Écrits* (pp. 755–758). B. Fink (Trans.). New York, NY-London: W. W. Norton & Company.

Lacan, J. (2006[1962]). Kant with Sade. In *Écrits* (pp. 645–668). B. Fink (Trans.). New York, NY-London: W. W. Norton & Company.

Lacan, J. (2006[1964]). Position of the Unconscious. In *Écrits* (pp. 703–721). B. Fink (Trans.). New York, NY-London: W. W. Norton & Company.

Lacan, J. (2006[1965]). Science and Truth. In *Écrits* (pp. 726–745). B. Fink (Trans.). New York, NY-London: W. W. Norton & Company.

Lacan, J. (2006[1966a]). *Écrits*. B. Fink (Trans.). New York, NY-London: W. W. Norton & Company.

Lacan, J. (2006[1966b]). Overture to this Collection. In *Écrits* (pp. 3–5). B. Fink (Trans.). New York, NY-London: W. W. Norton & Company.

Lacan, J. (2006[1966c]). On My Antecedents. In *Écrits* (pp. 51–57). B. Fink (Trans.). New York, NY-London: W. W. Norton & Company.

Lacan, J. (2006[1966d]). Remarks made at the 1960 Bonneval Colloquium, rewritten in 1964. In *Écrits* (p. 703). B. Fink (Trans.). New York, NY-London: W. W. Norton & Company.

Lacan, J. (2007[1991]). The Seminar. *Book XVII, The Other Side of Psychoanalysis (1969-'70)*, J.-A. Miller (Ed.) R. Grigg, Trans., New York, NY: W.W. Norton & Company.
Lacan, J. (2008[2005]). My Teaching, its Nature and its Ends. In *My Teaching* (pp. 57–89). D. Macey (Trans.). London-New York, NY: Verso.
Lacan, J. (2011[1974]). La troisième. *La cause freudienne. Nouvelle revue de psychanalyse*, 79: 11–33.
Lacan, J. (2013[1953]). The Symbolic, the Imaginary, and the Real. In *On the Names-of-the-Father* (pp. 1–52). B. Fink (Trans.). Cambridge-Malden, MA: Polity.
Lacan, J. (2013[1971*a*]). Lituraterre. D. Nobus (Trans.). *Continental Philosophy Review*, 46(2): 327–334.
Lacan, J. (2013[1971*b*]). Lituraterre. B. Khiara-Foxton and A. Price (Trans.). *Hurly-Burly: The International Lacanian Journal of Psychoanalysis*, 9: 29–38.
Lacan, J. (2013[2005]). The Triumph of Religion. In *The Triumph of Religion preceded by Discourse to Catholics* (pp. 53–85). B. Fink (Trans.). Cambridge-Malden, MA: Polity Press.
Lacan, J. (2014[2004]). *The Seminar. Book X: Anxiety (1962-'63)*. J.-A. Miller (Ed.). A. R. Price (Trans.). Cambridge-Malden, MA: Polity.
Lacan, J. (2015[2001]). *The Seminar. Book VIII: Transference (1960-'61)*. J.-A. Miller (Ed.). B. Fink (Trans.). Cambridge-Malden, MA: Polity.
Lacan, J. (2016[1975]). Joyce the Symptom. In *The Seminar. Book XXIII: The Sinthome (1975-'76)* (pp. 141–148). J.-A. Miller (Ed.). A. R. Price (Trans.). Cambridge-Malden, MA: Polity.
Lacan, J. (2016[2005]). *The Seminar. Book XXIII: The Sinthome (1975-'76)*. J.-A. Miller Ed.). A. R. Price (Trans.). Cambridge-Malden, MA: Polity.
Lacan, J. (2017[1998]). *The Seminar. Book V: Formations of the Unconscious (1957-'58)*. J.-A. Miller (Ed.). R. Grigg (Trans.). Cambridge-Malden, MA: Polity.
Lacan, J. (2017[2011]). *Talking to Brick Walls: A Series of Presentations in the Chapel at Sainte-Anne Hospital (1971-'72)*. A. R. Price (Trans.). Cambridge-Medford, MA: Polity.
Lacan, J. (2018[1976]). Preface to the English Edition of *Seminar XI*. R. Grigg (Trans.). *The Lacanian Review: Journal of the New Lacanian School and the World Association of Psychoanalysis*, 6: 23–27.
Lacan, J. (2018[1979]). Joyce the Symptom. A. R. Price (Trans.). *The Lacanian Review: Journal of the New Lacanian School and the World Association of Psychoanalysis*, 5: 13–18.
Lacan, J. (2018[2011]). *The Seminar. Book XIX: … or Worse (1971-'72)*, J.-A. Miller (Ed.). A. R. Price (Trans.). Cambridge-Malden, MA: Polity Press.
Lacan, J. (2019[1947]). British Psychiatry and the War. Ph. Dravers and V. Voruz (Trans.). *Psychoanalytical Notebooks*, 33: 13–57.
Lacan, J. (2019[1974]). The Third. Ph. Dravers (Trans.). *The Lacanian Review: Journal of the New Lacanian School and the World Association of Psychoanalysis*, 7: 83–109.
Lacan, J. (2019[2013]). *The Seminar. Book VI: Desire and Its Interpretation (1958-'59)*. J.-A. Miller (Ed.). B. Fink (Trans.). Cambridge-Medford, MA: Polity.

Lacan, J. (2020[1933]). Motives of Paranoiac Crimes. The Crime of the Papin Sisters. R. Grigg (Trans.). *The Lacanian Review: Journal of the New Lacanian School and the World Association of Psychoanalysis*, 10: 17–31.
Lacan, J. (2020[1974]). The Lacanian Phenomenon. D. Collins (Trans.). *The Lacanian Review: Journal of the New Lacanian School and the World Association of Psychoanalysis*, 9: 17–43.
Lacan, J. (2020[1994]). *The Seminar. Book IV: The Object Relation (1956-'57)*. J.-A. Miller (Ed.). A. R. Price (Trans.). Cambridge-Medford, MA: Polity.
Lacan, J. and Cénac, M. (2006[1950]). A Theoretical Introduction to the Functions of Psychoanalysis in Criminology. In J. Lacan, *Écrits* (pp. 102–122). B. Fink (Trans.). New York, NY: W. W. Norton & Company.
Lacoue-Labarthe, Ph. (1991). De l'éthique: à propos d'Antigone. In M. Cardot, Y. Duroux, P. Guyomard, Ph. Lacoue-Labarthe and R. Major (Eds), *Lacan avec les philosophes* (pp. 21–36). Paris: Albin Michel.
Lacoue-Labarthe, Ph. and Nancy, J.-L. (1990[1973]). *Le titre de la lettre. Une lecture de Lacan*. Paris: Galilée.
Lafont, R. (1966). Les 'Leys d'Amors' et la mutation de la conscience occitane. *Revue des langues romanes*, 76: 13–59.
Lagache, D. (1953). *Letter to Michael Balint of 26 November 1953*. Michael Balint Papers. Archives of the British Psycho-Analytic Society, London.
Langer, M. M. (2010). *Nietzsche's Gay Science: Dancing Coherence*. Basingstoke: Palgrave Macmillan.
Laplanche, J. (1980). *Problématiques III. La sublimation*. Paris: Presses Universitaires de France.
Laplanche, J. and Leclaire, S. (1966[1960]). L'inconscient: Une étude psychanalytique. In H. Ey (Ed.), *L'inconscient. VIe Colloque de Bonneval* (pp. 95–130). Paris: Desclée De Brouwer.
Laplanche, J. and Leclaire, S. (1972[1960]). The Unconscious: A Psychoanalytic Study. P. Coleman (Trans.). *Yale French Studies*, 48: 118–175.
Laplanche, J. and Pontalis, J.-B. (1967). *Vocabulaire de la psychanalyse*. Paris: Presses Universitaires de France.
Laplanche, J. and Pontalis, J.-B. (1973[1967]). *The Language of Psychoanalysis*. D. Nicholson-Smith (Trans.). New York, NY-London: W. W. Norton & Company.
Laurent, E. (1995). Alienation and Separation (1/2). In R. Feldstein, B. Fink and M. Jaanus (Eds). *Reading Seminar XI: Lacan's Four Fundamental Concepts of Psychoanalysis* (pp. 19–38). Albany, NY: State University of New York Press.
Laurent, E. (2002[1999]). The Purloined Letter and the Tao of the Psychoanalyst. M. Thomas and V. Woollard (Trans.). *Psychoanalytical Notebooks*, 9: 31–65.
Laurent, E. (2011). Lacan and Feminine Jouissance. M. Andersson (Trans.). *Lacanian Ink*, 38: 86–101.
Lauret, M. (2014). *L'énigme de la pulsion de mort. Pour une éthique de la joie*. Paris: Presses Universitaires de France.
Lavin, I. (2007). *Visible Spirit: The Art of Gianlorenzo Bernini*, vol. 1. London: The Pindar Press.
Leader, D. (1997). *Promises Lovers Make When It Gets Late*. London-Boston, MA: Faber and Faber.
Lebovits, A. (2007). Gai savoir. *La lettre mensuelle*, 258: 23–25.

Lee, J. S. (1990). *Jacques Lacan*. Amherst, MA: The University of Massachusetts Press.
Le Gaufey, G. (2012). *L'objet* a. *Approches de l'invention de Lacan*. Paris: EPEL.
Léglu, C. (2008). Language in Conflict in Toulouse: Las Leys d'Amors. *The Modern Language Review*, 103(2): 383–396.
Lehmann, H.-T. (1989). Das Erhabene ist das Unheimliche. Zur Theorie einer Kunst des Ereignisses. *Merkur: Deutsche Zeitschrift für europäisches Denken*, 43(487): 751–764.
Lehrer, R. (1995). *Nietzsche's Presence in Freud's Life and Thought: On the Origins of a Psychology of Dynamic Unconscious Mental Functioning*. Albany, NY: State University of New York Press.
Leonard, M. (2003). Antigone, the Political and the Ethics of Psychoanalysis. *The Cambridge Classical Journal*, 49(1): 130–154.
Leonard, M. (2005). *Athens in Paris: Ancient Greece and the Political in Post-War French Thought*. Oxford: Oxford University Press.
Leonard, M. (2006). Lacan, Irigaray, and Beyond: Antigones and the Politics of Psychoanalysis. In V. Zajko and M. Leonard (Eds), *Laughing With Medusa: Classical Myth and Feminist Thought* (pp. 121–139). Oxford: Oxford University Press.
Letiche, H. (2004). Jean Baudrillard. In S. Linstead (Ed.), *Organization Theory and Postmodern Thought* (pp. 127–148). London-Thousand Oaks-New Delhi: Sage.
Letiche, H. and Essers, J. (2004). Jean-François Lyotard. In S. Linstead (Ed.), *Organization Theory and Postmodern Thought* (pp. 64–87). London-Thousand Oaks, CA-New Delhi: Sage.
Levey, H. B. (1939). A Critique of the Theory of Sublimation. *Psychiatry: Journal for the Study of Interpersonal Processes*, 2(2): 239–270.
Lévi-Strauss, C. (1955). The Structural Study of Myth. *The Journal of American Folklore*, 68(270): 428–444.
Lévi-Strauss, C. (1958[1955]). La structure des mythes. In *Anthropologie structurale* (pp. 227–255). Paris: Plon.
Lévi-Strauss, C. (1960). *Leçon inaugurale, faite le 5 janvier 1960, Collège de France, Chaire d'anthropologie sociale*. Nogent-le-Rotrou: Daupeley-Gouverneur.
Lévi-Strauss, C. (1963[1955]). The Structural Study of Myth. In *Structural Anthropology* (pp. 206–231). C. Jacobson and B. Grundfest Schoepf (Trans.). New York, NY: Basic Books.
Lévi-Strauss, C. (1967[1960]). *The Scope of Anthropology*. S. Ortner Paul and R. A. Paul (Trans.). London: Jonathan Cape.
Lévi-Strauss, C. (1973[1966]). *From Honey to Ashes. Introduction to a Science of Mythology*, vol. 2, J. Weightman and D. Weightman (Trans.). London: Jonathan Cape.
Lévi-Strauss, C. (1983[1960]). The Scope of Anthropology. In *Structural Anthropology*, vol. 2 (pp. 3–32). M. Layton (Trans.). Chicago, IL-London: The University of Chicago Press.
Lévi-Strauss, C. and Éribon, D. (1991[1988]). *Conversations with Claude Lévi-Strauss*. Chicago, IL-London: The University of Chicago Press.
Lévy-Valensi, J., Migault, P. and Lacan, J. (1931). Troubles du langage écrit chez une paranoïaque présentant des éléments délirants du type paranoïde (schizographie). *Annales médico-psychologiques*, 13(2): 407–408.

Lévy-Valensi, J., Migault, P. and Lacan, J. (1975[1931]). Écrits 'inspirés': Schizographie. In J. Lacan, *De la psychose paranoïaque dans ses rapports avec la personnalité, suivi de Premiers écrits sur la paranoïa* (pp. 365–382). Paris: du Seuil.
Liart, M. (1996). La pulsion après la traversée du fantasme. *Quarto*, 60: 55–57.
Linstead, S. and Thanem, T. (2007). Multiplicity, Virtuality and Organization: The Contribution of Gilles Deleuze. *Organization Studies*, 28: 1483–1501.
Lomas, D. (2000). *The Haunted Self: Surrealism, Psychoanalysis, Subjectivity*. New Haven, CT-London: Yale University Press.
Longinus (1995). On the Sublime. W. H. Fyfe and D. Russell (Trans.). In *Aristotle/Poetics, Longinus/On the Sublime, and Demetrius/On Style* (pp. 159–305). Cambridge, MA: Harvard University Press.
Loraux, N. (1986). La main d'Antigone. *Mètis. Anthropologie des mondes grecs anciens* 1(2): 165–196.
Loraux, N. (1991). Antigone sans théâtre. In M. Cardot, Y. Duroux, P. Guyomard, Ph. Lacoue-Labarthe and R. Major (Eds), *Lacan avec les philosophes* (pp. 42–49). Paris: Albin Michel.
Loriot, P. (1966). Satisfaction au Seuil. *Le nouvel observateur*, 30 novembre-6 décembre: 37.
Loudmer, G. (1991). *Jacques Lacan: Lithographies, cartes—bibelots, sièges et meubles, divan d'analyse, table de travail*, Catalogue de 5 octobre 1991.
Luepnitz, D. A. (2020). Antigone and the Unsayable: A Psychoanalytic Reading. *American Imago*, 77(2): 345–364.
Lysy-Stevens, A. (1993a). Raser le sens: le gay sçavoir. *Quarto*, 51: 80–85.
Lysy-Stevens, A. (1993b). A propos du 'gay sçavoir'. *Les Feuillets du Courtil*, 6: 25–47.
Macey, D. (1988). *Lacan in Contexts*. London-New York, NY: Verso.
Macey, D. (1994). Introduction. In J. Lacan, *The Seminar. Book XI: The Four Fundamental Concepts of Psychoanalysis (1964)* (pp. vii–xxxviii). J-A. Miller (Ed.). A. Sheridan (Trans.). Harmondsworth: Penguin.
Macmillan, M. (1997). *Freud Evaluated: The Completed Arc*. Cambridge, MA-London: The MIT Press.
Major, R. (2001). *Lacan avec Derrida: Analyse désistentielle*. Paris: Flammarion.
Malévitch, K. (1975). *Écrits*. Paris: Champ libre.
Mannoni, M. (1964). *L'enfant arriéré et sa mère*. Paris: du Seuil.
Mannoni, O. (2003[1969]). 'I Know Well, But All the Same …'. G. M. Goshgarian (Trans.). In M. A. Rothenberg, D. Foster and S. Žižek (Eds), *Perversion and the Social Relation* (pp. 68–92). Durham, NC-London: Duke University Press.
Marcuse, H. (1966). *Eros and Civilization: A Philosophical Inquiry into Freud*. Boston, MA: Beacon Press.
Marder, E. (2009). The Sex of Death and the Maternal Crypt. *Parallax*, 15(1): 5–20.
Martin, P. (1984). *Argent et psychanalyse*. Paris: Navarin.
Masschelein, A. (2011). *The Unconcept: The Freudian Uncanny in Late Twentieth-Century Theory*. Albany, NY: State University of New York Press.
Masson, J. M. (Ed.) (1985). *The Complete Letters of Sigmund Freud to Wilhelm Fliess 1887–1904*. J. M. Masson (Trans.). Cambridge, MA-London: The Belknap Press of Harvard University Press.
Maurer, B. (2006). The Anthropology of Money. *Annual Review of Anthropology*, 35: 15–36.

Mazzoni, C. (1996). *Saint Hysteria: Neurosis, Mysticism, and Gender in European Culture*. Ithaca, NY-London: Cornell University Press.
McDougall, J. (1995). *The Many Faces of Eros: A Psychoanalytic Exploration of Human Sexuality*. London: Free Association Books.
McGuire, W. (Ed.) (1974). *The Freud/Jung Letters—The Correspondence Between Sigmund Freud and C.G. Jung*. R. Manheim and R. F. C. Hull (Trans.). Princeton, NJ-London: Princeton University Press.
McNeill, D. N. (2011). Antigone's Autonomy. *Inquiry*, 54(5): 411–441.
Meltzer, F. (2011). Theories of Desire: Antigone Again. *Critical Inquiry*, 37(2): 169–186.
Mendelssohn, M. (1997[1761]). On the Sublime and Naive in the Fine Sciences. In *Philosophical Writings* (pp. 192–232). D. O. Dahlstrom (Ed. and Trans.). Cambridge: Cambridge University Press.
Meyer, C. (Ed.) (2005). *Le livre noir de la psychanalyse. Vivre, penser et aller mieux sans Freud*. Paris: les arènes.
Miller, J.-A. (Ed.) (1976). *La scission de 1953. La communauté psychanalytique en France—1*. Paris: Navarin.
Miller, J.-A. (Ed.) (1977). *L'excommunication. La communauté psychanalytique en France—2*. Paris: Navarin.
Miller, J.-A. (1983). Pas de clinique sans éthique. *Actes de l'École de la Cause freudienne*, 5: 28–32.
Miller, J.-A. (1985). *Entretien sur Le Séminaire avec François Ansermet*. Paris: Navarin.
Miller, J.-A. (1994). L'homologue de Málaga. Remarques sur la logique de la cure présentées en cloture des Journées de Málaga, le 28 février 1993. *La cause freudienne. Revue de psychanalyse*, 26: 7–16.
Miller, J.-A. (1998). *… du nouveau. Introduction au Séminaire V de Lacan*. Paris: rue Huysmans.
Miller, J.-A. (2000). Paradigms of *Jouissance*. J. Jauregui (Trans.). *Lacanian Ink*, 17: 10–47.
Miller, J.-A. (2001). Pas-à-lire. In J. Lacan, *Autres Écrits* (back cover). Paris: du Seuil.
Miller, J.-A. (2006[1966a]). Classified Index of the Major Concepts. In J. Lacan, *Écrits* (pp. 851–857). B. Fink (Trans.). New York, NY-London: W. W. Norton & Company.
Miller, J.-A. (2006[1966b]). Commentary on the Graphs. In J. Lacan, *Écrits* (pp. 858–863). B. Fink (Trans.). New York, NY-London: W. W. Norton & Company.
Miller, J.-A. (2011). The Economics of Jouissance. A. Alvarez (Trans.). *Lacanian Ink*, 38: 6–63.
Miller, J.-A. (2018). *Del síntoma al fantasma. Y retorno (1982-1983)*. S. E. Tendlarz (Ed.). S. Baudini (Trans.). Buenos Aires: Paidós.
Miller, J.-A. (2020[2011]). Lacan's Daemon: An Interview with Jacques-Alain Miller. D. Collins and R. Grigg (Trans.). *The Lacanian Review: Journal of the New Lacanian School and the World Association of Psychoanalysis*, 10: 129–167.
Miller, P. A. (2007a). Lacan's Antigone: The Sublime Object and the Ethics of Interpretation. *Phoenix*, 61(1/2): 1–14.

Miller, P. A. (2007b). *Postmodern Spiritual Practices: The Construction of the Subject and the Reception of Plato in Lacan, Derrida, and Foucault*. Columbus OH: Ohio State University Press.

Milovanovic, D. (2003). *Critical Criminology at the Edge: Postmodern Perspectives, Integration, and Applications*. Boulder, CO: Lynne Rienner Publishers.

Moberly, L. G. (1917). Inexplicable. *The Strand Magazine: An Illustrated Monthly*, 54(324): 572–581.

Moberly, L. G. (1992[1917]). Inexplicable. J. Quackelbeen and D. Nobus (Trans.). *Quarto*, 48/49: 88–95.

Moberly, L. G. (1993[1917]). Onverklaarbaar. D. Nobus and J. Quackelbeen (Trans.). *Psychoanalytische Perspektieven*, 19/20: 43–53.

Moi, T. (2004). From Femininity to Finitude: Freud, Lacan, and Feminism, Again. *Signs*, 29(3): 841–878.

Molière (1959[1666]). A Doctor In Spite of Himself. In *The Misanthrope and Other Plays* (pp. 165–199). J. Wood (Trans.). Harmondsworth: Penguin Books.

Monaco, J. (1975). Le gai savoir: Picture and Act—Godard's Plexus. *Jump Cut: A Review of Contemporary Media*, 7: 15–17.

Monson, D. A. (1999). The Troubadours at Play: Irony, Parody and Burlesque. In S. Gaunt and S. Kay (Eds), *The Troubadours: An Introduction* (pp. 197–211). Cambridge: Cambridge University Press.

Morel, G. (2010). D'un éclat féminin qui suscite la dispute. Lectures croisées d'*Antigone* de Sophocle par Jacques Lacan et Jean Bollack. In C. König and D. Thouard (Eds), *La philologie au présent. Pour Jean Bollack* (pp. 185–199). Villeneuve d'Ascq: Presses Universitaires du Septentrion.

Morlock, F. (1997). Doubly Uncanny: An Introduction to 'On the Psychology of the Uncanny'. *Angelaki: Journal of the Theoretical Humanities*, 2(1): 17–21.

Mormando, F. (2011). *Bernini: His Life and His Rome*. Chicago, IL-London: The University of Chicago Press.

Moyaert, P. (1994). *Ethiek en sublimatie. Over* De ethiek van de psychoanalyse *van Jacques Lacan*. Nijmegen: SUN.

Munch, M. (2011). *Écrits*. Dijon: Les presses du réel.

Murdin, L. (2012). *How Money Talks*. London: Karnac Books.

Murnaghan, S. (1986). *Antigone* 904-920 and the Institution of Marriage. *American Journal of Philology*, 107: 192–207.

Musée d'Orsay. *Gustave Courbet—L'origine du monde, notice d'œuvre*. http://www.musee-orsay.fr/fr/collections/catalogue-des-oeuvres/notice.html?nnumid=69330. Accessed on 3 October 2012.

Nacht, S. (1963). *La présence du psychanalyste*. Paris: Presses Universitaires de France.

Nancy, J.-L. and Lacoue-Labarthe, Ph. (1992[1990]). *The Title of the Letter: A Reading of Lacan*. F. Raffoul and D. Pettigrew (Trans.). Albany, NY: State University of New York Press.

Napoleone, C. (1998). Bernini e il cantiere della Cappella Cornaro. *Antologia di belle arti*, 55-58: 172–186.

Nasio, J.-D. (2014). Fondation de l'École freudienne de Paris. https://francearchives.fr/fr/commemo/recueil-2014/38835, accessed on 5 June 2021.

Naveau, L. (2011). Lacan avec Antigone. *La cause freudienne. Revue de Psychanalyse*, 79: 231–234.
Neill, C. (2011). *Lacanian Ethics and the Assumption of Subjectivity*. Basingstoke: Palgrave Macmillan.
Neuburg. M. (1990). How Like A Woman: Antigone's 'Inconsistency'. *Classical Quarterly*, 40(1): 54–76.
Nietzsche, F. (1974[1887]). *The Gay Science, With a Prelude in Rhymes and an Appendix of Songs*. W. Kaufmann (Trans.). New York, NY: Vintage.
Nietzsche, F. (1988). Nachlaß 1880-1882. In *Kritische Studienausgabe*, vol. 9. G. Colli and M. Montinari (Eds). Berlin: Deutscher Taschenbuch Verlag.
Nietzsche, F. (1996). *Selected Letters of Friedrich Nietzsche*. Indianapolis IN: Hackett.
Nietzsche, F. (1996[1878]). *Human, All Too Human: A Book For Free Spirits*. R. J. Hollingdale (Trans.). Cambridge: Cambridge University Press.
Nietzsche, F. (1997[1881]). *Daybreak: Thoughts on the Prejudices of Morality*. M. Clark and B. Leiter (Eds). R. J. Hollingdale (Trans.). Cambridge: Cambridge University Press.
Nietzsche, F. (1998[1887]). *On the Genealogy of Morals*. D. Smith (Trans.). Oxford: Oxford University Press.
Nietzsche, F. (2002[1886]). *Beyond Good and Evil*. R.-P. Horstmann and J. Norman (Eds). J. Norman (Trans.). Cambridge: Cambridge University Press.
Nietzsche, F. (2005[1888]). Ecce Homo: How To Become What You Are. In *The Anti-Christ, Ecce Homo, Twilight of the Idols and Other Writings*. J. Norman (Trans.) Cambridge: Cambridge University Press.
Nietzsche, F. (2011[1887]). *The Gay Science, With a Prelude in German Rhymes and an Appendix of Songs*. J. Nauckhoff and A. Del Caro (Trans.). Cambridge: Cambridge University Press.
Nobus, D. (1993). Freud versus Jentsch: Een kruistocht tegen de intellectuele onzekerheid. *Psychoanalytische Perspektieven*, 19/20: 55–65.
Nobus, D. (2000). *Jacques Lacan and the Freudian Practice of Psychoanalysis*. London-New York, NY: Brunner-Routledge.
Nobus, D. (2001). Littorical Reading: Lacan, Derrida and the Analytic Production of Chaff. *Journal for the Psychoanalysis of Culture and Society*, 6(2): 279–288.
Nobus, D. (2002). Illiterature. In L. Thurston (Ed.), *Re-inventing the Symptom: Essays on the Final Lacan* (pp. 19–43). New York, NY: Other Press.
Nobus, D. (2012). (E)valuating Words: Money and Gain in the Therapeutic Economy. In R. Vanderbeeken, F. LeRoy, C. Stalpaert and D. Aerts (Eds). *Drunk on Capitalism: An Interdisciplinary Reflection on Market Economy, Art and Science* (pp. 65–78). New York, NY: Springer.
Nobus, D. (2013). Annotations to Lituraterre. *Continental Philosophy Review*, 46(2): 335–347.
Nobus, D. (2016). Psychoanalytic Violence: An Essay on Indifference in Ethical Matters. *Psychoanalytic Discourse*, 1(2): 1–20.
Nobus, D. (2017a). En rencontrant le gai savoir: La fin de l'analyse comme l'analyse de la fin. *Psychoanalytische Perspectieven*, 35(3): 251–259.
Nobus, D. (2017b). *The Law of Desire: On Lacan's 'Kant with Sade'*. Cham: Palgrave Macmillan.

Nobus, D. (2019). From Sense to Sensation: Bacon, Pasting Paint and the Futility of Lacanian Psychoanalysis. In B. Ware (Ed.). *Francis Bacon: Painting, Philosophy, Psychoanalysis*. (pp. 95–116). London: Thames & Hudson.

Nussbaum, M. C. (1994). *The Therapy of Desire: Theory and Practice in Hellenistic Ethics*. Princeton, NJ: Princeton University Press.

Nussbaum, M. C. (2001). *The Fragility of Goodness: Luck and Ethics in Tragedy and Philosophy*, Updated Edition. Cambridge: Cambridge University Press.

Ohayon, A. (1999). *L'impossible rencontre. Psychologie et psychanalyse en France 1919–1969*. Paris: La découverte.

Onfray, M. (2010). *Le crépuscule d'une idole. L'affabulation freudienne*. Paris: Grasset.

Otto, R. (1958[1917]). *The Idea of the Holy: An Inquiry into the Non-rational Factor in the Idea of the Divine and its Relation to the Rational*. J. W. Harvey (Trans.). Oxford: Oxford University Press.

Parsons, W. B. (2003). Let Him Rejoice in the Roseate Light! Teaching Psychoanalysis and Mysticism. In D. Jonte-Pace (Ed.), *Teaching Freud* (pp. 79–99). Oxford-New York NY: Oxford University Press.

Paskauskas, R. A. (Ed.) (1993). *The Complete Correspondence of Sigmund Freud and Ernest Jones 1908-1939*. Cambridge, MA-London: The Belknap Press of Harvard University Press.

Passerat, G. (2000). L'Église et la poésie: les débuts du *Consistori del Gay Saber*. In J.-L. Biget (Ed.), *Église et culture en France méridionale (XIIe-XIVe siècle)* (pp. 443–473). Toulouse: Privat.

Paul the Apostle (1997). Epistle to the Romans. In *The Bible. Authorized King James Version with Apocrypha—The New Testament* (pp. 189–205). Oxford-New York, NY: Oxford University Press.

Pearson Geiman, C. (2001). Heidegger's *Antigones*. In R. Polt and G. Fried (Eds), *A Companion to Heidegger's* Introduction to Metaphysics (pp. 161–182). New Haven, CT-London: Yale University Press.

Perlove, S. K. (1990). *Bernini and the Idealization of Death: The Blessed Ludovica Albertoni and the Altieri Chapel*. University Park, PA: Penn State University Press.

Petersson, R. T. (2002). *Bernini and the Excesses of Art*. Firenze: Maschietto Editore.

Pinkard, T. (2018). Introduction. In G. W. F. Hegel, *The Phenomenology of Spirit* (pp. ix–xxxvi). T. Pinkard (Trans.). Cambridge: Cambridge University Press.

Pippin, R. B. (2011). *Nietzsche, Psychology, and First Philosophy*. Chicago, IL-London: The University of Chicago Press.

Pischel, R. (1893). Zu Sophokles Antigone 909-912. *Hermes*, 28(2): 465–468.

Plato (1998). *Cratylus*. C. D. C. Reeve (Trans.). London: Hackett.

Plato (2003). *The Symposium*. C. Gill (Trans.). Harmondsworth: Penguin.

Plato (2005). *Phaedrus*. C. Rowe (Trans.). London: Penguin Books.

Plato (2007). *The Republic*. D. Lee (Trans.). London: Penguin Books.

Plato (2011). *Phaedrus*. H. Yunis (Ed.). Cambridge: Cambridge University Press.

Poe, E. A. (1988[1844]). The Purloined Letter. In *The Complete Illustrated Stories and Poems of Edgar Allan Poe* (pp. 319–333). London: Chancellor Press.

Polizzotti, M. (2009). *Revolution of the Mind: The Life of André Breton*. Revised and updated edition. Boston, MA: Black Widow Press.

Pop, A. (2019). *A Forest of Symbols: Art, Science, and Truth in the Long Nineteenth Century*. New York, NY: Zone Books.

Porge, E. (2005). *Transmettre la clinique psychanalytique. Freud, Lacan, aujourd'hui.* Ramonville Saint-Agne: Érès.
Porge, E. (2018). *La sublimation, une érotique pour la psychanalyse.* Toulouse: Érès.
Porret, Ph. (2004). Un mur de lumière. *Le Coq-Héron*, 178: 139–148.
Porter, J. I. (2015). Jacob Bernays and the Catharsis of Modernity. In J. Billings and M. Leonard (Eds), *Tragedy and the Idea of Modernity* (pp. 15–41). Oxford: Oxford University Press.
Prawer, S. S. (1963). Reflections on the Numinous and the Uncanny in German Poetry. In A. Closs (Ed.). *Reality and Creative Vision in German Lyrical Poetry* (pp. 153–173). London: Butterworths.
Previtali, G. (1962). Il Costantino messo alla Berlina o bernina su la porta di San Pietro. *Paragone Arte*, 13, 145: 55–58.
Psaroudakis, S., Parker, I. and Burman, E. (2012). Lacan's hairdresser. http://mentholmountains.blogspot.co.uk/2012/05/lacans-hairdresser.html. Accessed on 29 August 2012.
Quackelbeen, J. and Nobus, D. (1992). Á propos de l'élucidation d'une référence freudienne: l'Inexplicable de L. G. Moberly. *Quarto*, 48/49: 83–87.
Quackelbeen, J. and Nobus, D. (1993). Over een opgehelderde referentie bij Freud. Het 'Inexplicable' van L. G. Moberly. *Psychoanalytische Perspektieven*, 19/20: 35–42.
Rabaté, J.-M. (2001). *Jacques Lacan: Psychoanalysis and the Subject of Literature.* Basingstoke: Palgrave.
Rabaté, J.-M. (2014). *The Cambridge Introduction to Literature and Psychoanalysis.* Cambridge: Cambridge University Press.
Rabaté, J.-M. (2019). *Rire au soleil. Des affects en littérature.* Paris: CampagnePremière/.
Rath, C.-D. (2019). *Sublimierung und Gewalt. Elemente einer Psychoanalyse der aktuellen Gesellschaft.* Gießen: Psychosozial-Verlag.
Rauchfleisch, U. (1990). Psychoanalytische Betrachtungen zur musikalischen Kreativität. *Psyche: Zeitschrift für Psychoanalyse*, 44(12): 1113–1140.
Reich, W. (1971). *The Sexual Revolution: Towards a Self-governing Character Structure.* T. P. Wolfe (Trans.). New York, NY: Farrar, Straus and Giroux.
Reik, T. (1968). The Psychological Meaning of Silence. K. M. Altman (Trans.). *The Psychoanalytic Review*, 55: 172–186.
Reinhardt, K. (1979[1933]). *Sophocles.* H. Harvey and D. D. Harvey (Trans.). London: Wiley-Blackwell.
Reiss-Schimmel, I. (1993). *La psychanalyse et l'argent.* Paris: Odile Jacob.
Rémy, A.-R. (1991). *Beau comme la rencontre fortuite …: La psychiatrie et la psychanalyse dans l'œuvre d'André Breton.* Thèse de médecine. Université Louis Pasteur—Strasbourg.
Rey, P. (1989). *Une saison chez Lacan.* Paris: Robert Laffont.
Ricœur, P. (1965). *De l'interprétation. Essai sur Freud.* Paris: du Seuil.
Ricœur, P. (1970[1965]). *Freud and Philosophy: An Essay on Interpretation.* D. Savage (Trans.). New Haven, CT-London: Yale University Press.
Rigaut, J. (1970). *Écrits.* Paris: Gallimard.
Rose, J. (1982). Introduction—II. In J. Mitchell and J. Rose (Eds). *Feminine Sexuality: Jacques Lacan and the école freudienne* (pp. 27–57). New York, NY-London: W. W. Norton & Company.

Rosenkranz, K. (1844). *Georg Wilhelm Friedrich Hegel's Leben*. Berlin: Verlag von Duncker und Humblot.
Roudinesco, E. (1990[1986]). *Jacques Lacan & Co.: A History of Psychoanalysis in France 1925-1985*. J. Mehlman (Trans.). London: Free Association Books.
Roudinesco, E. (1997[1993]). *Jacques Lacan*. B. Bray (Trans.). New York, NY: Columbia University Press.
Roudinesco, E. (2005). La liste de Lacan. Inventaire de choses disparues. In E. Marty (Ed.), *Lacan & la littérature* (pp. 181–195). Houilles: Manucius.
Roudinesco, E. (2014[2011]). *Lacan: In Spite of Everything*. G. Elliott (Trans.). London-New York, NY: Verso.
Roudinesco, E. and Plon, M. (1997). *Dictionnaire de la psychanalyse*. Paris: Fayard.
Roustang, F. (1990). *The Lacanian Delusion*. New York, NY: Oxford University Press.
Royle, N. (2003). *The Uncanny*. Manchester: Manchester University Press.
Rudnytsky, P. L. (1987). *Freud and Oedipus*. New York, NY-Oxford: Columbia University Press.
Ruskin, J. (1906[1856]). Of the Pathetic Fallacy. In *Modern Painters. vol. 3: Of Many Things.* (pp. 161–177). London: George Allen.
Russo, L. (Ed.) (1987). *Da Longino a Longino. I luoghi del Sublime*. Palermo: Aesthetica Edizioni.
Ruti, M. (2012). *The Singularity of Being: Lacan and the Immortal Within*. New York, NY: Fordham University Press.
Ruti, M. (2015). *Between Levinas and Lacan: Self, Other, Ethics*. London-New York, NY: Bloomsbury.
Ruti, M. (2017). *The Ethics of Opting Out: Queer Theory's Defiant Subjects*. New York, NY: Columbia University Press.
Sade, D.-A.-F. de (1968[1797]). *Juliette*. A. Wainhouse (Trans.). New York NY: Grove Press.
Sade, D.-A.-F. de (1995[1775–1778]). *Voyage d'Italie*. Paris: Fayard.
Saint Girons, B. (1993). *Fiat Lux. Une philosophie du sublime*. Paris: Quai Voltaire.
Saint Girons, B. (2005). *Le Sublime. De l'antiquité à nos jours*. Paris: Desjonquères.
Sartre, J.-P. (1990). *Écrits de jeunesse*. M. Contat and M. Rybalka (Eds). Paris: Gallimard.
Saussure, F. de (1959[1916]). *Course in General Linguistics*. W. Baskin (Trans.). New York NY: Philosophical Library.
Sauverzac, J.-F. de (2000). *Le désir sans foi ni loi. Lecture de Lacan*. Paris: Aubier.
Schadewaldt, W. (1929). Aias und Antigone. *Neue Wege zur Antike*, 8: 61–117.
Schama, S. (2006). *The Power of Art*. London: BBC Books.
Scheidhauer, M. (2010). *Freud et ses visiteurs Français et Suisses francophones (1920-1930)*. Strasbourg: Arcanes.
Schelling, F. W. J. (2006[1809]). *Philosophical Investigations Into the Essence of Human Freedom*. J. Love and J. Schmidt (Trans.). Albany, NY: State University of New York Press.
Schiller, F. (1998[1793]). On the Sublime. In *Essays* (pp. 22–44). W. Hinderer and D. O. Dahlstrom (Eds). D. O. Dahlstrom (Trans.). London: Continuum.
Schneiderman, S. (1983). *Jacques Lacan: The Death of an Intellectual Hero*. Cambridge, MA-London: Harvard University Press.

Schoonejans, S. (2008). *Le geste de Lacan. Chronique des années 1970*. Bruxelles: Éditions Luc Pire.
Schopenhauer, A. (2017[1851]). On Ethics. In *Parerga and Paralipomena: Short Philosophical Essays*. vol. 2 (pp. 183–216). A. Del Caro and C. Janaway (Eds and Trans.). Cambridge: Cambridge University Press.
Schumpeter, J. A. (1976[1942]). *Capitalism, Socialism and Democracy*. London: Routledge.
Schur, M. (1972). *Freud: Living and Dying*. London: The Hogarth Press.
Sedley, D. (2003). *Plato's Cratylus*. Cambridge: Cambridge University Press.
Shaw, Ph. (2017). *The Sublime*. London-New York, NY: Routledge.
Shephard, B. (2000). *A War of Nerves: Soldiers and Psychiatrists 1914-1994*. London: Jonathan Cape.
Shepherdson, Ch. (2008a). *Lacan and the Limits of Language*. New York, NY: Fordham University Press.
Shepherdson, Ch. (2008b). The Atrocity of Desire: Of Love and Beauty in Lacan's Antigone. In *Lacan and the Limits of Language* (pp. 50–80). New York, NY: Fordham University Press.
Sheriff, M. D. (2004). *Moved by Love: Inspired Artists and Deviant Women in Eighteenth-Century France*. Chicago, IL-London: The University of Chicago Press.
Silvain, M. (1732). *Traité du sublime*. Paris: Pierre Prault.
Sipos, J. (1994). *Lacan et Descartes. La tentation métaphysique*. Paris: Presses Universitaires de France.
Sjöholm, C. (2004). *The Antigone Complex: Ethics and the Invention of Feminine Desire*. Stanford, CA: Stanford University Press.
Sjöholm, C. (2014). Bodies in Exile: From Tragedy to Performance Art. In T. Chanter and S. D. Kirkland (Eds), *The Returns of Antigone: Interdisciplinary Essays* (pp. 281–295). Albany, NY: State University of New York Press.
Slade, C. (1995). *St. Teresa of Avila: Author of a Heroic Life*. Los Angeles/Berkeley, CA-London: The University of California Press.
Slonimsky, N. (Ed.) (1984). *Baker's Biographical Dictionary of Musicians*. 7th Edition. New York, NY: Collier MacMillan.
Smith, G. (1981). *Letter of 2 October 1981 to John Forrester*. John Forrester Papers. Albert Sloman Library, University of Essex. Unlisted Collection.
Söderbäck, F. (Ed.) (2010). *Feminist Readings of Antigone*. Albany, NY: State University of New York Press.
Sokal, A. and Bricmont, J. (1998[1997]). *Intellectual Impostures*. London: Profile Books.
Sollers, Ph. (2005). *Lacan même*. Paris: Navarin.
Sollers, Ph. (2011). Le corps sort de la voix. *Le diable probablement*, 9: 16–28.
Solms, M. (1997). *The Neuropsychology of Dreams: A Clinico-Anatomical Study*. Mahwah, NJ: Lawrence Erlbaum Associates.
Solms M. and Turnbull, O. (2002). *The Brain and the Inner World: An Introduction to the Neuroscience of Subjective Experience*. London-New York: Karnac Books.
Sophocle (1947). *Théâtre de Sophocle*. R. Pignarre (Trans.). Paris: Garnier.
Sophocles (1984). Antigone. In *The Three Theban Plays: Antigone, Oedipus the King, Oedipus at Colonus*. R. Fagles (Trans.). London: Penguin Books.

Sophocles (1998). *Antigone, Women of Trachis, Philoctetes, Oedipus at Colonus*. H. Lloyd-Jones (Trans.). Cambridge, MA-London: Harvard University Press.

Sophocles (1999). *Antigone*. M. Griffith (Ed.). Cambridge: Cambridge University Press.

Sourvinou-Inwood, C. (1989). Assumptions and the Creation of Meaning: Reading Sophocles' *Antigone*. *Journal of Hellenic Studies*, 109: 134–148.

Spankie, R. (2015). *Sigmund Freud's Desk: An Anecdoted Guide*. London: Freud Museum London.

Spear, R. E. (2003). Scrambling for *Scudi*: Notes on Painters' Earnings in Early Baroque Rome. *Art Bulletin*, 85: 310–320.

Spector, J. J. (1972). *The Aesthetics of Freud: A Study in Psychoanalysis and Art*. London: Allen Lane.

Spinoza, B. de (1996[1677]). *Ethics*. E. Curley (Trans.). Harmondsworth: Penguin.

Starobinski, J. (2003[1999]). *Action and Reaction: The Life and Adventures of a Couple*. S. Hawkes and J. Fort (Trans.). New York, NY: Zone Books.

Stavrakakis, Y. (2008). Subjectivity and the Organized Other: Between Symbolic Authority and Fantasmatic Enjoyment. *Organization Studies*, 29: 1037–1059.

Steiner, G. (1984). *Antigones: The Antigone Myth in Western Literature, Art and Thought*. Oxford: Clarendon Press.

Sterba, R. (1930). Zur Problematik der Sublimierungslehre. *Internationale Zeitschrift für Psychoanalyse*, 16(3/4): 370–377.

Stevens, J. (1986). *Words and Music in the Middle Ages: Song, Narrative, Dance and Drama, 1050-1350*. Cambridge: Cambridge University Press.

Stewart-Steinberg, S. (2011). *Impious Fidelity: Anna Freud, Psychoanalysis, Politics*. Ithaca, NY-London: Cornell University Press.

Stirling, J. H. (1972[1865]). *The Secret of Hegel: Being the Hegelian System in Origin, Principle, Form and Matter*. Dubuque, IA: William C. Brown.

Strachey, J. (1957). Papers on Metapsychology: Editor's Introduction. In *The Standard Edition of the Complete Psychological Works of Sigmund Freud*, vol. 14. (pp. 105–107). J. Strachey (Ed. and Trans). London: The Hogarth Press and the Institute of Psycho-Analysis.

Stuttard, D. (Ed.) (2018). *Looking at Antigone*. London-New York, NY: Bloomsbury.

Szlezák, T. A. (1981). Bemerkungen zur Diskussion um Sophokles, *Antigone* 904-920. *Rheinisches Museum* 124: 108–142.

Tallis, R. (1997). The Shrink From Hell. *The Times Higher Education Supplement*, 31 October: 20.

Tauber, A. I. (2010). *Freud, the Reluctant Philosopher*. Princeton, NJ-London: Princeton University Press.

Taylor, Ch. (1995). Overcoming Epistemology. In *Philosophical Arguments* (pp. 1–19). Cambridge, MA-London: Harvard University Press.

Themi, T. (2014). *Lacan's Ethics and Nietzsche's Critique of Platonism*. Albany, NY: State University of New York Press.

Todorov, T. (Ed.) (1966). *Théorie de la littérature. Textes des formalistes russes*. Paris: du Seuil.

Todorov, T. (1978). Autour de la poésie. In *Les genres du discours* (pp. 99–131). Paris: du Seuil.

Trist, E., Higgin, G., Murray, H. and Pollock, A. (1963). *Organizational Choice*. London: Tavistock Publications.
Trist, E. and Murray, H. (Eds) (1990). *The Social Engagement of Social Science, vol. 1: The Socio-psychological Perspective*. London: Free Association Books.
Turquet, P. (2014). *Le rapport Turquet*. Paris: Cahiers de l'Unebévue.
Vailland, R. (2008[1957]). *The Law*. P. Wiles (Trans.). London: Eland Books.
Vallois, P. (2003). Le gai savoir de Lacan. *Letterina—Bulletin de l'ACF Normandie*, 35: 69–76.
van Braam, P. (1912). Aristotle's use of Αμαρτία. *The Classical Quarterly*, 6(4): 266–272.
van der Sterren, H. A. (1948). *De lotgevallen van Koning Oedipus volgens de treurspelen van Sophocles. Een psychologische studie*. Amsterdam: Scheltema & Holkema.
van der Sterren, H. A. (1952). The 'King Oedipus' of Sophocles. *The International Journal of Psycho-Analysis*, 33: 343–350.
Van Haute, Ph. (1998). Death and Sublimation in Lacan's Reading of *Antigone*. In S. Harasym (Ed.), *Levinas and Lacan: The Missed Encounter* (pp. 102–120). Albany, NY: State University of New York Press.
Van Haute, Ph. (2002[2000]). *Against Adaptation: Lacan's 'Subversion of the subject' – A Close Reading*. P. Crowe and M. Vankerk (Trans.). New York NY: Other Press.
Van Haute, Ph. and Westerink, H. (Eds) (2017). *Deconstructing Normativity? Re-reading Freud's 1905 Three Essays*. London-New York, NY: Routledge.
Van Haute, Ph. and Westerink, H. (2021). Reading Freud's *Three Essays on the Theory of Sexuality*: From Pleasure to the Object. London-New York, NY: Routledge.
Vanheule, S., Hook, D. and Neill, C. (Eds) (2019). Introduction to 'Reading the Écrits': *La trahison de l'écriture*. In *Reading Lacan's* Écrits: *From 'Signification of the Phallus' to 'Metaphor of the Subject'* (pp. xvii–xxi). London-New York, NY: Routledge.
Vanheule, S., Lievrouw, A. and Verhaeghe, P. (2003). Burnout and Intersubjectivity: A Psychoanalytical Study From a Lacanian Perspective. *Human Relations*, 56: 321–338.
Vanheule, S. and Verhaeghe, P. (2004). Powerlessness and Impossibility in Special Education: A Qualitative Study on Professional Burnout from a Lacanian Perspective. *Human Relations*, 57: 497–519.
Van Reeth, A. and Nancy, J.-L. (2014). *La jouissance. Questions de caractère*. Paris: Plon/France Culture.
Van Rillaer, J. (2019). *Freud et Lacan des charlatans? Faits et légendes de la psychanalyse*. Bruxelles: Mardaga.
Vasse, D. (2008). *L'homme et l'argent*. Paris: du Seuil.
Vereecken, C. (1987). Le gay sçavoir du seigneur des Accords. *Quarto*, 26: 30.
Vergote, A. (1997). *La psychanalyse à l'épreuve de la sublimation*. Paris: du Cerf.
Verhaeghe, P. (1998). Causation and Destitution of a Pre-ontological Non-entity: On the Lacanian Subject. In D. Nobus (Ed.). *Key Concepts of Lacanian Psychoanalysis* (pp. 164–189). New York, NY: The Other Press.
Verhaeghe, P. (2004). *On Being Normal and Other Disorders. A Manual for Clinical Psychodiagnostics*. New York, NY: The Other Press.

Verhaeghe, P. (2019). Position of the Unconscious. In S. Vanheule, D. Hook and C. Neill (Eds), *Reading Lacan's Écrits: From 'Signification of the Phallus' to 'Metaphor of the Subject'* (pp. 224–258). London-New York, NY: Routledge.

Verlaine, P. (1976). *Lettres inédites à divers correspondants*. G. Zayed (Ed.). Genève: Droz.

Verrier, A.-J. and Orillon, R. (1908). *Glossaire étymologique et historique des patois et des parlers de l'Anjou*, vol. 1. Angers: Germain & G. Grassin.

Vidaillet (2007). Lacanian Theory's Contribution to the Study of Workplace Envy. *Human Relations*, 60: 1669–1700.

Vidaillet, B. and Gamot, G. (2015). Working and Resisting When One's Workplace Is Under Threat of Being Shut Down: A Lacanian Perspective. *Organization Studies*, 36: 987–1011.

Viderman, S. (1992). *De l'argent en psychanalyse et au-delà*. Paris: Presses Universitaires de France.

Voltaire (1964[1747]). Zadig. In *Zadig and L'ingénu* (pp. 17–104). J. Butt (Trans.). Harmondsworth: Penguin Books.

Vuillerod, J.-B. (2020). *Hegel féministe. Les aventures d'Antigone*. Paris: Vrin.

Walker, K. (2012). The Dialectic of Beauty and Agency. *Philosophy and Social Criticism*, 39(1): 79–98.

Weber, A. (1990). *Teresa of Ávila and the Rhetoric of Femininity*. Princeton, NJ-London: Princeton University Press.

Weber, S. (2004). Antigone's *Nomos*. In *Theatricality as Medium* (pp. 121–140). New York NY: Fordham University Press.

Weibel, W. (1976[1909]). The Representation of Ecstasy. M. Armstrong and G. C. Bauer (Trans.). In G. C. Bauer (Ed.), *Bernini in Perspective* (pp. 77–89). Englewood Cliffs, NJ: Prentice-Hall, Inc.

Weil, S. (1998[1936]). Antigone. In *Intimations of Christianity Among the Ancient Greeks* (pp. 18–23). London-New York, NY: Routledge.

Weinberg, S. (2015). *To Explain the World: The Discovery of Modern Science*. London: Allen Lane.

Weiser, J. (2019). Illness Narrative, Hysteria, and Sainthood: Santa Teresa as a Case Study. In M. Bengert and I. Roebling-Graud (Eds). *Santa Teresa: Critical Insights, Filiations, Responses* (pp. 219–242). Tübingen: Narr Francke Attempto Verlag.

Weissman, Ph. (1964). Antigone—A Preoedipal Old Maid. *Journal of the Hillside Hospital*, 13(1): 32–42.

Wheen, F. (2004). *How Mumbo-Jumbo Conquered the World: A Short History of Modern Delusions*. London: Fourth Estate.

Whitman, C. H. (1951). *Sophocles: A Study of Heroic Humanism*. Cambridge, MA: Harvard University Press.

Widmaier-Haag, S. (1999). *Es War das Lächeln des Narziß: Die Theorien der Psychoanalyse im Spiegel literatur-psychologischen Interpretationen des 'Tod in Venedig'*. Würzburg: Königshausen & Neumann.

Williams, B. (2001). Introduction. In F. Nietzsche, *The Gay Science, with a Prelude in German Rhymes and an Appendix of Songs* (pp. vii–xxii). J. Nauckhoff and A. del Caro (Trans.). Cambridge: Cambridge University Press.

Wilson, C. C. (1999). Saint Teresa of Ávila's Martyrdom: Images of Her Transverberation in Mexican Colonial Painting. *Anales del Instituto de Investigaciones Estéticas*, 74/75: 211–233.

Wittgenstein, L. (1961[1921]). *Tractatus Logico-Philosophicus*. D. F. Pears and B. F. McGuinness (Trans.). London: Routledge & Kegan Paul.

Wittkower, R. (1955). *Gian Lorenzo Bernini: The Sculptor of the Roman Baroque*. London: Phaidon.

Wolin, R. (2004). *The Seduction of Unreason: The Intellectual Romance with Fascism from Nietzsche to Postmodernism*. Princeton, NJ-Oxford: Princeton University Press.

Wycherley, R. E. (1947). Sophocles *Antigone* 904-20. *Classical Philology*, 42(1): 51–52.

Zafiropoulos, M. (2019). *Œdipe assassiné? Œdipe roi, Œdipe à Colone, Antigone ou L'inconscient des modernes. Les mythologiques de Lacan 2*. Toulouse: Erès.

Zalkind, A. B. (2001[1929]). Половое Воспитание Юных Пионеров, in *Педология: Утопия и реальность* (pp. 345–362). Moscow: Agraf.

Zilcosky, J. (2018). 'The Times in Which We Live': Freud's *The Uncanny*, World War I, and the Trauma of Contagion. *Psychoanalysis and History*, 20(2): 165–190.

Žižek, S. (1989). *The Sublime Object of Ideology*. London-New York, NY: Verso.

Žižek, S. (1994). *The Metastases of Enjoyment: Six Essays on Woman and Causality*. London-New York NY: Verso.

Žižek, S. (1999). Death and the Maiden. In E. Wright and E. Wright (Eds). *The Žižek Reader* (pp. 206–221). Oxford-Malden, MA: Blackwell.

Zupančič, A. (2000). *Ethics of the Real: Kant, Lacan*. London-New York, NY: Verso.

Zupančič, A. (2002). *Esthétique du désir, éthique de la jouissance*. Lecques: Théétète.

Zupančič, A. (2003). Ethics and Tragedy in Lacan. In J.-M. Rabaté (Ed.), *The Cambridge Companion to Lacan* (pp. 173–190). Cambridge: Cambridge University Press.

Acknowledgements

With one exception, all the essays included in this book have been published before, and I wish to thank the editors and publishers for granting me permission to reprint a version of them here. All of the essays have been thoroughly revised and updated for this volume, also in order to take account of the latest research and the most recent translations, and to avoid duplication between them. I have added cross-references between the chapters wherever I deemed it useful and all translations from source materials not originally published in English are mine, unless otherwise indicated in the bibliography.

As to the provenance of the individual chapters, Chapter 1 is an expanded version of the opening Keynote Lecture delivered on 21 September 2018 at the International Conference on Lacan's *Écrits*, which was held at the University of Ghent. The revised text of the lecture was subsequently published as "*Écrits* Revisited: On Writing as Object of Desire" in *Psychoanalytische Perspectieven*, 2018, 36(4), 345–374. A slightly different Portuguese version, courtesy of Paulo Beer, was published as "O *Escritos* de Lacan revisitado: Sobre a escrita como objeto de desejo" in *Lacuna: Uma Revista de Psicanálise*, 2019, 4(7), 6–43. Part of the argument also served as the basis for a paper entitled "Écrire les *Écrits*: Quelques réflexions sur le lecteur, le style et le désir, which was presented via Zoom on 17 April 2021 under the auspices of the "Société Internationale de Psychanalyse et de Philosophie", on the occasion of the publication of *Lacan, style des écrits* by Bruno Vincent (Lormont: Editions Le Bord de l'Eau, 2019). I am grateful to Stijn Vanheule, Derek Hook, and Calum Neill for inviting me to speak at the Ghent conference and to Paulo Beer for giving me the opportunity to participate in the discussion of Vincent's work. I am also grateful to the two anonymous readers for *Psychoanalytische Perspectieven*, who forced me to clarify my argument in various places. Finally, Bruno Vincent's own response to my paper on 17 April 2021 helped me to revise various sections of the text.

Chapter 2 started life as public lectures presented at the Lacanian School of Psychoanalysis in San Francisco, CA, on 3 November 2012; at the

Jan Van Eyck Academy in Maastricht on 7 November 2012; and at the Boston Graduate School of Psychoanalysis in Boston, MA, on 20 April 2013. I would like to extend my thanks to Raul Moncayo, Dominiek Hoens, and Siamak Movahedi for arranging these lectures and to all those participants who contributed to the further elaboration of my ideas with their questions and critical comments. I am especially grateful to Mladen Dolar, whose astute observations after the Maastricht lecture enabled me to rethink substantial parts of the argument. An earlier version of the chapter subsequently appeared under the same title as this chapter in *Modern Psychoanalysis*, 2013, 38(2), 157–188, and in Slovene as "Koliko so vredne besede? Lacan in kroženje denarja v psihoanalitični ekonomiji", *Problemi*, 2013, 9/10, 167–196.

Chapter 3 originates in a public lecture delivered at the University of Vermont on 11 April 2011, under the title "Crazy Little Thing Called Object *a*". I am grateful to Todd McGowan for extending the invitation, and to him and his students for their invariably challenging questions. A second iteration of this lecture was subsequently presented as a seminar for the Lacanian School of Psychoanalysis in San Francisco, CA, on 29 October 2011, for which I am grateful to Raul Moncayo and all those who participated in the discussion. The text of these lectures was subsequently published as an essay entitled "That Obscure Object of Psychoanalysis" in *Continental Philosophy Review*, 2013, 46(2), 163–187. For this, I am grateful to Dominiek Hoens, who edited the special journal issue, and to the anonymous reviewers. The chapter as it appears in this volume is a revised and updated version of this essay.

The origin of Chapter 4 is a keynote lecture delivered at the International Conference "Civilization and Its Blisscontents: Violence and Psychoanalysis" at Fordham University in New York, NY, on 3 May 2015. A new version of this lecture was subsequently presented at the California Institute for Integral Studies in San Francisco, CA, on 14 November 2015. I wish to express my thanks to Manya Steinkoler, Vanessa Sinclair, and Raul Moncayo for inviting me to these events and to all the participants for their stimulating questions. The essay on which this chapter is based appeared under the same title in *The Comparatist*, 2015, 39(1), 22–46, for which I am grateful to Zahi Zalloua and the journal's anonymous reviewers. Carlos Eire did not read the essay until quite some time after it was published, but his exceptionally generous remarks encouraged me to make some additional revisions to it for this chapter.

Chapter 5 is based on the opening keynote address I delivered at the International Conference "Re-working Lacan at Work", which was held on 14 June 2013 at ESCP-Europe in Paris. I am grateful to Gilles Arnaud for the invitation, for introducing me to ESCP-Europe, and for his valuable critical comments on my presentation. A revised version of this presentation subsequently informed a public lecture for the Lacanian School of Psychoanalysis in San Francisco, CA, which was delivered at the California Institute for Integral Studies on 19 November 2016, and a public lecture at the Freud Museum London on 25 April 2018. For arranging these events, I am grateful to Raul Moncayo and Lili Spain. The essay on which this chapter is based was also published under the same title in *Psychoanalytische Perspectieven*, 2016, 34(4), 355–378. The anonymous reviewers for the journal offered another round of critical comments, which helped me re-shape the argument, and which also to some extent informed the revisions to the essay I made in preparing the chapter for this book.

A first approximation of the argument in Chapter 6 was presented as the closing address for the Study Days of the Affiliated Psychoanalytic Workgroups on "Psychoanalysis and Laughter", which were held at Fordham University in New York, NY, on 27 and 28 April 2013. The paper I presented there was subsequently expanded for a public lecture at Stanford University, which was delivered on 7 November 2013 under the title "Jacques the Fantasist and His Master: A Portrait of the Analyst as a Gay Man". Portions of the argument were also included in a keynote lecture entitled "For a New Gaya Scienza of Psychoanalysis", which I presented at the International Conference "Psychoanalysis on Ice" in Reykjavik on 10 October 2014. The Reykjavik lecture was published in *Division/Review: A Quarterly Psychoanalytic Forum*, 2016, 15, 17–23. The more substantial argument subsequently crystallized in an essay published under the same title as this chapter in P. Gherovici and M. Steinkoler (Eds), *Lacan, Psychoanalysis, and Comedy* (Cambridge: Cambridge University Press, 2016), pp. 36–59. For all these events and opportunities, I wish to express my thanks to Dan Collins, Manya Steinkoler, Ben Davidson, Vanessa Sinclair, Jamieson Webster, and Patricia Gherovici.

Preliminary versions of Chapter 7 were presented as public lectures at Duquesne University (9 October 2011), Edinburgh Napier University (17 February 2016), the University of Essex (4 May 2016), the California Institute for Integral Studies (18 November 2016), Dublin City University (3 December 2016), the University of Ghent (27 January 2017), the State University of New York—Buffalo (1 March 2017), and the Centre for Freudian Analysis and Research in London (21 October 2017). I would like to thank all the participants at these seminars for their constructive criticisms and insightful comments, and in particular those people who invited me to speak: Bruce Fink, Dan Collins, Calum Neill, Jochem Willemsen, Matt ffytche, Raul Moncayo, Marcelo Estrada, Carol Owens, Gerry Moore, Paul Verhaeghe, Eline Trenson, Steven Miller, Ewa Ziarek, Pat Blackett, and Darian Leader. As it appears in this book, the text is an amplified version of the essay commissioned by Ankhi Mukherjee for an anthology in the "After"-series by Cambridge University Press. As such, an earlier version was published as "Psychoanalysis as Poetry in Lacan's Clinical Paradigm" in A. Mukherjee (Ed.), *After Lacan: Literature, Theory, and Psychoanalysis in the 21st Century* (Cambridge: Cambridge University Press, 2018), pp. 74–92. Apart from extending my thanks to Ankhi for inviting me to contribute to the anthology, I would also like to express my gratitude to the anonymous readers appointed by Cambridge University Press for their detailed reading and valuable criticisms.

In its first iteration, Chapter 8 was a public lecture delivered for the School of Fine Arts at the University of Nebraska—Omaha on 13 April 2004, under the title "Working Through the Creative Impulse". The argument subsequently served as the basis for a plenary lecture at the International Conference on "The Image and the Creative Act", which was held on 24 June 2005 at the Baltic Gateshead Centre for Contemporary Art in Newcastle-upon-Tyne. The elaboration of the second, clinical part of the argument took place at Mission Mental Health in San Francisco, CA, on 2 November 2012, where I delivered a seminar entitled "Creative Sublimation in the Endgame of Psychoanalysis". The final draft of the text was then presented as a public lecture at the Centre for Freudian Analysis and Research on 7 December 2019, and published under the same title as this chapter in A. Casement, Ph. Goss and D. Nobus (Eds), *Thresholds and Pathways between Jung and Lacan: On the Blazing Sublime* (Routledge, 2021), pp. 123–152. I would like to extend my profound gratitude to all those people who were involved in these events, and especially to Tom Svolos, Jasper Joseph-Lester, Raul Moncayo, and Pat Blackett for inviting me to speak. My revision of the text for this book also benefited from the critical observations of Ben Ware, who meticulously read through the entire piece, offering numerous valuable comments and various suggestions for improvement.

Chapter 9 is a substantially revised and significantly expanded version of an essay that was originally commissioned by Carol Owens for an anthology of papers on Lacan's *Seminar VII*. As such, an abridged version of it is scheduled to appear in C. Owens (Ed.), *Studying Seminar VII* (London-New York NY: Routledge, 2022). Parts of the argument also formed the basis for a seminar on the finality of the psychoanalytic treatment presented for the postgraduate programme in psychoanalytic psychotherapy at the Faculty of Psychology and Pedagogical Sciences, University of Ghent, on 18 December 2020, and for a public lecture at the Centre for Freudian Analysis and Research in London on 6 March 2021. I am grateful to Lesley Van Hoey for inviting me to share my ideas at the seminar in Ghent, and to Pat Blackett for giving me a platform at CFAR, much as I am also grateful to all the participants at these events for their questions and observations. The final version of the text benefited tremendously from the critical comments of Armand d'Angour, who kindly verified my interpretations of the ancient Greek for general accuracy and philological consistency. Elissa Marder also read through the entire text and made various valuable criticisms. Finally, my ideas benefited from the numerous stimulating discussions on *Antigone* I had with Nektaria Pouli, ever since we had been fortunate enough to admire, from the first row, Juliette Binoche play Sophocles' heroine at the Barbican in London in March 2015.

Photo Acknowledgements

The author wishes to thank the sources of illustrative material below for granting permission to reproduce it. In the interest of completeness, the locations of artworks are also stated below.

Figure 4.1. p. 88: Gian Lorenzo Bernini (1598–1680), *The Cornaro Chapel* (1647–1652), Church of Santa Maria della Vittoria, Rome. Photo courtesy of Adam Eastland via Alamy Stock Photo.

Figure 4.2. p. 94: Gian Lorenzo Bernini (1598–1680), *L'Estasi di Santa Teresa* (*Saint Teresa in Ecstasy*) (detail) (1647–1652), Church of Santa Maria della Vittoria, Rome. Photo courtesy of INTERFOTO via Alamy Stock Photo.

Figure 4.3. p. 96: Gian Lorenzo Bernini (1598–1680), *Beata Ludovica Albertoni* (*The Blessed Ludovica Albertoni*) (1674), Church of San Francesco a Ripa, Rome. Photo courtesy of the Picture Art Collection via Alamy Stock Photo.

Figure 4.4. p. 97: Gian Lorenzo Bernini (1598–1680), *Beata Ludovica Albertoni* (*The Blessed Ludovica Albertoni*) (detail) (1674), Church of San Francesco a Ripa, Rome. Photo courtesy of the Picture Art Collection via Alamy Stock Photo.

Index

Notes: *Italicized* page numbers refer to figures. Page numbers followed by "n" refer to notes.

a (imaginary book) (Lacan) 33, *34*
Abraham, Karl 71, 72, 74
abreaction 205
absolute knowledge (*savoir absolu*) 142
Accademia Musicale di Santa Cecilia 132
activation-synthesis hypothesis 82n5
Adams, Parveen 194n14
AE *see* Analyst of the School (AE)
Aesthetics (Hegel) 209–210, 227–228n10
affect 32, 52, 58, 75, 113, 127, 134, 146, 188, 190, 199, 205, 220
Agamben, Giorgio 168n16
Agard, Walter R. 230n22
Air d'être sujet (Lacan) 161–162
Air du poète (Fargue) 153, 154, 159, 161
Albertoni, Ludovica 95
Alexandrian, Sarane 176
Alfandary, Isabelle 40n22
alienation 76–79
Allaigre-Duny, Annick 168n16
Allouch, Jean 43, 44, 166n5
Althusser, Louis 82n10
AME *see* Analyst Member of the School (AME)
analysand 10, 12, 15, 38n12, 43, 46–55, 59, 59n5, 60n13, 144, 164
"Analysis Terminable and Interminable" (Freud) 189
Analyst Member of the School (AME) 124–126
Analyst of the School (AE) 124–126, 130n11
Anderson, Mary Margaret 111n35
André, Serge 109n26

Anglade, Joseph 137
Ansell-Pearson, Keith 149n10
Anthropologie Structurale (Lévi-Strauss) 218–219
Antigone (Sophocles) 15, 199–209, 220–225; brilliance, cathartic effect of 204–210; desire and 210–219
anxiety 13, 28, 64, 74, 85n32, 104, 178
Apollinaire, Guillaume 171n27
Aristotle 202, 205, 208, 213, 220, 228n12, 228n14, 230n23, 232n34, 232n37; material cause 80; *Nicomachean Ethics* 203, 232n34; *Poetics* 204
Armstrong, Richard H. 177
Arnaud, Gilles 61n15, 112, 113
Arnoux, Danielle 39n19
ars poetica 151
art 18, 49, 57, 89, 97, 113, 144, 165, 173, 175, 177, 181–183, 185, 188–190, 195n19, 196n20, 196n23, 196n24; appreciation 63; objects 59n2; sublime 181, 188, 221
Assoun, Paul-Laurent 150n24
Atkins, Peter 63–64
Aufhebung 180, 190, 194n16
authentic leadership 112
Aux frontières du langage poétique (Dragonetti) 149n11
Avery, Charles 109n16
Ávila, Teresa of 88, 90, 96, 102, 106n2, 108n9, 111n35

Babich, Babette E. 149n10
Backès, Jean-Louis 138

Badiou, Alain 223, 235n56
Balaska, Maria 227n5
Balint, Michael 193n5
Bally, Charles 19
Barcham, William 106n2
Barnet, Marie-Claire 167n15
Barthes, Roland 22
Barzilai, Shuli 41
Bataille, Georges 38n14; *Eroticism* 93
Beattie, Tina 112
Beatitudes 120, 121
Beaufret, Jean 29
Being, potentiality of 79–81
Beiser, Frederick C. 62
Benardete, Seth 230n22
Berger, Brenda 57
Bergounioux, Gabriel 232n33
Berkeley, George: empirical idealism 62
Bernanos, Georges 167n8
Bernays, Jacob 228–229n14
Bernfeld, Siegfried 192n5
Bernini, Gian Lorenzo: *Blessed Ludovica Albertoni, The* 95–96, *96*, *97*, 109n16; *Saint Teresa in Ecstasy* 87–111, *94*; *Vision of Constantine, The* 89
Bernini, Pietro Filippo 87
Berrebi, Emilie 39n19
Berthold-Bond, Daniel 231n27
Beucler, André 166n5
Beyond Good and Evil (Nietzsche) 192n4
"Beyond the Pleasure Principle" (Freud) 67
Bhagwan Shree Rajneesh 48
Bicknell, Martin 113
Bion, Wilfred Ruprecht 116–118, 122, 123, 125, 126, 128
Birth of Tragedy, The (Nietzsche) 149n13
Black Square (Malevich) 18, *19*
Blanchet, Réginald 169n24
Blessed Ludovica Albertoni, The 95–96, *96*, *97*, 109n16
Bloom, Harold 113, 178, 179
Böckh, August 208
bodily ego 68
body 95, 101–103, 106, 133, 160, 201, 207, 211, 217, 219, 224; jouissance of the 98; parts 57; physical 100
Boehm, Rudolf 159
Böhme, Jakob 157
Boileau, Nicolas 192n3
Bollack, Jean 229n14

Bollas, Christopher 82n9
Bonaparte, Marie 13, 108n12, 129n6, 191n2
Bonnet, Marguerite 175, 176
Borch-Jacobsen, Mikkel 3, 83n12, 83n13, 86n34
Born, Bertran de 138
Borromean knot 106
Boucher, Bruce 109n16
Boudet, Monique 39n19
Bousseyroux, Michel 170n24
Boussidan, Gabriel 109n26
Bowra, Cecil Maurice: *Sophoclean Tragedy* 233n41
Brabant, Eva 227n7
Breton, André 175, 193n6, 193n7; *Les Vases Communicants* 176; *L'immaculée conception* 193n6; *Nadja* 157
Breuer, Josef 82n7, 90, 114, 228n13; *Studies on Hysteria* 189, 204–205, 220
Bricmont, Jean 3; *Intellectual Impostures* 4
Brosses, Charles de 89, 90
Buekens, Filip 3
Burckhardt, Jacob 89
Burke, Edmund 192n3
Burke, Victoria I. 231n27
Burman, Erica 59n4
Burrell, Gibson 113
Butler, Judith 82n10, 177, 226n5

Cairns, Douglas 227n6
Calder, William M. 229n15
Careri, Giovanni 109n16
Carrington, Anca 61n15
Carter, Pippa 113
Cassin, Barbara 61n18, 109n22
castration 13, 84n22, 85n32, 104, 146, 178, 222
catastrophe theory of creativity 179
catharsis 204, 205, 210, 211, 220, 228n12, 228n13, 228–229n14, 232n37
Caudill, David S. 115
causality 37n8
cause 12, 28, 32, 33, 74, 80
Caws, Mary Ann 107n6
Cederström, Carl 113–115
Chandler, Albert R. 227n7
Chanter, Tina 226n5, 231n27
Chapsal, Madeleine 131–132, 141, 148n2, 150n16, 168n19

Charcot, Jean-Martin 90, 92, 99, 107n5
Chasseguet-Smirgel, Janine 184
Chiesa, Lorenzo 109n26
Cho, K. Daniel 115
circular organization (*organisation circulaire*) 123, 125, 127
"Civilization and its Discontents" (Freud) 83–84n17, 84n18, 173
"Classified Index of Major Concepts" (Miller) 25
Clausewitz, Carl von 38n14
Clavreul, Jean 10–11, 60n7
Clemens, Justin 226n5
Clewis, Robert R. 193n10
Cohn, Jan 192n4, 193n11
Conklin, William 231n27
consciousness 66, 82n3, 198n23; inner 48; perception-consciousness 67; self-consciousness 62, 64, 69
Consistori de la Gaya Sciensa 137
Contu, Alessia 113
Cook, Méira 103
Cooper, David 134
Copjec, Joan 149–150n15, 226n5
Cornaro, Federico Baldissera Bartolomeo 88
Cornaro chapel *88*, 89, 91–92, 106
"Così Fan Tutti" (Irigaray) 107n8
Costas, Jana 112
Cottet, Serge 149n15
Courbet, Gustave: *L'origine du monde* 41
Courrier des Ardennes 166n8
Course in General Linguistics (Saussure) 18, 53
Cowles, Henry M. 82n2
creationism 189–190
"Creative Writers and Day-dreaming" (Freud) 187
Critchley, Simon 236n57
Critique of Judgement (Kant) 227n9
Crockett, Clayton 193n10, 194n14
Cropp, Martin 230n22
Crowther, Paul 193n10
Cusanus, Nicolaus 144
customer care 51

Dada movement 176
Dalí, Salvador 90
Danto, Elizabeth A. 60n12
Dasein 159
Daudet, Alphonse: *Les femmes d'artistes* (*Artists' Wives*) 166n8

Davis, Colin 84n24
Davis, Frederick B. 176–177
Daybreak (Nietzsche) 192n4
Dean, Tim 147
death drive 78
de Beauvoir, Simone 33; *Second Sex, The* 108n12
De Boer, Karin 231n27
de Frutos Salvador, Ángel 38n13
Deharme, Lise (Anne-Marie Hirtz) 157; *Le Phare de Neuilly* 158
De Kesel, Marc 194n14, 226n5, 232n38, 235n54
Delacroix, Eugène: *La liberté guidant le peuple* 18
De l'interprétation. Essai sur Freud (Ricœur) 22, 38n12
delusion 143, 212
demand 14, 45, 73
de Maré, Patrick Baltzar 117
de Mijolla, Alain 129n6
de Mijolla-Mellor, Sophie 192n5
democratic psychiatry 116
Depoortere, Frederiek 110n31
Deri, Frances (Franziska Herz) 192n5
Derrida, Jacques 22, 23, 39n22, 40n22, 105, 113, 167n13, 231n27; "Double Session, The" 178
de Sade (*see* Sade)
Descartes, René 64; *res cogitans* and *res extensa*, distinction between 62
desire 210–219
Desire and its Interpretation (Lacan) 179, 183, 202
Devereux, Georges 65; *From Anxiety to Method in the Behavioral Sciences* 64
Die Fröhliche Wissenschaft (Nietzsche) 135–136, 146, 149n9
dignity 180–181, 190
"Direction of the Treatment and the Principles of its Power, The" (Lacan) 51
disavowal (*Verleugnung*) 146
discourse 20, 33, 34, 58, 59, 74, 76, 91, 100, 105, 112, 113, 115, 126, 128, 142, 144, 156, 182, 189, 212, 216, 224
divided subject 76–81, 128
docta ignorantiae 144
Donougho, Martin 231n27
Doran, Robert 193n10
Dosse, François 39n17; *History of Structuralism* 35n2

"Double Session, The" (Derrida) 178
doubt 100, 108n12, 132, 208, 210, 214, 215, 217
Douglas, Mary 144
Dragonetti, Roger 138, 139; *Aux frontières du langage poétique* 149n11
dream 12, 66, 82n5, 142, 166n8, 176, 186
drive 66, 73, 74, 82n9, 102, 173, 174, 180, 207; death 78, 203, 222; partial 70, 83n15; sexual 70, 72, 73, 179
Driver, Michaela 112, 113
duality of mind 62
Duchamp, Marcel 182
Dufour, Dany-Robert 59n3, 168n16
D'un discours qui ne serait pas du semblant (Lacan) 36n4, 109n25
Duras, Marguerite 25
Durcharbeitung (working through) 123
Du symptôme au fantasme, et retour (Miller) 197–198
Dutronc, Jacques 16
"dynamics of transference, The" (Freud) 82–83n11

Eagleton, Terry 226n5
Earlie, Paul 40n22
Eastman, Max 146
Ecce Homo (Nietzsche) 136
Eckermann, Johann Peter 208
École de la cause freudienne 54, 130n11, 197, 198
École Française de Psychanalyse 10
École Freudienne de Paris (EFP) 10, 12, 35, 118, 119, 122–126, 134, 169n24; 7th Conference of 132
École Normale Supérieure 8, 13, 20, 139
École pratique des Hautes Études 20
Écrits (Lacan) 9–10, 16–40, 81, 84n24, 168n19, 170n24; features of 22–24; "Kant with Sade" 27, 32–33, *33*, 39n16, 40n23, 234n48; "Metaphor of the Subject" 25; "Position of the Unconscious" 25, 38n12; *Schriften* (German translation) 26; "Science and Truth" 39n16; "Subversion of the Subject" 25
Écrits de jeunesse (Sartre) 19
Écrits politiques (Hugo) 19
Edmundson, Mark 191n2
EFP see *École Freudienne de Paris* (EFP)
Egan, Gerard 49
Egginton, William 86n35

ego 10–17, 80, 81, 82n10, 177, 187, 195n23; alter 84n21; bodily 68; super-ego 67, 69, 76, 82n8, 110n28
"Ego and the Id, The" (Freud) 67
ego-psychology movement 86n33
ego-subject 66–69, 78
Ehrenreich, Barbara 4
Eire, Carlos 108n9
Eissler, Kurt R. 46, 55–56, 129n6, 193n6
ekstasis 111n35
Eliade, Mircea 178
Eliot, Thomas Stearns: "Waste Land, The" 142
Ellison, David 192n12, 227n9
Ellmann, Richard 184
Éluard, Paul: *L'immaculée conception* 193n6
Emerson, Ralph Waldo 136, 138, 139, 149n9, 149n13
empirical idealism 62
Encore (Lacan) 98–101, 103, 105, 106, 110n32
Enlightenment 18, 36n4, 89
Ensor, James 166n8
epistemology 17, 64, 65, 79, 81, 92, 144
Éribon, Didier 37n5, 218
Eroticism (Bataille) 93
Esman, Aaron H. 176
esprit de corps 116–118, 127, 128
Essers, Juup 113
Etchegoyen, Ricardo Horacio 120
eternal feminine 103
ethical idealism 62
Ethics (Spinoza) 145–146
ethics of psychoanalysis 197–236
Ethics of Psychoanalysis, The (Lacan) 179, 183, 190, 199, 202, 218, 220, 221, 223
Euripides: *Phoenician Women* 227n6
Ey, Henri 30, 38n12
Eyers, Tom 40n22

Falzeder, Ernst 227n7
fantasy 32, 33, 58, 74, 77, 81, 91, 93, 112, 128, 131–134, 141, 143–145, 185–189, 191, 195n23, 195–196n24, 196n25, 197, 212, 222, 225, 232n35; and artistic/creative impulse, connection between 187; definition of 188
Fargue, Léon-Paul 166n4, 166n7, 167n10, 169n22; *Air du poète* 153, 154,

159, 161; *Ludions* 153; Papouète 154; Pouasie 154, 161
father 201, 206, 211, 212, 216
femininity 90, 97, 100, 101, 103, 105, 108n10, 111n23, 112n31
Fenichel, Otto 13
Ferenczi, Sándor 129n9, 173, 191n2, 193n5
fetish 13, 53, 85n32
Fichte, Johann Gottlieb 164, 168n17; ethical idealism 62
Fink, Bruce 4, 32, 36n4, 39n16, 47, 48, 50, 85n26, 85n28, 101, 109n26, 148n5, 168n19
Finkelde, Dominik 226–227n5
Finnegans Wake (Joyce) 152, 185, 189
Fleming, Katie 231n25
Fliess, Wilhelm 168n18
Flournoy, Olivier 192n5
Foley, Helene P. 230n22
Forrester, John 38n9, 55–56, 61n15
Fotaki, Marianna 113
Foucault, Michel 22, 73, 82n10, 113; *History of Sexuality, The* 73
"Founding Act" (Lacan) 129n8
Four Fundamental Concepts of Psychoanalysis, The (Lacan) 188–189
Fraenkel, Théodore 175
Fragility of Goodness, The (Nussbaum) 226
freedom 85n29, 116, 130n10, 182, 183, 217
Freeland, Charles 226n5, 229n17
Freud, Ernst L. 227n7
Freud, Sigmund 49, 71, 73, 74, 76, 120, 133, 145, 151, 172–196, 204; "Analysis Terminable and Interminable" 189; attitude towards art 173; "Beyond the Pleasure Principle" 67; "Civilization and its Discontents" 83–84n17, 84n18, 173; "Creative Writers and Daydreaming" 187; *Durcharbeitung* (working through) 123; "dynamics of transference, The" 82–83n11; "Ego and the Id, The" 67; ego-subject 66–69, 78; *Interpretation of Dreams, The* 176–177; "Moses of Michelangelo, The" 208–209; "Mourning and Melancholia" 74, 84n23; "Negation" 13, 21; Oedipus complex 71, 72, 83n15, 104; "On Beginning the Treatment" 52; "Outline of Psycho-Analysis, An" 174; "Perception-Consciousness" (Pcpt.-Cs.) 67–68; *Project for a Scientific Psychology* 83n16, 194n18; psychoanalysis 2, 6–9, 12–14; on psychoanalytic fee 56–57, 60n12, 61n15; "Recommendations to Physicians Practising Psycho-Analysis" 49; *Studies on Hysteria* 189, 204–205, 220; theory of sublimation 180, 192n5; *Three Essays on the Theory of Sexuality* 70, 177, 179–180, 184; "'Uncanny,' The" 178, 193n13; *Verneinung* 11, 12, 25; *Zur Vorbereitung der Metapsychologie* (In Preparation for the Metapsychology) 192–193n5
Freudian School of Paris 10
Frey, Karl 229n15
Fröhliche Wissenschaft (Nietzsche) 138, 147
From Anxiety to Method in the Behavioral Sciences (Devereux) 64
Fromm, Erich 227n7
"Function and Field of Speech and Language in Psychoanalysis, The" (Lacan) 139
Fundamentals of Psychoanalysis, The (renamed as *The Four Fundamental Concepts of Psychoanalysis*) (Lacan) 9
Funke, Hermann 229n14
Furedi, Frank 60n8
furor pecuniam 50, 55

gai saber, psychoanalysis as 131–150; episteme of laughter 145–148; gay psychoanalysis 141–145
Gallagher, Cormac 98
Gallop, Jane 109n39
Gamot, Grégory 113
Gamwell, Lynn 177
Garnier, Robert 228n11, 233n43
Gasser, Reinhard 150n24, 192n4
Gatian de Clérambault, Gaëtan: *Infirmerie Spéciale de la Préfecture de Police* 157
Gaunt, Simon 149n11
Gay, Volney Patrick 192n5
gaya scienza (gay science) 136, 137, 139–141, 145
gay intelligence 137
gay knowledge 137

gay learning 137
gayness 133
gay psychoanalysis 141–145
gay saber 138
Gay Science, The (Nietzsche) 136, 146, 149n13
gay thinking 15
gaze 93, 108n10, 110n31
Geblesco, Elisabeth 60n5
Gemes, Ken 192n4
Genette, Gérard 22
genitality 71–72
Germond, Janine 39n19
Ghandi, Indira 139
Gherovici, Patricia 129n7, 148n1
Giampieri-Deutsch, Patrizia 227n7
Gibeault, Alain 61n15
Gide, André 30
Giroud, Françoise 49, 148n2
Glover, Ernest 192n5
Glynos, Jason 113
God 34, 75, 84n21, 87n30, 89, 93, 100, 102, 107–108n9, 110n28, 111n35, 156, 174
Godard, Jean-Luc 150n15
Godin, Jean-Guy 44, 59n5
Goebel, Eckart 192n5
Goethe, Johann Wolfgang von 103, 208
Golden, Leon 232n34
Goldsack, Christopher 166n4
González, Gloria (Lacan's secretary) 43
González Moreno, Beatriz 193n12
Goux, Jean-Joseph 61n15
grammatocentric project 35
Greimas, Algirdas Julien 22
Griffith, Mark 226n5
Grigg, Russell 160, 169n24, 170n24
Grimstad, Paul 149n9
Groot, Ger 229n15
Grubrich-Simitis, Ilse 193n5
Grünbaum, Adolf 82n4
Gudmand-Høyer, Marius 113
Guéguen, Pierre-Gilles 54
guilt 236n59
Guyomard, Patrick 226n5, 233n40
Guyotat, Pierre 143

Haas, Norbert 26
Haddad, Gérard 44–45, 59
Hadewijch of Antwerp 90
Hahn SJ, Guillaume 107n5
happiness 47, 138, 201, 203, 224, 226

Harari, Roberto 164n5
Harding, Nancy 115
hate 11
Harris, Oliver 227n5
Harrison, Tom 116, 117
Harvey, Ruth 138
"hateloving" (*hainamoration*) 11
Hayes, Tom 110n29
Heath, Stephen 97–98, 109n19
Hegel, Georg Wilhelm Friedrich 21, 64, 139, 192n3, 194n18, 196n25, 203, 204, 215, 221, 227n9, 231n27, 233n41; absolute knowledge 142; *Aesthetics* 209–210, 227–228n10; *Aufhebung* 180, 190, 194n16; *Lectures on the History of Philosophy* 227n10; *Phenomenology of Spirit, The* 18, 19, 208, 209, 234n44; subject-object identity 63, 65
Heidegger, Martin 1, 29, 159, 194n18, 206, 209, 229n19, 230–231n25; *Dasein* 159; Hölderlin's Hymn "The Ister" 209, 223, 230n25; *Introduction to Metaphysics* 222–223, 230n25; "Logos" 194n18; *Sein und Zeit* 159
Heller-Roazen, Daniel 171n29
Hendrickx, Wilfried 236n60
Hendrix, John S. 112
Henri-Rousselle Hospital 104
hermeneutics 38n12, 143, 155, 164
Herodotus 233n43; *Histories* 208
Herrbach, Olivier 112
Hertz, Neil 193n12
heteroglossia 34
hiatus irrationalis (Fichte) 168n17
"Hiatus Irrationalis" (Lacan) 157, 158, 163
Hibbard, Howard 109n16
Higgins, Kathleen Marie 149n10
Hinrichs, Hermann Friedrich Wilhelm 208
Hinterberger, Heinrich 193n6
Histories (Herodotus) 208
History of Sexuality, The (Foucault) 73
Hitler, Adolf 191n2
Hobson, John Allan 82n5
Hoedemaekers, Casper 113–115
Hölderlin, Friedrich: "Ister, The" 223
Hollywood, Amy 108n12
Homer, Sean: *Jacques Lacan* 2
Homo Ludens (Huizinga) 149n12
homo oeconomicus 114
Honig, Bonnie 226n5

Hook, Derek 24
Hôpital Sainte-Anne 8
Houbbalah, Adnan 60n6
How Mumbo-Jumbo Conquered the World (Wheen) 4
Hugo, Victor: *Écrits politiques* 19
Huizinga, Johan: *Homo Ludens* 149n12
Human, All Too Human (Nietzsche) 192n4
Hunt, Jamer Kennedy 59n3, 150n16
Hurst, Andrea 40n22, 226n5
Huxley, Aldous 178, 209
hypokeimenon 80
Hyde, Isabel 232n34
Hyppolite, Jean 13, 38n9; on Freud's "Negation" 21; on Freud's *Verneinung* 25
hysteria 67, 90, 103, 107n5, 143, 189, 222, 233n41

identification 8, 10, 68, 82n10, 183, 191
ignorance 12, 67, 101, 105, 144, 196n25
image 4, 16, 36n3, 84n19, 84n24, 90, 124, 133, 139, 146, 186, 225
Imaginary 106, 222
Infirmerie Spéciale de la Préfecture de Police (Clérambault) 157
inhibition 185
inside/outside distinction 8
Intellectual Impostures (Sokal and Bricmont) 4
intellectual uncertainty 178
International Psycho-Analytic Association (IPA) 8, 26, 118–121, 124, 129n6, 198
Interpretation of Dreams, The (Freud) 176–177
Introduction to Metaphysics (Heidegger) 222–223, 230n25
IPA *see* International Psycho-Analytic Association (IPA)
Irigaray, Luce 91–93, 98, 101; "Così Fan Tutti" 107n8
"Ister, The" (Hölderlin) 223

Jackson, Norman 113
Jacob, August Ludwig Wilhelm 207–208
Jacobs, Carol 226n5
Jacques Lacan (Homer) 2
Jacquot, Benoît 148n3
Jagger, Mick 134
Jagentowicz Mills, Patricia 231n27

jagodzinski, jan 112
Jagose, Annamarie 109n24
Jakobson, Roman 171n29, 226n4
Janáček, Leoš 19
Janaway, Christopher 149n10
Janicaud, Dominique 230n25
Jaques, Elliott 114, 129n3
Jaramillo, Jorge Iván 226n5
Jebb, Richard Claverhouse 230n22
Jentsch, Ernst 178, 193n9
Johnsen, Rasmus 113
Jones, Campbell 113
Jones, Ernest 30, 172, 173, 192n5, 229n14
jouissance 28, 47, 84n22, 115, 140, 142; of being 98; of the body 98; ethics of 223; feminine, iconography of 87–111; knowledge of 98–104; of the Other 100–102; perverse 98; phallic 91, 98, 101–103, 105; sexual 98; surplus (*plus-de-jouir*) 98
Joyce, James 144, 150n21, 159, 165–166n3, 184–185; *Finnegans Wake* 152, 185, 189
"Joyce the Symptom" (Lacan) 165n3
Juliette (Sade) 206, 232n35
Jung, Carl Gustav 16, 49, 178, 182, 184, 185, 189, 192n4

Kant, Immanuel 30, 32, 89, 142, 178, 181, 192n3, 193n9, 194n15, 206, 213, 231n29; *Critique of Judgement* 227n9; transcendental "*Ding an Sich*" (thing-in-itself) 181; transcendental idealism 62, 65
Kanzer, Mark 227n7
Kaufmann, Pierre 231n29, 234n49
Kaufmann, Walter 135–136, 192n4, 230n22, 231n29, 234n49
Kay, Sarah 149n11
Kenny, Kate 113
Kern unseres Wesen 76
Khan, Mohammed Masud Raza 169–170n24
King, Pearl 117
Kirkwood, Gordon M. 230n22
Kitto, Humpfrey Davy Findley 229n15
Klein, Melanie 72, 74, 144
Klossowski, Pierre 138
knowledge 46, 63–64, 66, 67, 81, 85n27, 92, 95, 97, 140, 157, 225; absolute (*savoir absolu*) 142, 145; affected 145;

economy 145; gay 136–137, 147; of jouissance 98–104; libidinal 142; production 65, 76, 137, 144; psychoanalytic 8, 14, 15, 27, 37n4, 103, 105, 124, 128, 133, 144, 146, 170n24, 175; transmission 35; virtuous 143
Knox, Bernard 207, 215, 233n41, 235n53
Köhler, Joachim 148n7
Kojève, Alexandre 209, 231n26, 234n44
Kosmala, Katarzyna 112
Kowsar, Mohammad 226n5
Koyré, Alexandre 157
Kripal, Jeffrey 113n30
Kritische Studienausgabe (Colli-Montinari—Nietzsche) 148n8
Krueger, David W. 57
Kusnierek, Monique 149n15

Labbie, Erin Felicia 149n15
Lacan, Jacques: *Air d'être sujet* 161–162; with Antigone 197–236; clinical artistry 172–196; clinical paradigm, psychoanalysis as poetry in 151–171; *Desire and its Interpretation* 179, 183, 202; "Direction of the Treatment and the Principles of its Power, The" 51; *D'un discours qui ne serait pas du semblant* 36n4; *Écrits* 9–10, 16–40, 81, 84n24, 168n19, 170n24; *Encore* 98–101, 103, 105, 110n32; *Ethics of Psychoanalysis, The* 179, 183, 190, 199, 202, 218, 220, 221, 223; *Four Fundamental Concepts of Psychoanalysis, The* 188–189; "Freudian Thing, The" 168n19; "Function and Field of Speech and Language in Psychoanalysis, The" 139; "function of the written, the" (*la fonction de l'écrit*) 20; *Fundamentals of Psychoanalysis, The* (renamed as *The Four Fundamental Concepts of Psychoanalysis*) 9; as gay psychoanalyst 134–141, 147; gay thinking 15; "Hiatus Irrationalis" 157, 158, 163; idiosyncratic technique 54, 57; *a* (imaginary book) 33, *34*; "Joyce the Symptom" 165n3; "Le champ freudien" 36n3; *L'éthique de la psychanalyse* 197, 198, 226n4; *L'insu que sait de l'une-bévue s'aile à mourre* 152; "Lituraterre" 20, 36n4, 37n4, 134, 135; "Names-of-the-Father, The" 9, 121–122; new signifier 152–156; object *a* 69–76; as organizational theorist 112–130; "Parenthesis of Parentheses" 23; *Pas à lire* (imaginary book) 28, 29, *30*; "Presentation of the Suite" 23; psychoanalysis 1–15; (*see also individual entries*); reading of Bernini's *Saint Teresa in Ecstasy* 87–111; "Rome Discourse" 5–7, 14, 23, 53, 120, 139, 149n14, 153, 166n5; at *Santa Maria della Vittoria* 90; "Seminar on 'The Purloined Letter,' The" 23, 27, 30–31, 39n16, 62n13; *Seminar II* 52; *Seminar V* 29; *Seminar VII* 179, 180, 182, 194n15, 197–198, 202, 210, 223, 227n8, 228n12, 231n31; *Seminar XI* 60n10, 159, 160, 162, 169n24, 170n24, 188–189; *Seminar XVI* 53; *Seminar XXIII* 159, 165n3, 169n23, 194n16; *Seminar XXIV* 154–156, 159, 163, 164; "Situation of Psychoanalysis and the Training of Psychoanalysts in 1956, The" 120; theory of sublimation 185, 187; "Variations of the Standard Treatment" 49; wealth 41–61
Lacan in Contexts (Macey) 108n10
Lacan: In Spite of Everything (Roudinesco) 18
La Compagnie des mainteneurs du Gai Savoir 137
Lacoue-Labarthe, Philippe 39n22, 86n34, 226n5; *Le titre de la lettre* 28; *Title of the Letter, The* 85n26
Ladvocat, Pierre-François 166n8
Lafont, Robert 137
Laing, Ronald David 134
La liberté guidant le peuple (Delacroix) 18
La loi (Vailland) 183–184
Langer, Monika M. 149n10
language 6, 13, 34, 38n12, 40n22, 63, 73, 76, 80, 81, 91, 100, 102, 103, 106, 137, 138, 143, 144, 151, 155, 156, 159, 164, 165, 181, 183, 190, 211
Laplanche, Jean 38n12, 175, 192n5
"*Lasciate ogni speranza*" 29
Las Leys d'Amors (*The Laws of Language*) (Molinier) 137
latency period 71
Laurent, Eric 37n4, 85n28, 110n33, 165n3

Lavin, Irving 89–90
law 110n28, 179, 183–184, 207, 209, 211, 212–214, 228, 228n11
Leader, Darian 280
leaderless group project 117
Le Bon, Gustave 177
Lebovits, Anaëlle 149n15
"Le champ freudien" (book series—Lacan) 36n3
Leclaire, Serge 38n12
Lectures on the History of Philosophy (Hegel) 227n10
Lee, Jonathan Scott 226n5
Le Gaufey, Guy 84n20
Léglu, Catherine 137
Lehmann, Hans-Thies 193n12
Lehrer, Ronald 150n24, 192n4
Le médecin malgré lui (A Doctor in Spite of Himself) (Molière) 228n14
L'enfant arriéré et sa mère (Mannoni) 39n17
Leonard, Miriam 226n5
Le Phare de Neuilly (journal—Deharme) 158
Les Échos 131
Les femmes d'artistes (Artists' Wives) (Daudet) 166n8
Les Temps Modernes (journal) 131
Les Vases Communicants (Breton) 176
L'ethique de la psychanalyse (Lacan) 197, 198, 226n4
Le titre de la lettre (Lacoue-Labarthe and Nancy) 28
L'étourdit (Lacan) 109n25, 110n33, 132
letter 20, 27, 31, 32, 36–37n4, 37nn4–7, 40n22, 52, 60n13, 75, 81, 84n24, 126, 131, 152, 162, 168n18, 169n24, 172, 173, 185, 189–191
Levey, Harry B. 192n5
Lévi-Strauss, Claude 22, 37n5, 142, 222, 234–235n49, 235n50, 235n51; *Anthropologie Structurale* 218–219; "Structural Study of Myth, The" 218–219
Lévy-Valensi, Joseph 30, 150n20
L'évolution psychiatrique (journal) 116, 117, 121
Lewis, Clive Staples 178
L'express 131, 132
Leys d'Amors 137–138
libertine dementia 33

libido 68, 71, 72, 83n14, 83n15, 109n15, 174
Liefooghe, Andreas 113
Lievrouw, An 113
L'immaculée conception (Breton and Éluard) 193n6
linguistics 27, 53, 112, 222
Linstead, Stephen 113
L'insu que sait de l'une-bévue s'aile à mourre (Lacan) 152
Little Shoes 120
"Lituraterre" (Lacan) 20, 36n4, 37n4, 134, 135
Lloyd-Jones, Hugh 206, 212–213
Loewenstein, Rudolph 157
logical time 96
"Logos" (Heidegger) 194n18
Lomas, David 176
Longinus 192n3
Loraux, Nicole 226n5
L'origine du monde (Courbet) 41
Loriot, Patrick 35n2
Loudmer, Guy 59n2
love 11, 13, 51–56, 61n16, 71, 72, 75, 89, 95, 96, 103, 131, 140, 163, 164, 203, 216
Low, P. 166n4
Ludions (Fargue) 153
Luepnitz, D. A. 227n5, 236n57
Lysy-Stevens, Anne 149n15

Macey, David 9, 98; *Lacan in Contexts* 108n10
Macías, Bianca Pérez-Mora de 134
Macmillan, Malcolm 82n4
Maderno, Carlo 87
Magritte, René: *La trahison des images* 24
Major, René 40n22
Maklès, Sylvia 42, 59n3, 150n16
Malevich, Kazimir: *Black Square* 18, *19*
Mannoni, Maud 134; *L'enfant arriéré et sa mère* 39n17
Mannoni, Octave 29, 147
Marcuse, Herbert 73
Marder, Elissa 226n5
Marx, Karl: surplus-value 74
masculinity 13
Masschelein, Anneleen 193n9
Masson, Jeffrey Moussaieff 43, 166n5, 169n5, 171n18
master 3, 10, 15, 34, 45, 46, 71, 90, 91,

105, 121, 125, 126, 128, 133, 142, 176, 189
material cause 80
Maurer, Bill 61n14
Mazzoni, Cristina 92
McCarley, Robert W. 82n5
McDougall, Joyce 184
McGonagall, William 154, 158
McGuire, William 49, 192n4
McNeill, David N. 234n43
Meltzer, Françoise 226n5
Mendelssohn, Moses 192n3
Menzies Lyth, Isabel 114
Merleau-Ponty, Maurice 25, 26, 37n5
metaphor 23, 57, 78, 105, 133, 155, 229n19
Meyer, Catherine 82n4
Migault, Pierre 30, 150n20
Miles, Thomas H. 192n4, 193n11
Miller, Jacques-Alain 21, 23, 29, 107n7, 109n26, 110n27, 119–121, 141, 148n3, 150n23, 150n24, 194n15, 194n16, 199, 226nn1–3, 231n29, 234n48, 235n55; "Classified Index of Major Concepts" 25; *Du symptome au fantasme, et retour* 197–198
Miller, Paul Allen 115
Milovanovic, Dragan 112
Moberly, Lucy Gertrude 193–194n13
Moi, Toril 103, 109n23
Molière (Jean-Baptiste Poquelin): *Le médecin malgré lui* (*A Doctor in Spite of Himself*) 228n14
Molinier, Guilhem: *Las Leys d'Amors* (*The Laws of Language*) 137
Monaco, James 150n15
money, as symbolic gift 53
money-back guarantee 51
Monson, Don A. 149n12
Morel, Geneviève 226n5
Morelli, Giovanni 208
Moreno, Jacob 116
Morlock, Forbes 193n9
Mormando, Franco 107n3, 108n9, 108–109n15
"Moses of Michelangelo, The" (Freud) 208–209
motherhood 13
"Mourning and Melancholia" (Freud) 74, 84n23
Moyaert, Paul 194n14
Munch, Edvard 19

Murdin, Lesley 57
Murnaghan, Sheila 230n22
Musee d'Orsay 43
Mutter, Anne-Sophie 191

Nacht, Sacha 60n10, 119, 169n24
Nadja (Breton) 157
"Names-of-the-Father, The" (Lacan) 9, 121–122
Nancy, Jean-Luc 28, 39n22, 86n34, 109n22; *Le titre de la lettre* 28; *Title of the Letter, The* 85n26
Napoleone, Caterina 106n2
narcissism 68
Nasio, Juan-David 129n8
Naveau, Laure 226n5
"Negation" (Freud) 13, 21
Neill, Calum 24, 226n5
neo-liberal organizational culture 115
neuro-scientific theory of dreams 82n5
neurosis (*Neurosenwahl*) 13
Newman, Stephanie 57
New York State Psychiatric Institute 193n6
Nicomachean Ethics (Aristotle) 203, 232n34
Nietzsche, Friedrich 134, 138–139, 147–148, 150n24, 173; *Beyond Good and Evil* 192n4; *Birth of Tragedy, The* 149n13; *Daybreak* 192n4; *Die Fröhliche Wissenschaft* 135–136, 138, 146, 147, 149n9; guesses and intuitions [*Ahnungen und Einsichten*] 146; *Human, All Too Human* 192n4; *On the Genealogy of Morality* 149n13, 192n4; *Thus Spoke Zarathustra* 134, 149n13
Nussbaum, Martha C. 227n9; *Fragility of Goodness, The* 226

object *a* (*objet petit* a) 27, 31–34, 40n23, 69–76, 79–81, 84n20–22, 84n24, 112, 115, 128, 222
objectivity 62–66
object of desire 16–40, 115
obsessional neurosis 222
"Obstacles" (Tudal) 166n5
Oedipus at Colonus (Sophocles) 231n28
Oedipus complex 71, 72, 83n15, 104, 204
Oedipus Rex/Oedipus the King (Sophocles) 204, 234n48
"On Beginning the Treatment" (Freud) 52

Onfray, Michel 82n4
On the Genealogy of Morality (Nietzsche) 149n13, 192n4
organization studies 113–114
Orillon, René 159
Other 73, 76–81, 98–106, 110n31, 114, 152, 162, 183, 196n25, 198, 217
Otto, Rudolf 178, 193n11
"Outline of Psycho-Analysis, An " (Freud) 174
Overbeck, Franz Camille 146

Pallière, Aimé 45
Paluzzi, Paluzzo 95
"Parenthesis of Parentheses" (Lacan) 23
Pareto, Vilfredo 53
Parisot, Thérèse 139
Paris Psychoanalytic Society 6, 139
Parker, Ian 59n4
Parsons, William B. 110n30
Partialtrieb 83n15
Partie de campagne (Renoir) 59n
Paskauskas, R. Andrew 193n5
Passerat, Georges 137
pass, procedure of the 126, 144
pathetic fallacy 62
Paul the Apostle 110n28
Pearson Geiman, Clare 231n25
"Perception-Consciousness" (Pcpt.-Cs.) 67–68
переключение (switching) 179
Perlove, Shelley K. 109n16
Petersson, Robert T. 109n16
Perrier, François 129n8
perverse jouissance 98
perversion 98, 147, 183, 184
Phaedrus (Plato) 215
phallic jouissance 91, 98, 101–103, 105
phallus 4, 71, 84n22, 86n32, 91, 100, 102, 103, 105, 106, 109n23, 112n31, 222
Phenomenology of Spirit, The (Hegel) 18, 208, 209, 234n44
philosophy 9, 38n12, 39n22, 62, 64, 65, 69, 79, 81, 157, 167n15, 206, 227n9
Phoenician Women (Euripides) 227n6
Pinkard, Terry 19
Pippin, Robert B. 149n9
Pischel, Richard 230n22
Plato 84–85n24, 202, 216, 217n9, 233n39, 233n42; *Phaedrus* 215
pleasure principle 67, 68, 222, 225
Poe, Edgar Allan 30–32, 37, 52, 75, 84n24, 85n25; "Purloined Letter, The" 36n4, 74, 219
Poetics (Aristotle) 204
poetry, psychoanalysis as 151–171
Polizzotti, Mark (2009) 179
Pollock, Jackson 182
Pontalis, Jean-Bertrand 175
Pop, Andrei 195n19
Pope Clement X (Emilio Bonaventura Altieri) 95
Pope Gregory XV (Alessandro Ludovisi) 88
Pope Pius VI (Count Giovanni Angelo Braschi) 206
Porge, Erik 86n21, 194n14
Porret, Philippe 166n5
Porter, James I. 229n14, 229n16, 229n17, 229n19, 230n24, 234n46, 236n58
Portrait imaginaire de D.A.F. de Sade (Man Ray) 198–199
postmodernism 4
potentiality of being (*Sein können*) 79–81
pre-genital love 71
"Presentation of the Suite" (Lacan) 23
Previtali, Giovanni 107n4
Project for a Scientific Psychology (Freud) 83n16, 194n18
projection 17, 68
Psaroudakis, Stavros 59n4
psychoanalytic creativity, sublime and 184–189
psychoanalytic economy, circulation of money in 41–61
psychosexuality, developmental stages of 71
psychosis 23
pun 27
"Purloined Letter, The" (Poe) 36n4, 74, 219

Quackelbeen, Julien 194n13
quality of the "analytic service" 51

Rabelais, François 139
Rabaté, Jean-Michel 167n10, 193n7, 230n5
"Radiophonie" (Lacan) 132
Rauchfleisch, Udo 191n1
Ray, Man (Emmanuel Radnitzky): *Portrait imaginaire de D.A.F. de Sade* 198–199

Real 40n22, 106, 156, 157, 162, 164, 198, 222, 223
reality 17, 33, 54, 63, 69, 76, 105, 145, 168n12, 185, 187, 188, 195n22, 225
reality principle 225
"Recommendations to Physicians Practising Psycho-Analysis" (Freud) 49
Reich, Wilhelm 73
Reik, Theodor 50
religion 45, 89, 93, 95, 103, 219
Reinhardt, Karl 234n45
Reiss-Schimmel, Ilana 57
Rémy, Ariane-Rachel 175
Renduel, Eugène 166n8
Renoir, Jean: *Partie de campagne* 59n3
repetition 175, 177
repression 73, 84n18, 174, 175, 177, 183–186, 195n20
res cogitans and *res extensa*, distinction between 62
resistance 52, 60n9, 133, 173
Rey, Pierre 59n5
Rickman, John 116, 117
Ricœur, Paul 35n3; *De l'interprétation. Essai sur Freud* 22, 38n12
Rigaut, Jacques 19
Rockefeller, Edith 184
"Rome Discourse" (Lacan) 5–7, 14, 23, 53, 120, 139, 149n14, 153, 166n5
Rose, Jacqueline 102, 105, 109n21
Rosenkranz, Karl 228n10
Rothko, Mark 182
Roudinesco, Élisabeth 3, 9, 21, 22, 24, 35n2, 39n17, 42, 60n11, 90, 114, 119, 131, 145, 226n5, 230n25; *Lacan: In Spite of Everything* 18
Roustang, François 3
Royal Army Medical Corps 121
Royle, Nicholas 193n9
Rudnytsky, Peter L. 227n7
Ruskin, John 62–63
Russo, Luigi 192n3
Ruti, Mari 226n5, 236n57

Sade, Donatien-Alphonse-François Comte de 30, 32–33, 40n23, 89, 90, 142, 229n18, 232n35, 234n48; *Juliette* 206, 232n35
Saint Girons, Baldine 192n3
Saint John of the Cross 90, 108n2

Saint Teresa in Ecstasy (Bernini) 87–111, *94*
San Francesco a Ripa 95
Santa Maria della Vittoria 87, 90, 108n2
Santa Susanna 87
Sartre, Jean-Paul: *Écrits de jeunesse* 19; *Les Temps Modernes* 131
Satie, Erik 153
Saussure, Ferdinand de 19; *Course in General Linguistics* 18, 53; structuralist semiotics of money 53
Sauverzac, Jean-François de 226n5
Schadewaldt, Wolfgang 230n22
Schama, Simon 87
Scheidhauer, Marcel 176
Schelling, Friedrich Wilhelm Joseph 62, 80
Schiller, Friedrich 192n3
Schneiderman, Stuart 46, 59n5
Schoonejans, Sonja 60n5
Schopenhauer, Arthur 192n3
Schumpeter, Joseph A. 180
Schur, Max 191n2
science 6, 63–65, 79, 81, 82n3, 151, 152, 165; *gaya scienza* (gay science) 136, 137, 139–141, 145, 147, 149n9
Sechehaye, Albert 19
Second Sex, The (de Beauvoir) 108n12
Sedley, David 233n42
Shaw, Philip 193n10
Shephard, Ben 117
Shepherdson, Charles 226n5
Sein und Zeit (Heidegger) 159
self-consciousness 62, 64, 69
self-engendering 78
semblance 81, 99
"Seminar on 'The Purloined Letter,' The" (Lacan) 23, 27, 30–31, 39n16, 62n13
Seminar VII (Lacan) 179, 180, 182, 194n15, 197–202, 210, 223, 227n8, 228n12, 231n31, 234n44
Seminar VIII (Lacan) 231n31, 234n48
Seminar XI (Lacan) 159, 160, 162, 169n24, 170n24
Seminar XVI (Lacan) 53
Seminar XXIII (Lacan) 159, 165n3, 169n23, 194n16
Seminar XXIV (Lacan) 154–156, 159, 163, 164
separation 76–79
sexuality 13, 70, 90, 176, 177; feminine

91, 105, 109n21; homosexuality 135, 148n7; Klein's theory of 72; psychosexuality 71; repressive hypothesis of 73
sexual jouissance 98
sexuation 104
SFP *see Société Française de Psychanalyse* (SFP)
shame 134, 187, 211, 212
Sheldrake, Rupert 16
Sheridan, Alan 160
Sheriff, Mary D. 97
short session 46, 60n7; treatment 114
sign 9, 84n21, 95, 157, 168n16, 230n25
"signature of things" (*signatura rerum*) 157
signifier 17, 27, 31, 32, 40n22, 45, 53, 60n13, 61n15, 84n24, 106, 111n34, 152–156, 162–164, 167n12, 169n24, 183, 189, 191, 196n25, 198, 208
Silvain 192n3
Sipos, Joël 85n28
"Situation of Psychoanalysis and the Training of Psychoanalysts in 1956, The" (Lacan) 120
Sjöholm, Cecilia 226n5
Slade, Carole 108n9
Slonimsky, Nicolas 172
Smith, Gordon 35
Sobregaya Companhia del Gay Saber 136–137
Société Française de Psychanalyse (SFP) 5, 119, 121, 222, 226n4
Société Psychanalytique de Paris (SPP) 5, 108n12, 124; Teaching Committee 119; Training Institute 120
Söderbäck, Fanny 226n5
Sokal, Alan 3; *Intellectual Impostures* 4
Sollers, Philippe 141, 143
Solms, Mark 82n5
Sonnenfeld, Paul 193n6
Sophoclean Tragedy (Bowra) 233n41
Sophocles 15, 199–201, 203, 207–210, 212–214, 216–218, 220, 221, 223, 226n2, 227n6, 227n7, 227n10, 228n11, 229n20, 230n23, 231nn30–32, 232n35, 232n36, 233n40, 233n41, 233n43, 233nn45–47, 235n53; *Antigone* 15, 199–225; *Oedipus at Colonus* 231n28; *Oedipus Rex/Oedipus the King* 204, 234n48

Sophocles: A Study of Heroic Humanism (Whitman) 233n43
Sourvinou-Inwood, Christiane 230n22
Spankie, Ro 193n7
Spear, Richard E. 106n2
Spector, Jack J. 179
sphinx 104–106
Spicer, André 113
Spinoza, Baruch de: *Ethics* 145–146
"splitting of the ego" (*Ichspaltung*) 76, 85–86n32
SPP *see Société Psychanalytique de Paris* (SPP)
Starobinski, Jean 228n13
Stavrakakis, Yannis 113
Steiner, George 228n10, 235n11, 235n53
Steinkoler, Manya 129n7, 148n1
Sterba, Richard 192n5
Stevens, John E. 137, 149n15
Stewart-Steinberg, Suzanne 227n7
Stirling, James Hutchison 194n17
Strachey, James 193n5, 193n11, 195n21, 205
"Structural Study of Myth, The" (Lévi-Strauss) 218–219
structuralism 84n24, 183, 184, 219
Studies on Hysteria (Breuer and Freud) 189, 204–205
stupidity 232n34
Stuttard, David 227n6
subjectivity 62–66
sublation (*Aufhebung*) 180, 182–183, 191, 194n17
sublimation (*Sublimierung*) 174–175, 188, 190, 191, 192n3, 192n4, 195n20; as creative destruction 175–184; and sexual satisfaction 179; theory of 180, 185, 187, 192n5
"sublimation of the instincts" [*Sublimierung der Triebe*] 173
sublime 178, 181, 182, 190, 191, 192n4, 194n18; and psychoanalytic creativity 184–189
superego 67, 69, 82n8, 110n28
surplus jouissance (*plus-de-jouir*) 98
surplus-value 74
suspended leadership 118, 126
sustine et abstine 179
Swenson Jr., James B. 40n23
Symbolic 40n22, 106, 222

symptom 5, 48, 49, 54, 58, 60n9, 105, 116, 142, 155, 185, 187, 195n20, 205
Szlezák, Thomas Alexander 230n22

Tabourot, Etienne 144
Taheri, Alireza 112
Tallis, Raymond 3
Tauber, Alfred I. 83n12
Tavistock Institute of Human Relations 114
Taylor, Charles 65
Television (Lacan) 12, 73, 132, 133, 140, 143–145
Teresa of Ávila 88, 90, 108n2
Thanem, Torkild 113
Themi, Tim 226n5
Thomán, István 172
Thomán, Mária 172, 173, 190, 191, 191n1, 191n2
Three Essays on the Theory of Sexuality (Freud) 70, 177, 179–180, 184
Thus Spoke Zarathustra (Nietzsche) 149n13
time 13, 14, 58, 96
Tiresias 105
Title of the Letter, The (Nancy and Lacoue-Labarthe) 85n26
Todorov, Tzvetan 22, 171n26
To Explain the World: The Discovery of Modern Science (Weinberg) 152
transcendental "*Ding an Sich*" (thing-in-itself) 181
transcendental idealism 62, 65
transference 52, 54, 55, 60n10, 60n13, 143; work 118–124, 126–128
trauma 228n13
Trist, Eric Lansdown 114, 129n3
Truly Necessary 120, 121
truth 2, 7, 16, 28, 76, 86n34, 104, 122, 144, 145, 151, 206, 208, 209, 218, 234n46
Tudal, Antoine 166n6; "Obstacles" 166n5
turmoil 229n18
Turnbull, Oliver 82n5
Turquet, Pierre 119, 121

"'Uncanny,' The" (Freud) 178, 193n13
unconscious 76, 85n28
use-value 195n19

Vailland, Roger: *La loi* 183–184

Vallois, Pascalle 149n15
van Braam, Paul 232n14
van der Sterren, Hendrik A. 227n7, 230n22
Van Haute, Philippe 115, 193n8, 226n5
Vanheule, Stijn 24, 112, 113
Van Reeth, Adèle 109n22
Van Rillaer, Jacques 3
Vappereau, Jean-Michel 142, 158, 159, 161, 163
variable-length session 50–51, 62n7
"Variations of the Standard Treatment" (Lacan) 49
Vasse, Denis 57
Vereecken, Christian 150n21
Vergote, Antoine 192n5
Verhaeghe, Paul 85n28, 113
Verlaine, Paul 166–167n8
Verneinung (Freud) 11, 12, 25
Verrier, Anatole-Joseph 159
Vidaillet, Bénédicte 113
Viderman, Serge 57
Vienna Psychoanalytic Society 50
Vision of Constantine, The (Bernini) 89
Voltaire (François-Marie Arouet) 209
Vuillerod, Jean-Baptiste 231n27

Waelhens, Alphonse de 159
Wahl, François 25, 39n17
Walker, Kathryn 227n9
War Office Selection Boards 117, 121
"Waste Land, The" (Eliot) 142
Weber, Alison 108n14
Weber, Samuel 226n5
Weibel, Walther 94–95
Weil, Simone 234n46
Weinberg, Steven: *To Explain the World: The Discovery of Modern Science* 152
Weiser, Jutta 107n5
Weissman, Philip 235n53
Wells, Richard 177
Westerink, Herman 193n8
Wheen, Francis: *How Mumbo-Jumbo Conquered the World* 4
Whitman, Cedric H.: (*Sophocles: A Study of Heroic Humanism*) 233n43
Widmaier-Haag, Susanne 191n1
Williams, Bernard 136
Wilson, Christopher Chadwick 108n11
Winnicott, Donald Woods 134
Wittgenstein, Ludwig 227n9
Wittkower, Rudolf 89

Witz 144–145
Wolin, Richard 4
work transference (*transfert de travail*)
 118–124
Wycherley, R. E. 230n22

Zadig-Morelli method 208
Zafiropoulos, Markos 227n5
Zalkind, Aron Borissovich 179

Zilcosky, John 193n13
Zayed, Georges 167n8
Zhuravleva, Lyudmila Vasilyevna 140
Žižek, Slavoj 81, 110n31, 223, 226n5,
 235n56, 235–236n57
Zupančič, Alenka 223, 226n5, 235n56
Zur Vorbereitung der Metapsychologie
 (In Preparation for the
 Metapsychology) (Freud) 192–193n5

Printed in the United States
by Baker & Taylor Publisher Services